DATE DUE

NOV 2 2 2009	
FEB 0 7 2014	

BRODART, CO.   Cat. No. 23-221-003

STRANGERS

Also by Graham Robb

BALZAC

VICTOR HUGO

RIMBAUD

Graham Robb

STRANGERS

Homosexual Love in the
Nineteenth Century

W. W. Norton & Company
New York London

For information about permission to reproduce selections from
this book, write to Permissions, W. W. Norton & Company, Inc.,
500 Fifth Avenue, New York, NY 10110

Manufacturing by The Maple-Vail Book Manufacturing Group

Library of Congress Cataloging-in-Publication Data
Robb, Graham, 1958–
Strangers : homosexual love in the nineteenth century /
Graham Robb.—1st American ed.
p. cm.
Also published in London by Picador, 2003.
Included bibliographical references and index.
ISBN 0-393-02038-X
1. Homosexuality—Europe—History. 2. Homosexuality—
United States—History. 3. Gays—Europe—History. 4. Gays—
United States—History. 5. Homophobia—Europe—History. 6.
Homophobia—United States—History. I. Title: Homosexual
love in the 19th century. II. Title
HQ76.3.E8R63 2004
306.76´6´094—dc22   2003066239

W. W. Norton & Company, Inc.
500 Fifth Avenue, New York, N.Y. 10110

W. W. Norton & Company Ltd.
Castle House, 75/76 Wells Street, London W1T 3QT

1 2 3 4 5 6 7 8 9 0

Contents

Contents

List of Illustrations

25. 'Berlin Census in a Thoroughly Modern Home', by Erich Wilke. (Taylor Institution)
26. Havelock Ellis. (Bodleian Library)
27. Richard Burton in Arab dress. (National Portrait Gallery)
28. Caricature of Frank Harris, by Max Beerbohm. (Bridgeman Art Library)
29. 'Merry Robin stops a Stranger in Scarlet'. (Bodleian Library)
30. From the English translation of Adolphe Belot's *Miss Giraud, My Wife*. (Bodleian Library)
31. Sherlock Holmes and Irene Adler. (Bodleian Library)
32. Jean Delville, *L'École de Platon*. (Bridgeman Art Library)

1

Prejudice

I have seen with my own eyes the most beautiful examples of something that we know only from Greek traditions. I was able to observe, as an attentive scientist, its physical and moral aspects. It is a subject about which one can hardly speak, let alone write, and so I shall save it for future conversations.

Goethe to Duke Karl August, Rome, 29 December 1787

[. . .] that most horrid, detestable, and sodomitical crime (among Christians not to be named) called Buggery.

Indictment of Rev. John Church, Surrey Assizes, 1817

MORE THAN ONCE, while working on this book, I left the age of top-hats and bustles to find the world outside strangely similar. A librarian, whispering to a colleague, referred to the titles I had requested from a closed collection as 'naughty books'. A French bookseller kept the gay and lesbian books behind the cash register so that they had to be asked for in person. The Director of the State photographic archive in St Petersburg refused to supply a photograph that would be used in a book about homosexual love. Acquaintances volunteered ancient ideas about homosexuality as if blandly introducing a pet dinosaur or a Cro-Magnon parent. Sympathy was expressed for members of my family who might be asked what I was writing. I was praised, disconcertingly (and mistakenly) for my courage and teased for my opportunism – dabbling in prurience to sell more books. I was asked which famous people I was hoping to 'out', usually with the implication that my suppositions would be wrong. Some people wondered whether the book would be 'for' or 'against'. Others, knowing the subject to be homosexuality, offered scraps of information on Victorian child molesters and spectacular sex crimes. Scholars in Britain, France and the United States wished me a speedy return to biography and literary history.

Few subjects give such a vivid sense of the living past. In fact, most of the chapters in this book overshot their intended finishing-line (the First World War) and ended up in the late 20th century. In Proust's À la recherche du temps perdu, a character jokes that if Baron de Charlus, a notorious 'invert', keeps fluttering his eyelashes at the conductor, the train will start going backwards. This joke, in various forms, is still being told. Public behaviour towards gay men and women has changed enormously, but private ideas about homosexuality are much what they were 200 years ago.

On reflection, none of this was surprising. I had my own unexamined sludge of preconceptions, but one important advantage: a familiarity with the novels of Balzac, the lives of Rimbaud and Verlaine, and the complicated reasons behind Baudelaire's first choice of a title for his poems, Les Lesbiennes. Over a period of about fifteen years, this research had turned up some curious fragments of what seemed to be a vanished civilization. Most of it was news even to friends with an interest in gay history. It seemed a good idea to pass on the information and to spend three years reading everything I could find about the lost world.

*

THE SUBJECT OF this book is homosexual love in Europe and America – the obstacles it encountered and the societies it created. It is not intended to be a check-list of famous homosexuals. Prominent people who left a written record of their feelings inevitably account for a large proportion of the evidence, but a social history should leave as much room as possible for the mass of humanity known as 'ordinary people'. It is no more accurate to make Oscar Wilde the emissary of 19th-century homosexuality than it is to see Queen Victoria as a typical Victorian. Though some of the texts quoted in this book might come as a surprise to some readers, this is not an exercise in pinning sexual labels on conspicuous individuals.

The 'strangers' of the title are lesbians as well as gay men. In sexual history, lesbians are often treated separately, for political and practical reasons, but the similarities in the lives of gay men and women are strong and significant enough to make them part of the same story. Whatever the intention, the historical segregation of men and women aggravates the lack of evidence and helps to keep lesbian history in the dark.

Perhaps the trickiest problem lay in the fact that almost everyone already has a theory about homosexuality – its history and its causes. The commonest notions appear to be a) that homosexuality never used to be mentioned and was not even known to exist; b) that homosexuality is on the increase.

These theories are impressions, not conclusions. It is remarkable how often a person who insists that homosexuality is a very recent development will, if kept on the subject, eventually remember several earlier instances, both male and female, in or outside the family, of the species that was supposed not to exist.

The idea that homosexuality is peculiar to certain periods reflects a natural tendency to confuse one's own history with the history of society. In almost everyone's experience, sexual activity is always on the increase, from infancy to early adulthood and sometimes far beyond. If the theory of homosexual proliferation had always been correct, the 'strangers' of this book would have been heterosexual rather than homosexual. For a thousand years at least, people have been complaining that sodomites, margeries, homosexuals or gays are more prevalent than ever before.

> *1102* – 'This sin is now so frequent that no one blushes for it any more, and many indulge in it without perceiving its gravity.' (St Anselm)
>
> *1663* – 'Sir J Mennes and Mr Batten both say that buggery is now almost grown as common among our gallants as in Italy, and that the very pages of the town begin to complain of their masters for it.' (Samuel Pepys)

1749 – 'Till of late Years, Sodomy was a Sin, in a manner unheard of in these Nations.' 'We have but too much Reason to fear, that there are Numbers yet undiscover'd, and that this *abominable Practice* gets Ground ev'ry Day.' ('Plain Reasons for the Growth of Sodomy in England', in *Satan's Harvest Home*)

1811 – 'The grand feature, I take it, in the last year of our history, is the enormous increase of Paiderastia [. . .] At no place or time, I suppose, since the creation of the world, has Sodomy been so rife.' (C. S. Matthews to Byron)

c. *1850* – 'The increase of these monsters in the shape of men, commonly designated *Margeries, Pooffs,* &c., of late years, in the great metropolis, renders it necessary for the sake of the public, that they should be made known.' (*Yokel's Preceptor*)

1881 – 'Immorality, used in a special sense, which I need not define, has been of late increasing among the upper classes in England, and specially in the great cities. [. . .] There is amply sufficient ground for alarm that the nation may be on the eve of an age of voluptuousness and reckless immorality.' (Canon J. M. Wilson, *Morality in Public Schools*)

1884 – 'Since my lectures on this subject in 1881, anal deformations caused by this unnatural act have regrettably become more and more numerous, proving that lustful acts are increasing by the day. [. . .] Sapphism and sodomy are growing at an unheard-of rate.' (Dr Louis Martineau, *Leçons sur les déformations vulvaires et anales*)

1930 – 'The question of homosexuality hovers over society like a ghostly scarecrow. In spite of all the condemnation, the number of perverts seems to be on the increase.' (Alfred Adler, *Das Problem der Homosexualität*)

The complementary notion that homosexuality has a particular cause is more durable. Information about homosexuality from books, the media, personal experience and gossip still tends to be treated as diagnostic rather than descriptive, as if the ultimate aim were still to find a cure.

The following brief deluge of commonly adduced causes will at least make it possible to see personal favourites in a broader context. Most of these explanations were seriously proposed and sometimes formed the basis of a career in medicine, psychiatry, criminal anthropology or sociology. The list is based on about 350 texts dating from the late 18th century to the early 20th century. Many of these 'causes' will be mentioned later on. The idea at this stage is simply to show the general direction of thought. For the sake of convenience, the explanations are divided into approximate categories.

Physiological

- regional or ethnic features such as beauty, ugliness or genital conformation (especially size)
- climate (especially temperature and altitude)
- chemical imbalance caused by diet or soil
- impotence or sterility (congenital or accidental – e.g. excessive horse-riding)
- 'abnormal conditions of the anterior lobe of the pituitary body'
- a failure to pass through puberty due to poor diet and living conditions
- excessive meat-eating
- lack of physical exercise
- physical impediments to intercourse
- venereal disease
- epilepsy
- anaemia
- masturbation
- drug abuse (especially opium and alcohol)
- atavistic hermaphroditism
- a foetal deformation causing the genital nerves to end at the rectum
- excessive application of enemas
- castration or ovariotomy
- parents of widely different ages (especially old father and young mother)

Psychological and Parapsychological

- fear of contracting venereal disease ('syphilophobia')
- fear of pregnancy
- population density, large family or physical degeneracy triggering an instinctive form of contraception
- regression to a prehuman era when the hindquarters were the primary visual stimulant
- curiosity or boredom

- books about homosexuality
- misogyny or androphobia
- sexual abstinence or indulgence
- homosexual rape, especially in childhood
- lack of parental love
- overbearing mothers
- disappointment in heterosexual love
- celibacy
- marriage
- shyness
- insanity (e.g. satyriasis, nymphomania or 'erotic delirium')
- sexual position adopted by parents at the moment of conception
- the mother's desire for a child of the other sex
- the absence of the father during pregnancy
- the mother's reading (e.g. oriental tales) or unusually strong desire for men during pregnancy
- planetary alignments at birth (especially Uranus)

Social

- migrations (the westward spread of Bulgarians, the Norman Invasion, etc.)
- religious influences (Catholic, Protestant, Muslim, pagan, etc.)
- atheism and lack of religious constraints
- unisexual institutions such as convents, boarding-schools, prisons and the armed forces
- foreign fashions and bad examples (especially Oscar Wilde)
- polygamy (in the Orient) leading to satiety in the upper classes and lack of women in the lower classes
- aristocratic over-refinement
- plebeian brutishness
- the social acceptability of non-procreative sex
- the emancipation of women
- the decriminalization of homosexual acts
- 'loosening of moral fibre'

It is not as easy as one might hope to arrange these explanations of homosexuality in chronological order. Some are still quite popular in the 21st century: homosexuality is a love of physical beauty inherited from the Ancient Greeks; homosexuality is a result of mental

or physical immaturity; homosexuality is caused by other homosexuals, especially by those who work in schools or the mass media.

These apparently diverse explanations – the social, the physical and
the metaphysical – are fundamentally similar. They all reflect a desire
to find a cause. Whether homosexuals are thought to originate in the
Garden of Eden with Adam's first wife Lilith, at the dawn of evolution in sexually undifferentiated organisms, or in a gene in the Xq28
region of the X chromosome, the essential idea is that they must have
come from somewhere.

The tail-chasing nature of this search for origins is especially
obvious in the lively domain of sexual geography. This book was
to have contained a comprehensive map of the imagined spread of
homosexuality in the western world, but early sketches quickly produced an illegible mass of two-directional arrows. While 'the Italian
vice' crept into Britain, 'il vizio inglese' (also applied to flagellation)
was heading south to Naples and Capri. In France, 'l'amour allemand'
crossed the Rhine like an invading army. Meanwhile, 'die französische
Krankheit', carried by pornography and dilettantes, conducted a
counter-offensive, turning cities into open-air brothels and respectable women into lesbians.

Romanians traced homosexuals back to Turkey, Turks traced
them to Persia, and Persians to a remote Persian province. In 1810,
when a flourishing club of 'mollies' was discovered in a London
pub, two newspapers blamed 'the evil' on the Napoleonic wars:
too many foreign servants and too many Englishmen exposed to
foreign customs. In Paris, a supposed increase in 'pederasty' in the
1840s was attributed to the conquest of Algeria: according to
the Marquis de Boissy, troops had brought the 'mal d'orient' home
like a tropical disease. Later, the surge of bourgeois sex tourists
from Britain, France and Germany convinced Algerians (according
to André Gide) that 'these tastes came to them from Europe'. Even
the Atlantic Ocean was useless as a cordon sanitaire. In 1842, a New
York journal called the Whip noted with some relief that, among the
sodomites infesting the city, 'we find no Americans as yet – they are
all Englishmen or French'.

These sexual trade routes may reflect regional variations in the
acceptability of homosexual behaviour, and they certainly reflect

the international nature of gay culture. When a French dictionary in 1870 illustrated the word '*pédéraste*' with the phrase, 'There are many pederasts among the Greeks and Italians', it should have pointed out that many of these 'pederasts' were French. But these geographical theories have no value whatsoever as explanations of sexual preference.

Most ideas about homosexuality survive, often for centuries, not because they match real experience, but because they tell an interesting tale. This is partly why, in the early days of sexology, literature and science were so mutually dependent. From about 1870 to 1920, scientific studies of lesbianism increased in exactly the same ratio as novels with lesbian characters. The theories of homosexuals themselves tended to be disappointingly banal. Most people who were interviewed on the subject simply claimed that they had been 'that way' for as long as they could remember.

The 'scientific' approach to homosexuality nearly always involves a logical fallacy. The 1994 *National Survey of Sexual Attitudes and Lifestyles* in Britain finds that the only obvious distinguishing feature of British homosexuals apart from sexual orientation is a tendency to live in London. Anecdotal and forensic evidence suggests that this internal migration has been going on for at least 200 years, and probably for as long as large settlements have existed. Towns and cities offered a more tolerant or indifferent population and a more varied social life. On arriving in a big city, many 19th-century homosexuals were amazed to find that they were not unique after all. The city might have altered their behaviour and even revealed their sexuality to them, but few gay people thought of their sexuality as a side-effect of urban living.

The storytelling instinct, however, presented this demographic trend not as a reflection of practical arrangements but as dramatic evidence that cities breed sexual perverts. The bright lights and polluted air of New York, London, Paris and Berlin were the fire and brimstone that destroyed Sodom and Gomorrha. This notion was reinforced by popular expressions like 'Sodom on the Spree' (Berlin) or 'Sodom by the Sea' (San Francisco), and titles like *Sodom in Union Square* (1879) or *Paris-Gomorrhe* (1894). The connection between the mythical past and the mysterious present was so firmly established that physical explanations for the disappearance of Sodom and Gomorrha, by earthquake or the ignition of subterranean bitumen lakes, were sometimes treated as arguments in favour of sexual tolerance: the Sodomites were not sinners, they were victims of a natural catastrophe.

The habit of attaching colourful causes to banal effects is not peculiar to popular notions of homosexuality. The same sort of logic seems to have inspired the enduring psychological idea that homosexuals are produced by weak or absent fathers and over-protective mothers (first expressed scientifically in Freud's 1910 essay on Leonardo da Vinci). Far from identifying a cause, this appears to describe a common parental reaction to sons who were either homosexual or effeminate: mothers tended to sympathize, fathers tended to sever all ties.

Freud's idea satisfied the two main requirements for a successful theory. First, it chimed with popular prejudice – in this case, the belief that gay men are 'mummy's boys'. Second, it was almost indestructibly elastic. If the father was sympathetic, he could still be described as weak. Similarly, most mothers could be said to have exercised a degree of emotional domination at some stage in the child's development, especially in the early years.

Similar theories can be found throughout the 19th and 20th centuries. However thick the layers of subsequent elaboration, almost every 'scientific' explanation of homosexuality can be traced back to a rudimentary fact:

Fact: Homosexuals are less likely to marry than heterosexuals.
Theory: Homosexuality is caused by celibacy.

Fact: Homosexual acts were illegal.
Theory: The homosexual is a criminal type.

Fact: Many homosexuals studied by doctors had suffered blackmail, arrest, public mockery and a humiliating medical examination.
Theory: Homosexuals are neurotic.

Fact: Lunatic asylums provided pathologists with large numbers of more or less compliant experimental subjects.
Theory: Homosexuals are insane.

As Marc-André Raffalovich complained in *Uranisme et unisexualité* (1896), the silent majority of 'unisexuals' was unknown to doctors and legislators precisely because it was silent. By sheer force of circumstance, the typical unisexual, in the eyes of many doctors, was a garrulous transvestite with a hectic sex-life and a history of mental illness.

Naturally, most of these ideas seemed to come true after the fact. Homosexuals who were treated as criminals sometimes committed suicide, which proved that they were mentally unstable. Some were grateful to doctors for listening to their tales of woe and tried to live up to their new, scientific persona. In exchange for a friendly ear, they provided evidence of hysterical behaviour, moral weakness or a family tree infested with lunatics and drug addicts.

The scientists themselves had ever more reason to believe their own theories. Any doctor who had peered into a thousand anuses looking for the physiological signs of 'inversion' was unlikely to conclude that his theory had led him down a cul-de-sac.

Theories, then and now, can make the gay past seem much poorer and more dismal than it was. More importantly, calls for equal treatment based on a theory of sexuality ultimately depend on the niceness of whoever applies the theory. Karl Heinrich Ulrichs, who campaigned openly for legal and social acceptance of homosexuality in the 1860s and 1870s, believed that 'Uranians' were congenitally different from the rest of the human race. Heinrich Himmler, who caused the deaths of thousands of homosexuals in Nazi death camps, held the apparently less sinister view that boys became homosexual through lack of opportunity, especially in cities, where, according to Himmler, high-rise apartments prevented them from clambering through girls' bedroom windows.

From a late-20th-century theoretical point of view, Himmler's idea would be more acceptable because it stressed the element of choice. Ulrichs' innateness theory, though it helped to change attitudes, would be seen as a cringing concession to prejudice: homosexuals should be tolerated because they can't help it.

*

THE FIRST MODERN HISTORIANS of homosexual love worked under severe personal and professional constraints but still managed to supply a vast amount of reliable information without losing their patience or their sense of humour. However, apart from one or two high-speed aerial reconnaissance projects, most books on the subject were confined to one country or one language and were vulnerable to local distortions. One of the main ambitions of this book was to make 'Europe' mean something more than Britain and a variety of continental holiday destinations, and especially to make the discoveries of European historians better known in the English-speaking world. Gay men and women in Europe and America were remarkably cosmopolitan, but this is not always reflected in histories of the subject.

The biggest surprise was the blanket influence of Michel Foucault's theory of social construction (see p. 42), developed in his *Histoire de la sexualité* (1976–84). The great advantage of this theory was that it allowed sexuality to be studied in the light of history and sociology. Unfortunately, it has popularized the view that gay people have no real heritage before the 1870s. The basic idea is that sexuality is not innate but 'constructed' by a particular set of circumstances, notably by the rise of competitive capitalism and its handmaidens, modern science and bureaucratic control. In its extreme form, the social constructionist approach suggests that 'homosexuality' did not exist until the word was invented. Before then, supposedly, sexuality was just a certain repertoire of acts, not a personality trait.

This approach not surprisingly had a wide appeal beyond the scholarly gay community: it meant that there was no continuous gay culture and that Socrates or Michelangelo could not be seen as 'gay'; it seemed to promise an automatic avoidance of anachronism, and it attributed enormous influence to the theorists' academic predecessors. It also allowed very small amounts of evidence to be presented as insights into an entire period and culture. It is no coincidence that the biggest theories tended to come from the smallest articles.

The theory that homosexuality came into being at a particular moment closely matched popular notions of sexual history. Early Christian theologians, Romantic poets and 20th-century queer theorists all espoused the view that, after a cataclysmic moment in human history – the Fall of Man, the death of God, the modernist 'fracturing' of thought and knowledge – a Golden Age of sexual indeterminacy came to an end. This ideological perception of a less guilty and simpler sexual past is suspiciously similar to the convenient attitudes of some Victorian colonists. In places that are foreign by time or distance, causal links are often invisible and their apparent absence tends to create an impression of unusual spontaneity and freedom. This unadministered world would have been unrecognizable to the natives of the 19th century.

First, there always were people who were primarily or exclusively attracted to people of their own sex. They had no difficulty in identifying themselves as homosexual (or whichever word was used), often from a very early age. Second, these people were known to exist and were perceived to be different. They did not call themselves 'homosexual' or 'gay', and they lived in a society that would be in many ways profoundly shocking and mostly unrecognizable to inhabitants of the 21st century. But early Victorian 'sodomites', 'mollies', 'margeries' and 'poufs' had a great deal in common with the later 'Uranians', 'inverts', 'homosexuals' and 'queers': very similar daily experiences, a shared culture, and of course an ability to fall in love with people of their own sex.

*

No HISTORY OF a human trait can claim to be comprehensive. 'Homosexuality' is a huge generalization and the word itself conveys a fearsomely clinical notion of love. It reinforces the vulgar association of gay love with anal intercourse (also commonly practised by women and heterosexual men). Strangely, though, the commonest objection to the word, since its invention in 1868 (see p. 67), has been that it combines Greek (*homos*, same) with Latin (*sexus*). (The same complaint could be made of 'television' and 'sociologist'.)

A more serious problem is the lack of evidence. Some countries, like Spain and Canada, are largely uncharted territory. In all countries, private papers were destroyed, thoughts were never recorded, lives were cloaked in conventionality, and a plague of euphemisms wiped out the traces of homosexual love.

It is difficult in any case to give a fair and concise description of

social attitudes at any one time. The inevitable tendency is to caricature a period so that it can be contrasted with another period. The
following four statements, for instance, could be used to characterize
the attitudes of a particular society to homosexuality:

- Homosexuality 'may be tolerated by the French, but we are
  British – thank God.'
- Homosexuality 'is entirely precipitated by the abnormal sexual
  behaviour of parents during pregnancy.'
- God has visited a 'dreadful plague' on 'perverts' who 'offend the
  laws of God and nature'.
- Homosexuals should be hanged, flogged, castrated and 'sent
  home'.

These apparently archaic opinions were published in Britain in
1965, 1977 and 1986. One day, they might allow 22nd-century readers
to feel sorry for people who had to suffer through the benighted end
of the 20th century. But few people alive today would consider this a
balanced description of sexual attitudes in modern Britain.

The tabloid image of a mean-spirited population of ignoramuses
consumed by fear and envy can of course be corrected by personal
experience. But when the period in question lies beyond living
memory, the distortions are harder to correct.

One of the main sources of information on homosexuality is literature. Since, at first sight, the literary record says very little on the
subject, it looks as though homosexuality was relatively unimportant
or unusual in the past. But literature has only rarely been the free and
encyclopedic expression of a whole society. Other common aspects of
human life are also missing from the record.

In fact, the subject of homosexuality was far more prevalent than
it seems. Words, gestures and symbols, even from one half-generation
to the next, become almost prehistorically obscure. 'Lavender aunts',
'musical' young men, crooked fingers and green carnations are no
longer widely understood as references to homosexuality. But the
evidence is there. Newspapers could refer to homosexual scandals
with the faintest of allusions, and city crowds obviously knew why
they were hurling dead cats and offal at sodomites in the pillory.
The 'crime not to be named among Christians' exists even in the

supposedly genteel world of Jane Austen: 'Certainly', says Mary Craw-
ford in *Mansfield Park* (1814), 'my home at my uncle's brought me
acquainted with a circle of admirals. Of *Rears*, and *Vices*, I saw enough.
Now, do not be suspecting me of a pun, I entreat.'

*

THIS BOOK IS divided into three parts. Part One describes the treatment of gay men and women by the legal and medical professions
and by society in general. Part Two describes their lives and loves –
how they discovered themselves and made contact with like-minded
people. This part ends with the dawn of homosexual solidarity and
the early gay rights movement. Part Three is devoted to some crucial
aspects of gay culture.

A social history that ranges over one and a half continents and one
and a half centuries can have nothing precise to say about the likely
future, but it might provide some credible reasons to take a more
cheerful view of the past.

Part One

2

In the Shadows

Lord Darlington: Do you know I am afraid that good
people do a great deal of harm in this world. Certainly
the greatest harm they do is that they make badness of
such extraordinary importance.

Oscar Wilde, *Lady Windermere's Fan*, Act 1

ONE OF THE RICHEST sources of information on the gay past has
to do with the capture and punishment of homosexuals: laws,
court records and criminal statistics.

This is unfortunate for several reasons. By lumping homosexual
men and women together with insane or violent people, the criminal
evidence paints a grim and antiquated picture of the 19th century.
Like the earliest psychiatric studies of homosexuality, it places the
people who were popularly and legally known as 'sodomites' in
the same sexual zoo as exhibitionists, paedophiles and sex-murderers.
Since the law was concerned with acts, not with desires, it turns
homosexual history into a long tale of sodomy and prostitution.

The fact that sodomy was punishable by death in England and
Wales until 1861 suggests that many people lived their lives in the
shadow of the gallows, and that the official and social homophobia
of the 20th century was a continuation of a Victorian trend rather
than something peculiarly modern. Bathed in the red glow of crime,
the whole Victorian age looks like a homophobic hell from which

gay people eventually liberated themselves. In this view, a happy gay heritage dates back only a few decades, or, missing out the period of supposed persecution, to a remote and poorly understood group of cultures labelled 'Ancient Greece'. All but the last generation and a half of gay culture is reduced to a simple reaction against oppression.

The view from the courtroom also obliterates lesbians almost completely, whilst conferring a perverse kind of prestige on homosexual men. There have been attempts to show that lesbians also suffered legal as well as social persecution. Sexual acts between women were outlawed in some European countries (Prussia until 1851; Austria until 1971; Spain, briefly, until 1976), but the laws were almost never applied. Most cases from the 13th to the 18th century involved another crime – usually deception or, in one case, the use of dildos by two 16th-century Spanish nuns. A woman like Mary Hamilton, who was publicly whipped and sent to prison for 'marrying' three unsuspecting women – as described in Henry Fielding's *The Female Husband* (1746) – was punished, not as a female sodomite, but as someone who had 'by false and deceitful practices endeavoured to impose on some of his Majesty's subjects'.

Finally, in the vast muddle of sexual history, statistics seem to provide fixed reference points. This has endowed them with a huge, undeserved influence on notions of the gay or not-so-gay past. It is all the more surprising that, until Harry Cocks's thesis, *Abominable Crimes: Sodomy Trials in English Law and Culture, 1830–1889* (University of Manchester, 1998), no book or article had presented more than a few years' worth of statistical evidence for England and Wales. The figures that were doled out in various studies, to prove various points, formed an amorphous puzzle that looked different, but always bleak, whenever it was assembled.

One aim of this chapter, therefore, is to demonstrate the relative unimportance of its subject, to present the forensic evidence but also to suggest that punishment was rarely systematic and never a vital element of gay culture. The following proliferation of legal fact should be seen as a spring-cleaning, after which the realities of individual lives should be easier to find.

*

A COMPLETE STATISTICAL STUDY of legal persecution in Europe and the United States would be impossibly complex and full of gaps. Most of the following figures refer to England and Wales, for which reliable and fairly consistent information is available. Other countries, discussed later in this chapter, either had no laws against homosexual acts or did not apply the laws with the seeming diligence shown by English courts. This means that, although the conclusions are widely applicable, much of this chapter is devoted to an unusually punitive jurisdiction. From a purely statistical point of view, a homosexual man was better off living in Spain under the Inquisition or Russia under the Tsars than in Victorian England.

Graph 1 (Appendix I, p. 272) shows indictments for sodomy and related offences (assault with intent to commit sodomy, incitement and soliciting) per 100,000 of population, from 1810 to 1900.

These figures cast immediate doubt on the presumption of systematic punishment. First, there was no significant increase in indictments of 'sodomites' in 19th-century England and Wales. An apparent slight increase disappears once the rise in population is taken into account. If anything, there was an overall decrease from the mid-1840s to the end of the century, despite the fact that, after 1892, the figures include the offence of indecency. Conviction rates also remained quite steady: 67 per cent of prosecutions led to a conviction in the 1810s, 57 per cent in the 1890s, with an average for the whole century of 49 per cent. These rates were not unusual and do not suggest that, within the terms of the law, sodomites were treated with unusual severity.

The second surprise is that the variations form no significant pattern. None of the factors that are sometimes supposed to have caused trends had any observable effect: changes in the law; war and unrest; economic recession; public scandals – except where the scandal itself inflated the figures.

When comparatively small numbers of people were involved, a single incident, like the Vere Street scandal of 1810, could affect the figures disproportionately. Of the twenty-seven men rounded up at the Vere Street 'molly house' near the Strand in London, six were found guilty of attempted sodomy. This single police raid accounts for over 11 per cent of all convictions for sodomy and related offences in 1810, and several other convictions were probably related to the same raid. Faced with the horrific and possibly fatal humiliation of the pillory, some people preferred to suffer a bad conscience and informed on their fellows.

A similar absence of long-term trends has been found in sodomy trials in 18th-century Amsterdam. Trials tended to come in groups. As in the Vere Street case, one detailed confession could lead to several arrests, but the effect was always temporary and there is no evidence of persistent, methodical persecution. The most dramatic purge of sodomites in Dutch history – twenty-four men and boys strangled and burned at the stake in the village of Faan in 1731 – was the work of a single magistrate, who seems to have used sodomy as an excuse to eradicate his personal enemies. This freak incident accounts for 4 per cent of all Dutch sodomy convictions in the 18th century.

In earlier periods, when buggery and sodomy were treated as forms of heresy, there was occasionally a clear correlation between religious zeal and the punishment of sexual deviants. But a more pragmatic, secular view seems to have prevailed throughout continental Europe from the mid-17th century.

Other fluctuations in the 19th-century figures can be attributed to passing causes like 'social purity' campaigns and moral crusades against prostitution and child abuse (England in the 1860s and 1880s, the United States in the 1880s and later) or a reconfiguration of existing laws: a rise in what might appear to be homosexual prosecutions occurred in the United States when sodomy laws were modified to include oral sex (heterosexual or homosexual).

Legal changes directly affecting homosexual men were also surprisingly inconsequential. In this respect, the biggest non-event on Graph 1 is the famous Labouchere Amendment, under which Oscar Wilde was prosecuted. This Amendment (Section XI of the Criminal Law Amendment Act, 1885) came into force on 1 January 1886 and, supposedly for the first time, made all homosexual acts between men illegal, 'in public or private'. In fact, homosexual acts were already illegal, whether or not they took place in private. If Oscar Wilde had been convicted at any time in the previous 200 years, he would probably have received the same sentence. Conviction rates in the ten years before and after the Amendment were practically identical (55 per cent and 56 per cent), and there was no significant rise in prosecutions until the 20th century.

Not all the faces behind these statistics belonged in any case to what would later be called homosexuals. The term 'sodomite' was widely used in much the same way as 'pédéraste'* still is in France, to refer to men who fell in love with other men, but in legal terms, 'sodomite' was a broader category than the later 'homosexual'. Sodomy became a civil crime in England in 1533, but the 'detestable and abhomynable vice' defined by the 1533 statute could be committed with 'mankynde [i.e. man or woman] or beaste'. The sex partner of one of the sodomites convicted in England in 1834 was a ewe, and even that sub-category was contentious. In 1877, reviewing the case of a Warwickshire man accused of committing an 'unnatural offence with a fowl', the Attorney General decreed that a fowl is 'not an animal' and granted the man a free pardon.

The term 'unnatural' was equally capacious. The 'unnatural' offence of buggery was associated at various times with oral sex and the use of contraception ('unnatural' because non-procreative). In Amsterdam, before the introduction of the French penal code in 1811, most of the eighteen prosecutions from 1800 to 1810 involved men who tried to have sex with children. In the United States, of eighty-nine reported sodomy cases from 1880 to 1925, only twenty-five involved consensual sodomy between two men. In the other sixty-four cases, the act was committed by a man with a woman, a child or an animal, or was part of a violent attack.

The fact that men who had sex with other men were placed in the same category as paedophiles, zoophiles and rapists can be interpreted as a sign of institutional homophobia. On the other hand, if the 'homosexual' was not a recognized variety of human being, the legal persecution of homosexuals could only be described as accidental. Only one kind of sexual act was considered licit, and this view was metaphysical rather than social. The buggery laws, for instance, were not inspired by concern for animal welfare but by notions of what constituted 'vice'.

* From *pais* (boy) and *erastes* (lover).

There was little change in this respect throughout the 19th century. Medical and criminological approaches to sexual deviance simply (but with endless scholarly complications) redefined 'vice' in their own professional terms. If one particular classification system had prevailed, homosexuals might have been legally separated from thugs and lunatics and treated differently; but this did not occur until much later.

*

SOME MORE PLAUSIBLE attempts have been made to detect patterns of persecution. According to one of the most popular arguments, prosecutions of homosexuals increased in times of war or civil unrest. Evidence of a surge of anti-sodomitical activity in wartime was first presented in 1976 and 1978 in studies of British naval court-martials. The theory was later extended, without evidence, to the civilian population.

The idea that social turmoil creates waves of homophobia looks plausible because of the widespread belief that homosexuals are effeminate and that a nation with a large homosexual population is an easy prey for a virile foe. This notion was used at various times to explain the fall of Rome, the capture of Constantinople by the Crusaders, and the defeat of the decadent French Second Empire by Prussia in 1870. More recently, it was used in Britain and the United States to oppose the admission of gay men and women to the armed forces.

It turns out, however, that the spate of buggery cases in the Royal Navy during the Seven Years' War and the Napoleonic wars (nine death sentences for sodomy from 1797 to 1805) coincides exactly with a sudden huge increase in the size of the Navy. War brought mass conscription. The argument that there was an ideological purge of buggers is not fundamentally implausible, but it should take account of the fact that there were more sailors to prosecute. Even then, buggery accounted for only 5 per cent of all capital convictions from 1756 to 1806 (19 out of 371 – the remainder comprising murderers, mutineers, deserters and men who had struck an officer).

There is, at first sight, more convincing evidence of a campaign of persecution in the fact that the death penalty was also applied to

civilian sodomites in England and Wales until 1835. Even if, as was often the case, the executed man had also committed rape or murder, it seems likely that the mere suspicion of sodomy could provoke an unusually savage response.

The last execution of a sodomite in France took place in 1783, when a defrocked monk was burned at the stake for murdering a boy who refused to have sex with him. The last execution for sodomy anywhere in continental Europe took place in Holland in 1803; but in England, executions continued until 1835. Forty-six people were executed for sodomy between 1810 and 1835. A further thirty-two were sentenced to death but reprieved. The remaining 713 who were convicted of sodomy or a related offence received a milder sentence – pillory (until 1816) or imprisonment. Of the 1,596 prosecutions between 1810 and 1835, 805 ended in acquittal.

However, Graph 2 (Appendix I, p. 272) shows that even this apparently definitive statistic should be treated with caution. Although the death penalty for sodomy was not abolished in England and Wales until 1861 (1889 in Scotland), the change in the law was anticipated by a quarter of a century. No sodomites were executed after 1835. This unofficial abolition of the death penalty coincided with an increase in the number of death sentences, as if judges and juries now felt free to issue their grisly warnings.

Harsh laws, in other words, may foster leniency, and vice versa. If the sentence is death and if juries suspect that the guilty man will die, they may be fussier about the evidence and more reluctant to convict.

It is, to say the least, a statistical error to view these forty-six executions as evidence of 'genocide'. Some ancient laws, which survived like hideous living fossils, have been used to paint a picture of continual, savage persecution. But there is no evidence that sodomites were ever buried alive (as prescribed by a 13th-century English law). Nor did sodomitical women in the United States ever have half-inch holes cut through the cartilage of their noses (as recommended by Thomas Jefferson and others when revising the laws of Virginia in 1777). The mere existence of a law says even less about the character of a society than a statement of moral principles does about the behaviour of an individual.

Sodomy was undoubtedly a special case. It remained a capital offence in England and Wales long after the death penalty had been abolished for crimes such as house-breaking, horse-stealing and sacrilege. This may reflect deliberate repression, or simply a reluctance by legislators to debate the matter in public. When politicians or journalists were asked to come up with an opinion, they generally expressed horror at the 'unmentionable' crime. In private, many thought it inhumane or pointless to punish a crime that had no victim (see Chapter 7). The death penalty was after all abolished. A bill of 1841 passed the House of Commons but was rejected by the House of Lords. The 1861 bill passed both Houses. The new sentence – ten years to life – could hardly be described as permissive, but it did show a willingness to modernize and humanize the law, even in such a controversial case.

The underlying problem is that the very process of singling out prosecutions of homosexuals suggests that homosexuals were singled out for special treatment. For most of the 19th century, in sexual matters, women had more to fear from the law than homosexual men. Under the English Divorce Act of 1857, a wife who committed a small, private, heterosexual indiscretion could be divorced and effectively condemned to social death. A husband's adultery was insufficient grounds for divorce, unless it involved sodomy. In France, public indecency and corruption of the young – often applied to sodomites – carried a maximum prison sentence of six months. Adultery – applied almost exclusively to women – carried a maximum sentence of two years.

The separation of homosexual crimes from the other statistics also makes an anachronistic perception of the punishment almost inevitable. It may not seem that much leniency was being shown to men who were clamped in pillories and exposed for several hours to a self-righteous mob of sadists armed with barrowfuls of excrement and dead animals. But these public displays of self-righteous cruelty were not reserved for sodomites, and there is no real evidence that juries were unusually vindictive. The pillory was the lightest sentence available. In early-19th-century England, a person could be hanged even for minor theft. (The pillory was abolished in 1816 for all crimes except subornation and perjury, and abolished completely in 1837.)

The more dramatic the punishment, the greater the opportunities for misrepresentation. It has been pointed out that, in 1806, there were more executions for sodomy than for murder, and that, in 1810, four out of five convicted sodomists were hanged, but these facts are extremely misleading when viewed in isolation.

Graph 3 (Appendix I, p. 273) shows that, while sodomy remained a capital offence, executions for sodomy were a small percentage of total executions.

Sodomy – usually with violence – accounted for less than 3 per cent of all executions in England and Wales from 1805 to 1835. Murder accounted for 21 per cent. By far the largest number of executions were for crimes against property, many of which would now seem too trivial even for imprisonment.

Until the mid-20th century, this seems to have been the case wherever sodomites were prosecuted. In the United States, according to William Eskridge, 'sodomy arrests remained a tiny portion (a fraction of one percent) of total arrests in all cities' from 1900 to 1920. In British India, there were only seven prosecutions and three convictions until 1929 under the 1860 law prohibiting 'carnal intercourse against the order of nature'. Most of these cases involved assaults on children.

However iniquitous the spirit of the law, conviction rates in England and Wales suggest that trials for sodomy were just as fair (or unfair) as trials for other offences. Once arrested, a sodomite was just as likely as any other criminal to be acquitted, and he could expect the sentence to reflect a proven fact rather than mere prejudice or rumour. After 1781, to convict a man of buggery, it was necessary to prove both penetration and emission of semen, and although the latter criterion was removed in 1828, the change was inspired, not by a desire to persecute sodomites, but by a concern that rapists were escaping too easily.

The lack of detailed court reports may suggest that sodomites were convicted on flimsy or non-existent evidence. Newspaper reports were sketchy and euphemistic and left their readers to imagine the unimaginable. Typically, *The Morning Chronicle* of London reported on 6 April 1815 that 'a hoary miscreant, a workhouse pauper [was executed for] a crime at which nature shudders, not a syllable of the evidence on which we can state'. Clearly, then, evidence had been given. But reporters were often instructed by judges to omit the loathsome details, either for the sake of decency or to guard against the possibility that readers might try out the unspeakable acts for themselves and cause an epidemic of unnatural vice.

Throughout the 19th century, silence was by far the commonest tactic, not just in Britain. The usual view was expressed by Napoleon, when confronted with evidence of a thriving sodomite community in Chartres in 1805: 'Nature has seen to it that [these offences] are not frequent. The scandal of legal proceedings would only tend to multiply them.' In a modern democracy, the bureaucratic concealment of official punishments would look like an attempt to disguise repression. In the 19th century it was founded on concern for public welfare. Sodomy was widely believed to be a vice that thrived on publicity.

The court reports that have survived suggest that the evidence heard in English courts was sufficiently explicit. The following testimony comes from the unpublished record of a sodomy trial held on 26 June 1807:

> Pearce unbutt'd my Breeches & put up my Shirt I asked him wt he was going to do he said I was to be quiet and lie still I told him he ought to be quiet & lie still because I wanted to go to sleep he took his Yard and put [it] to my Fundament. I told him it was worth his Life to do any such thing. [. . .] he did not say a word but proceeded on he went to put his Yard into my Fundament it went in a little way not far.

Official discretion sometimes prevented cases from coming to trial at all. Sodomites, especially those in high places, were often allowed to leave the country. When the Cleveland Street affair of 1890 revealed the sordid secrets of male brothels and the part-time activities of London telegraph boys, the Government seemed curiously slow to prosecute. This has given rise to a feeble conspiracy theory concerning Queen Victoria's homosexual grandson, Prince Eddy. It is more likely, as Harry Cocks suggests, that the Government was simply trying to cover up its usual reluctance to advertise the activities of sodomites. In this case, its hand was forced by campaigning journalists and by an enthusiastic police constable who clearly enjoyed the investigation.

A clergyman called Veck and a clerk called Newlove received prison sentences of four and nine months, but the most prominent culprit, Lord Arthur Somerset, was able to flee to the South of France where he spent the remaining thirty-seven years of his life with a male companion.

*

Beyond Britain, generalizations about legal persecution are unavoidably speculative, either because sodomy laws were inconsistent or unevenly applied, or because there was no specifically anti-homosexual legislation. In France, the revolutionary Code Pénal of 1791 decriminalized sexual relations between men by deliberately omitting any reference to them. This reform was incorporated into the Code Civil of 1804 and subsequently imposed, adopted or imitated, at least for a time, in Holland and many of the German states. Before the end of the 19th century, homosexual acts between consenting adults were no longer prohibited in Belgium, Italy, Luxembourg, Monaco, Portugal, Romania and Spain (depending on the interpretation of 'abusos deshonestos' in the 1822 legal code). Brazil removed sodomy from its criminal code in 1830. In the United States, where the 1533 English statute was adopted, but without the death penalty, convictions were rare until the 1880s.

This is not to say that a homosexual Englishman had only to cross the Channel to find peace and happiness. The mere absence of anti-sodomitical laws did not bring immunity from harassment and prosecution. France, with its revolutionary code, is sometimes mentioned as an example of modern tolerance, but 'pederasts' could still be punished under laws on public indecency, corruption of the young and even vagrancy. The notorious 'lewd-vag' (public lewdness and vagrancy) arrests of 1950s California were not a new idea.

This supple use of legislation makes it hard to discover the true extent of official persecution. When Paul Verlaine was arrested in Brussels in 1873 for shooting his lover Arthur Rimbaud in the wrist, he received the maximum sentence of two years. A medical examination had revealed 'traces of habitual pederasty, both active and passive', and although Verlaine's sexuality was strictly irrelevant, it seems to have influenced the jury.

Despite the legal tolerance of homosexuality, France was more dangerous for homosexuals than England. For most of the 19th century, raids on homosexual clubs and cruising-grounds were even more common in Paris than they were in London. In the 1850s, official campaigns were launched to 'clean up' the streets or (as one police doctor put it) to take soundings in the sea of 'filth'. A particularly energetic series of raids in 1865 caused a small diaspora of 'pederasts', about 10 per cent of whom were foreigners. In Paris alone, from 1860 to 1870, 1,282 pederasts were prosecuted. A further 1,631 were caught *in flagrante delicto*. By contrast, in all of England and Wales, there were 1,210 indictments for sodomy and related offences in the same period.

These extraordinary efforts certainly reflect a degree of institutional prejudice. François Carlier, who ran the Paris vice squad in the 1860s, thought that 'pederasty' deprived the sufferer of courage, family feeling and patriotism. 'Normal' prostitutes, who were registered by municipal doctors, performed a useful function, in his view, by sating the lusts of potential rapists, whereas pederasts were inherently useless and should not be tolerated.

Prejudice against 'pederasts', however, is by no means the only explanation. Mass round-ups were standard police procedure for dealing with prostitution (approximately 12,000 female prostitutes were arrested each year), and French policemen seem to have found it impossible to distinguish between male prostitutes and their customers. Many of the men arrested were caught having sexual intercourse in surprisingly public places like the shrub-lined avenues of the Champs-Élysées. Their arrest for indecency was not a specific result of their sexuality. Public intercourse of any kind was liable to punishment.

Carlier himself was mainly concerned with child prostitutes and blackmailers, who often masqueraded as policemen, and sometimes *were* policemen. The heaviest sentences were reserved for blackmail – often forced labour for life in New Caledonia. Carlier's colleague, Louis Canler, head of the Sûreté, dealt with 'antiphysicals' (*antiphysique* = 'unnatural') and blackmailers in the same chapter of his memoirs. Like most writers on the subject, he considered blackmailers a lower life-form than antiphysicals and painted an almost approving picture of a model homosexual couple whose lifestyle preserved them from the wiles of blackmailers and pimps:

> A wealthy foreign gentleman of seventy years, allied to one of the great families of northern Europe, settled in a sumptuous townhouse in Paris. [...] He brought with him a boy of eighteen (silky moustache, retroussé nose, feminine voice and appearance) whom he passed off as his nephew. [...] They spent the daytime shut up in the apartment. The young man, dressed as a woman, would devote himself to needle-work, either embroidery or tapestry. At dinner time, the 'nephew' would put on male clothing again and, after dinner, the two insepar-ables would climb into their carriage and go to the café for a cup of coffee and to read the newspapers. At ten o'clock, they climbed back into the carriage and returned home.

Of course, the fact that their daily routine was known to the police shows that they were not exactly free. But they were unlikely to be arrested. Many prosecutions in France were the result, not of direct police action, but of specific complaints: from members of the public who heard unseemly noises coming from public urinals, or from other homosexuals who used the law as a convenient means of revenge. The files of the Préfecture de Police show that many lovers' quarrels ended with an anonymous letter to the vice squad.

There was also some concern about false arrests and weak evidence. In 1881, after complaints about the dubious trial of a well-known pianist, Louis-Marcel Voyer, only ten arrests were made in Paris for 'male prostitution', compared to 165 in 1879 and 120 in 1880. (In 1882, normal service was resumed: eighty-two arrests.)

The main lesson of the French evidence is, first, that many law-enforcers who came into contact with real homosexual men, rather than with a shadowy, abstract notion of 'pederasty', quickly changed their minds and developed an anthropological fascination with these strange creatures who fell in love with people of their own sex. Second, despite the threat posed by police campaigns against prostitutes and blackmailers, there was – to anticipate the second part of this book – a thriving homosexual community with a highly politicized sense of its sexual rights, a calendar of events and anniversaries, its own villains and living legends, social clubs with international links, cafés and brothels, and well-established cruising-grounds with organized patrols.

Something similar could be said of most major cities, whatever the laws and however active the police. Some form of homosexual community seems to have existed in any city large enough to provide anonymity. In most European and American cities, there was a place or even a district where homosexual men – and, more rarely, women – could meet in relative safety (see Chapter 6): the waterfront in San Francisco, Broadway and Central Park in New York, parks, alleyways and toilets in Toronto (from about 1890), Montmartre in Paris, Unter den Linden in Berlin, the Retiro in Madrid, the docks in Barcelona, the Boulevard Ring in Moscow, the square in front of Copenhagen town hall, about seventeen different places in Amsterdam, and almost everywhere in Naples.

Even in countries where new laws were enacted against sodomy – Russia in 1835, the German Empire in 1871 – there were few prosecutions. The notorious paragraph 175 of the German Imperial Code (1871, from a Prussian law of 1851) made 'unnatural vice committed by two persons of the male sex or by people with animals' an imprisonable offence. Lists of homosexuals were drawn up by the sinister-sounding 'Päderasten Abteilung' ('Pederasty Division') of the German police, but the 'Rosa Listen' ('Pink Lists') were almost never used and were intended in any case to serve as a weapon in the fight against blackmailers. The Head of the Division, Leopold von Meerscheidt-Hüllessem (d. 1900), working closely with the enlightened psychologist Albert Moll, came to the conclusion that homosexuality was not a vice, and even tried to bequeath the Pink Lists to the organization that campaigned for homosexual equality.

The overall picture, then, is not unremittingly bleak. Nineteenth-century homosexuals lived under a cloud, but it seldom rained. Most of them suffered, not from the cruel machinery of justice, but from the creeping sense of shame, the fear of losing friends, family and reputation, the painful incompatibility of religious belief and sexual desire, the social and mental isolation, and the strain of concealment. Loveless marriages caused more lasting grief than laws, and still do.

Even so, as doctors and policemen discovered to their amazement, many 'pederasts' were perfectly happy with their strange condition and had no desire to change. Some of them had fulfilling, long-term relationships. Others relished the thrills of a night of 'public outrage' on the Champs-Élysées. Most of them never tangled with the law. As the head of the Paris vice squad observed, there was nothing he could do about 'orgies in private homes'.

*

As far as law enforcement is concerned, it was in the 20th century that the Dark Ages began.

Unlike Graph 1 (1810–1900), Graph 4 (1900–2000) (Appendix I, p. 274) shows a clearly significant change. (Both graphs take account of population growth.) The huge increase in 'buggery' (formerly, 'sodomy') offences in 20th-century England and Wales (buggery, indecent assault on males and gross indecency between males) partly reflects the increase in all crimes of violence, but the annual rate of increase for buggery and related offences was much higher. As the century progressed, buggery loomed ever larger in the eye of the law. In the late 1890s, it accounted for 5 per cent of all Crimes Against the Person. In the late 1950s, the percentage had risen to 21.

Seen as a percentage of all recorded crimes (Graph 5, Appendix I, p. 274), the mid-century peak is even more dramatic: 0.24 per cent in 1905; 1.52 per cent in 1955; 0.09 per cent in 1995. (The figures for homicide in the same years are 0.3 per cent, 0.06 per cent and 0.01 per cent.)

The key fact here is the contrast with the 19th century. The crime figures do not support very detailed arguments, especially over such a long period. Prosecutions for buggery increasingly involved children and probably reflect a growing awareness of child abuse and greater willingness to report it. (The offence of 'gross indecency with a child' was introduced in 1983.) But the specific offence of 'gross indecency between males' meant homosexual acts, usually between consenting males over the age of twenty-one. Figures for this offence, which did *not* include all consensual homosexual acts, follow the same upward trend.

For all the apocalyptic pronouncements of Victorian moralists, nothing like this had been seen before. In 1955, 2,322 cases of indecency between males were recorded. Applying a common average for the homosexual population of 4 per cent, and assuming that each offence involved two people (and no reoffenders), this would mean that one in every 125 homosexual men in England and Wales became a criminal statistic in 1955. Nineteenth-century homosexuals were comparatively unmolested. It was not until the 1930s that, as Quentin Crisp put it, the police began to think of homosexuals 'as North American Indians thought of bison [and] cast about for a way of exterminating them in herds'.

Allowing for incomplete figures and complex variations in State legislation, a similarly dramatic rise can be seen in many other European countries and in the United States (Graph 6, Appendix I, p. 275).

By the mid-20th century, the earlier effects of the Enlightenment on law reform had either evaporated or were visible only in the form of massive state interference. France had no explicitly anti-homosexual law until 1942, when the Pétain régime made homosexual acts with men under the age of twenty-one an imprisonable offence. This law was retained after the Liberation. Prosecutions of homo-sexuals very soon outnumbered all previous sodomy prosecutions in France (approximately seventy, from the 14th century to the Code Pénal of 1791). In 1960, the penalties for homosexual indecency were increased (six months to three years in prison, and a fine of 1,000 to 15,000 francs). Homosexuality was defined as a 'social scourge', along with alcoholism, prostitution and tuberculosis. The 'Brigade Mondaine' of the Paris police force ran a special archive on drug dealers, drug addicts, pimps, prostitutes and 'real or "fake" homosexuals' (i.e. hookers and blackmailers). The law was finally repealed in 1982.

In Germany, paragraph 175, which had narrowly escaped repeal, was reinforced instead in 1908. The Nazis introduced a more strin-gent version in 1935, outlawing any 'criminally indecent activities between men'. A kiss or a squeeze of the hand could send a man to jail. Like the French law, the Nazi law survived the Second World War. Some of the few surviving homosexuals (and gypsies) who had been incarcerated and tortured by the Nazis were transferred to prison when the camps were liberated. In West Germany, the maximum penalty was increased in 1957 from five to ten years. The law was abolished in East Germany in 1968 but lived on in West Germany, in a milder form, until 1994. Holland introduced a similar law in 1911. It remained in force until 1971.

The Soviet Union lagged behind Europe, so to speak, by legalizing sodomy between consenting adults in 1922. Even before the Revolution, there had been calls to repeal the sodomy law – notably by Vladimir Nabokov, the novelist's father. But in 1934, homosexual intercourse was pronounced a decadent 'social crime', along with sabotage and spying. It was not decriminalized until 1993.

Despite enormous changes since the 1960s, the legal effects of this counter-Enlightenment are still apparent today.*

Because of its uninterrupted history of anti-sodomy legislation, England provides the clearest evidence of a high tide of homophobia. The purge of publicly active homosexuals in mid-20th-century England was surely one of the most successful and futile police operations of all time. A policeman once complained to my father, who was a probation officer in Manchester in the early 1950s, that his tobacco always stank of chlorine because he had to spend so much time in public toilets. In the 19th century, a 'snowball' effect had sometimes produced little flurries of trials and scandals. Now, the snowball was vast and apparently unstoppable. Moralizing legislators could point to the statistics and warn of an alarming proliferation of perverts, and when cases came to court, there was a new willingness to prosecute. In 1920, the dangerously vague 'attempt to commit

---

* In fifteen European nations – Albania, Armenia, Austria, Belarus, Bulgaria, Cyprus, the Faeroe Islands (Denmark), Georgia, Hungary, Ireland, Lithuania, Moldova, Portugal, Romania and Serbia – and some British outposts – Gibraltar, Guernsey, Jersey and the Isle of Man – the law in 2002 still distinguished between homosexual and heterosexual acts, usually in the age of consent. In the United Kingdom (but not Northern Ireland), the age of consent for homosexuals and heterosexuals was equalized in January 2001, but until 2003 the notion of 'abuse of trust' allowed some men who had consensual sex with boys between sixteen and eighteen to be placed on the Sex Offenders Register. Homosexual age-of-consent offenders are treated far more harshly than heterosexual offenders. Consensual sodomy is outlawed in thirteen American states. The ban applies only to homosexual sodomy in Kansas, Missouri, Oklahoma and Texas.

buggery' (later, 'indecent assault on males') took over from buggery and indecency between males as the commonest of the three homosexual offences.

The modern figures show, once again, that legislation is a poor guide to reality. The punitive Labouchere Amendment of 1886 had not produced a rise in prosecutions. But the progressive 1967 Act, which legalized homosexual acts in private between two consenting men of twenty-one and over (except in the armed services and the merchant navy) was followed by a surge of cases of 'indecency between males'. The prosecution rate was 31 per cent in 1967 but 60 per cent in 1971. These figures began to fall only recently: 1,159 recorded cases in 1990; 167 in 2000.

Roy Walmsley of the Home Office suggests that this unexpected increase was caused by the introduction of summary trial for the offence of indecency between males. Indecent men could be dealt with, like drunkards, in less than a day. But obviously someone had to arrest them in the first place. Old police habits died hard.

It may seem flippant or callous to play down the perils of homosexual life in the Victorian age by contrasting it with the 20th century. The point is that the criminal statistics distort and darken the lives of real people. Graphs are a poor guide to the daily experience of individuals. Even the apparently grim state of affairs that prevailed for most of the 20th century is not final evidence of a homosexual hell on earth. Not everyone lived the sort of life that put them within the chlorinated grasp of policemen. And not everyone knew – or cared – that their sexual activities were punishable by law.

Police raids and famous trials, as parts of this book will show, could even have an encouraging effect. They proved that like-minded people existed and that not all 'sodomites' lived in fearful isolation. Legal-medical textbooks and newspaper reports were the unwitting media of a virtual community, a society of strangers that was informed of its own existence by its persecutors. Even a horrific case like the Vere Street scandal of 1810 could be a consolation and a rallying-cry.

It was in this positive spirit that Byron's friend Charles Matthews kept His Lordship up to date with all the latest sodomite news from England:

Your Lordship's delicacy w^d I know be shocked by the pillorification (in the Hay M.) of a club of gents who were wont to meet in Vere Street (St Clement's) – how all London was in an uproar on that day, & how the said gents were bemired and beordured. [. . .] Every Newsp that one casts one's eye upon, presents one with some instance.

With your friends the Turcomans to be sure, [sodomy's] value (compared with fornication) is as five to two. But that wch you get for £5 we must risque our necks for; and are content to risque them.

*

The relatively cheerful display of bleak statistics in this chapter is an attempt to reduce the weight of the statute books in notions of the gay past. The once common view of the Victorian age as a hellishly inconvenient century populated by dangerous eccentrics and downtrodden victims has affected homosexual history even more than other fields of social history. Information is scarce, and so the criminal evidence plays an important role, but it should not be allowed to dominate every scene.

Even in the tidy world of statistics, significant trends are hard to detect. A history of homosexuality in the 19th century would be much easier to write if epoch-making moments did rise up like volcanic peaks in the ocean of fact, but, as the figures suggest, few such moments exist. When the whole century is taken into account – and not just the oscillations of a few years – the grand narratives disappear.

The same thing occurs when any particular case is examined, even if it appears to be unusually representative.

The remainder of this chapter is devoted to the most famous and supposedly emblematic case of all.

*

On 18 February 1895, the paranoid Marquis of Queensberry, whose son Lord Alfred Douglas was Oscar Wilde's lover, set a 'booby-trap' (Wilde's expression) by leaving a card at the Albemarle Club 'For Oscar Wilde, posing somdomite' (*sic*). Unwisely, Wilde decided to sue for criminal libel.

During the trial, evidence of 'unnatural habits, tastes and practices' was discovered in Wilde's writings – *The Picture of Dorian Gray* and some flowery letters to Alfred Douglas with his 'red, rose-leaf lips'. The homosexual undercurrent of the Aesthetic Movement was cruelly exposed. The exquisite Wilde was seen to have consorted with pimps and rent-boys. His flippant remarks show that he was either bent on self-destruction or too flattered by the court's appreciative laughter to notice the danger.

> *Edward Carson (prosecuting):* Did you ever kiss [Walter Grainger]?
> *Oscar Wilde:* Oh, no, never in my life; he was a peculiarly plain boy.
> *Carson:* He was what?
> *Wilde:* I said I thought him unfortunately – his appearance was so very unfortunately – very ugly – I mean – I pitied him for it.

Not surprisingly, Wilde lost the case. Legally, he was now a sitting duck. Queensberry's solicitor sent the trial notes and testimonies to the Director of Public Prosecutions. Several people urged Wilde to take the boat-train to the Continent, but he stayed on in London. Later that day (5 April 1895), he was arrested at the Cadogan Hotel and charged with indecency. The jury failed to reach a verdict. He was released on bail but still refused to leave England. At the second trial, he was found guilty and sentenced to two years' hard labour.

This sad and avoidable sequence of events is still the biggest single influence on perceptions of Victorian homosexuality. In their repercussions, the Wilde trials belong more to the 20th century than to the 19th. They not only helped to impose a music-hall view of homosexuality as the preserve of camping aesthetes and seedy sex-workers, they also provided modern homosexuality with a date of birth, a charismatic martyr and some memorable legends. According to the famously unreliable Frank Harris, for instance, the arrest of Oscar Wilde was followed by a mass emigration of homosexuals to the Continent: trains to the coast and the cross-Channel ferries were crammed with wealthy sodomites, fleeing to France and Italy. 'Never was Paris so crowded with members of the English governing classes.' This melodramatic fantasy has little more basis in fact than the medieval legend according to which all sodomites died on the day that Christ was born. Both show a tendency to treat all homosexuals as a neurotic, undifferentiated mass, prone to catastrophe and essentially separate from the rest of humanity.

Historically, the trials of Oscar Wilde, like the Amendment under which he was prosecuted, are a huge distraction. Homosexuality was only part of the story. The charge was indecency, not sodomy, for which Wilde could have received a life sentence instead of two years. In purely legal terms, as Wilde himself acknowledged, the conviction was fair, and public opinion was by no means unanimously hostile. The comments of bigots like the *Daily Telegraph* reporter, who blamed him for all modern sins – atheism, Impressionism, disrespect for parents, and so on – are simply more memorable and quotable than the sensible or humane comments.

Even after the shocking revelations of a homosexual underworld, there was widespread support for Wilde. An Anglican clergyman paid half of his bail; the other half was paid by the Marquis of Queensberry's eldest surviving son. A Jewish businessman offered him the free use of his yacht as a means of escape. The servants of his friends the Leversons expressed sympathy with 'poor Mr Wilde'. The painter Louise Jopling exchanged a 'sorrowful' glance with the newsboy who told her of the verdict. W. B. Yeats, whose father urged him to testify for Wilde, brought letters of support from several Irish writers. 'Cultivated London', said Yeats, 'was now full of his advocates.' When Wilde gave his moving speech on 'the Love that dare not speak its name', the hissing from the public gallery was drowned out by applause.

After the trial, there were letters to the press protesting at Wilde's treatment. The popular journalist W. T. Stead pointed out that Wilde's 'unnatural' propensities were not unnatural for him, and that if he had committed adultery with his friend's wife or corrupted young girls instead of boys, 'no one could have laid a finger upon him'. Even *The Illustrated Police Budget* was sorry that 'one of the most brilliant wits, epicures, and epigrammatists we have seen in England for years' had 'passed from the light of freedom'.

Wilde may have been 'crucified' on the cross of public morality, but he supplied the hammer and the nails. Before and after his arrest, he was given every chance to leave the country but ignored the advice of friends and lawyers. In court, he improvised brilliantly, but he also lied stupidly and antagonized his prosecutors by hinting (as Solicitor-

General Lockwood put it) that they were 'too low to appreciate' his art.

The Wilde trials, in other words, cannot be treated as straightforward evidence of homophobia, though that certainly played a part. As usual in such public cases, homosexuality was a symbol. Sodomy was the sin that stood for all the others. Wilde's sexual habits were shocking, but so was the blatant disregard for class divisions that seemed to go with them. Wilde had had the 'disgraceful audacity' to dress up a common boy, found on the beach at Worthing, in 'public school colours'. His 'associates', said the Solicitor-General, 'ought to have been his equals and not these illiterate boys whom you have heard in the witness box'.

Worse still, Wilde had made a brilliant career of poking fun at English society and did nothing to apologize for his success. As Yeats pointed out, 'the rage against Wilde was also complicated by the Britisher's jealousy of art and the artist'. 'This hatred is not due to any action of the artist or eminent man; it is merely the expression of an individual hatred and envy, become collective because circumstances have made it so.'

Finally, Wilde was not English. His Irishness was never mentioned in court, but it is remarkable that so many of the famous British sodomy scandals had an Irish connection: the arrest of the Bishop of Clogher, the suicide of Castlereagh (accused of desiring 'unnatural union' between Britain and Ireland), the Dublin Castle affair, the Wilde trials and the trial of Roger Casement. Both Casement and Wilde were Irish nationalists. The first person to be prosecuted under the Labouchere Amendment had been a troublesome Irish MP, Edward Samuel Wesley de Cobain, who had previously complained about the brutality of British policemen in Ireland.

To reduce this complex muddle to a simple tale of 'martyrdom' (as both Wilde and Douglas later saw it) is to amplify the effects of anti-sodomy legislation. The melodramatic approach fashions a weapon of sexual oppression out of a jumble of laws that were often casually enacted, sporadically applied and aimed primarily at acts of violence. It promotes a highly localized and pejorative view of homosexuality. It suggests that gay people were defined entirely by their sexuality and that they participated in 'normal' society only as impostors. It creates a largely invented oppressor and the possibility of a correspondingly fictitious 'liberation'. Acceptance – or, as it came to be known, 'tolerance' – appears in this light as a relatively recent development attributable to political agitation and legal reform rather than to general human characteristics like compassion or indifference.

These well-intentioned exaggerations have little to tell us about the Victorian age. They belong, not to the maligned 19th century, but to the more openly repressive age that began with the death of Oscar Wilde in 1900.

3

Country of the Blind

Into whatever houses I enter, I will go into them for the benefit of the sick, and will abstain from every voluntary act of mischief and corruption; and, further, from the seduction of females or males, of freemen and slaves.

Hippocratic Oath; tr. F. Adams

The psychoanalytic press regularly reproaches us with neglecting love and the erotic. We are not trained for that and are therefore not obliged to consider all mental phenomena from that point of view. We had more important things to do.

Alfred Adler, *Das Problem der Homosexualität*, 1930

A S FAR AS 'SODOMITES' were concerned, the legal system was underpinned and eventually almost replaced by the medical system.

For centuries, physicians had been examining prisoners for traces of sodomy. The two Belgian doctors who described Verlaine's genitals in such loving detail in 1873 were practising an ancient art. Like soothsayers inspecting entrails, they saw things that the uninitiated would dismiss as insignificant. As Dr Brouardel, a friend and colleague of Marcel Proust's father, explained, 'There is more variety in the shape and size of the penis than there is in the face.'

Throughout the 19th century, as the medical profession gained in confidence and prestige, medical views of homosexuality became increasingly specialized and ingenious. Homosexuality was one of the undiscovered continents on which doctors could stake a claim to originality and build a career. Their investigations now sound ludicrously ill-informed or simply hostile, but they had a beneficial side-effect. Unprecedented amounts of information were gathered on the lives of gay men and women who would otherwise have vanished altogether.

As the roll-call of 'causes of homosexuality' on pp. 5–6 suggests, a history of medical approaches to homosexuality would be a slice of the history of the whole medical profession. Practically every new theory and technique was applied – and still is being applied – to the 'problem' of homosexuality. This source of information therefore has some of the disadvantages of the legal evidence. It imbues accounts of homosexual life with the disinfectant smell of theory and favours certain groups: criminals and lunatics, fee-paying middle-class patients, and literate, liberated homosexuals, some of whom were medical practitioners themselves.

It also creates the false impression that most homosexuals were permanently suicidal. Desperate people were more likely to resort to doctors, and the doctors often assumed that homosexuals could not be happy. Since few people go through life without at least a glance at the emergency exit, a determined interviewer could always turn up evidence of suicidal misery.

The interviewers themselves were not necessarily typical of their profession. Medical science did after all make enormous advances in the 19th century. It was rarely at its best when dealing with sexual behaviour. Most doctors who tried to cure, comfort or castigate relied on common prejudice and hazy notions of sexuality. They confused the people they called 'sodomites' and 'pederasts' with rapists and paedophiles. Few were at the cutting-edge of their science and, until the 1890s, very few had access to any useful information. Even the hastiest modern gay historian has read far more medical literature on the subject than almost any Victorian doctor.

The real value of the medical literature lies in the patients' own accounts. A huge amount of information about 19th-century homosexuality comes from these accounts. It is all the more important to know about the circumstances in which they were produced. It is also worth knowing that this was not an entirely one-sided relationship: the views of doctors were determined to a large extent by the information they received from their patients.

The muddle of medical theories should not be treated with too much respect. To present these theories in chronological order is to conjure up the image of a long, straight road to truth rather than an intellectual swampland in which ancient superstitions thrived and diversified. Some lingered on into the 21st century; others had a delayed effect. The year on the surgery calendar was no guide to the advice that would be dispensed by the doctor. Even now, Victorian notions of homosexuality are being energetically applied by religious groups like JONAH (Jews Offering New Alternatives to Homosexuality) and psychiatrists purporting to treat 'prehomosexual' children.

There is one other reason why medical views deserve attention. A dramatic suggestion made by Michel Foucault in 1976, based on a 19th-century idea, is now widely accepted as the historical truth. Despite growing academic scepticism, it appears quite regularly in newspaper articles and conversations. The idea is that, before 1870, the exclusively homosexual person did not exist. 'The homosexual' supposedly was a creature invented by Victorian doctors. The earlier 'sodomite' had simply indulged in certain acts. The new 'homosexual' was a distinct personality, characterized by an 'internal androgyny, a hermaphrodism of the soul'. 'The sodomite had been a sinner, the homosexual was now a species.'*

Foucault, whose father had been a surgeon and a professor of anatomy, proposed 1870 as the 'date of birth' of this new category of human being and the *Archiv für Neurologie* as the place of birth. He was referring to a journal (actually the *Archiv für Psychiatrie und Nervenkrankheiten*) edited by a Berlin asylum doctor called Carl Westphal (see p. 55). In an article published in the *Archiv* in 1870,

---

* 'Sinner' is a translation of '*relaps*' (a person who has relapsed into heresy after abjuring it). The standard English version mistranslates '*relaps*' as 'a temporary aberration'.

Westphal defined 'contrary sexual feeling' as a neuropathic condition. By opening his journal to the psychiatric study of homosexuality, Westphal helped to create the new sub-discipline to which Foucault himself belonged.

Foucault never intended his idea to be treated as the final word. Like any theory, it was supposed to be tested, not ingested whole. Unlike some of his followers, he never claimed that homosexuality itself began in 1870 (phrases like 'hermaphrodism of the soul' had been in use since the 18th century), and he certainly never said that homosexuality waited to exist until a word was invented for it. Foucault seems not to have read Westphal's article and his theory simply repeated a commonplace of early French psychiatry. According to Léon Thoinot in 1898, for instance, the god-like Westphal had 'extracted from the chaos of inverted love a clear and precise morbid type: congenital inversion'. 'There was light, and the scientific phase began, following the phase of chaos.'

This fantasy about the power of academic discourse, which effectively devalues all gay experience before the advent of psychiatry, has been a Trojan horse of homophobia. It draws attention to the fact that our notions of sexuality are peculiar to our own society and age, but it also implies that the medical profession impinged on the lives of gay men and women to such an extent that they eventually saw themselves through the doctors' eyes and became their own oppressors. Ironically, the idea itself has had such a huge effect on modern perceptions of the gay past that it is now its own best proof.

*

DESPITE THEIR APPARENT complexity, medical views of homosexuality are remarkable for their persistent uniformity.

The basic divisions of homosexuality into the physiological and the mental, the innate and the acquired, the persistent and the circumstantial go back to the dawn of medicine. Several ancient authors – Herodotus, Parmenides and Soranus – saw 'the Scythians' madness' (high-pitched voices, transvestism and womanly pursuits) as a disease of the mind. They also believed that it could be inherited. Hippocrates, on the other hand, attributed the condition to physiological changes caused by excessive horse-riding. (The same view was expressed over 2,000 years later by Dr William Hammond of New York who rediscovered the illness in the Pueblos of New Mexico.)

Most Victorian doctors would not have found parallels with ancient writers insulting. Hippocrates was still being quoted in the 1850s as a medical authority. Until the mid-19th century, the main authority on 'pederasty' was Paolo Zacchias's *Quaestiones medico-legales* (Rome, 1621–5), which was heavily indebted to Hippocrates. One of the most influential theories of sexuality in the 19th century – in less literal forms – was the idea humorously expounded by Aristophanes in Plato's *Symposium* in the 4th century BC.*

The physiological school remained dominant for most of the 19th century, partly because most treatises on the subject were written by doctors whose job was to provide courts with evidence of sodomy. Even when psychiatry shifted attention from the genitals to the brain, physiology was still thought to play a part. In the early 20th century, Sigmund Freud and the English sexologist Havelock Ellis were still inclined to believe that 'inversion' might be related to primitive herm-aphrodism.

Some doctors simply registered the signs of 'unnatural' intercourse such as anal infections and relaxed sphincters. Others thought that genital anomalies might *precede* the immoral acts and that physio-logical deformity could produce aberrant sexual behaviour. In most cases, a simple kind of logic prevailed. It was widely assumed that a man who felt sexual desire for another man must be in some way female and that the signs of his femininity could be detected. By the same token, lesbians were thought to have over-developed clitorises which they used like penises. This childish notion survived a complete lack of evidence (a study of Parisian prostitutes in 1836 discovered no significant abnormalities) and could still be found in a medical dictionary of 1849, a marriage manual of 1862, a French dictionary of 1874 and the Larousse encyclopedia in 1876. Even in 1897, Havelock Ellis thought it necessary to refute the idea, though he did

---

* The three original sexes – male, female and hermaphrodite, each with four hands, four legs and two faces – were cut in half by Zeus. Since then, every human has tried to find its original 'other half': men who come from hermaphrodites are attracted to women (and vice versa), women who came from the female love women, and men who came from the male love men.

accept the findings of a German voice specialist who discerned 'a very decidedly masculine type of larynx' in '23 inverted women'.

Thinking on the subject was, to say the least, confused, and perhaps further muddled by a few genuine cases of pseudo-hermaphrodism (genital deformation). In his *Rapports du physique et du moral de l'homme* (1802), which contains one of the earliest modern medical descriptions of homosexuality, Georges Cabanis showed a typically non-committal approach to the question of physical causes:

> I have encountered some of these ambivalent individuals who not only had shriller voices, weaker muscles and softer, more flaccid flesh, but also that greater proportional width of the pelvis which, as we have said, characterizes the bone structure of the female body; and conse-quently they walked like women, describing a greater arc around the centre of gravity. In such cases, the physical condition always seemed to me to be accompanied by an exactly matching mental condition.

The association of physiology and mental state appealed to a sense of completeness. Medical theorists, like novelists, were in the business of piecing together miscellaneous bits of information to create a convincing whole. The same hotchpotch of moral, mental and physical traits underlies Balzac's luscious description of the young poet Lucien de Rubempré in the first part of *Illusions perdues* (1836–7):

> His face had the distinguished lines of classical beauty: a Grecian brow and nose, the soft whiteness of a woman's skin [. . .] The smile of sad angels hovered over lips whose coral hues were heightened by beautiful teeth. He had the hands of a well-born person, elegant hands which women longed to kiss and whose every gesture men felt compelled to obey. [. . .] Looking at his feet, any man would have been tempted to take him for a girl in disguise, especially since, like most men with subtle, not to say cunning minds, his hips were shaped like those of a woman. This is nearly always a reliable clue to character and was so in Lucien's case.

Balzac was accused of encroaching on medical territory, which shows that homosexuality was felt to be a medical subject long before psychiatry laid claim to it. In fact, Balzac was so far ahead of his time that he is barely recognizable as a pioneer. His homosexual characters are not 'sodomites'. They fall in love like other people, but with a heroic intensity that reflects the forbidden nature of their passion. Many doctors noticed the extraordinary degree of sexual excitement enjoyed by 'pederasts' and 'sapphists', but only Balzac recognized this as an effect of repression rather than as a sign of depravity.

In the 'construction' of homosexuality, entertaining novels like Balzac's *Illusions perdues* or Gautier's *Mademoiselle de Maupin* were surely far more influential than obscure, turgid texts written by academic doctors. Over a century later, Kenneth Walker's *The Physiology of Sex* (1940) showed that the tortoise of medical science was not merely slow, it feigned forward motion:

> The distinctive characteristics of the more obvious types of invert are well known. Their skins are delicate and feminine, they have deposits of fat over their buttocks and thighs, they often talk in high-pitched voices and their mode of walking resembles that of a woman. [Arthur] Weil states also that their pelvic measurements approximate to those of the female rather than the male.

It was this imaginative paranoia that produced the great classic of the physiological school: Ambroise Tardieu's forensic handbook, *Étude médico-légale sur les attentats aux mœurs* (Paris, 1857).* Tardieu was not a medical pioneer: his supposed discoveries – notably the 'infundibular' (funnel-shaped) anus – were already widely accepted as tell-tale signs. His real contribution was to introduce an appearance of precision into the art of detecting 'pederasts'.

Tardieu, perhaps misled by homosexual fashions, believed that passive pederasts had enormous bottoms: 'I have seen one pederast whose buttocks were joined and formed a single, perfect sphere.' In active pederasts, the penis was deformed: it bulged like a snout or tapered like a dog's penis, and, for a reason easily imagined, it had a distinctive corkscrew shape. As a result, pederasts were unable to urinate in a straight line.

> Curled hair, painted face, open collar, waist tightly corseted so as to accentuate the figure, fingers, ears and breast loaded with jewels,

---

* 7th edition: 1878. Translated into German (1860), Spanish (1882) and Italian (1898). No English translation exists.

the whole person giving off the smell of the most pungent perfumes, a handkerchief, flowers or some needlework in the hand – this is the strange, repulsive and quite rightly suspect physiognomy that betrays a pederast.

A no less characteristic trait, which I have observed a hundred times, is the contrast of this false elegance and attention lavished on appearance with the sordid uncleanliness that would on its own be enough to make one shun these wretches.

Tardieu's neurotic details proved to be utterly fascinating. His book became a bestseller far beyond the medical world. Tardieu, who had met over 200 'pederasts', had a real gift for expressing that eerie sense of contact with a strange tribe living side by side with the rest of the human race.

From now on, a great deal of pseudo-anthropological ingenuity would be devoted to the task of identifying the species. This, more than any theoretical or practical position, was one of the main forces in 19th- and 20th-century homosexual science. It proclaimed the doctor's usefulness, the efficiency of his profession or sub-discipline, and his divinatory skill.

It is revealing that, as the study of sexual deviance became more complex and specialized, the detection of signs became increasingly unscientific. It was as if the terminology had been invented to allow prejudice and superstition to survive in a modern idiom. Some terms, in fact, were taken directly from myth. 'Succubus' and 'incubus' (for passive and active pederast) were still in medical use at the end of the 19th century.

Constitutional features like body hair and bone size were confused with acquired habits like smoking and drinking. Many of the supposed signs – a mincing walk or a penchant for perfume – reflected growing awareness of homosexual urban life. Most reflected simple, orthodox notions of masculinity and femininity. The idea that homosexual men were unable to whistle or spit probably had a popular origin, but it was incorporated into the medical literature and seriously discussed. This accounts for one of the odder themes of Havelock Ellis's *Studies in the Psychology of Sex*: 'He never succeeded in his attempts to whistle'; 'I am, perhaps, a better whistler than most men'; 'It may be added that inverted women are very often good whistlers; Hirschfeld even knows two who are public performers in whistling.'

For lesbians, the diagnostic process was simply reversed: they smoked (in severe cases, cigars), had deep voices and big muscles, liked sport, and were able to spit, whistle, curse and throw.

Some of the most popular theories – that men and women could masturbate themselves into a state of sexual inversion, or that an inability to urinate in a straight line was a sign of homosexuality – must have given rise to some anxious self-examinations. These medical fairy tales served a practical purpose. The precise definition of what constituted a homosexual allowed the species, in theory, to be sectioned off and securely identified. By implication, a man who walked stiffly, never looked around in the street and never used eau de cologne could not be homosexual, whereas a left-handed man with small hands and feet, warm skin and feminine handwriting was probably suffering from a serious disorder.

Ironically, precise definitions also allowed homosexuals to refine their disguises. In 1869, one of Karl Heinrich Ulrichs' homosexual correspondents sent him a photograph of himself and told him not to be surprised by the cigar in his hand: 'I must show myself to the world in the fashions of a man.' In 1891, Albert Moll revealed that 'Uranists deliberately try to become heavy smokers to put people off the scent.' For Englishmen, an ability to grow a moustache and to bowl overarm at cricket were valuable assets. In Proust's *À la recherche du temps perdu*, a bone-crushing handshake is said to be typical of German homosexuals. This presumably explains Proust's own remarkable floppiness. When his friend Antoine Bibesco advised him to grip the hand more firmly, Proust exclaimed: 'But people would take me for an invert!'

The identification game, with its promise of instant wisdom, became a stubborn habit. The supposed ability of homosexuals to recognize one another at a glance was a challenge to medical science. Doctors prided themselves on their ability to replicate by 'rational' means the instinctive insights of homosexuals. Throw an object at the lap of a sitting homosexual, said the Berlin doctor Magnus Hirschfeld in 1913, and he will automatically open his legs to catch it. A lesbian, being a natural trouser-wearer, will close her legs.

Homosexual men sat on the toilet seat; lesbians stood. Dr Hirschfeld also described the workings of the 'sidereal pendulum' – a gold wedding-ring on a thread tied around the right index finger and held over a silver tablespoon. The direction of swing reveals the person's sexuality: longitudinally or at right angles = heterosexual; oblique swinging = homosexual.

The popularity of these parlour games shows how little difference there was between science and popular wisdom. Little had changed in 2,000 years. Dio Chrysostom (1st century AD) knew of a man from Tarsus who could recognize the character of any individual in an instant. One man left him baffled. 'But just as the fellow was leaving, he sneezed, whereupon our friend immediately cried out that the man was a catamite.'

Increasingly in the 20th century, this identification game seemed to reflect homophobic paranoia rather than scientific ambition. Raphael Kirchner's pseudo-sociological handbook, *Woran erkennt man Homosexuelle?* (1908) ('How to Recognize Homosexuals'), was written 'for employers, managers and men in key positions'. In 1963, the *Sunday Mirror* (London) published a two-page guide on 'How to Spot a Possible Homo' ('shifty glances', 'dropped eyes' and 'a fondness for the theatre'). Six years later, Clifford Allen's *Textbook of Psychosexual Disorders* (2nd edition, Oxford University Press, 1969) was still offering comforting advice to those who feared the presence of undetected strangers:

> It is not necessary to be homosexual to be able to detect inverts in casual social life. Although I am normal I have seen many homosexuals and am able to observe them in a crowd by minute gestures, tones of speech, and so on. Even on the wireless one can tell them by their speech which is either excessively soft and slightly slurred or else grating and harsh.

*

THE OTHER MAIN CURRENT of medical thought also had little to do with science, though it ran through almost every work on the subject. Medicine was used to justify morality and to confirm religious beliefs.

Attempts to reconcile medical fact with sexual myth had a long history. Herodotus attributed the Scythians' disease to the plundering of the temple of Aphrodite: the goddess of love had taken revenge by making them effeminate. In a similarly imaginative vein, an anatomical treatise by Le Baillif de la Rivière in 1580 claimed that burns caused by the caustic Dead Sea (the fall-out from Sodom and Gomorrha) could be cured only by menstrual blood. He also claimed that sodomy was punished with a disease called gonorrhoea, which he associated with 'Gomorrha'.

With the advent of modern medicine, the notion of vice was translated into pathological terms. In the 1880s, Cesare Lombroso argued that homosexuality was a sign of evolutionary back-sliding. Now that his skull-measuring science is known to be spurious, Lombroso looks more like a Grand Inquisitor than a scientist. His new-fangled terms – 'degenerative', 'atavistic', 'criminaloid', etc. – are far less common in his writing than old favourites like 'lascivious', 'perverted' and 'turpitude'. A typical Lombroso sentence simply adds a dash of mathematics to the moralizing: 'If several women are brought together in a prison, their erotic shamelessness is cubed.'

Even with the introduction of professional tools and terminology, most medical writers still proclaimed their disgust, if only to create the rhetorical conditions in which the untouchable subject could be discussed. In 1813, François Fodéré began the 'Sodomy' section of his forensic manual with a typical show of revulsion: 'Oh, that I could avoid sullying my quill with the foul obscenity of pederasts!' Later, distaste was conveyed with ugly abstractions. No one who talked of 'congenital sexual inversion' or of 'cerebro-spinal' perverts could be accused of showing undue sympathy. Later still, morality appeared in the form of pity for 'unfortunate cases' or in the notion of redemption. According to Kenneth Walker's *The Physiology of Sex*, which was still being reprinted by Penguin in 1965, homosexuals often regain their 'self-respect' by 'devoting themselves with enthusiasm to various forms of social and philanthropic work'.

The story of Sodom lurked in the back of every doctor's mind. Sodomites had survived the fire and brimstone, but their bodies bore the marks of their perversion and they suffered from horrible diseases. For some doctors, these stigmata had purely logical explanations: anal intercourse or venereal disease. Real medical problems did of course exist and must have placed 'sodomites' in an impossible position. Byron was said by one of his Greek servants to have consulted an English doctor in Greece about his boyfriend Giraud's 'ragged fundament, arising from the frequent distension of the *podex* in antiphysical concubinage'. The only consolation was that this embarrassing complaint had an interesting pedigree, having been 'frequent among the ancient Greek and Roman *cinaedi*'.

The other commonly recorded complaint was a pustular venereal disease called crystalline, also known as 'the Ganymedes' syphilis'. A male brothel in Paris in the 1820s retained doctors who specialized in the treatment of the disease. Paresis (dementia and paralysis caused by syphilis) was also thought at one time to be a homosexual disease, hence the name given to a meeting place for 'fairies' in 1890s New York: Paresis Hall.

Most sodomite illnesses existed only in doctors' minds. Samuel Tissot claimed in his famous treatise on onanism (continually in print in several languages from 1758 to 1905) that 'sapphists' were prone to 'cancers in the womb', 'caused by movements and by frictions which are far from natural'. Several German doctors, from the 1830s, thought that pederasty led to tuberculosis, dropsy and typhoid. Some suggested that genital deformities associated with 'unnatural' acts were a pathological trait of 'pederasts', whether or not they performed the acts in question.

'Disease' had been used as a metaphor for homosexuality long before the 19th century, but as doctors became more skilled at finding connections, local complaints could be interpreted as signs of a more profound disorder. Pustules, cancers and ragged fundaments were a warning from Nature that she did not after all tolerate sexual deviance. The writer of the 'Orgasme' article (1874) in the Larousse encyclopedia scrupulously admitted that 'artificial means' (those used by homosexuals) would produce a bona fide orgasm, but he went on to observe, with obvious relief, that Nature concurred with morality, 'for many diseases come from unnatural pleasures'.

The notion that AIDS was a special punishment for gay people was just the latest version of an ancient idea.

*

THE DOMINANCE OF LOCAL moral attitudes in medical approaches to homosexuality is also visible in the geographical spread of sexologists.

Almost all the early works on the subject were French or German. There was increasing interest in Italy and the United States from the mid-1880s. But in Britain, there was almost total silence. Sir Alexander Morison included 'monomania with unnatural propensity' in his *Physiognomy of Mental Diseases* (1838), and there was an article on the phrenological concept of 'Adhesiveness' in *The Lancet* of 6 August 1836:

> ADHESIVENESS. – I knew two gentlemen whose attachment to each other was so excessive, as to amount to a disease. When the one visited the other, they slept in the same bed, sat constantly alongside of each other at table, spoke in affectionate whispers, and were, in short, miserable when separated.

Little else of a medical nature was said in Britain until Havelock Ellis's *Sexual Inversion*, which struggled into print in 1897.* Even the fearless Malthusian, George Drysdale, whose *Elements of Social Science* (1854) called for open debate of 'the sexual questions', avoided the subject. There were English translations of Casper (1861–5) and Krafft-Ebing (1892) (see pp. 58, 57), but for decades, practically the only British medical authority was *The Principles and Practice of Medical Jurisprudence* (1865) by Alfred Taylor, who merely alluded to false charges made 'by soldiers and a bad class of policemen'. He preferred to leave the matter to lawyers. Later editions covered the topic with two picturesque cases of transvestism.

The *British Medical Journal* remained pruriently hostile well into the 20th century. In 1902, it recommended Krafft-Ebing's book as a handy source of toilet-paper. In 1909, in a review of Edward Carpenter's *The Intermediate Sex*, it suggested that homosexuals should emigrate *en masse* and leave 'serious people in England' in peace.

This British black-out has sometimes been attributed to a prag-

---

* Written in collaboration with the scholar and poet J. A. Symonds, it first appeared in Germany as *Das konträre Geschlechtsgefühl* (Leipzig, 1896). The entire print-run of the first English edition was bought up and destroyed by Symonds' heirs. The 2nd edition, without Symonds' name, appeared under the fictitious imprint, 'Watford University Press'.

matic reluctance to indulge in flowery Continental theorizing, but it surely has more to do with prudery. The Larousse encyclopedia (1864–76) contains enough material for a very large book on homosexuality from prehistory to the present. The 1911 *Encyclopaedia Britannica* is comprehensively silent. 'Lesbian' appears in the index, but only as an architectural term: 'Lesbian leaf'.

On the Continent, doctors were less squeamish, but even there, social and professional considerations were more consistently influential than medical findings.

Before the 1870s, most writers owed their information to ancient texts or to first-hand experience. Glimpses of a thriving and widespread homosexual culture appeared in studies of prostitutes, convicts and criminals. In 1791, Karl Philipp Moritz had published accounts of two men 'who manifested an enthusiastic love for persons of their own sex'. In 1852, a forensic doctor, Johann Ludwig Casper, revealed the amazing world of 'mental hermaphrodites': his article 'On Rape and Pederasty' was based on the confiscated diary of a Count who had belonged to a very active 'Pederasts Club' that seemed to contain a fair cross-section of German society. Even more dramatically, in 1864, a journalist and former jurist called Karl Heinrich Ulrichs published the first of twelve texts calling for legal reform (see p. 181). Ulrichs himself was homosexual and his theory that 'Urnings'* were a separate sex was adopted by several doctors, usually in Latin: '*anima muliebris in corpore virili inclusa*' ('a woman's soul shut up in a man's body').

In the 1870s and 1880s, doctors, mostly French and German, began to reduce this soup of information to something that could be divided up along disciplinary lines. The same authorities appeared again and again, as thesis directors, journal editors and preface writers. A professional community was taking shape. Before the end of the century, conferences and journals had given certain approaches a dynastic respectability. Each doctor's conclusions reflected his training and his preferred field of action. Anatomists clung to the genital

---

* Ulrichs' neologisms, 'Urning' (Uranist or Uranian) and 'Dioning' (Dionian), come from Plato's *Symposium*, where 'heavenly love' is associated with Aphrodite, daughter of Uranus, and 'common love' with Aphrodite, daughter of Dione.

explanation. Public health experts worried about epidemics of inversion. Alienists saw sexual deviance as a sign of madness. Determinists warned of degeneration. Few doctors found evidence to suggest that their own approach was not the best.

By the end of the 1880s, the medical profession was supplying enough information of its own, packaged in the correct terminology, to do without outside help. Julien Chevalier's 520-page study of sexual inversion (1893) was based on second-hand cases (actually, third-hand, since the patients' accounts had already been digested by doctors). Chevalier's book in turn was used by later writers. Spectacular, untypical cases were recycled and had a disproportionate effect. One of the 'classic' early case studies, described in Claude Michéa's 'Des déviations maladives de l'appétit vénérien' (1849), was a man convicted of necrophilia.

Medical self-confidence thrived on an ability to reach conclusions no matter what. The most original aspect of Freud's *Three Essays on the Theory of Sexuality* (1905) is not the separation of sexual instinct from sexual object but the quite exceptional confession of partial ignorance: 'It will be seen that we are not in a position to base a satisfactory explanation for the origin of inversion upon the material at present before us.'

The main problem was not a lack of intelligence or hatred of homosexuals but a professional desire to wring fresh ideas out of a subject that could not support them. Doctors who thought long and hard about homosexuality even after exhausting its capacity to produce reliable conclusions trod a backward path from common sense to make-believe. Freud's disciple, the Hungarian doctor Sándor Ferenczi, is a typical example. In 1906, he urged his colleagues in Budapest to accept 'uranism' as a naturally occurring form of sexuality and called for decriminalization. The following year, he discovered Freud, decided that uranism was a kind of neurosis, and began to develop theories of his own. He concluded that homosexuality was a form of coprophilia (an abnormal interest in faeces), expressed in a fondness for perfume and the arts.

*

SURPRISINGLY, THIS CONFIDENT and lively confusion about homosexuality brought with it something that eventually looked very much like progress. In 1868, Wilhelm Griesinger, a doctor at the Charité asylum in Berlin, had published an article 'On a Little-Known Psychopathic Condition'. He defined homosexuality as an inherited, mental condition and called for study of the patient's mind. The article appeared in a new journal founded by Griesinger, the *Archiv für Psychiatrie und Nervenkrankheiten*. In the same journal, the following year, Griesinger's successor, Carl Westphal, published his report on a session of the Berlin Medical-Psychological Society in which various pathological and ethnographic cases were discussed, and then, in 1870, his article on 'contrary sexual feeling'.

The definition itself was not the turning-point. The association of homosexual behaviour with a mental condition had been common-place since the early 19th century and was more widely accepted than the small number of texts might suggest. Long before Westphal – without always specifying the vice in question – doctors had described 'vicious tendencies' and 'guilty passions' as forms of instinctive behaviour caused by a 'psycho-organic predisposition'. Pleas of insanity were lodged in English sodomy trials at least as early as 1822. In 1841, Hubert Lauvergne had discovered a 'third sex' in the prison hulks at Toulon – a special variety of human being with its own physical and mental features, discernible to a trained eye: wispy beard, moist eye, indolence, etc. The term 'third sex', also used by Gautier and Balzac, suggested that these strange creatures occupied a natural or social niche of their own. In 1853, a Prussian doctor, Hieronymous Fränkel, after studying a homosexual curtain-hanger called Süsskind Blank, applied the old Roman term '*homo mollis*' to the new species (*mollis* = 'soft' or 'effeminate').

From this point of view, '*homo mollis*' could hardly be defined by something as superficial as genital misuse. If, as Casper claimed, the condition was innate, it was of no immediate concern to forensic medicine.

The real change, which was gradual rather than sudden, lay not in the definition of homosexuality as a mental state but in the relation-ship of homosexual and doctor. Both Griesinger and Westphal were liberal reformers who opposed the use of restraints in the treatment of psychiatric patients. Their innovation was to urge a kind of practical sympathy. Patients should be listened to instead of being treated as perverts. Faces, not genitals, should be the focus of attention.

Unlikely as it might now appear, the definition of homosexuality as a mental illness or congenital flaw seemed to many people, on both sides of the doctor's table, to be a step in the right direction. It implied some awareness that homosexuality was a state of being rather than an acquired habit. It presented legal reformers with a powerful though demeaning argument (see p. 184). And it changed the nature of what for some was the only chance for honest self-expression: the medical consultation.

However ignorant or insensitive, the new breed of doctor could be treated as a confidant or confessor. This was an obvious improvement. Until the 1880s, most meetings of doctor and homosexual had taken place in prisons and hospitals. Even then – though the following pages might suggest a sudden enlightenment – older forms of treatment survived. The psychiatrists' predecessors, who were taught to look for visible signs, continued to treat homosexuals like livestock. Charles Vibert's *Précis de médecine légale* (1893) is a late but typical example:

> *Examination of Pederasts.* – For this, the individual is placed in a well-lit room, made to bend his torso so that the head is almost touching the floor, the buttocks are parted with one hand, one notes the appearance of the anus, then one introduces a finger into the orifice, so as to appreciate fully the resistance of the sphincter. [Etc.]

Some doctors explained precisely how to overcome resistance. Acts of love were often prudishly cited in Latin. The same precaution was rarely used for hardcore descriptions of scientific rape. At a medical conference in Berlin in 1890, Carl Liman described a case in which the patient had been probed, in a single session, by eight 'lubricated fingers'. The eight doctors subsequently issued eight reports which all contradicted one other. As Dr Brouardel pointed out in an article of 1880, the classic sign of pederasty – the famous funnel-shaped anus – could easily be produced by the cold hands of an energetic doctor. This would explain why doctors' findings became more consistent as they perfected their inspection techniques.

Anal inspection was the last stand of physiologists against the rising discipline of psychiatry. It became increasingly rare as a diagnostic tool towards the end of the century, though it was used for a long time in municipal inspections of French brothels. (Female prostitutes in French North Africa knowingly referred to the intrusive instrument as 'the Government's penis'.)

Although physical characteristics remained a preoccupation, greater importance was now attached to the words of the patients themselves. Case studies in the epic *Psychopathia sexualis* (1886) by Richard von Krafft-Ebing* usually contained a few remarks on physiology (voice, body hair, hip size, etc.) and a summary of perversion and illness in the family, but the bulk was made up of the patient's autobiography, albeit in reported speech:

> Case 163. *Homosexuality.* S.J., 38, governess. Sought my medical advice for a nervous problem. Father was intermittently insane and died of a brain disease. Patient is an only child. Even in early infancy, suffered from anxiety and excruciating fancies – e.g. waking up in a coffin after it had been closed, inadvertently saying something shameful in confession. [. . .]
>
> The patient has never been attracted to a member of the opposite sex and has considered marriage only as a means of support. She did however feel strongly attracted to girls. At first she interpreted her proclivity as friendship, but the fervour of her attachments and the constant deep yearning for her friends made her realize that these feelings were something more than friendship. [. . .]
>
> The patient, who looks entirely feminine and highly respectable, claims never to have felt that she was playing a particular [sexual] role with her friends, even in happy dreams.
>
> Feminine pelvis, large mammaries, no hint of beard growth.

Quite unexpectedly, *Psychopathia sexualis* and later compendia of case studies served as a kind of international bulletin board for homosexual men and women. There was a huge repressed demand for a public forum. Within four years of its publication, Otto de Joux

---

* 14th revised edition in 1912. Translations: Italian (1889), English (Philadelphia and London, 1892) and French (1895).

received 736 letters thanking him for writing his defence of homo-sexual love, *Die Enterbten des Liebesglückes* (1893) ('The Disinherited of Love's Happiness'). Already in 1864, after the publication of his first two pamphlets on 'The Riddle of Man-Manly Love', Ulrichs had been inundated with letters from 'Urnings near and far'. His later pamphlets, which incorporate his correspondents' views, are a talking-shop rather than a soap-box. The 1st edition of Krafft-Ebing's study (1886) contained forty-five cases; the 12th edition (1903) con-tained 238. Some of these books were bestsellers and were reprinted many times. Casper's single case, described in an article (1852) and then in his *Practisches Handbuch* (1858), spawned several other accounts, often supplied by anonymous readers who were clearly neither criminal nor insane. A 5th edition appeared in 1871, revised by his nephew Carl Liman. Other cases were published by Casper in his *Klinische Novellen* (1863). Until about 1880, articles on the subject outnumbered case studies. In 1870, Westphal could refer to only a handful of cases. In 1913, Magnus Hirschfeld's *Die Homosexualität* was based on more than 10,000 cases.

Even digested and medicalized by the doctor, the case history was a literary form that allowed otherwise silent individuals to discuss their sexuality. It also made medical texts more accessible to the general public. Of course, this was hardly a perfect state of affairs. Aleister Crowley supposed, with a touch of envy, that Krafft-Ebing's book had 'attained its enormous popularity' because it was used as pornography. If so, it was a fearsomely hygienic form of eroticism in which the key passages were printed in surgical Latin: 'She found sexual satisfaction only *in corpore feminae*' (Krafft-Ebing); 'Only excep-tionally did he dare to *socios concumbentes tangere et masturbationem mutuam adsequi*' (Krafft-Ebing); 'When the Uranist thinks that no one is looking, he likes to direct his gaze *in eam directionem ubi membrum virile est*' (Moll).

To view these clinical consultations through the one-way mirror of the distant present is to be painfully aware of vast discrepancies between the patient's experience and the doctor's opinions. Accounts that might have been quite rational acquired an air of insanity or depravity in the retelling. A man called Franz E... had been arrested in 1871 for making 'obscene propositions' to a watchman and was committed to an asylum. The case was described by Dr Servaës in Westphal's *Archiv für Psychiatrie und Nervenkrankheiten* in 1876:

> He confesses that he has had sexual relations with men and that he experienced the greatest possible pleasure. He interprets Holy Scripture so as to glorify his vice. He has an insurmountable aversion for women and has never been able to have relations with them. He advocates marriage between men, and claims that he could easily prove its legitimacy and worth. He adds, 'I recognize men like myself at a glance, just from their expression. I have never approached such people in vain.'

Franz E. . .'s intuition seems (but perhaps only seems) to have deserted him in the asylum. 'He invites the doctor to share his bed', noted the dispassionate Servaës.

*

BEYOND THE ASYLUM and the surgery, the theories of the early sexologists were not necessarily pernicious. The alleged causes of homosexuality stirred the imagination and made it possible for homosexual men and women to view their sexuality as an inherent part of life's pattern rather than as an aberration. Theories were not just abstractions: they were stories that identified common traits and prevented individual cases from surviving in isolation. Medical concepts like 'contrary sexual feeling' and 'the intermediate sex' were the templates of tales that could make sense of life in all its details: the shape of one's hand, the behaviour of one's parents, a predilection for the colour green.

The autobiographical accounts tended to project a view of homosexuality that was more in keeping with common experience than with medical prejudice. The idea that it was a psychopathic condition or a vice looked increasingly dubious. With the exception of four mid-life transvestites, all forty-four homosexuals studied by Krafft-Ebing (seventeen women and twenty-seven men aged between twenty-two and fifty-five) had always been attracted only to people of their own sex. All of them identified their sexual inclination – often quite happily – as a deviation from the norm. All had become aware of their feelings at puberty or long before. The average age of first awareness for the men who gave a date was just under ten, but several others used phrases like 'from the beginning', 'very early' and 'as long as I can remember'. For the women, the average was just over fourteen. Two of them traced their feelings back to 'earliest infancy'.

The sudden availability of homosexual autobiographies is more significant than their individual details. Once published, they could be read and reinterpreted without the scientific trimmings. Many people who had thought themselves unique were thrilled to read about a world in which they were normal. It is easy to imagine the reaction of lonely readers to these revelatory accounts. This letter, for example, was sent anonymously to Dr Casper by a young man who had read his article 'On Rape and Pederasty':

> I was so unhappy because I thought I was the only such strange creature in existence. Many times the pistol lay before me. Only my religious upbringing prevented me from committing a crime.
>
> You may laugh when I say this, but it's the pure truth: often in my sadness I threw myself down in the dust before God – or, if you prefer, the Devil. Yet in my heart a voice spoke so clearly that I thought that someone was in the room. It said, 'Go to the Linden!' [the promenade in Berlin] [. . .] A week later, I went back there and formed an acquaintance that has had a huge influence on my life. He was a beautiful young person of the highest society – happily dead now for years! Before long, we loved each other tenderly, and, through him, I came to know several other fellow sufferers.
>
> I went to England; then I buried my love. Later, I spent more time in Paris, Italy and Vienna, and everywhere I found poor creatures like myself! [. . .] On the Righi [above Genoa], in Palermo, in the Louvre, in the highlands of Scotland, in St Petersburg and at the docks in Barcelona I found people I had never seen before but who became attached to me in an instant, and I to them. Can this really be a crime? [. . .] I may never see them again but I think of them as often as they think of me and we shall never forget one another. Even now, I am hastening away to the South [. . .]

Similar journeys from darkness to light were described by many other patients. A thirty-one-year-old bachelor in Krafft-Ebing's *Psychopathia sexualis* had enjoyed an active sex life since the age of fourteen: 'I could write volumes about my acquaintances, who number over 500.' Another had lived with a man for years 'like husband and wife'. Relatively few had had difficulty in finding partners, which suggests a much sunnier climate than the words 'Victorian underworld' imply. When writing his memoirs (unpublished until 1984), J. A. Symonds only suspected that his condition was 'commoner than I imagine'. After reading Casper and Krafft-Ebing, he was happily 'aware that my history is only one out of a thousand'.

This accidental, therapeutic function of the medical profession is perhaps its only lasting contribution to homosexual happiness. Even if some readers had no access to the urban networks, they could still find relief in the act of confession. The doctor was a representative of society and the confessional letter was a kind of coming out, albeit very private and polite. Krafft-Ebing's patients were grateful, not for his anxious expertise, but for his attentive ear:

> No one suspects my true nature. You, a stranger, are the only one who knows me, and you know me more intimately, in the most important respect, than father, mother, friend or lover. It has done me good to be able to divulge that bizarre, oppressive secret.
>
> First, I must beg your forgiveness, dear Sir, for importuning you with my writing. I had lost all self-control and become a monster in my own eyes. I disgusted myself. But then your writing restored my courage and I resolved to get to the bottom of the matter and to look back over my life, no matter what the result. [. . .]
>
> I hope, after reading your works, that if I fulfil my duties as doctor, citizen, father and husband, I may count myself among those who deserve something better than scorn.

These reports from the unknown continent also helped to enlighten friends and relatives. The lesbian heroine of Radclyffe Hall's *The Well of Loneliness* (1928) discovers, after her father's death, that he had been poring over Krafft-Ebing in an attempt to understand his daughter. Magnus Hirschfeld knew of a man in Berlin who suspected his son of sexual abnormality. He read the medical literature, identified the boy as 'a born homosexual' and gave his blessing to him and his partner. Even if understanding came too late, there was still the hope of a posthumous reconciliation. A suicide note, written by a man called Alfred Slova, was published by Otto de Joux in 1897:

> Father, Mother, forgive me! *I cannot help it*! Dear Mizzi, forgive me too. Read *Psychopathia sexualis* and you will no longer curse me for having left you in such a shameful fashion. [. . .] Forgive me as I have forgiven you.

Case studies became so popular, so quickly, that some doctors began to complain about the glut of information. At the third Congress of Criminal Anthropology in Brussels in 1892, Dr de Rode claimed to be swamped with 'repulsive details' of 'pitiful triviality'. His patients were using medical science, he felt, to exonerate themselves. Dr Fritz Strassmann complained in 1895 that no Urning ever visited the surgery without bringing along a ready-to-publish manuscript. Some doctors thought that incredible accounts of a flourishing homosexual underworld proved that homosexuals were constitutional liars, addicted to gossip and navel-gazing.

People who were wrestling with their sexuality and who were asked to talk about their problems were often understandably verbose. It took a certain amount of autobiographical fluency to describe a life of shame and secrecy or, for that matter, a life of defiance and illicit pleasure. The young Italian aristocrat who sent his 'human document' to Émile Zola, hoping to be immortalized in one of his novels, would have been just as vain with a different sexual inclination. As he discovered when passing a bookshop one day, Zola had sent his letter to a doctor called Georges Saint-Paul. It was published in Saint-Paul's study of inversion in 1896 as the 'Novel of a Born Invert'.

> I wrote these pages this evening with the most intense enjoyment. The room is very cheerful with its warm carpets, all the gas lamps lit, and the sounds of a busy hotel. I am almost happy; but how long will it last? [. . .]
>
> This will have to be the last page, otherwise I'd never finish and I'd send you a whole book which would eventually wear you out. I always think I've finished and then I always find something else to tell you; besides which, I enjoy writing about my little self so much that I'd never stop summoning up my image and looking at it in these pages. It seems to me that one can never tire of talking about oneself and

studying oneself in the tiniest detail, especially if Nature has made one
– as it made me – such an exceptional being.

On 30 April 1897, a French philosophy teacher called Georges
Hérelle wrote a long reply to the book by Saint-Paul. The letter was
never sent. He bequeathed it, along with a large file of notes on
Greek love and the minutes of conversations with like-minded friends,
to the library of Troyes. Publication was out of the question: his only
readership was the faceless future. But the medical literature at least
allowed him to enjoy a semblance of dialogue. This was surely a
common reaction to the medical colonization of homosexuality:

> Books like yours, Monsieur, produce in minds like mine a swirl of
> contradictory thoughts and feelings – first, passionate curiosity, then,
> depending on the chapter or the paragraph, deep delight or angry
> frustration [. . .]; and finally, when the storm has passed, a kind of
> gratitude.
>
> [. . .] I am not expecting you to cure me; I do not consider myself
> ill in the usual, accepted sense of the word. But you have spoken to
> me at length about myself, my inner life, the most intimate, essential
> and secret part of myself. This makes you a confidant and a friend,
> even when you offend me.
>
> Thanks to you, for a few hours or days, I have been able to feel
> stirring within myself thoughts that are stifled by the monotony of life.
> I have felt the passion that is deadened by social constraints and the
> need for constant secrecy. And so I readily forgive you the occasional
> epithet such as 'repulsive', 'disgraceful', etc. What do I care about your
> opinion anyway, I who am unknown and anonymous – a mere case?

At this stage, it was still possible to feel some sense of a collabor-
ative endeavour. Simply by writing about homosexuality, doctors were
also taking risks – small in comparison, but real none the less. The
French prospectus for the 1893 French translation of Albert Moll's
Die conträre Sexualempfindung was prosecuted by moral campaigners.
In England, Havelock Ellis's *Sexual Inversion* (1897) was indicted as a
'lewd, wicked, bawdy, scandalous libel'.

Some doctors used pseudonyms. Saint-Paul wrote as 'Dr Laupts'.
Those who wrote under their real names were careful to specify their
audience. On page xxiv of his study of sexual inversion (1893), Julien

Chevalier told women that they were not to read it. He also took the unusual step (so he claimed) of making it extremely difficult to read. 'I sincerely hope that my book will have limited publicity and a merely local success.' The sale of Dr W. C. Rivers' pamphlet on *Walt Whitman's Anomaly* (London, 1913) was 'restricted to members of the legal and medical professions', and Earl Lind's *Autobiography of an Androgyne*, prefaced by Dr Alfred Herzog (New York, 1918), was 'sold only, by mail order, to physicians, lawyers, legislators, psychologists, and sociologists'. Most books on the subject were unobtainable in the United States without a note from the doctor.

This uneasy situation continued for some time, especially in Britain. Readers at the Bodleian Library are still reminded of the censorship that was silently practised by individuals. Even dour, unillustrated works on homosexuality that were not legally banned were catalogued away into the 'Phi' (Φ) collection, as late as the 1970s. Until 2002, they had to be requested in person and consulted under observation in a special room.*

*

ACCORDING TO THEORIES inspired by Foucault, the laboratorial approach, even in a benign form, replaced fear of the law with self-loathing. The medical 'invention' of homosexuality, in this view, transfused society's homophobia into the homosexual bloodstream. The old religious sanctions were internalized and experienced as feelings of guilt and inadequacy. After a few decades of medical discourse, every homosexual, even without living the sordid life of Wilde's Dorian Gray, would have a hideous portrait of himself hidden away in the attic.

The real situation was far more confused. The well-travelled young man who wrote to Casper felt shame and self-loathing long before psychiatric interest in the subject. Krafft-Ebing's correspondent, the self-proclaimed 'monster' quoted above, began to think of himself as

---

* For example, Raffalovich, *Uranisme et unisexualité* (1896); Symonds, *A Problem in Greek Ethics* (1908); Hirschfeld, *Sexualgeschichte der Menschheit* (1929); several editions of Iwan Bloch's sociological studies (1901–38); Cory, *The Homosexual Outlook* (1953); Humphreys, *Tearoom Trade* (1970); Karlen, *Sexuality and Homosexuality* (1971); Hocquenghem, *Homosexual Desire* (1978).

a respectable person only *after* reading other case studies. Many people who confided in doctors considered themselves diseased but without necessarily feeling shame for that reason. Seeking treatment was not always a sign of self-hatred. In turn-of-the-century America, Earl Lind and Claude Hartland consulted doctors even while enjoying a busy sex life.

Homosexual men and women consulted doctors for various complex reasons: self-exploration, the pleasure of divulging a secret, the desire to find a limited form of social integration, or simply an attempt to cope with problems caused by homosexuality rather than with homosexuality itself.

The full humiliating effect of medical discourse was not felt until well into the 20th century, when superstitions adopted by the medical profession returned to the community emblazoned with technical terms. Liberated gays like Edmund White and Martin Duberman spent years looking for a psychoanalytic cure. Nineteenth-century homosexuals were untroubled in comparison.

The main source of suffering was not theoretical but social. J. A. Symonds wrote of 'a perpetual discord between spontaneous appetite and acquired respect for social law'. Earl Lind visited many doctors and read the medical literature, but this only strengthened his conviction that he had a right to be congenitally different:

> Is it right to chastise a horse because he prefers to munch hay out of a manger instead of walking into his owner's dining-room; throwing himself backwards into an enormous chair; squeezing with difficulty a spoon between his two front hoofs; and with it carrying to his mouth ice-cream and French pastry?

This equine self-portrait was inspired by Lind's experience of American society, not by medical textbooks. A fifty-five-year-old woman, 'Miss L.', who consulted Krafft-Ebing was positively delighted to learn that she was abnormal: 'I am comforted by the thought that moral laws were made only for normal people and cannot be binding on abnormal people.'

A surprisingly common source of anxiety caused by medical texts seems to have been the simple realization that homosexual acts were disapproved of or against the law:

Miss M. can see nothing wrong in her feelings; and, until, at the age of 28, she came across the translation of Krafft-Ebing's book, she had no idea 'that feelings like mine were "under the ban of society" as he puts it, or were considered unnatural and depraved'. (Ellis, case 37)

After reading *Psychopathia sexualis*, he became terrified of himself and of the possibility of legal punishment. He forced himself to avoid sexual relations with men. This abstinence caused him many wet dreams and also neurasthenia. For that reason he sought medical help. (Krafft-Ebing, case 154)

Evidence of a negative effect on the homosexual psyche could be found in the fact that homosexual men and women seem to have adopted the medical terminology almost as soon as it was invented. But schoolchildren often acquire an astonishingly detailed knowledge of educational theory without changing their behaviour. It is easy to be misled by statements made to doctors. (The doctors could of course select the accounts that proved their theories.) Heterosexuals wrote with a tacit, unconscious assumption of a fundamentally sympathetic audience. In homosexual writings, a neutral context can never be assumed.

Self-accusations were often opportunistic. Claude Hartland was able to publish an account of his sexual experiences by subtitling his *Story of a Life* 'for the consideration of the medical fraternity' (St Louis, 1901). Oscar Wilde's famous self-diagnosis as a mental invalid was not a personal confession, it was part of a petition for his release written while he was at Reading Gaol: 'the terrible offences of which [I] was rightly found guilty [. . .] are forms of sexual madness [. . .] diseases to be cured by a physician rather than crimes to be punished by a judge.'

Sometimes, abject self-diagnosis was a kind of courtesy to the listener. Georges Hérelle told Dr Laupts that 'all true inverts' not only took what doctors said with a pinch of salt, they also believed that the doctors themselves were homosexual and that all their talk about aberrations was just a large and garish fig-leaf: 'Be in no doubt: this is why your desk is flooded with confessions.'

In fact, there is just as much evidence for the 'construction' of medical discourse by homosexuals as there is for the medical construction of homosexuality. Benedict Friedländer even suggested in 1907 that doctors were beginning to abandon the 'sickness' theory of homosexuality under pressure from their patients: 'They had to, of course, or their clients would have left them.'

Many of the classification systems and technical terms that sound as though they were imposed by doctors were actually invented and publicized by homosexuals – even the more elaborate systems: those of Karl Heinrich Ulrichs, whose theories were more influential than those of any Victorian doctor (see p. 181), and Magnus Hirschfeld's, who devised four scales of 'sexual intermediacy' including eighty-one fundamental types.

There was a simple, practical advantage in devising technical terms. Classification systems made it easier to discuss 'the nameless sin'; they helped to distinguish 'normal' homosexuals from prostitutes, transvestites and the criminally insane; and they gave homosexual desire a kind of legitimacy. Some of the terms were borrowed from botany (unisexual, monosexual, bisexual, etc.) and implied that homosexuality was part of the grand plan of Nature. Above all, classification led to the revolutionary idea that other people were not normal, they were simply heterosexual. If there were 'Uranians' (in Ulrichs' scheme), there must also be 'Dionians'.

The word '*Homosexualität*' itself was invented, not by a doctor, but (probably) by a peripatetic Hungarian man of letters called Kertbeny (Karl Maria Benkert, 1824–82). It was first used, along with '*Homosexualisten*', in a letter to Ulrichs in 1868 and then in two pamphlets (Leipzig, 1869). The word was intended as a neutral term, applicable to both men and women, and was probably coined at the same time as '*Heterosexualität*', which first appeared in a text of unknown date later printed in Gustav Jaeger's *Die Entdeckung der Seele* in 1880. '*Homosexualität*' and foreign equivalents were not commonly used until the early 20th century.

Clearly, then, these awkward encounters of two strange tribes, exchanging terms and trading insights, were seldom one-sided. Not all homosexuals were the passive victims of interfering ideologues and medical missionaries. One doctor even discovered in the course of treatment that he himself was homosexual. 'Thereafter he adopted inverted practices and ceased to find any attraction in women.'

The traditional view of 19th-century homosexuals as a helpless, silent minority, blinking in the torchlight of investigative doctors, should at least be called into question. Compared to what now looks like a rubbish-heap of superstitions dressed up as science, the contributions made by homosexual men and women to medical science are a monument to common sense. Their influence was broad and beneficial. Notions of 'Nature' were shown to be hopelessly crude and contradictory. Standard definitions of masculinity and femininity proved to be scientifically worthless. Sickness and perversion began to look like relative concepts. Historical and anthropological precedents showed that Victorian society was not the only state of civilization. The sexuality of any individual – homosexual or not – was seen to have its own peculiarities. The old bugbear of anal intercourse turned out not to be peculiar to the homosexual population.

Inspected at close quarters, the entire human race appeared to be 'abnormal'. If, as many claimed, there was a direct link between 'onanism' and 'uranism', and if, as Dr J. Christian supposed in the *Dictionnaire encyclopédique des sciences médicales* in 1881, 'solitary manoeuvres were almost universally practised', did that not mean that practically everyone was a 'pervert' or might become one at any moment?

The immense power attributed to theorizing doctors has concealed the splendid irony: the repressed homosexual minority had a huge and stimulating effect on the world of ideas. The medical profession, by contrast, devoted much of its ingenuity to avoiding the insights provided by its patients.

The real, tangible deterioration wrought by medical interference was practical, not psychological. The medicalization of homosexuality threatened to replace the judge and the prison guard with the doctor and the asylum nurse. The definition of homosexuality as a mental illness opened the way to a practice that was both benign and sinister: the treatment of something that was not susceptible to treatment.

*

SYSTEMATIC ATTEMPTS to cure homosexuality were rare before the 1880s. Until then, most 'cures' were either legal (imprisonment or death) or religious (penance or death). In January 1852, when Gogol confessed his sinful leanings to a priest, he was advised to abstain from sleep and food until his soul was clean. He died of starvation in February. The priest was unrepentant: 'A physician is not blamed when the seriousness of the illness makes him prescribe strong medicine to his patient.'

The only widely applied medical cures were developed to combat masturbation, which was thought to be a cause of homosexuality. Usually, this meant cold showers. Katherine Mansfield seems to have been sent to take a cold-water cure in Bavaria because of her 'unnatural relationships'. The same remedy was applied by Dr Kiernan of Chicago in 1884 to a young lesbian who later married her lover's brother. (Kiernan concluded that the treatment had been successful.) William Acton preferred 'the tepid sponge-bath', while Dr Hammond of New York complemented the cold baths with outdoor exercise and the study of mathematics.

If homosexuality had a specific cause, it followed that the cause had simply to be removed. Sexual ardour should be cooled, the idle should be put to work, boys from boarding-schools should be introduced to girls, and libertines should be inspired with the fear of God.

Prevention rather than cure was the norm. Boys at Wellington School in the 1870s lay in their cubicles at night, staring up at the barbed wire that Headmaster Benson had installed to prevent nocturnal depravity. Adults were simply advised to remove themselves from temptation.

The more ingenious and drastic cures seem to have been applied by homosexuals to themselves before they ever occurred to physicians. Albert Moll had a patient who asked to be cured by castration. The first known person to think of using electricity to combat homosexual passion was a gay French engineer in 1878.

Most Victorian doctors were more cautious and more sensitive to the evidence than their 20th-century descendants. When they were confronted with normal inhabitants of the strange new world, and not just with the few mad or criminal cases captured on raids, it became apparent that something was wrong. Many doctors were bemused by an apparent lack of pathological or physiological defects. There was, it seemed, such a thing as an intelligent, happy and healthy homosexual. Some were astonished to observe the clear signs of true love. As Krafft-Ebing reported,

Many even lack awareness that their condition is an illness. Most Urnings feel happy in their perverse sexual feeling and drive, and unhappy only insofar as social and legal constraints prevent them from achieving satisfaction.

Often, 'illness' was more heartily desired than health: 'I seek no remedy for this sickness of my constitution, for I owe it far too many unforgettably sweet moments' (Krafft-Ebing, case 144). An English 'high society' correspondent of Dr Saint-Paul suggested that the higher incidence of nervous complaints in 'uranists' was due to nothing more than the fact that laws and prejudice prevented them from 'satisfying their sexual or genital leanings in a simple and easy fashion'.

Even in the furiously moralizing mind of Ambroise Tardieu, the relentless inspector of penises, a window of sympathetic recognition briefly opened:

> I have often had occasion to read the correspondence of self-confessed pederasts, and have found, couched in the most passionate forms of language, epithets and images borrowed from the most ardent trans- ports of true love.

The idea that homosexuality might be a form of love, and that a desire to propagate the species was not the root of all romance, had been expressed in some serious studies of Greek love (Ramdohr's *Venus Urania* in 1787; Hössli's *Eros* in 1836), in the novels of Balzac and in Hubert Lauvergne's study of lovesick convicts: *Les Forçats considérés sous le rapport physiologique, moral et intellectuel* (1841). A great deal of time and ingenuity could have been saved if doctors had read more widely or trusted their patients.

Even so, the medical discovery of homosexual normality was much earlier and less controversial than might be supposed. When Evelyn Hooker showed in 1957 that there was no difference between the psychological profiles of gay and straight people, her findings pro- voked more professional outrage than they would have done seventy years before. A medical encyclopedia published in Leipzig and Vienna in 1885 insisted that 'aberrations of the sexual feeling appear not only in the case of nervous and mental illness, but also in individuals for whom neither any kind of disturbance of the psychic functions nor any anomaly in the nerve centre may be demonstrated'. Sexual 'aberrations', it said, were more frequent in sane people.

The need to distinguish between perversity (vice) and perversion (an instinctive, congenital state) was a commonplace of late-19th-century psychiatry. In 1885, Enrico Morselli, professor of psychiatry at Turin from 1889, went so far as to group perversion *and* perversity under the term 'omosessualismo', reserving the term 'uranismo' for homosexuality, 'that truly extraordinary phenomenon of the sexual psyche'.

In a famous article on 'Inversion du sens génital' in the *Archives de neurologie* in 1882, Valentin Magnan and Jean Charcot described a sociable, kind and erudite man of thirty-one with a big moustache and a military bearing who had become a University professor at the age of thirty. Apart from fluttering eyelashes, the occasional *'crise hystérique'* and a helpless attraction to men, he appeared strangely sane:

> One would certainly not make oneself popular if one told his listeners that the distinguished professor whose eloquence, logic and judgment they admire every day was in reality a sick man whose brain is tormented by the strangest ideas and who may, from one moment to the next, be compelled in spite of himself to behave in the most shamefully promiscuous fashion.

For the first time in history, real scenes of forbidden passion appeared in the clinical environment of forensic textbooks. Albert Moll described 'Uranists weeping with despair in my consulting room'. Paul Garnier, in *La Folie à Paris* (1890), espoused the theory of 'mental degeneration', but the notes of his 'pederast' sounded for all the world like the cries of any passionate lover: 'Oh, dear sad memories! How I used to kiss that beautiful body, that pretty face without a wrinkle, that sweet mouth that asked to be kissed, those lovely eyes I used to worship . . .' In the *Archives d'anthropologie criminelle* in 1894, Marc-André Raffalovich made the astonishing claim that 'one can, without much risk (or even any risk at all), make friends with a congenital invert'.

There were even hints that, far from being a close cousin of bestiality, homosexual passion might betoken a kind of superiority.

In his study of *La Folie érotique* (1888), Benjamin Ball, who held the first chair of psychiatry in France, contended that 'sexual perversion can coexist with a perfectly normal mental state and even with the most brilliant intellectual faculties'. Lists of eminent homosexuals – Shakespeare, Michelangelo, Byron, etc. – were already a common form of self-affirmation in homosexual circles. With Albert Moll's sensitive study of 1891, these lists began to acquire some scientific respectability.

The implication was that a cure might be the mental equivalent of amputating a healthy limb. Some patients seemed to need nothing but encouragement to regain their health. As one of Krafft-Ebing's early patients exclaimed: 'Ever since I gave free rein to my Uranian nature, I have been happier, healthier and more productive!'

This is where the eventual importance of Westphal's 1870 article on 'contrary sexual feeling' and its possible treatment becomes ominously apparent. Westphal had presented himself as the investigator of a phenomenon that had been 'described little or not at all', but his notion of 'innate inversion [*Verkehrung*] of sexual feeling' was neither new nor particularly convincing. The article was based on two cases: a man masquerading as a countess who earned a living by theft, and a woman suffering from violent rage and a desire to have sex with women. The man might have had a 'morbid desire' to dress as a woman, as Westphal asserted, but he also had a professional reason for doing so. Transvestite disguise was a common criminal ploy. (The French and German laws against transvestism were aimed at criminals, not at sexual deviants.) There was no sign that he had ever been sexually attracted by men. The woman, as Westphal acknowledged, seemed perfectly normal. She was worried about spending two months in a lunatic asylum and later befriended one of the more pathetic inmates, not because she wanted sex, but because she felt sorry for her.

The description of homosexuality as a neuropathic state was hardly a great advance. The real significance of Westphal was that he gave long and detailed accounts, with direct quotations, then showed how homosexuality could be saved for the medical profession. He stamped it with psychiatric authority and made it sound like a treatable condition. In fact, Westphal had been inspired partly by the recent legal debate in Germany. If the law was repealed and 'contrary sexuals' were no longer sent to prison, doctors, 'in whose domain they belong', would receive more and more such patients. It was important therefore to prepare for the rush and to make sure that they knocked at the right door.

Westphal was well equipped to become a 'pioneer'. Unlike Ulrichs, he was not a homosexual and so could not be accused of 'special pleading'. He knew how to make the most of small quantities of information, and he edited the *Archiv für Psychiatrie und Nervenkrankheiten*. This was his real contribution. In the long term, Westphal made it easier for doctors who were not simply performing their forensic, hygienic duty to talk about the shameful subject without risking their reputations.

The only problem now was to show that all cases – even the healthy, happy ones – fell under the doctor's jurisdiction. The military doctor Julien Chevalier coined the oxymoron 'lucid psychopaths', which at least assigned that anomalous creature, 'the born invert', to a branch of the pathological tree. Not surprisingly, even in apparently sane inverts, symptoms of degeneration could always be found, if only an asymmetrical face, a jutting jaw, big ears or a tapering penis.

From now on, there would be a witch-ducking logic about the treatment of homosexuals. If mentally ill, the subject was not responsible and should be locked away. If, on the other hand, there were no signs of illness, then the person was a healthy invert and thus a simple debauchee who should be punished. As Dr Chevalier decreed in 1893, 'No half measures: either *chastise* or *sequester*.'

*

MANY DOCTORS WHO TRIED to develop a cure for homosexuality were inspired by the idea that a bridge could be built between abnormality and normality. For example, a man who was attracted to boys could be encouraged to fall in love with boyish women. In a novella by Heinz Tovote, *Erlöst* (1895), a homosexual man is introduced by his doctor to an angelic *garçon manqué* with short hair. Marriage follows, the man becomes increasingly heterosexual and, after the first child, the wife is told that she can now safely grow her hair.

Dr Saint-Paul wondered in 1896 whether this treatment might not be used to cure a male homosexual and a lesbian at the same time. The lesbian would become enamoured with the womanly man, and the man with the manly woman. He also suggested that an invert, placed in an exclusively female environment, might invert himself a second time and become normal, as it were, by a process of 'double inversion'.

The 'bridge' idea was based on an assumption that heterosexuality would naturally reassert itself like a stream that had been dammed or diverted. Abraham Brill, a psychiatrist at Columbia University, reported in 1913 that some doctors 'invariably resort to bladder washing and rectal massage when they are consulted by homosexuals'. According to one doctor, the idea was to kill the homosexual cells so that normal cells could take their place.

This 'Nature will out' view was also held by doctors who had no interest in developing elaborate procedures. The advice reported by one of the interviewees in Gordon Westwood's *Report on the Life of the Male Homosexual in Great Britain* (1958) is typical of most medical prescriptions for at least a century and a half: 'He told me to pull up my socks, find myself a nice girl and get married.'

Even the ingenious Dr Brouardel, who made a study of (illusory) sex changes in the corpses of boy prostitutes, favoured a simple, practical approach. When André Gide consulted him shortly before becoming engaged to Madeleine Rondeaux in 1895, he was told not to make a fuss:

> Get married and don't worry. You'll soon see that it's all in your imagination. You're like a starving man who has been trying to feed himself on nothing but gherkins. [...] Once you're married, you'll understand in no time at all what natural instinct is.

These doctors who so breezily sacrificed the happiness of women to their male patients' sexual and moral health looked no further than the genitals. The great thing was to achieve intercourse and to procreate. Social responsibility was more important than sexual fulfilment. The proper repository for sperm was a wife – the passive piggy-bank that would eventually pay dividends in the form of a son and heir. This seemed particularly urgent in France after the defeat by Prussia in 1870. The population was growing too slowly, and almost a third of all conscripts were judged too puny to fight. (An even greater preponderance of male weediness was discovered in Britain at the time of the Boer War.) Practitioners of 'unnatural vice' were obvious scapegoats. In 1871, Ambroise Tardieu came up with the idea of a fiscal cure: a tax on bachelors and childless widows under thirty.

Some doctors went a step further and tried to kick-start the 'natural instinct'. Albert Moll, who lost his youthful common sense, used literary descriptions of boudoirs and harems, and pictures of 'lightly-clad female persons'. Baron Albert von Schrenck-Notzing, a Munich psychiatrist with boundless powers of self-persuasion, prescribed frequent visits to the brothel, preceded by large doses of alcohol. The idea was that an experienced prostitute would know how to generate the correct response, even in a nervous, drunken invert. (Female patients were referred only to their husbands.) The patient would then be able to marry, have children and, of course, pass on any venereal infections picked up during the treatment.

Freud's teacher, Jean Charcot, used the same sordid cure on a Belgian law professor, as he boasted to his literary friends, Daudet and Goncourt. The man had emerged from the brothel crying, 'I can do it! I can do it!' If true, this was extremely unusual. Albert Moll, who described the brothel cure as a training in debauchery and a source of continually renewed despair, knew a patient who fled in horror just as the woman was removing her clothes. Claude Hartland claimed to prefer the dentist's chair.

It should be said that brothel therapy, like most other 19th-century cures, was not invented by the medical profession. Along with abstinence and suicide, it was one of the commonest self-applied remedies. Naturally, these dismal experiments were worse than futile. After his release from prison, Oscar Wilde was persuaded by Ernest Dowson to visit a prostitute in Dieppe in order to acquire 'a more wholesome taste'. When he emerged from the brothel, a small crowd, supposedly, had gathered in the street. He whispered to Dowson, 'The first these ten years, and it shall be the last. It was like chewing cold mutton!' Then, in a louder voice: 'But tell it in England, for it will entirely restore my character!'

A slightly more subtle form of therapy involved the use of hypnosis.

Even the pragmatic Krafft-Ebing saw hypnosis as the best hope, though he considered it to be little more than 'dressage' and used it mainly to express sympathy:

> When a contrary-sexual demands treatment on ethical, social or other grounds, it should not be refused. It is the doctor's sacred duty to give whatever help and advice he can to those who seek it. The client's health should always come before the well-being of society as a whole.

In practice, he felt that the only real success consisted in rendering the patient 'sexually neutral' (i.e. sexually neutralized).

The bleak suggestions made to patients under hypnosis bring to mind the 'cure' devised by well-meaning doctors for the sighted man in H. G. Wells's *The Country of the Blind*. A young businessman treated by Krafft-Ebing was made to repeat depressingly prophylactic sentences like this: 'I abhor love of my own sex and will no longer find any man beautiful.' The following series of suggestions was made to a twenty-nine-year-old bachelor in December 1888:

1. I abhor onanism, for it makes me sick and miserable.
2. I am no longer attracted to men, for loving men is against religion, Nature and the law.
3. I am attracted to women, for women are lovely and desirable and created for man.

This particular case was described as a 'success'. After four sessions, 'the patient even asked for the address of a brothel'. A year and a half later, when Krafft-Ebing met him on a journey, he was copulating happily and 'thinking seriously of marriage'. Dr Bernheim of Nancy contented himself with programming his patient, a travelling sales-man, to have 'spontaneous erections' on nights when he would share a bed with his wife.

These hypnotic cures sometimes lasted several years and more than 100 sessions. They were the Victorian equivalent of long-term, voluntary psychoanalysis. Their apparent popularity is understand-able: the prize of normality was always just out of reach, and the length, cost and futility of the treatment gave patients a good reason to feign success. Freud himself believed that some people had been cured by hypnosis. The idea that homosexuals were constitutional liars was usually set aside when they claimed to be cured.

Hypnosis was also tremendously flattering to the doctor. The charismatic American Dr Quackenbos claimed in 1899 to have cured his patients of various complaints including kleptomania, tobacco addiction, dishonesty and homosexuality. An employee of 'one of our great insurance companies' was restored to an appearance of normality by being made to associate 'unnatural lust' with 'moral, mental and financial ruin'. 'Would I dare to soil a soul so completely at my mercy with a single untoward thought?' Dr Quackenbos wondered with barely concealed megalomania. His hypnotic red carnelian on a gold pencil turned him into 'the vice-regent of the Almighty'.

Compared to later refinements, this was mere showmanship. Psychoanalysis was more insidious and just as ineffective. Instead of simply curbing his sexual desires, the patient would be sent on a wild goose chase inside his own mind, in search of domineering mothers, feeble fathers and masochistic tendencies. Psychoanalysis gave common prejudice a much larger repertoire of disguises, and the patient could always be blamed for the doctor's failure. As Edmund Bergler decreed in *The Counterfeit Sex* (1958): 'There are no happy homosexuals; and there would not be, even if the outer world left them in peace.' 'The reason is an internal one. Unconsciously they want to be disappointed.'

*

HYPNOSIS WAS ONE OF the cures that seemed to be dying a natural death when it was revived in the early 20th century and plugged in to the ever-expanding grid of technological innovation.

The homosexual became a walking laboratory. The cure was no longer an attempt to heal, it was a means of testing medical theories and procedures. Or rather, the doctor's expertise determined his view of homosexuality. Alienists experienced in the use of hydrotherapy and anaphrodisiacs believed that homosexuals were sexually overcharged. Doctors who liked to lecture their patients on morality adduced moral weakness: in 1894, Dr Kiernan of Chicago, when treating a lesbian, found that 'sympathy' had a 'poisonous' effect – 'there is entirely too much sympathy wasted on these patients, since sympathy to them is as poisonous as to the hysteric whose mental state is very similar'. Hypnotists naturally refused to believe that homosexuality was innate. If the condition turned out to be congenital, suggestion therapy would be largely redundant. This is why Dr Schrenck-Notzing described the idea that homosexuality was not an illness as 'therapeutic nihilism'.

The idea that medical views of homosexuality were determined by the available treatments and technology is not particularly interesting from a theoretical point of view, but it does account for the increasing ingenuity brought to bear on the matter. In the 1930s, in Europe and America, brutal aversion therapies were applied with increasing indifference to failure. In 1935, Dr Louis Max induced vomiting while showing pictures of naked men. After an injection of testosterone, the naked men were replaced with naked women. Similar therapies were still routinely used in Australia in the 1960s.

The modest pharmaceutical procedures of the 19th century – bromide of potassium prescribed for masturbating boys and women who were thought to have been stimulated by excessive use of sewing-machines; morphine, camphor and strychnine, or simply a spartan diet – gave way to radiation and hormone treatments (from the 1930s). Electrical therapy or 'faradization' had been used for various complaints since the 1830s, but most 19th-century doctors were sceptical. Later, it was used quite freely.

Surgical cures also became more popular. Early interest had been shown in the United States. In 1889, Dr Frank Lydston suggested removing the ovaries or the clitoris of sexual deviants. He also cited a doctor who repeatedly cauterized the back of the patient's neck, 'basing this treatment upon the theory that the disease takes its origin in over-excitation of the nerve fibres of the cerebellum or some of the ganglia in the neighborhood'. In 1893, Dr F. E. Daniel of Austin, Texas recommended castration as a humane alternative to death: 'We are warranted in at least making the experiment on a scale large enough to test the operation as a therapeutic measure.' By 1917, Dr Lydston was a champion of sterilization: '*No sexual pervert should be allowed to procreate.*'

These brutal treatments sometimes met with public opposition, but other surgical cures were widely applied: trepanning (from the 1890s), testicle transplants (early 20th century), lobotomy (mainly in the United States in the 1940s). The cure, increasingly, was a con-version process that turned the victim into a textbook case. The cure did not remove the complaint; it endowed the patient with the abnormality from which he was supposed to be suffering. The math-ematician Alan Turing, after his arrest in Manchester in 1952, was given oestrogen injections to reduce his libido. As a result, he began to grow breasts. Before the treatment, Turing was a normal person who fell in love with other men. After the treatment, he looked more like the androgynous freak that the police had imagined they were arresting. He committed suicide in 1954.

This dismal state of affairs should not be seen as the inevitable result of the medical discovery of homosexuality. Real progress did occur. In the thirty-eight years between Casper's *Practisches Handbuch* (1858) and Ellis's *Sexual Inversion* (1896), many myths were exploded: homosexual men could be virile and lesbians could be womanly; passive and active roles were fluid and the 'passive' partner was not always the more effeminate; transvestism and the act of sodomy were more common among heterosexuals; most surprising of all, contrary sexuals, Uranians and inverts could lead happy, fulfilling lives.

The long-term effects of these Victorian explorations should also be seen in more cheerful developments. In the 19th century, self-loathing was the first sign that the homosexual might be cured. Since 1973, 'ego-dystonic homosexuality' – a frantic, futile desire to be heterosexual – is the only category of homosexuality listed as a disorder in the American Psychiatric Association's *Diagnostic and Statistical Manual of Mental Disorders*. (Naturally, the removal of homosexuality from the manual met with fierce opposition. It has since crept back in as 'Gender Identity Disorder' or 'Deficit'.) This enlightened non-interference has its roots in the 19th century – in Krafft-Ebing's advice to avoid excessive abstinence, or in Magnus Hirschfeld's 'adaptive therapy' (1913): make sure that the patient is homosexual; explain that homosexuality is a misfortune only because of social pressure; counteract the sense of isolation by telling the patient about eminent homosexuals in history and the present; stop all medical treatments and introduce the patient to other homo-sexuals.

When Freud wrote to an American woman who was troubled by

her son's homosexuality in April 1935, he was writing as a student of 19th-century medicine. The insulting theory of arrested development came from the Victorian age, but so did the pragmatism and the humanity:

> Homosexuality is assuredly no advantage, but it is nothing to be ashamed of, no vice, no degradation, it cannot be classified as an illness; we consider it to be a variation of the sexual function produced by a certain arrest of sexual development. Many highly respectable individuals of ancient and modern times have been homosexuals, several of the greatest men among them (Plato, Michelangelo, Leonardo da Vinci, etc.). It is a great injustice to persecute homosexuality as a crime, and cruelty too.

*

THIS CHAPTER INEVITABLY paints a somewhat grisly picture of homosexuality in the surgery, and so it seems a good idea to end with an example of what medical science could achieve when it allowed first-hand experience to threaten its disciplinary integrity.

Albert Moll's *Die conträre Sexualempfindung* (1891), written and published before he was thirty, was a summing up and sweeping out of the 'knowledge' amassed by the fledgling discipline. It may well be the first major work on homosexuality produced by a homosexual from within the medical establishment. Moll never married and he had unusually good access to first-hand information. His book was based on hundreds of interviews with Berlin 'uranists' and on the testimony of the sympathetic Head of the German Pederasty Division. It says a lot about the tenacity of prejudice that its findings might still seem extraordinary to some people, 112 years after its publication.

Homosexuality, in Moll's view, was not 'picked up' like a vice or a habit. It appeared in early childhood and was probably congenital. All the supposed 'causes' were imaginary. Masturbation had nothing to do with it, nor did sexual excess. By the same reasoning, overactive homosexuals would turn themselves into heterosexuals: 'One is no more likely to see an individual glutted with cakes and pastries develop a sudden taste for the filth and rubbish in the street.'

Unusually for a doctor whose cases were predominantly criminal,

Moll claimed that homosexuality was not the mark of a bad character. Homosexuals were not particularly prone to mistreating or killing one another. Paedophiles were just as likely to be heterosexual. Homosexuality was found in all times and places and there were no racial variations. As many Jews as Gentiles were homosexual. (Moll himself was a Protestant of Jewish descent.) Its incidence – especially in women – was greatly underestimated.

Moll did claim to find some inherent traits – hysteria, gossiping, effeminate gestures – and he threw in the occasional 'repulsive', but he rejected the more spectacular suppositions. There was no connection between physical hermaphrodism and sexual inversion. Hairy women were not predisposed to tribadism, and homosexual penises did not point in a different direction from those of other men. Smoking was just as common among male homosexuals, and the range of whistling ability was the same.

Instant recognition was also a myth, though many homosexuals believed it. Moll had interviewed two Berlin uranists independently: though they both believed in an instinctive ability to recognize men like themselves, neither knew that the other was homosexual. Apparently, when they were shown photographs, they tended to associate a sidelong glance with homosexuality. As for Mantegazza's theory that the genital nerves of homosexuals ended at the anus, Moll pointed out that one would have to conclude that men who received sexual stimulus from their toes or forehead had penile nerves in their feet or face.

Homosexuality was a cause of suffering but not a disease. The unhappiness of homosexuals was caused by society. Many passions lasted a lifetime, and if liaisons were often brief, it was not because homosexuals were promiscuous but because they were not bound by the social conventions of family and marriage.

Perhaps the most radical aspect of Moll's study was the definition of homosexuality as a naturally occurring variety of human sexuality. The 'unnatural' argument was specious: 'Man generally performs the sexual act with woman, not with the conscious aim of producing children, but to satisfy an irresistible urge.' A homosexual who had sex with another homosexual was performing a natural act.

Over half a century before the Kinsey Report, Moll replaced the quasi-ethnic division of humanity into hetero- and homo-sexual with the notion of a sexual continuum:

> One can easily see that sexual inversion is not isolated from normal sexual life by an unbridgeable gulf. In bisexuality, as in all other domains, one finds intermediate cases ranging from a mere trace of homosexual love to the most pronounced uranism.

The practical conclusions were obvious. The law should be changed, and 'cures' should be abandoned. Illnesses suffered by homosexuals were caused, not by mental or physical abnormality, but by fear, guilt and sexual deprivation. 'Since abstinence has been proved to aggravate the morbid state of uranists, we can only encourage them to indulge in homosexual acts.'

This remarkable book was written by a young man who was sufficiently confident, commonsensical and witty to undermine the discipline to which he owed his reputation and his salary. If his conclusions were adopted, medical categories would be seen to be little more than metaphors. The whole field would be shattered into individual cases: 'To make a complete study [of sexual perversions, heterosexual and homosexual], one would have to [. . .] take account of the individual features of each invalid and the peculiarities of his perversion.' Nevertheless, his work was read and admired not just by outsiders like Ellis and Carpenter but also by other doctors.

Sadly, Moll fell prey to his own profession. He came to believe that cures were possible after all and insisted that homosexuals should obtain a medical opinion before pronouncing themselves sane. Like most of his colleagues, he found that reasons to change his mind became increasingly scarce. He became obsessed with professional rivalries. He and Freud made a show of despising one another, perhaps because they owed so much to each other's work. In 1913, Moll helped to found the International Society for Sex Research as a rival to Hirschfeld's Medical Society for Sexology. He wanted to 'open the eyes of educated people to the dangers of homosexual agitation'. In such belligerent circumstances, partisan theories were always likely to prevail.

Albert Moll died on the same day as Sigmund Freud (23 September 1939). By then, from Nazi Germany to the United States, the theoretical view of homosexuality had become a hereditary perversion of the medical profession.

4

Outings

On one of those foggy nights when sounds are strangely lugubrious, I heard the cries of distress of a man who was being beaten up and, it seemed, butchered. I have since learned what this strange drama was about, but I neither can nor will say what it was.

George Sand, *Histoire de ma vie* (IV, 9), apparently associating the incident with the Marquis de Custine (see p. 87)

One evening after we had lived together a month, I returned from work to find my apartment in the condition in which burglars would have left it, locked closets and drawers broken open, and their contents scattered around. [. . .]

The following evening I was amazed at learning that the manuscript of this autobiography had been returned by *parcels post*. The package had been inadvertently opened by my landlord, and I therefore decided to confess my androgynism. Moreover, on account of the expected call from criminally-minded blackmailers, it was desirable to appeal to him for protection. His marvellous and hardly expected sympathy greatly relieved my distress. I proposed vacating his house, but he would not hear of it.

Earl Lind, *Autobiography of an Androgyne*, 1900; published 1918

IN THE PREVIOUS TWO CHAPTERS, Uranians, inverts and homosexuals have been seen in exceptional – and exceptionally
unpleasant – circumstances. In this chapter, the institutional doors
are thrown open onto the bigger institution outside.

Any description of the relations of gay men and women with the
rest of society relies on generalization. Some communities and periods
were more tolerant than others; some people were eventually quite
happy to be 'outed', others suffered lifelong humiliation. Yet the
similarities are just as striking and significant as the differences. This
would not have surprised the thousands of men and women who
found groups of like-minded strangers in other countries and social
classes, or who recognized their plight and passion in books and
paintings from a distant age.

The first part of this chapter is devoted largely to well-known
middle- or upper-class people who had special claims to the public's
attention. This is partly because the evidence is more copious, but it
also provides a basis for understanding the experience of less extraordinary people. The widely reported misadventures and triumphs of
prominent homosexuals helped to shape the self-image and social
identity of people who were otherwise alone and adrift.

*

THE LIVES OF men and women who belong to an unorganized
minority are often representative to an unusual degree, however
various the individuals.

A homosexual French aristocrat, for instance, whose father and
grandfather were guillotined in the Revolution, who grew up in a
medieval castle in Brittany, whose mother was Chateaubriand's mistress and who wrote one of the finest travel books of the Romantic
period (*La Russie en 1839*), can hardly be described as typical. But
even the life of Astolphe de Custine could give shivers of recognition
to people who belonged to very different worlds.

In 1818, unaware that some people referred to the sensitive young
marquis as 'Mlle de Chateaubriand', the Duchesse de Duras set her
sights on Astolphe as a husband for her daughter Clara. Astolphe's
mother knew about his inclinations but saw no reason to prevent the
marriage. Her son must have an heir.

At first, Astolphe seemed to show interest but then withdrew, pleading some mysterious impediment. In public, he wrapped himself in a fashionable Romantic cloak. He was suffering from an indefinable malady of the soul: 'Ever since I came into this world, my heart has been an enigma that no other heart has solved [. . .] and that I myself am less able to explain than anyone else.' 'Sitting on the ruins of my life, I stare insensibly at the torrent that bears me off with my shattered hopes.' It was perfectly possible to talk like this in 1818 without arousing suspicions.

Word went round that the mysterious problem was impotence. Custine's prospective mother-in-law expressed her worries by writing a puzzling novel, *Olivier, ou le Secret* (1822), in which a shrinking violet called Olivier oddly refuses to marry the perfect woman. Even now, Olivier's 'bizarre secret' is sometimes said to be impotence. But when Olivier complains that 'the only feelings of which my heart is capable are those that honour forbids', is he really referring to genital malfunction?

Olivier is a parlour game in which the truth emerges by a process of elimination: the only theory left standing at the end is the unmentionable one. The Duchesse de Duras was not a novice. She was obviously intrigued by her daughter's reluctant suitor, and the result of her analysis was the first sympathetic novel in modern literature about a homosexual man. Of course, sympathy had to be disguised as something else. At the end of the novel, Olivier blows his brains out and his fiancée goes mad. But this is the death of an innocent tragic hero, not the comeuppance of a pervert.

Custine's friend Rahel Varnhagen von Ense also guessed the truth: 'Few people', she told him, 'truly know the needs of their own nature, even those of their physical nature.' Women, too, were likely to be judged either sexless or depraved and were often better able to understand the predicament. Custine's closest male friend, Édouard de La Grange, was completely mystified and spent the next two years trying to find out what was wrong: 'Is this misfortune the misfortune of nature?' he asked his diary. 'Is it the fault of misdirected leanings? Oh my friend, how you hurt me, and how guilty I feel to have such thoughts!'

Like most people in his position, Custine suffered more from the need to deceive his friends than from fear of discovery. Deception was a form of mental suicide. In his unsigned novel *Aloys* (1829), without specifying the source of his anguish, he gave one of the first psychological analyses of life in the closet. This was something more insidious than social inconvenience. The undiscovered homosexual was an exile in his own land, an invisible man who was also blind to his surroundings:

> As long as we speak only in response to other people's disapproving silence, and as long as our words are but an apology, we ourselves are unable to judge the world fairly. Our life is an enigma to others, but their lives are an enigma to us, and our attempts to communicate with them are futile: we see them always as an audience, and in their eyes we are actors. No mind or character can withstand such false relations. They affect not only our behaviour but also our most intimate feelings.

In 1823, Custine suddenly seemed to solve his problem. His mother gave him an innocent orphan to marry. A son was born – thus ruining the 'impotence' excuse – but died a few years later. At about the same time, Custine found a new friend in the homosexual underworld of Paris: the son of an English judge called Edward Sainte-Barbe. Edward, Astolphe and his wife Léontine formed an amicable *ménage à trois*. Edward nursed Léontine through her final illness. She died in July 1823.

Just when the 'ruins' of his life were beginning to look habitable, Custine's secret was brutally revealed. In November 1824, several newspapers reported that a 'Marquis de C . . .' had been beaten up by some soldiers on the road to Saint-Denis. The Prefect of Police wanted to reassure people that the streets were safe and made sure that details leaked out. Custine had had an assignation with a young soldier. The soldier's comrades had decided to 'teach him a lesson'. They shaved Custine's head, tore off his clothes and left him to make his way back to Paris in the rain. This lynching had the savage, ritualistic features of what would later be called 'queer-bashing'. The soldiers had taken a stone and smashed his hand in order to remove his wedding-ring.

Custine's friends were appalled, but not by the violence. One of them saw the incident as a sign of the times: 'My God, what a sordid combination of Romanticism, mysticism and Germanism!' Even La Grange was battered into recognition: 'The man is sunk, sullied, branded with the mark of reprobation.' To think that 'every mother wanted him as a son-in-law!'.

The not entirely regrettable result was that Custine was ostracized by the snobs of the Faubourg Saint-Germain and spent more time travelling. He shared his house at Fervaques with Sainte-Barbe and sometimes with other friends like the German historian F. C. Schlosser ('a stranger to everything but Greek and philosophy'). Disgrace washed off quite easily. Custine entertained lavishly, corresponded widely and was admired by some of the greatest writers of the age, including Balzac, Stendhal and Baudelaire.

The brutal outing of the Marquis de Custine was a kind of liberation. Everyone knew his secret, he was able to live an honest life with his lovers, and since most of the pedants and prudes had been driven away, the quality of his social life improved enormously. His heterosexual guests might have twittered about his 'black depths' and his 'limp and sticky hand', but they enjoyed his hospitality and his conversation. Now that their diaries and letters have been published, Custine's world looks forbiddingly homophobic, but daily reality was different, even in the nervous, sectarian world of Restoration France. The rewards of Custine's company outweighed the pleasures of condemnation. In the end, sexuality mattered less than gender. A woman who had suffered sexual disgrace and who continued to live with more than one lover would have found the road back to respectability impossibly long and stony.

*

IT IS UNLIKELY that French society invented a special response just for Custine. Other homosexual households were already known to exist. Of course, the fact that they were famous marks them out from the crowd. They were more vulnerable to common prejudice, but they also had the financial and intellectual means to counteract it. Their voices could be heard. Joseph Fiévée, who served Napoleon as a secret agent in London and Paris, lived quite openly with his friend, the playwright Théodore Leclercq. The two men had lived as a couple in England, Germany and in Fiévée's official residence when he was Prefect of the Nièvre. Far from being ostracized, they were a very popular couple. They staged Leclercq's satirical playlets at their home in front of large and appreciative audiences. When he died in 1851, Leclercq was buried next to his friend in the Père-Lachaise cemetery. As Fiévée pointed out, 'Any friendship that lasts more than thirty years eventually becomes respectable.'

Naturally, acceptance was not absolute. The words 'tolerance' and 'acceptance', used throughout this chapter, should be taken in a severely restricted sense. Fiévée's remark suggests a long apprentice-ship in respectability. 'Model' couples were contrasted, as they are today, with the unacceptable 'promiscuous' variety. The art critic Delécluze reported the gossip after a performance at Fiévée's home in 1826:

> They were barely in the street when everyone started talking about the *male household* of Fiévée and Leclercq. [. . .] One of the gentlemen spoke about the air of decency that reigns *chez* Fiévée and compared it with the liaison of the improvvisatore Sgricci with his young sten-ographer. The difference between Leclercq and Antonio, he said, is the same as the difference between a lawful wife and a mistress. Fiévée has found a way to make it almost respectable!

Tommaso Sgricci himself may have been more disreputable but he enjoyed a similar degree of tolerance, at least in Italy, where his genius for improvising poems on any subject made him a national hero. Byron wrote to John Hobhouse from Ravenna on 3 March 1820:

> Sgricci is here improvising with great success – he is also a celebrated Sodomite, a character by no means so much respected in Italy as it should be; but they laugh instead of burning – and the Women talk of it as a pity in a man of talent – but with greater tolerance than could be expected – and only express their hopes that he may yet be converted to Adultery.

Sgricci was publicly teased for his sexual tastes but he could respond to the jibes quite safely. In Florence, he was placed under police surveillance. Spies saw him standing at his window in the Via dei Bardi, pretending to write poems and flirting with boys and soldiers in the street. The protection of the Grand Duke of Tuscany might have saved him from prosecution, but his behaviour seems to have been accepted in any case. According to the Inspector of Police, Sgricci would leave the house at dusk, dressed for pleasure: ostentatious coiffure, open-necked shirt, 'almost skimpy and artificially tight-fitting clothes designed to show off the hips as much as possible'. (This had been a recognizably homosexual style of dress for several centuries.) 'And with an affected gait, he goes walking through the city in search of adventures in the manner of a lady of the night.'

Acceptance was clearly not the result of naivety. Custine's mishap on the road to Saint-Denis left no one in doubt about his private life, and even Fiévée's decent liaison was widely thought to be sexual, as various smutty epigrams suggest:

> Des soins divers, mais assidus
> De Fiévée occupent la vie;
> Comme B[ougre] il salit les cus,
> Comme écrivain il les essuie.*

Even people who were not visibly monogamous, like Sgricci or the French painter Girodet, could be seen as sexual oddities without fatal damage to their reputation. Girodet's paintings, especially the dreamy *Sleep of Endymion* (1792), were recognized as icons of homosexual love. French novelists used his name to hint at a character's sexual proclivity. Anecdotes were told about his private life: he had apparently been pestered by the actress Julie Candeille, who saw him as the perfect husband for her declining years. At first Girodet pleaded impotence, to which she replied, 'What does that matter at our age!' Then he claimed to be a 'bizarre and violent' man who was in the habit of beating up his servants: 'I am capable of every sort of excess!' This convinced her that she should look elsewhere.† (She eventually

---

* 'Fiévée devotes his life / To various exacting tasks. / As a B[ugger], he dirties arses, / And as a writer wipes them.'
† Beating up servants seems to have been a metaphor for homosexual acts. In an otherwise baffling episode of Stendhal's *Armance* (1827) – inspired by the Duchesse de Duras's *Olivier* – Octave, a frigid aristocrat 'with the most beautiful blond curls in the world', throws his servant out of the window, then adopts the man, becomes his 'servant' and eventually sends him away with a pension to buy his silence.

settled on a homosexual artist called Hilaire Périé who used to run about Paris dressed as an Ancient Greek.)

The absence of consistently extreme reactions makes it hard to tell a simple tale of outrage and persecution. There is at least as much evidence of a desire to live and let live as there is of rabid homophobia. Murderous rage was less common than curiosity, curiosity less common than indifference. Life for men like Custine or Sgricci could be almost simultaneously traumatic, moderately pleasant and deeply satisfying. The simple, inconvenient fact is that different views were applied at various times to the same person. Later parts of this book will suggest that similar remarks can also be applied to men and women who had no particular talent for entertaining an audience.

Evidence of ordinariness tends to be neglected because it lacks dramatic interest. The temptation is to fill up the canvas with mass events – hysterical mobs, purity campaigns, moral panics, and so on. This tends to reduce people to their sexual desires and to present them as helpless micro-organisms in the tide of majority opinion. But they were part of the societies which they helped to form. Like all social beings, they knew the art of compromise and concealment.

It could even be said that homosexual men and women revealed more of themselves than other people and were eagerly invited to do so. As Michel Foucault pointed out, far from being censored and 'driven back into some dark, inaccessible region', sex in the 19th century was increasingly brought into the open. Sex was reincarnated as the sphinx that could tell the final truth about a human being. The unmentionability of the 'nameless sin' was mentioned all the time. 'Sodomites' in these conditions could acquire an almost prophetic importance: they not only had more secrets to tell, they were also more likely to know the answers to other people's secrets.

*

FOUCAULT'S PERCEPTION might explain why something like gratitude was shown to sexual strangers. It would also explain why the two most famous 'outings' in European history had such unexpectedly pleasant results.

Johann Joachim Winckelmann (1717–68), whose studies of Greek art inspired the Classical revival, was commonly thought to have practised what he preached. As Walter Pater wrote in 1867 with unusual directness (for him):

> That his affinity with Hellenism was not merely intellectual, [. . .] is proved by his romantic, fervid friendships with young men. He has known, he says, many young men more beautiful than Guido's arch-angel. These friendships, bringing him in contact with the pride of human form, and staining his thoughts with its bloom, perfected his reconciliation with the spirit of Greek sculpture.

Winckelmann himself insisted that the glories of classical art would remain a mystery to 'those who are observant of beauty only in women, and are moved little or not at all by the beauty of men'. Casanova claimed to have seen him putting the idea into practice. Early one morning in Rome, he walked in on a trouserless Winckelmann lying on top of a beautiful boy. While pulling up his pants, the intrepid scholar explained that he was conducting an experiment: he was trying to enter the minds of his ancient heroes. This may never have happened (that is, Casanova may never have caught him at it), but Casanova's comic anecdote does reflect a common notion that sex could also be an intellectual adventure. Voltaire is said to have conducted a similar experiment with an Englishman at the court of Frederick the Great. A few days later, the Englishman told him that he had repeated the experiment, to which Voltaire replied: 'Once, a philosopher; twice, a sodomite.'*

Eight years later, in 1768, Winckelmann was stabbed and strangled in a tavern in Trieste by a man called Arcangeli. His scandalous death was thought to have lifted the veil on his sordid dealings with the homosexual underworlds of Europe. Arcangeli was an uneducated man and their liaison had clearly not been intellectual. After reports in all the European papers, Winckelmann's propensity was widely

---

* Cf. the more intrepid Flaubert, who paid to be 'handled' at the baths in Cairo in 1850: 'Travelling for our instruction and on a government mission, we considered ourselves duty-bound to practise that form of ejaculation.' 'You ask if I consummated the work begun in the baths. Yes, on a pock-marked young fellow wearing an enormous white turban. It made me laugh, that's all. *But* I'll do it again. To be properly carried out, an experiment must be repeated.'

(though not universally) known, and yet his reputation survived and was even enhanced.

His private letters began to appear shortly after his death and showed that 'Greek love' was not an ancient curio: it was a living tradition. Winckelmann had been cautious but not obscure:

> I am thinking of going to Naples on the 20th [. . .] How happy I should be to have you by my side! You rise with me and you sleep with me! You are the dream of my night. [. . .] I kiss your picture and I swoon.

> From the moment I first saw you, an incomprehensible attraction, aroused not only by your form and features, gave me an inkling of that harmony that passes human understanding. [. . .] Love at its strongest must express itself in whatever way it can.

> > I Thee, both as a man and woman, prize;
> > For a perfect Love implies
> > Love in all Capacities.

> > (Abraham Cowley, 'Platonick Love')

Goethe's edition of these extraordinary love letters appeared in 1805. In the accompanying essay, *Winckelmann und sein Jahrhundert*, he portrayed him as 'a complete man' whose quest for beauty had been fuelled by every aspect of his social, intellectual and emotional life:

> If the demands of friendship and beauty both find sustenance at the same time in a single object, the man's happiness and gratitude seem to exceed all bounds. [. . .] Thus we often find Winckelmann associating with beautiful young men, and never does he appear more animated and amiable than in often fleeting moments.

This was not euphemism. Goethe was not hampered by the non-existence of the word '*Homosexualität*'. He was describing the precise, exciting conjugation of desire and intellect, of circumstance and predisposition. Winckelmann was a hero of the modern mind and the modern world, and his 'unnatural' desires were the clues to a civilization that had been awaiting rediscovery for over 2,000 years.

Winckelmann's sexuality was seen to be central to his influence on European culture. His writings and admirers helped to establish the seemingly contradictory ideas that 'pederasty' was an intellectually superior form of passion and that 'Greek love' was not essentially chaste. Carl Justi's biography (1866–72) talked transparently of 'paroxysms of friendship' and 'a natural indifference to the other sex'. By the time Ludovic Dugas wrote his epic study of *L'Amitié antique* (1894), it was no longer possible to believe that 'boy love' was an ancient metaphor for intellectual endeavour, as some British scholars had insisted. The riddle, of course, was as puzzling as ever: 'How could these men who had such a keen sense of honour have lost all honour?'

*

SIXTY YEARS AFTER Winckelmann's death, another notorious 'outing' of a German writer showed that his case was not unique.

In 1829, the distinguished poet Count von Platen made a snide reference to Heinrich Heine's Jewishness in his drama, *Der romantische Ödipus*. Despite believing Platen to be 'a true poet', Heine now decided to destroy his reputation. Like other critics, he had been startled by 'yearnings for pederasty' in Platen's latest poems. In his *Reisebilder* (vol. 3), he called him a sexual ostrich who thought that by simply omitting the word '*Freund*' (male friend) from time to time, he could hide his enormous sin. 'He would have done better to stick his bottom in the sand.'

No one could possibly have doubted Heine's meaning. He called Platen 'a woman', 'a pathic', 'a male tribade', 'a bottom man' whose love 'has a passive, Pythagorean quality'. He used the common euphemism for homosexuals: '*warme Brüder*' or '*warme Freunde*'.* He

---

* 'Warm brothers' or 'warm friends' had been in use since at least the early 1770s. 'Warm' implies affection, though Magnus Hirschfeld traced the expression to the supposedly higher skin temperature of homosexuals. The anonymous *Briefe über die Galanterien von Berlin* (1782) shows that the term was not innocently used:

'Those seven men are warm.'

'Warm? What does that mean?'

'You've spent four months in Berlin and you don't know that? Amazing! [. . .] But you must have read something about Socratic love? Well, those men are genuine Socratic lovers.'

'How lovely!'

'It would be if they stopped at spiritual love, but they mix it up with every sort of carnal love as well.'

'Impossible! . . .'

also suggested that Platen's 'Romantic Oedipus' should have killed his mother and married his father.

Heine's vicious attack was not just another tirade against sodomy. It was one of the first perceptive studies of the ruses of a homosexual writer 'living in an age when he is not allowed to name his true feelings and when the moral code that opposes his love with unfailing hostility forbids him even to express his dismay openly'. 'His fear muffles the natural sound of his own voice and condemns him [. . .] to use the feelings of other poets to mask his own.' It was practically an invitation to rediscover Platen's poetry. Heine had removed the roof and exposed the fascinating interior – its intricate symbols, its Persian imitations, its unspeakable secrets. His remarks would have struck a chord with people who had never written a poem or published a book.

Platen pretended not to have seen the attack, but he was ill in bed for two months and spent most of his remaining years in Italy. However, there were also two unexpected results. Although Heine was not the only critic to deplore Platen's 'fervent praise of young boys' bodies' (as a reviewer put it in 1829), Heine was widely condemned for the attack. His reputation suffered more than Platen's. When Platen died in Sicily in 1835 of typhoid, Heine was widely blamed for his death. The real crime – naming the unnameable – had been committed, not by Platen but by Heine. Private vice was less disgraceful than a public breach of etiquette. Even the reviewer who had criticized the 'unwomanly' Platen broke off relations with Heine.

The second surprise is that, like Custine, Platen discovered a new freedom. Heine had helped his poems to reach their audience and confirmed the private impressions of many readers. Platen's technically perfect stanzas now looked like a disciplined expedition into the wild side of the mind. His sonnets on Venice (1825) had turned the city into the unreadable map of a homosexual heart:

> *Dies Labyrinth von Brücken und von Gassen,*
> *Die tausendfach sich ineinanderschlingen,*
> *Wie wird hindurchzugehn mir je gelingen?*
> *Wie werd ich je dies große Rätsel fassen?**

---

* 'This labyrinth of bridges and alleyways / That twist around themselves a thousandfold: / How shall I ever walk that maze / And solve its enormous riddle?'

Platen's circle of acquaintances grew and he was never again short of friends. He wrote fewer poems but led a happier life and overcame his self-disgust. At Venice he braved the excremental smells of summer to swim in the lagoon with young Venetians. He rediscovered Naples, where 'love between men is so frequent that one never expects even the boldest demands to be refused'.

In the early autumn of 1835, with cholera spreading through Italy, Platen sailed for Sicily. He died at Syracuse in December and was buried in the Protestant cemetery. His grave became one of the pilgrimage sites on the gay Grand Tour. Naturally, the shrine was decently discreet, the ironic epilogue to a life largely devoted to keeping up appearances. As if to underline the fact that he had been tolerated rather than accepted, the tomb was adorned with a bas-relief woman weeping over an urn.

*

THE TEARFUL WOMAN on Platen's grave is a more appropriate symbol for the treatment of homosexuals than the gallows or the padded cell. Silence was by far the commonest form of persecution. If the works of a sodomite gave pleasure to 'decent' people, it was customary to believe that the author was not a sodomite at all. In 1809, during an investigation of the German playwright August Wilhelm Iffland's 'immoral attraction to his own sex', an informer of the Viennese police recorded general incredulity that 'a devotee of sodomy' could write such 'moral' plays.

If evidence of 'vice' became overwhelming, it could still be sectioned off and treated as a professional weakness or a temporary aberration. Even Havelock Ellis took the view that Oscar Wilde was fundamentally heterosexual but became homosexual 'by the exercise of intellectual curiosity and esthetic interest'. Exceptions could always be made without weakening the general prejudice.

In the right circumstances, a limited form of 'coming out' could even act as a vaccination against homophobic aggression. Barbey d'Aurevilly, the dandified novelist and biographer of Beau Brummell, kept his sexuality secret by appearing to do the opposite. When challenged directly, he had the wit to respond with amusing half-admissions: 'My tastes incline me to it, my principles permit it, but the ugliness of my contemporaries repels me.' One of Heine's complaints about Platen was that he hid his feelings behind a mask of sobriety. No such complaint could be made about men like Barbey d'Aurevilly or the fifth Marquess of Anglesey who paraded along Piccadilly and the Paris Boulevards in the 1890s, rouged, powdered, perfumed and cradling an equally fragrant poodle festooned with pink ribbons.

Evidence of 'camp' behaviour is notoriously difficult to interpret and apparently more common in the late 18th and 19th centuries than in earlier periods. This may reflect the spread of more consistent views of what constituted a 'molly' or a 'pouf': once the image existed, it could be acted up to. Or it may reflect a more confident gay subculture, or simply the camouflaging effect of certain fashions: the *précieux*, the Regency 'fop', the Restoration dandy. Fashions passed between the homosexual and heterosexual worlds quite freely. Some types of information are simply unavailable – gestures, expressions, significant smiles.

There is however a noticeable continuity, from the performances of Leclercq and Sgricci to the 'queans' of Victorian and Edwardian London and the gay celebrities of 21st-century television. The Edwardian music-hall entertainer Fred Barnes, for instance, seems a distant relative of Sgricci or Count von Platen, but he was able to exploit the same exasperating double standard. Newspapers of the time slavered over the evidence of arrested sodomites, but the effeminate Fred ('Freda' to the boys in the gallery) delighted his audiences with brazen innuendos. His hit song 'The Black Sheep of the Family' (1907) caused a storm of applause when it was first performed. 'Only a few people', Fred remembered, 'glared at me as though I were a monstrosity.'

> It's a queer, queer world we live in
> And Dame Nature plays a funny game –
> Some get all the sunshine,
> Others get the shame.*

* 'Shame' was another code word for homosexual love – as in Alfred Douglas's 'In Praise of Shame' ('Of all sweet passions Shame is loveliest'). For 'queer', see p. 262.

The consistently ambiguous reaction to performing gays suggests that western societies – which seem to have been uniquely repressive – did after all provide a role for homosexual behaviour. Most of the evidence presented so far relates to prominent individuals and artists, but the partial immunity of public entertainers was also available, at the usual cost – self-mockery and humiliation, strict observance of the ever-changing rules, obligatory good humour and constant personal danger – to people with less lofty aspirations.

As pioneers and anthropologists discovered, most societies sanction some form of homosexuality. North American Indians were found to be extraordinarily accepting of sexual ambiguity in the form of the 'man-woman', the 'berdache', the 'bote', the 'agokwa', the 'alyhā' or the 'joya'. Noble savages had been seen doing needlework and washing dishes; missionaries and explorers were offered oral and anal intercourse by hospitable transvestites.

Remarkably few writers interpreted queer behaviour among the Indians as a sign of barbarism. Closer acquaintance showed that the 'berdache' played a precise role and lived under severe constraints. Many of them were revered for their prophetic powers, but they were also often seen as an unfortunate and hilarious aberration.

In the 1830s, the painter George Catlin found similar attitudes along the Missouri and the Ohio. The gorgeous 'dandies' who wore their hair like women, carried turkey-feather fans and spent the day preening themselves on beautiful ponies, were held in low regard and referred to as 'old women'. When Catlin asked to paint one of these 'gay and tinselled bucks', he was told that, if he did, he would have to destroy the portraits he had painted of the chiefs.

This orderly form of victimization would have been quite familiar to any Victorian 'pouf' who happened to be captured by a North American tribe. As one of the most famous Victorian sodomy trials showed, acceptance and ridicule were just as much the norm in central London as on the banks of the Ohio.

The protagonists of this tragi-comic trial were Ernest Boulton, twenty-two, the son of a stockbroker (a.k.a. Lady Arthur Clinton or 'Stella, Star of the Strand') and Frederick Park, twenty-three (known to his friends as 'Fanny'), who worked for a firm of solicitors. Fanny and Stella specialized in melodramas and operettas. They played to full houses from Scarborough to Southend and received ecstatic reviews. No one who sees their photographs will be surprised to learn that everyone knew that they were men. Sometimes, as in *Love and Rain* (1868), Stella's lucky husband was played by the young gentleman who fed, lodged and loved her: Lord Arthur Clinton, MP.

Off stage (if they ever were), they wore tight trousers and low-necked shirts, powdered their faces and flounced up and down the Strand and the Burlington Arcade, eyeing up the men.

Unfortunately, their 'giggling and chirruping' attracted the wrong sort of attention. The Metropolitan Police kept them under surveillance for a year. They were observed to light their cigarettes 'with gestures of unnecessary flamboyance'. 'They did not swing their arms like men, but walked like women do.' Worst of all, when her lace came unpinned one day at the Strand Theatre, Fanny availed herself of the facilities. 'Was she dressed as a woman?' the attendant was later asked. 'Dressed as a Lady. The Lady said, "Have you a Ladies' Room?", and I said, "Yes, madam, walk this way if you please."'

Outside, the constables were waiting. At Bow Street, Fanny's companion was found to be wearing a sleeveless, low-cut scarlet dress with white kid gloves. Further inspection revealed petticoats and stays, and, according to the police doctor, a distended anus. Fanny and Stella were charged with conspiracy to commit a felony (sodomy). The following morning (Friday, 29 April 1870), they appeared in court. Park's counsel, Mr Straight, failed to prove their innocence and they were bound over for trial at the Old Bailey.

One reporter called for 'these misguided youths' to be severely punished. A crime had been committed that should 'arouse the just indignation of every true Englishman'. This was a reference, not to sodomy, but to Mr Park's use of the ladies' room. The petticoated monster had 'had the unblushing impudence to apply to the female attendants to fasten up the gathers of his skirt'. Rome and Sodom had nothing to compare with 'the atrocious phases of London life as they exist in the nineteenth century'.

It would be an insult to Victorians to assume that this pompous blather represented a common view. At the main trial, the jury and the public gallery observed the parade of exhibits – silk stockings, curling irons, 'boxes of Violet Powder and Bloom of Roses', and twenty false chignons. They chortled at the testimony of at least twenty men who cruised the West End in drag. And when the girly-voiced Mr Thomas Gibbings, who hosted drag balls at Haxell's Hotel, said that he saw nothing wrong with 'going in drag', he was loudly applauded.

Boulton and Park had carried the stage into the courtroom. The trial was a bedroom farce, complete with a housemaid who had witnessed daily visits from the hairdresser and heard them call each other 'darling': 'I said to him [said the housemaid], I beg your pardon but I really think you are a man. He said he was Lady Arthur Clinton, he said, I am Lady Clinton, Lord Arthur's wife.' He even had a wedding-ring to prove it.

The prosecution exhibited the calling cards of homosexual prostitutes and tried to frighten the jury with plagues of sodomy: the 'national character' was at stake. The defence maintained, rather implausibly, that such public shenanigans were unlikely to be a front for sexual depravity. It asked the jury to prove by its verdict that the 'plague' did not exist. Anticipating the Wolfenden Report by eighty-seven years, Lord Chief Justice Cockburn wisely observed that the conspiracy charge 'operates unjustly, unfairly, and oppressively'.

When the acquittal was pronounced, applause broke out again and Fanny fainted in the dock.

The escapades of Boulton and Park and their sympathetic treatment by most of the court suggest that the two main interpretations of camp behaviour are both correct. 'Camp' has its own intricacies and rituals, and the idea that it simply parodies female behaviour depends on a very odd view of women. It appears to be a spontaneous feature of gay culture, from Ancient Rome and pre-conquest North America to the present day. At the same time, it can be seen as an example of 'minstrelization' – a tactful conformity to common prejudice designed to win a kind of condescending acceptance. The two interpretations are not mutually exclusive. Aspects of gay life that seem to have certain social advantages can be exaggerated for the benefit of a hostile audience. Similar survival techniques are practised by schoolchildren with similarly varying degrees of success.

In either case, the performance was precarious. As long as the 'disgraceful' behaviour was seen as part of an act – as it was in the theatrical setting of a courtroom and even in the street – it could be accepted and applauded. But if it seemed to be claiming a place in 'real life', it was once again a threat. Lord Arthur Clinton had appeared quite openly with his darling Stella, but when he saw his name in the papers in connection with the trial, he killed himself. He was thirty years old. The official cause of death was scarlet fever. Stella survived, but she lost a loving husband and, as far as we know, was never seen in public again.

*

IT WILL BE APPARENT by now that the title of this book might almost have been 'But Not in Britain'. In England especially, sodomites seem to have been treated more harshly than elsewhere. Whatever the causes – Protestant morals, the rise of the nuclear family, early industrialization reinforcing the sexual division of labour – the main observable difference in English attitudes is the ease with which connections were made between sodomy and other sins. In England, a sodomite was never just a sodomite.

The Bishop of Clogher, the 'mitred reprobate' who was caught with a handsome guardsman and his breeches round his ankles at the White Hart Inn in Westminster in 1822, represented 'The Crimes of the Clergy' (the title of a pamphlet of 1823).

Richard Heber, MP for Oxford University, who fled to Brussels in 1826 under suspicion of 'unnatural practices' (as his friend Walter Scott put it), William Bankes, MP, who compromised himself by the walls of Westminster Abbey (1833) and then in Green Park (1841), and Edward Protheroe, MP, who was accused in 1847 and 1850 of luring boys to his home, represented the moral bankruptcy of politicians.

Lord Arthur Somerset, who was implicated in the Cleveland Street brothel scandal of 1889, stood for the 'toffs' who thought that they could exploit the workers and then flee to sunny climes – as *The North London Press* complained:

> My Lord Gomorrah sat in his chair
> Sipping his costly wine;

He was safe in France, that's called the fair;
In a city some call 'Boo-line'.

The scapegoating of sodomites was not of course peculiar to England. In the late 19th and early 20th centuries, some of the biggest political scandals in France, Germany, Denmark and Austro-Hungary were fuelled by revelations of sodomy. Nevertheless, scapegoating seems to have been more consistently and enthusiastically practised in England. Even today, British tabloid newspapers devote more space than their foreign equivalents to the moral implications of homosexual buggery. English communities abroad could be just as savage. Edward Gibbon found it 'astonishing' that anyone should befriend William Beckford, who fled from England after a scandalous love affair with the teenage Viscount William Courtenay: 'Even supposing him innocent, still some regard was due to the opinion of the world.'

It is all the more surprising to find so many exceptions to the rule that the rule itself looks questionable. Trials and other investigations often turned up evidence of casual acquiescence. Of course, compared to other fields of social history, the evidence is scarce and tends to be concentrated in certain areas. There is, however, a noticeable gap between the lynch mentality of sensationalist newspapers and everyday behaviour. As Rictor Norton points out, not every heterosexual Londoner who was approached by a homosexual prostitute summoned a policeman, and 'even the law-abiding citizens who lived in the neighbourhood of a known molly house seldom heaped abuse upon its customers or brought the tavern to the attention of the police'. In 1810, two men were able to set up and furnish a molly house in Vere Street with a chapel for weddings and every sort of feminine necessity and run it for almost six months before it was raided.

American cities at the turn of the century were just as tolerant, according to a correspondent of Havelock Ellis:

> Ninety-nine normal men out of a hundred have been accosted on the streets by inverts, or have among their acquaintances men whom they know to be sexually inverted. Everyone has seen inverts and knows what they are. The public attitude toward them is generally a negative one – indifference, amusement, contempt.

Even the Metropolitan Police showed signs of moderation. In 1854, two bizarrely dressed men were arrested in London outside a drag ball that was regularly held at Druids' Hall in Turnagain Lane. One was 'completely equipped in female attire of the present day'; the other, a man of sixty, was clad 'in the pastoral garb of a shepherdess of the golden age'. The ball had been known to the police for eighteen months, but, as the magistrate learned to his amazement, the constable had been told by his sergeant not to interfere unless the perversions were carried on in public.

This relatively relaxed attitude, which may reflect the views of individual policemen rather than official policy, could still be found in 1889 when the homosexual prostitute Jack Saul was interviewed about his business:

'Were you hunted out by the police?'
'No, they have never interfered. They have always been kind to me.'
'Do you mean they have deliberately shut their eyes to your infamous practices?'
'They have to shut their eyes to more than me.'

The constables may of course have had their tolerance enhanced by money. Ellis's correspondent later reported an equally benign and well-oiled police force in American cities: 'The inverts have their own "clubs" [. . .] attached to *saloons*.' 'You will rightly infer that the police know of these places and endure their existence for a consideration; it is not unusual for the inquiring stranger to be directed there by a policeman.'

In the gaslit streets of Victorian London, famous 'margeries' like 'Fair Eliza' sallied forth each evening, courting customers and shocking decent citizens from Holborn to Regent Street (according to the *Yokel's Preceptor: or, More Sprees in London!*, *c.* 1850). 'Betsy H . . .', another 'notorious and shameless pouf', patrolled the Strand, St Martin's Court and Fleet Street, apparently with impunity. These metropolitan mollies were as much a tourist attraction as the 'fairies' of Broadway and Madison Square. Voyeuristic tours of gay districts were not a 20th-century invention.

Even when 'poufs' were molested, it was not necessarily because of their supposed inclinations. In October 1889, Inspector Ferret of 'H' Division arrived at Bromley Street in the East End to find 600 people surrounding Edward Hamblar, a sixty-one-year-old ship's joiner. Mr Hamblar was wearing a hat and veil, a print dress, two flannel petticoats and 'a large dress improver' (a bustle). 'All the people around the prisoner imagined he was "Jack the Ripper", and the excitement was very great in consequence.'

Outside London, away from the bulging eyes of journalists and the nightly parade of mollies, even the most notorious delinquents were not treated with universal revulsion. The disgraced Bishop of Clogher, after leading a jolly life in Paris, went to live in Glasgow and then in Edinburgh under an assumed name. Some of his neighbours discovered his true identity but 'kept the secret until after his death'. William Beckford, who returned to live behind a seven-mile wall in his fantastic Gothic palace at Fonthill, was liked and fêted by the locals. Most of his upper-class visitors knew of his so-called crimes but thought them either inconsequential or picturesque. Hester Thrale, the friend of Samuel Johnson, was astounded at how quickly Beckford's *favourite Propensity* was forgotten: 'I hear nothing said of Mr Beckford but as an *Authour*. What a World it is!!!!'

These pliant attitudes to homosexuality in almost all its forms were prevalent throughout the Victorian age. Odd couples were often silently condoned, even if they ignored distinctions of rank, age and nationality: the 'married' artists Charles Ricketts and Charles Shannon; the sculptor Lord Ronald Gower and his stunning Italian valet; J. A. Symonds and his gondolier with 'the wild glance of a Triton'; Edward Fitzgerald and his Lowestoft fisherman, 'Posh'. Local trawlermen interviewed in the 1900s appear to have taken the same calm view of the matter as Russia's urban serving classes took of what they called 'gentlemen's mischief'. 'Ah! Mr. FitzGerald was a *good* gennleman to him – that he *wuz*!' Posh himself was never ostracized for his attachment.

Sexuality in most cases was simply not the dominant concern. 'Strange stories' about the rural idyll of Edward Carpenter and his working-class lover George Merrill at Millthorpe near Sheffield might have been inspired by Carpenter's writings on 'homogenic love' (friends had warned him that 'a ménage without a woman' would look 'queer'), but the neighbours were more concerned about an influx of socialists and vegetarians. The local letter-writing fool, M. D. O'Brien, was just a mad exception: 'Is the infamy which is said to have brought destruction upon Sodom and Gomorrah likely to bring in one form or another anything less than destruction upon the trade of Sheffield?', he wondered in *Socialism and Infamy: the Homogenic or Comrade Love Exposed* (1909). Anyone who could call the gentle Carpenter a 'disseminator of filth and dirt vomited up from the foul pit of sin and death' and who worried about the effect of homosexuality on the steel industry was not representative; he was simply a lunatic with time on his hands.

The same mixture of the tolerant and the indifferent, with the occasional attention-seeking windbag, was apparent in reactions to the Aesthetic Movement of the 1870s and 1880s. The aesthetes' flowery excesses were mocked so affectionately that it is easy to assume that their audience was quite innocent of sexual subtexts until the unmasking of Oscar Wilde. But swooning aesthetes were seen to be suspiciously pederastic long before the Wilde trials. Elbow-nudging satires like W. H. Mallock's *The New Republic* (1877) and Robert Hichens' *The Green Carnation* (1894) 'confirmed the worst suspicions'. As Richard Ellmann and others have shown, Wilde's sexuality was already in doubt at the height of his popularity. He may even have married to stifle the rumours. In W. S. Gilbert's *Patience* (1881), the Wildean aesthete Bunthorne sings about 'an attachment *à la* Plato / For a bashful young potato / Or a not too French, French bean!' An audience in Texas in the early 1880s may not have grasped the reference to Plato but it still found Gilbert's mincing aesthetes almost worthy of a lynching. In 1883, *Punch* called Wilde a 'Mary-Ann', which was a common term for a homosexual prostitute, while *The Scots Observer* pretended to believe that Wilde had written *The Picture of Dorian Gray* (1890) for 'outlawed noblemen and telegraph boys' – a blatant allusion to the Cleveland Street scandal.

Even without textual analysis, the sexual subtext was all quite obvious to most people. Colleagues of Edward Shelley, the office boy at Wilde's publishers, teased him knowingly about his friendship: 'They implied scandalous things,' Shelley told the court. 'They called me "Mrs Wilde" and "Miss Oscar".'

Lord Alfred Douglas was certainly right to say that much of 'the violent prejudice which existed against homosexuality in those days' was 'simulated and hypocritical'. This single, unpleasant fact goes some way to explaining the impression of routine hostility: some of the most vociferous opponents of 'sodomites' – the Marquis of Queensberry, Edmund Gosse, Freud's paranoid judge Schreber and, later, Douglas himself – were homosexual. The young J. A. Symonds denounced the homosexual headmaster of Harrow just when he was becoming aware of his own sexuality. Trial reports and other memoirs show that the headmaster in Scott Moncrieff's 'Evensong and Morwe Song' (1908), who punishes boys for sins he had committed in his own youth, was not unusual. Scott Moncrieff himself was expelled from Winchester for publishing the story.

The sad phenomenon of homosexual treachery was described – and exemplified – by Proust in *Sodome et Gomorrhe* (translated by Scott Moncrieff during his voluntary exile in Italy):

> These descendants of the Sodomites [. . .] are so readily admitted into the most exclusive clubs that, whenever a Sodomite fails to secure election, the black balls are for the most part cast by other Sodomites, who make a point of condemning sodomy, having inherited the mendacity that enabled their ancestors to escape from the accursed city.

The mere absence of persecution hardly amounts to tolerance. Proust's black-balling sodomites could never abandon their camouflage and 'would repair to Sodom only on days of supreme necessity, when their own town was empty, at those seasons when hunger drives the wolf from the woods'. Few Victorians could discuss the subject publicly without flaunting their moral credentials. Prejudice also operated in invisible ways, through landlords, employers, family members and friends. And, as Jeremy Bentham pointed out, 'the antipathy itself [is] a punishment'.

*

ANY DESCRIPTION OF attitudes to homosexuality must take account of the argument that homosexuality in the modern sense did not exist. If, as Foucault's theory has it, 'the homosexual' was not 'socially constructed' until the end of the 19th century, before then homosexual people can hardly be said to have been tolerated or, for that matter, persecuted.

Evidence of surprisingly intimate behaviour can give the impression that, in Europe and America, libidos used to roam quite freely. In this view, the factory régime of breeding couples had yet to replace the free-range sexual economy. In 1837, a young lawyer called Abraham Lincoln arrived in Springfield, Illinois and asked a storekeeper, Joshua Speed, for the price of a 'single bedstead'. Speed took pity on the handsome bachelor and offered to share his double bed. The two men became close friends and slept together for the next four years. This justifies their inclusion in Jonathan Katz's *Love Stories. Sex Between Men Before Homosexuality* (2001), although the only approximation to 'genital contact' that can be cited is Speed's advice to Lincoln on where he can 'get some' (i.e. sex with women).

Lincoln's lodging arrangements show that two men could sleep together without raising eyebrows. However, this was true only if codes of conduct were observed. The point is made implicitly by another story discovered by Katz. In 1846, Edward McCosker of the New York Police Department was accused of touching a man's private parts. The owner of the parts had taken offence and shouted at Mc-Cosker, calling him 'pretty policeman' and other names. McCosker subsequently lost his job. But in his defence, his colleague Francis Donnelly stated that he had 'been in the habit of sleeping with said McCosker for the last three months, and that said McCosker never to deponent's knowledge acted indecent or indelicate'.

Whatever connotations these domestic practicalities might have today, this was clearly a society for which homosexual behaviour existed and was subject to punishment. The difference between sharing a bed and using it as a platform for sex was just as obvious as it is now.

This is not to say that changes in behaviour have not altered the emotional landscape so much that we now need a whole array of historical positioning equipment to find our way about in the world of our great-great-grandparents. The jitteriness of modern male friendships was quite foreign to the early 19th century. Some means of expressing affection have certainly been lost. Compared to his Romantic ancestors, 21st-century man has only a small repertoire of cautious gestures and words with which to make his feelings known to male friends. On the other hand, future historians will find ample evidence of homoerotic behaviour beyond the gay community: private letters, locker-room language, hugging and kissing on the football field, and so on.

The belief in a less discriminating sexual era is based, of course, on more than Lincoln's double bed. Some striking examples of what looks like unabashed homosexuality have been found in the letters of two young friends in the 1820s: a law student called Thomas Jefferson Withers, who later married Mary Chesnut (of Civil War diaries fame), and James Hammond, the future Governor of South Carolina. A historian with no experience of the writing habits of adolescent men, then or now, might detect clear signs of untrammelled eroticism in Withers' letter to Hammond on 15 May 1826:

> Dear Jim:
>
> [. . .] I feel some inclination to learn whether you yet sleep in your Shirt-tail, and whether you yet have the extravagant delight of poking and punching a writhing Bedfellow with your long fleshen pole – the exquisite touches of which I have often had the honor of feeling? Let me say unto thee that unless thou changest former habits in this particular, thou wilt be represented by every future Chum as a nuisance.

Four months later, Withers supposed that his friend's 'fleshen pole' or '*elongated protruberance*' (*sic*) was more active than ever and that Hammond must be 'charging over the pine barrens of your locality, braying, like an ass, at every she-male you can discover'.

This back-slapping style may reflect the indiscriminate lunges of an adolescent libido in a pre-homosexual age, but it can hardly be treated as a window onto the sexual mores of an entire period. At best, it shows the difference between public and private expression. A useful contrast can be found in the diary of Albert Dodd, who was a law student at Hartford, Connecticut in 1836. Dodd was supposed to be in love with a woman called Julia but was painfully besotted instead with a man called Anthony Halsey:

> How completely I loved him, how I doated on him! [. . .] Often too he shared my pillow – or I his, and then how sweet to sleep with

him, to hold his beloved form in my embrace, to have his arms about my neck, to imprint upon his face sweet kisses! It was happiness complete.

Dodd's passionate, private declaration, his happiness and despair, his longing for Halsey's 'youth, beauty and innocence', are quite different from the ironic celebration of Jim Hammond's peripatetic penis. Only a late-20th-century eye would confuse this ostentatious horse-play with Dodd's whole-hearted commitment to another human being. Hammond went on to marry a Charleston heiress and became a keen seducer of teenage girls. Dodd never married and drowned in the Mackinaw river when he was twenty-six.

Without telepathy, interpretations are always speculative. The photographs of 19th-century men embracing or holding hands in American photographers' studios – reproduced in *Affectionate Men: A Photographic History of a Century of Male Couples, 1850s to 1950s* (1998) or in *Dear Friends: American Photographs of Men Together, 1840–1918* (2001) – remain, as one of the compilers says, 'stubbornly ambiguous objects'. The impossibility of plotting every sign of passion on a sexual graph is what made the conviction of Boulton and Park – once the anatomical evidence had been discredited – so difficult to obtain. The prosecuting counsel could only resort to an impression (but an accurate impression, as it happened) of passionate, physical love and ask the jury to exercise its stylistic common sense:

> A man crying at parting for a few weeks with another man ... What language is that? ... A landlord examining Mr Boulton's thighs! ... What does it mean?

In the full colour of personal experience, the indeterminacy that seems to be a mark of the age of black and white simply did not exist. In a communal bed by the banks of the Genesee river in 1791, Chateaubriand knew immediately what to think when he felt the leg of his Dutch guide slide up against his own: he ran out with his bearskin to sleep in the moonlight, 'cursing the customs of our noble ancestors'. As the ranting author of *The Infamous Life of John Church* (1817) pointed out, acts of physical affection are always a matter of personal judgment:

[T. A. said] that the very affectionate *Vere-street* 'Mr Church kindly put his arms round my neck and kissed me twice, and asked me politely to sleep with him.' Lord, what has sin done! However the Reverend brother T. A. further adds, 'I declined the latter offer, of course', &c. but how far this statement may be true respecting his declining the latter offer, after his allowing that pious brute to kiss him twice, must be left with the reader to judge for himself.

Each case has its own peculiarities and shows a variety of different attitudes. Perhaps the best hope for a general conclusion lies in the concept of 'submersion'. The idea is that, in certain periods and places, fashions in clothing and behaviour allow certain forms of homosexual expression to pass unnoticed. They are as it were submerged in the wider culture. Custine was able for a time to mask his feelings with the *mal du siècle*. Lovers could kiss and embrace under the umbrella of 'Romantic friendship'. The erotic male nudes of David, Girodet and Géricault were surrounded on the walls of the Paris Salon by a host of other male nudes in the neoclassical style. Even if a painter of Ganymedes, wrestling Greeks and Saint Sebastians were suspected of unnatural desires, the followers of fashion could act as a shield. A proliferation of neoclassical genitals was almost as good as a fig-leaf.

'Submersion' could also take more concrete forms: single-sex boarding-schools, workhouses, prisons and penal colonies, ocean-going ships (Herman Melville's 'wooden-walled Gomorrahs of the deep'), mining camps in California, South Africa and Australia. In special circumstances, special rules applied. In 1853, an old American sailor expressed the view that buggery was fine on board ship but that, on land, buggers should be shot.

It is difficult in these extreme conditions to distinguish epidermic episodes from lasting, amphibious passion that thrived on land and sea. Pictures of waltzing Californian miners say nothing about the sexual desires of the dancers. The men who took the woman's part in the dance were not necessarily able to identify a deeper difference in themselves. Situations like these could be just as confusing to the participants as they are to the observer. Many people who turned out to be homosexual assumed that their experiences in the 'sexual cocytus' of public school had been the cause of their homosexuality. Many more looked (or claimed to look) on their puerile deflowering by classmates, prefects or teachers as a curious or regrettable incident with little or no effect on their future life.

Homo- and heterosexuality are concepts that bear the imprint of the periods in which they were invented. But to say that no such dichotomy existed until these terms were coined is to sit on the dictionary and expect it to function as a magic carpet. The jocular Withers and the love-lorn Dodd were both describing erotic behaviour and cannot be neatly assigned to a particular sexual category. For that matter, nor can anyone else. But this does not mean that they lived, loved and died in a sexual Wild West.

*

THE IDEA THAT TOLERANCE or acceptance of homosexuality is a non-subject until the late 19th century also takes a more popular form. Widespread awareness of homosexuality is often said to be a recent consequence of gay liberation. 'It used to be possible' – so the remark usually goes – 'for two women (or men) to live together without being suspected of homosexuality.'

Like most complaints about modern sexual mores, this idea is not peculiar to our own time. In the 1920s, a woman in Katharine Davis's survey of unmarried American female graduates identified 'the ethics of homosexual relationships' as 'the most serious problem the business or professional woman has to face today': 'In my city some business women are hesitating to take apartments together for fear of the interpretation that may be put upon it.'

The kinds of behaviour that trigger a censorious reaction change over time, but anxiety at perceived transgressions can be found in any period. In *The Intermediate Sex* (1908), Edward Carpenter complained that teachers were reacting to affectionate pupils with deliberate coldness for fear of 'a bastard public opinion' and its seedy misinterpretations:

> Rather than run such a risk as this he seals the fountains of the heart, withholds the help which love alone can give, and deliberately nips the tender bud which is turning to him for light and warmth.

In 1896, Colette's husband Willy worried that homosexual interpretations of Wagner's *Parsifal* would impose similarly ridiculous constraints on artists: 'So now every tragic character will be forced to encumber himself with a woman for fear of being taxed with homosexual inclinations?' The *Daily Telegraph*, reporting on the Boulton and Park trial, deemed any such anxiety a good thing:

> The most effeminate and foolish lad will hesitate before, even in joke, he puts his signature to amatory effusions addressed to some one of his companions. That this should be so is a marked benefit.

The fear of being branded homosexual is not a recent phenomenon. It was sufficiently common in 1871 for a French psychiatrist, Legrand du Saulle, to introduce a new category of persecution complex: 'Fear of being considered a sodomite'. He cited two cases from 1845 and 1868. The second patient, having read Dr Tardieu's description of the physical attributes of 'pederasts', asked to be examined by a doctor so that he could be officially certified as 'normal'.

Half a century before, in 1824, referring to James I's 'propensity to favourites' and the 'base passion' of close friends, Ralph Waldo Emerson described in his diary the contamination of private relationships by public suspicions:

> Who is he that thought he might clasp his friend in embraces so tight, in daily intercourse so familiar that they two should be one? [. . .] They foolishly trusted to each other the last secret of their bosoms, their weakness. [. . .] They erred in fancying that friendship would pardon infirmities & that a just confidence demanded that the last door of the heart should be unclosed, and even its secret sensuality revealed.

Coleridge had similar worries about Shakespeare and his supposedly pederastic sonnets. He knew that there was such a thing as 'the Disposition' (as opposed to 'the absurd & despicable Act'), but he denied that Shakespeare was guilty of it:

> O my Son! I pray fervently that thou may'st know inwardly how impossible it was for a Shakespere not to have been in his heart's heart chaste.

This tense denial suggests that Coleridge's meditations on his own romantic friendships and dreams of being sexually assaulted by men were not just bland perambulations in a garden of innocence. The determination to see homosexual men as sodomites and buggers was an attempt to keep strange love certifiably separate. Shelley also tried to locate the boundary between passion and appetite. In his unpublished 'Discourse on the Manners of the Antient Greeks Relative to the Subject of Love' (1818), he stretched a *cordon sanitaire* through 2,000 years of history – noble Greeks and Shakespeare on one side, decadent Romans and Cavaliers on the other:

> It may blunt the harshness of censure [of Greek love] also to reflect that in the golden age of our own literature a certain sentimental attachment towards persons of the same sex was not uncommon. Shakespeare has devoted the impassioned and profound poetry of his sonnets to commemorate an attachment of this kind, which we cannot question was wholly divested of any unworthy alloy. Towards the age of Charles 2^d it is said that this romantic friendship degenerated into licentiousness and this latter age bears the same relation to the former as the first of the Roman Empire to [a gap in the ms].

Not all attempts to separate the innocent from the guilty were so erudite. Smollett's Roderick Random (1748), when subjected to the oddly affectionate Earl Strutwell's defence of sodomy, worries that he might be suspected of sharing 'his taste in love'. For someone who was faced with an urgent, sodomitical Earl, the difference between permissible affection and outrageous love was almost tangible:

> I began to be apprehensive that his lordship finding that I had travelled, was afraid I might have been infected with this spurious and sordid disease abroad, and took this method of sounding my sentiments on the subject. Fired at this supposed suspicion, I argued against it with great warmth [. . .] and declared my utter detestation and abhorrence of it [. . .]
>
> The Earl smiled at my indignation, told me he was glad to find my opinion of the matter so conformable to his own, and that what he had advanced was only to provoke me to an answer, with which he professed himself perfectly well pleased.

The problem is not that homosexuality did not exist but that sexual behaviour changes as rapidly as fashions in dress. The continual fluctuations in notions of what constitutes erotic behaviour are even less perceptible over short periods than changes in hat-size and hemline. Rules seem to be fixed and are rigorously policed. But when two different periods are compared, the cumulative changes are spectacular. A 21st-century person transported to the early 19th century would be in a permanent state of shock. Modern television and film adaptations might impose more 'liberated' mores on Victorian dramas, but they also expunge the details that would unsettle or distract a modern audience: breast-feeding in the drawing-room, men sharing beds, fathers kissing daughters on the lips. At the same time, the artificial ageing of the past demands the removal of unexpected similarities with the present: husbands and wives celebrating their sex life in letters, fear of terrorist attack, concern about the brain-rotting effects of popular culture, and jokes about homosexuality.

Even in the same period and social class, behaviour differed from one region or one person to the next. Roderick Random is startled to be hugged and kissed 'with a seemingly paternal affection' by Earl Strutwell but does not suspect an ulterior motive until he learns that Strutwell is 'notorious for a passion for his sex'. A German traveller in London in 1818 warned his readers that 'The kiss of friendship between men is strictly avoided as inclining towards the sin regarded in England as more abominable than any other.' A generation before, public kissing had been quite common, to judge by the author of *Satan's Harvest Home* (1749) who complained about '*fulsome* Fellows *Slavering* every Time they meet, *Squeezing* each other's Hand, and other like *indecent Symptoms*'. In the United States, men kissing men – 'that salute of American comrades' (Whitman) – remained acceptable for most of the 19th century. Even so, William Cobbett felt that he could use the custom to attack Democratic-Republic clubs in the 1790s: 'Must not their gander-frolicks, and their squeezing, and hugging, and kissing one another, be expected to cause a good deal of pouting and jealousy [among women?]' Terms of endearment were also regulated – not just in the 19th century. On holiday in the Basque country, Bill Gorton tells the narrator of Hemingway's *The Sun Also Rises* (1926):

'Listen. You're a hell of a good guy, and I'm fonder of you than any-body on earth. I couldn't tell you that in New York. It'd mean I was a faggot.'

*

THE FACT THAT the line between Romantic friendship and pas-sionate love is hard to find does not mean that no line existed. But this is not quite so obvious in female friendships. In women, the difference was often less visible and perhaps less important. Con-vention allowed for more intimacy in body and word, and it would be easy now to assume that erotic, lesbian relationships existed primarily in the minds of male novelists and painters – as Anne Lister pretended to believe while flirting with Maria Barlow: 'We agreed it was a scandal invented by the men, who were bad enough for anything . . .'

The example of Anne Lister, an unusually independent young gentlewoman from Halifax, Yorkshire, shows that some women at least formed physical and emotional relationships that were recogniz-ably lesbian in a modern sense. It shows too that, when these relationships were condoned or tolerated, it was not always because of ignorance. People who knew Anne Lister in the 1820s discussed her sexuality and were quite aware that something set her apart from other spinsters. Local labourers made jocular remarks: 'That's a man'; 'Does your cock stand?' Her maid thought 'merely, that I have my own particular ways'. She could even discuss her 'oddities' with friends who were not 'odd' themselves:

> Brought on the subject of my own oddities of which Emma seems aware but to which she does not appear to object. In fact she thinks me agreeable & likes me. So does her husband. She looked pretty this evening & once or twice as if conscious of a peculiar feeling when I looked at her. (2 July 1821)

Anne Lister may be an exceptional case (though one would have to believe that she was extraordinarily lucky in finding other excep-tional cases), and perhaps her lively record of sexual adventures in a Paris pension is not the best evidence of general attitudes to female homosexuality. But even in the most famously innocent case of all, sharp distinctions were made between love and friendship.

In 1778, two Irish gentlewomen put on men's clothing and ran away together. Lady Eleanor Butler had received several offers of marriage but was determined to share her life with her friend Sarah Ponsonby. The runaways were discovered and brought home. A few months later they eloped again and found their way to Wales. Their families relented and granted them an income.

They spent the rest of their lives in a black and white house called Plas Newydd outside Llangollen, cultivating their garden, improving their minds and filling the house with clocks, cabinets and 'whirligigs of every shape and hue'. After the departure of an unsatisfactory footman, all the servants and most of the domestic animals were female, including a little dog called Sapho. To John Lockhart, who saw them with 'crop heads', wearing men's hats and huge shoes, they looked like 'a couple of hazy or crazy old sailors'.

Llangollen was on the road to the Welsh ports, and the Ladies were visited by a stream of luminaries: Lady Caroline Lamb, Wordsworth, the Duke of Wellington, etc. For decades, poets extolled their worthy ménage in execrable odes. The general idea was that the Ladies of Llangollen epitomized Romantic friendship. They showed that two women could contract a 'marriage' and still be chaste. Eleanor and Sarah were famous for being a good example. The odd couple who went about their humble business and served tea to visitors were the acceptable face of that fashionable French scourge: sapphism.

This was the implicit background to the idealization of the Ladies, the reason why the word 'pure' was so often attached to their friendship, for example in the odes of Anna Seward: 'so pure a shrine'; 'sacred Friendship, permanent as pure'; 'pure Friendship's spotless palm'. Wordsworth's sonnet 'To the Lady E. B. and the Hon. Miss P.' (1824) is typical in politely catapulting their liaison into a realm of impenetrable chastity:

> On Deva's banks, ye have abode so long;
> Sisters in love, a love allowed to climb,
> Even on this earth, above the reach of Time!

The Ladies themselves, as they appear in Eleanor's fearsomely innocuous journal, seem to have expressed their love in serenity and routine rather than arousal.

> Three o'clock dinner. Boiled Pork. Peas pudding. Half-past three my beloved and I went to the new garden. Freezing hard. I am much mistaken if there be not a quantity of snow in the sky. I read to my beloved No. 97 of the Rambler written by Richardson [etc.] (1 February 1788)

Not everyone however saw them as sexless maids. Hester Thrale called them 'damned Sapphists' and said that no woman would dare to spend the night at Plas Newydd without a man. Anne Lister made a pilgrimage to Llangollen in 1822 and could not 'help thinking that surely it was not platonic. Heaven forgive me, but I look within myself & doubt.' Long before Colette described 'les Dames de Llangollen' in *Le Pur et l'Impur* (1932) as forerunners of modern lesbians, the Ladies of Llangollen joined the pantheon of homosexual couples. When Byron imagined himself and his beloved John Edlestone outshining other famous lovers, he included the Ladies in the list: 'We shall put *Lady E. Butler*, & Miss *Ponsonby* to the *Blush*, *Pylades* & *Orestes* out of countenance, & want nothing but a *Catastrophe* like *Nisus* & *Euryalus*, to give *Jonathan* & *David* the "*go by*".'

The Ladies' marriage has been a bone of contention among social historians and queer theorists. For some, they were simply passionate friends. For others, the purification of the Ladies of Llangollen is a case of retrospective censorship. The terms of the debate, and a simple lack of information, make any final answer impossible. Further complications are caused by a tendency to see genital excitement as the defining feature of a gay relationship – as if passionate love cannot be expressed in abstinence as well as orgasm. The point was beautifully made by Colette in *Le Pur et l'Impur*. (The italicised phrase comes from Eleanor's journal.)

> Two women who are very much in love do not avoid physical pleasure, nor a kind of sensuality that is more diffuse and yet more passionate than the spasmodic variety. This unresolved, undemanding sensuality that finds happiness in an exchanged glance, in an arm around the

shoulder, in the smell of warm wheat that hides in hair – these delights of constant presence and routine are the source and justification of their fidelity. [. . .] Perhaps this love that is said to be an outrage to love evades the passing seasons and the ebbing of love on condition that it be governed with invisible severity and kept on a strict diet [. . .] – in such a way that by its grace half a century slips away like *a day of sweetly enjoyed retirement.*

Conflicting modern interpretations are not just a result of 20th-century sexual politics; they also reflect 18th- and 19th-century realities. A similar debate existed in the Ladies' lifetime. Sexual relations were already sufficiently polarized for people to believe that the Ladies must be either one thing or the other. And the Ladies themselves were aware or became aware of the distinction. They were happy to have their manless marriage celebrated in celestial metaphors, but they reacted sharply when a certain line was crossed.

In July 1790, *The General Evening Post* published an article under the title 'Extraordinary Female Affection'. The article praised the Ladies' 'elegance, neatness and taste', but it also raised the spectre of sexual identity:

> Miss Butler is tall and masculine, she wears always a riding habit, hangs her hat with the air of a sportsman in the hall, and appears in all respects as a young man if we except the petticoats which she still retains.
>
> Miss Ponsonby, on the contrary, is polite and effeminate, fair and beautiful.
>
> [. . .]
>
> Miss Ponsonby does the duties and honours of the house, while Miss Butler superintends the gardens and the rest of the grounds.

Significantly, Eleanor and Sarah were enraged by the article and wanted to sue the newspaper. Like many later couples in the public eye, they were stung by the journalistic implication. In 1790, 'Extraordinary Female Affection' was not an innocent phrase. Eleanor and Sarah read widely and certainly knew, as did Hester Thrale, that there were such things as 'sapphists' and 'tribades'. They knew – to use a later term – that they were being outed.

Fortunately, this had no lasting effect on their happiness. The stream of visitors and their fascination with the Ladies' extraordinary purity were undiminished.

*

THE KNOWING ACCEPTANCE described in the first part of this chapter should therefore be distinguished from what only looks like tolerance. Most homosexual men and women were able to identify their feelings as something quite distinct from normal friendship. Many heterosexual people could make the same distinction and had a less categorical view of homosexuality than the legal and medical literature would suggest. Unfortunately, there is very little good evidence of attitudes among peasants and the working class. Some quiet voices will never be heard.

The role played by ignorance in the fragile happiness of gay couples should not be exaggerated. It is of course possible that the theatrical triumphs of Boulton and Park, the popularity of Oscar Wilde and Fred Barnes, and the relatively unmolested households of Custine or Carpenter were the result of widespread naivety. Even so, one would still have to exclude from the ranks of the innocent all those – judges, juries, policemen, preachers, journalists, schoolteachers, friends, relatives, inhabitants of large cities and a few hundred thousand homosexual men and women – who knew the difference between passion and friendship.

This was hardly a golden age for gay people. The references and examples available in the 21st century, the fruitful complications and public campaigns for legal and social reform were unknown and, to most people, unimaginable. No one was compelled by etiquette to make a show of tolerance. Calls for legal reform were inspired by horror of cruelty rather than by sympathy for a sexual minority. There was some awareness that different societies had different notions of sex and some debate about the possibly innate nature of homosexuality, but there is little sign that these ideas were in a sufficiently focused state to influence popular perceptions.

Naivety could always be sustained when necessary, and there was probably more ignorance about some aspects of sexual life – and more opportunities for feigning ignorance. At the trial in 1811 of two Edinburgh schoolmistresses accused of having sex within earshot of one of their boarders, the famously naive view was expressed that the ladies must be innocent of the nameless crime because it is 'even doubtful if it can exist'. But the transcripts clearly show that all six judges knew that two women could satisfy each other sexually. (The testimony of the aggrieved pupil was explicit enough.) The question was: should the court be seen to believe that such things were possible?

Most evidence of Victorian naivety turns out to be dubious. The tale that Queen Victoria thought it futile to legislate against lesbian sex because no such thing was possible dates from the late 1970s and proves the exact opposite of what it was supposed to prove. The fact that this canard is widely believed shows that we can be just as naive about the 19th century, not to mention the period in which we live. Victorian pornography shows that almost everything to do with sex had already been thought of and could be conveyed to the reader with the minimum of explanation and often with a good deal of humour.

Recent attempts to recover the gay past have been characterized by a desire to avoid anachronistic thinking and to show how unexpectedly influential society is in shaping sexuality. But to draw an international date line between 21st-century sexualities and those of the Victorians is itself an exercise in anachronism. Simply to identify differences is not to avoid anachronism. Many things were surprisingly similar. There was the same heterosexual preoccupation with anal intercourse, the same readiness to make exceptions for personal acquaintances and 'characters', the same tyrannical double standard.

Nineteenth-century Europeans and Americans made sense of their world in their own ways. They were not necessarily stunted by a dearth of information. Most people were more familiar than their 21st-century descendants with what Balzac called 'the Underside of Contemporary History'. A greater proportion of their knowledge came in the unprocessed and more potent form of personal acquaintance. Aspects of life that would later be confined to institutions were displayed in the street and in the home. Their prejudices were pitted against stranger and more urgent realities than those of their great-great-grandchildren.

The tactical hypocrisy of the Victorians should not be seen as purposeful repression. Discrepancies between public and private opinions were signs of confusion and internal debate. They were the gaps in an apparently united front. What Iris Murdoch wrote in 1964 was just as true 100 years before: 'The facts that will cure this prejudice belong to the ordinary talk of ordinary people'.

Part Two

5

Miraculous Love

The driver pulled up at a place near the boulevard. Father Pirard ushered Julien into a suite of spacious salons. Julien noticed that there was no furniture. He was looking at a magnificent gilded clock, representing a subject which struck him as highly indecent, when a very elegant gentleman came up to him in a friendly fashion. Julien made a slight bow.

The gentleman smiled and placed his hand on Julien's shoulder. Julien gave a start and jumped backwards, red with anger. Father Pirard, for all his gravity, laughed until he wept. The gentleman was a tailor.

Stendhal, *Le Rouge et le Noir* (1830), II, 2

We felt to each other at once. The night was very stormy [. . .]. Walt had his blanket – it was thrown round his shoulders – he seemed like an old sea-captain. He was the only passenger, it was a lonely night, so I thought I would go and talk with him. Something in me made me do it and something in him drew me that way. [. . .] Anyway, I went into the car. We were familiar at once – I put my hand on his knee – we understood. He did not get out at the end of the trip – in fact went all the way back with me.

Peter Doyle, on first meeting Walt Whitman, *c.* 1865–66

THE FIRST PART OF this book has lingered in the shadows of oppression. The second part describes a long journey towards the light. Some people fell by the wayside; others never made the journey at all; but very few were only passive victims of prejudice. They fell in love and were rarely as wretched as they were supposed to be. In some places, they had their own societies and institutions, and their own culture.

The miserly acceptance described in the last chapter was of little practical use in any case. Seasoned, as it usually was, with distaste, pity or amusement, it could be worse than open hostility. On 28 September 1876, Pyotr Ilyich Tchaikovsky wrote to his brother Modest about his 'vices' and their sister Alexandra:

> I know that she guesses *everything* and *forgives* everything. Thus am I treated by very many people whom I love or respect. Do you really think that I am not oppressed by this awareness *that they pity and forgive me*, when in fact I am guilty of nothing! [. . .] In a word, I should like by my marriage or, in general, an open affair with a woman to shut the mouths of various contemptible creatures whose opinion I do not value in the least but who can cause pain to people close to me.

Gay history is full of opportunities to see men trying to cope with experiences more common in women's lives: the vain attempt to ward off condescension, the urge to conform out of weariness or in a spirit of self-destructive revenge, the unfair responsibility for other people's pain, the sense of inevitable exclusion. Some part of the mind always agreed with society. It would have taken an unusually independent person – homosexual or heterosexual – to ignore the majority and to delete precisely from his upbringing only those elements that stood in the way of his happiness. Tchaikovsky, according to his brother, 'could not help submitting to the influence of the general detestation of this very defect'.

In the year of *Swan Lake* (1877), Tchaikovsky married a mentally unbalanced music student. The marriage was a disaster. 'Various manipulations' failed to generate a sex-life. They separated after a few weeks. Tchaikovsky worried that his wife would try to blackmail him. His friend Nikolai Bochechkarov helped him to find relief with servants and male prostitutes. 'Sublime', Platonic feelings were reserved for people of Tchaikovsky's own class.

Like the swans that become human again for a few hours after midnight, Tchaikovsky came out, but only in certain settings – in Bohemian St Petersburg, or on 'Bulatov's country estate', which was 'nothing but a pederastic bordello': 'As if it were not enough that I had been there, I *fell in love* as a cat with his coachman!!!'

Tchaikovsky came closer than almost any other public figure to living an openly homosexual life, but society ensured that the beloved composer would remain in the closet. After his death, knowledge of his homosexuality spread beyond St Petersburg, but a counter-legend soon repaired the damage. The *Symphonie pathétique* was supposed to prove that, if Tchaikovsky was homosexual, at least he had the decency to be miserable about it. He was, as the German biographer of Brahms put it in 1930, 'inwardly torn by the tragedy of his unhappy disposition'. The groundless story that Tchaikovsky did 'the decent thing' and shot himself is more widely accepted now than it was a 100 years ago. In fact, he died of cholera or from resulting complications. The 'pathétique' of his title (*pateticheskaya*) means 'impassioned' rather than 'sad', and it was not his last work.

*

EVEN FOR TCHAIKOVSKY, the benevolent blind eye was hardly congenial. Reactions might have varied, but their diversity made it hard to find a lasting relationship with the rest of society. 'Coming out' is never a single moment, like a debutantes' ball or a bar mitzvah. The process has to be repeated indefinitely, and there is no corresponding ritual of acceptance from the other side.

The commonest solution was not to come out at all. Gay people who come out are still in the minority, but in the 19th century, with the unique exception of Karl Heinrich Ulrichs, there is not a single example of someone publicly declaring their homosexuality.

The basic problem was not a lack of courage or a sense of shame but the gulf between homosexual and heterosexual experience. Unlike gender, sexuality was not considered a determining feature of social identity. Ulrichs himself could not simply disclose his sexuality. When he came out to the Congress of German Jurists in 1867 (see

p. 182), he was forearmed with a rational theory of sexuality and a programme of legal reform that allowed him to reveal himself in terms that were comprehensible and even reassuring to his audience.

For most people, revealing their true selves would have been a waste of time. They would be describing something – like smallpox or colour-blindness – that was not thought to be constituent of a 'true self'. Apart from a few examples of cross-dressing – women who fought as soldiers or served as seamen – tales of 'coming out' in the 19th century rarely have anything to do with sex. They either involve a declaration of principles or they imply some kind of imposture: a person could 'come out' as an illegitimate child, a foreigner, an ex-convict or a parvenu; but a declaration of abnormal preference was unlikely to be construed as a courageous act of social authenticity.

Heterosexuals still tend to see coming out as a kind of attention-seeking exercise that belongs to the same category of discourse as the bumper-sticker or the T-shirt. People who take their relationship with society for granted are not always able to understand an attempt to renegotiate a relationship with something that seems quite abstract as long as it remains approving. Nowadays, explanations and examples are widely available. A hundred years ago, there was practically nothing. The image of a 'closet' would have seemed strangely innocuous to most gay people. When Edmund Gosse described the predicament of the closet gay, he used an image that had more to do with Gothic horror than domestic furniture:

> The position of a young person so tormented is really that of a man buried alive & conscious, but deprived of sleep. He is doomed by his own timidity and ignorance to a repression which amounts to death. [. . .] This corpse, however, is obliged to bustle around and make an appearance every time the feast of life is spread.

*

MOST ACTS OF COMING OUT were confined to the microcosm of the family. Even then they were quite rare. Only one of Havelock Ellis's interviewees had come out to his family, and though the family was not uniformly hostile, anyone who read his account might have been dissuaded from trying the experiment for themselves:

Two years ago I told my parents about my sexual condition. It was a frightful blow to them. My father had the circumstances explained to him; he never understood the matter and never discussed it with me. Had I told him earlier I feel quite certain that, with his despotic nature, he would have put me in a madhouse. My mother and sister have treated me very kindly always. My brother has disowned me.

Sometimes, seeds of awareness in the family could be nurtured or forced. Lytton Strachey engaged his mother in an argument about the homosexuality of Shakespeare. Joe Ackerley, exasperated by his mother's references to 'Miss Right', lectured her on Otto Weininger's theory of a sexual continuum. Mikhail Kuzmin told his mother everything after trying to kill himself: 'She became affectionate and candid, and we would chat for hours on end during the night or in the evening over a game of piquet', though, 'for some reason or other', only in French.

All three men were specialists in self-expression and, crucially, none of them had a wife. Nearly all the happy tales of coming out within the family involved parents and their children rather than husbands and wives. Magnus Hirschfeld (1905) and Edward Prime-Stevenson (1908) published some encouraging anecdotes about understanding parents. Hirschfeld even knew a mother who hoped that her second son would turn out to be homosexual because the first son had contracted a venereal disease. But most of Hirschfeld's patients were strangers in their own families. Christmas, for them, was not a celebration of family unity, it was the time of year when they reached for the revolver or the phial of prussic acid.

Usually, when the truth was known, it was not divulged, it seeped out or was revealed by accident. Three of Krafft-Ebing's patients knew that they had a homosexual brother or sister, but apparently did not discuss the matter. The five patients who had discussed it were all women. Three were referred to the doctor by a worried husband, one by a guardian 'because she ran away from home in men's clothing in order to wander the world and become an "artist" ', and one by some relatives who saw her return from a spa wearing short hair and riding-boots, talking in a deep voice and pining for a woman.

None of the men in Krafft-Ebing's casebook found it hard to believe that his wife was a lesbian. The experience was traumatic none the less, especially for the women. The young wife of a factory-owner, 'Frau von T.', had warned her husband before marrying him that she was a lesbian and that 'she esteemed him only for his intellectual qualities'. She endured sexual intercourse by imagining that her husband was a woman. Herr von T. had taken her to the doctor after a catastrophic dinner party: 'In the drawing-room, after dinner, she flung her arms around one of the ladies, kissing and caressing her, and thereby caused a scandal.'

Frau von T. might have come out to her husband, but she was quickly pushed back in again. After a course of hydrotherapy and hypnotism, designed to give her 'a respectable or at least a sexually neutral personality', she returned to live with her relatives. 'She has been there for some time now and is conducting herself in a very proper fashion.'

There is some evidence – but not very much – of 'lavender marriages' in which both partners were gay, like Vita Sackville-West and Harold Nicolson, for whom fidelity in marriage meant telling each other the truth, though it took a long time for them to discover the truth about themselves. Some people reached a practical agreement, thanks in part to low expectations of marriage. The lesbian sister of the woman who wrecked the dinner party gave her husband his 'freedom' and paid him not to have sex with her. An army doctor had a similarly frank relationship with his wife, whom he called his 'Raphael'. The couple had managed to have four sons, but then gave up. 'My wife knows my mental state. Her kindness and love allow her to make light of it.'

Coming out within a marriage was the closest thing to finding a compromise with society. Both partners could, in theory, enjoy the benefits of respectability without stifling their desires. But these 'new marriages' could hardly be described as ideal. The paragon of openness in this respect is Edith Lees, who married Havelock Ellis in 1891, then fell in love with an old friend and explained it all to Havelock with every expectation that he would understand. Marriage gave her the freedom and security to pursue several other relationships with women, but the Ellises were forced to summon up all their ideological seriousness to survive. Convention was not a barrier that could simply be pushed to one side. Ellis described the sad dilemma in *My Life* (1916):

> As soon as she perceived this new emotional outflow towards her old friend Claire (as I will call her) she wrote to tell me of it with all her native trustful confidence, simple, direct and spontaneous. [. . .] But, after all, I was human. There remained beneath the surface the consciousness of a flaw in the ideal of married love I had so far cherished, and a secret wound of the heart 'not so deep as a well nor so wide as a church door',* but enough to kill that conception of mutual devotion in marriage.
> [. . .] I remained her 'boy', her 'child', always her 'comrade', and 'the one person in the world who understands me'.

Gay love has its 'martyrs', but so does the love that suddenly finds itself without an object. These experiences could fill another book: the subtle impoverishment of what had seemed a loving relationship, the faces in the photograph album – wives and husbands, children and parents – suddenly replaced by strangers. The misery caused by the ban on homosexual love was not peculiar to homosexual men and women. Constance Wilde was never the adorable innocent of Oscar's dreams, and Madeleine Gide was repeatedly crushed by the juggernaut of André's quest for 'authenticity'. As he acknowledged after her death, she knew from various articles that he was homosexual, but 'carefully hid from me the sufferings they might have caused her'. Gide had convinced himself that respectable women had no sexual desires and that Madeleine would be happier living with a man who had satisfied his own. 'Until *Les Faux Monnayeurs* [1926], everything I wrote was an attempt to convince her and persuade her. It was nothing but a long speech for the defence.' This speech had an audience of millions but it was never made to Madeleine herself.

*

IN THIS WORLD OF slow deaths by mutual deception, the systematic self-revelation of Karl Heinrich Ulrichs is an amazing exception.

---

* *Romeo and Juliet*, III, 1. (Mercutio describing his fatal wound.)

There is nothing to compare with his campaign for recognition until the public statements of Edward Carpenter and André Gide. Even so, Carpenter and Gide declared themselves on paper and were protected to some extent by age and reputation. Carpenter made his first direct statement when he was seventy-two, in *My Days and Dreams* (1916). Gide's awkward 'defence of pederasty', *Corydon* (1911, 1920 and 1924), was confessional only by implication. His first unambiguous statement was published when he was fifty-seven, in *Si le grain ne meurt* (1926).

Karl Heinrich Ulrichs (1825–95) had qualified as a jurist and served the state of Hanover for six years. In 1854, he resigned for an unknown reason, perhaps connected with his homosexuality, and worked as a freelance journalist. By now, quite certain that his attraction to men was innate and not perverse, he had decided to share his knowledge with the world. Attempts to discuss the matter at the Scientific Institute in Frankfurt led to his membership being removed in 1859. Perhaps it was this that encouraged him to refine his arguments in a family debate.

Karl's sister Ulricke and her husband, a pastor, already knew about his oddness. Ulricke's views can be deduced from the letter Karl sent to her on 22 September 1862. She was asked to send the letter on to six other members of the family:

> My dear sister, it is ABSOLUTELY IMPOSSIBLE for me to love even the most beautiful of women. [. . .] *No one can make himself* LOVE *a particular person or sex by sheer willpower.* I have ALWAYS been this way. If you were right, I would once have felt at least a glimmer of love for Dorette K., Auguste H., Louischen Ü, or one of the many other young girls I danced with. [. . .]
>
> There was no reason in the world for me to say, 'Oh, if only I could love a girl!' When I danced with the ladies and paid court to them, I was simply fulfilling the demands of politeness. And even then, Aunt U. and others had to keep reminding me, 'You must be nice to the ladies.' [. . .]
>
> Dear sister, I never said that I had a *general* aversion to women; my aversion concerns only *sexual love.* [. . .]
>
> So you are really quite mistaken when you exclaim, 'Oh, if only you had never gone to Berlin!'

Ulricke had considered the matter carefully and was more bemused than hostile, unlike some of the other relatives. Her husband the pastor and a man called Ludewig agreed with St Paul that homosexuality was a perversion. Wilhelm Ülzen called it 'devilish madness', and Uncle Wilhelm thought that Karl should be sent to prison or an asylum.

The next stage was to send a second letter to the same eight people. Karl was proposing to publish his findings in a pamphlet and asked for the family's opinion. This historic document was dated Frankfurt, 28 November 1862, and marked 'For circulation and return as soon as possible'. The tone was ironically reminiscent of St Paul:

My dear ones,

I now have reason to hope that in a short time from now there will be light between you, my nearest and dearest, and myself.

[. . .] Uranism is innate, but not in the sense that 'sinful proclivities' are innate, as Sister U. has been maintaining, or like 'pyromania', as Wilhelm contended in a manner which I must say was a little unkind. [. . .] The Uranian is a species of *man-woman*. Uranism is a natural anomaly, a trick of Nature of which there are thousands of examples in Creation.

[. . .] The Dioning [heterosexual] majority has no right whatsoever to make human society exclusively Dioning.

Most of the stunned recipients managed a response. Two of the men opposed Karl's plan to publish on the grounds that it would not further his interests. Wilhelm Ülzen thought that 'if such people exist, they should start a society of their own'. Ulricke's husband deemed the pamphlet 'inadvisable', gave up the struggle as 'hopeless' and begged to be spared any further disquisitions: 'May God bring about what men apparently cannot.'

Old Uncle Ü. also advised against publication but said that he would suspend judgement until he saw the proofs of the article. 'It saddens me, dear Karl, that you persist in justifying something that I am convinced cannot be justified. Auntie and Karl send their greetings.'

Considering the fact that Karl was intending to publish his views, the family handled it quite well. Of course, at this stage, they were assuming that he would remain safely anonymous.

*

IN 1862, ULRICHS was already several steps beyond the no-man's-land in which most of his fellow Uranians spent their lives. By coming out to himself, he had already conquered the greatest obstacle of all.

Few people came out in private without first negotiating the maze of self-deception. The early awareness described by most gay men and women was nearly always retrospective. It was only after falling in love or failing to satisfy a wife or a husband that they allowed themselves to interpret their childhood 'abnormalities' as symptoms of homosexuality. J. A. Symonds tried to 'stimulate a romantic feeling for women' by looking at pictures of Josephine Butler and Jenny Lind, and 'coaxed up' some emotion for a fifteen-year-old Swiss girl. André Gide lost his virginity to an Arab boy but still refused to acknowledge his 'instincts' and made a vain 'attempt at "normalization"' with a beautiful Arab girl.

One of the commonest forms of self-deception used the association of homosexuality with effeminacy: the homosexual Baron de Coubertin's re-creation of the Olympic Games in 1896 was a celebration of virtuous masculinity (women were excluded), as were the early German youth movements. Bernarr Macfadden, whose body-building *Physical Culture* magazine delighted several generations of gay men with its muscly male nudes, saw himself as the nemesis of 'perverts' – those 'shoals of painted, perfumed, Kohl-eyed, lisping, mincing youths that at night swarm on Broadway in the Tenderloin section, or haunt the parks and 5th avenue, ogling every man that passes and – it is pleasant to relate – occasionally getting a sound thrashing or an emphatic kicking', as he put it in *Superb Virility of Manhood* (1904). He would have been appalled to see his works advertised in the gay sections of online bookstores.

Walt Whitman used the equation of feebleness with perversion to remind his readers that there was nothing unhealthy about 'robust American love'. 'Powerful Matrons' abound in *Leaves of Grass*, though most of them sound more like ancient Greek athletes than Manhattan housewives:

[. . .] I will be the robust husband of those women.

They are not one jot less than I am,
They are tann'd in the face by shining suns and blowing winds,
Their flesh has the old divine suppleness and strength,
They know how to swim, row, ride, wrestle, shoot, run, strike,
    retreat, advance, resist, defend themselves,
They are ultimate in their own right [. . .]

Minds are always at their most inventive when fleeing from the truth. The self-awareness of homosexual diarists and autobiographers is all the more remarkable. Diaries were a means of coming out to oneself and to the future. For people who had no access to homosexual groups, a relationship with posterity was better than no relationship at all.

The Finnish writer, suffragette and cyclist, Hilda Maria Käkikoski (1864–1912), wrote an unsent letter on 'the secret motive' behind women's relationships 'which the world cannot see'. Minnie Benson (1841–1918), wife of the Archbishop of Canterbury and mother of three homosexual sons, composed the record of her love for Lucy Tait as if in the gloom of a deserted confessional, but the fact that the diary survived suggests that she had a wider audience in mind. The Swedish philosopher, Carl Pontus Wikner (1837–88), left his diaries to the Uppsala medical faculty, along with his 'Psychological Confessions' (1879), in which he defended the right of homosexuals to marry. The confessions were not to be published until after the death of his children. When he launched this message in a bottle, he could hardly have known how many other bottles would wash up on the distant shore:

> You, man, who read these lines, they are written to you by a brother who has suffered much. My thoughts are wrung from the deepest distress, yet still they try to find expression. O, that you could and would understand me! Some people are capable of deep, heartfelt, self-sacrificing love, yet the only possible object of their love is a person of their own sex. There are said to be such women, and I know that such men exist. I myself am such a man. These confessions contain a life of anguish.

There is a whole virtual gay literature of the 19th century that remained unread until the late 20th. Most of these time-capsule texts were discovered and read only when time had rendered them innocuous. Wikner's 'confessions' were published in 1971, in the same year as Forster's *Maurice*, written in 1913–14 and dedicated 'To a Happier Year'. Ackerley's *My Father and Myself* appeared in 1968, the year after the law changed in England and Wales. Both works were published posthumously.

Texts that did appear in their author's lifetime were often privately printed for a handful of friends, like the poems of Constantine Cavafy. Other texts were simply consigned to oblivion. As a young man, Symonds locked his early poems in a black tin box, then gave the key to his friend Henry Sidgwick, who threw it into the river Avon.

The few writers whose works left the closet and who were recognized as homosexual issued denials whenever someone tried to state the obvious. Walt Whitman had learned to stop worrying about his 'FEVERISH, *fluctuating, useless undignified pursuit of 16.4 – too long (much too long)* persevered in' and enjoyed a love affair of many years with Peter Doyle (16.4 = P.D.) – 'a great big hearty full-blooded everyday divinely generous working man'. But when Symonds naively asked him to clarify his position on 'the intimate and physical love of comrades and lovers', Whitman not surprisingly pulled down the blinds. After being pestered for almost twenty years, he finally gave an answer on 19 August 1890:

> Ab't the questions on Calamus pieces* &c: they quite daze me. L of G. [*Leaves of Grass*] is only to be rightly construed by and within its own atmosphere & essential character [...] – that the calamus part has even allow'd the possibility of such construction as mention'd is terrible – I am fain to hope the pp [pages] themselves are not to be even mention'd for such gratuitous and quite at the time entirely undream'd & unreck'd possibility of morbid inferences – wh' are disavow'd by me & seem damnable.

After locking away his poems, Whitman went on to say that, 'though unmarried', he had sired six children, two of whom were dead – and none of whom, of course, has ever been identified.

* A section of *Leaves of Grass* expressing 'the beautiful and sane affection of man for man'. Whitman calls the phallic calamus-root 'the token of comrades'.

The Belgian novelist Georges Eekhoud effectively came out before the end of the century. He published articles defending homosexuality and was mentioned as a homosexual writer in Iwan Bloch's *Das Sexualleben unsere Zeit* (Berlin, 1907). But when he was asked in 1909 to declare himself in a German review, *Sexuale Probleme*, he took refuge in scholarship and humanitarian concern:

> I have never professed or confessed to homosexuality. It was objectively, as a novelist, that I studied that interesting variety of pauper and outcast (cast out by society, not by nature), and the concern I feel for them would have been sanctioned by the Gospels.

Self-censorship was a practical necessity, but it was also part of the process of self-discovery, which makes it doubly unreasonable to accuse writers like Proust or James of failing to support the cause. Far more damage was done by the mutilations and incinerations of embarrassed readers. A diarist might turn his closet into a time-machine, but when it arrived in the future heirs and editors would be waiting to barricade the doors.

Some crude attempts at censorship are easily reversed – *him*s replaced with *her*s, and so on – but a great deal of the unread corpus was destroyed for ever. Edmund Gosse and the librarian of the London Library organized Symonds' papers into a pile in the library garden and set fire to them. Richard Burton's extensive research notes on 'pederasty' were probably destroyed by his widow. Minnie Benson's son Arthur left behind 'a packet of letters of very dangerous stuff' and another packet 'that had to be burnt unopened', according to his brother Fred. Edward Lear's papers seem to have been selectively destroyed after his death by the man for whom Lear had harboured a 'thwarted, frustrated, impossible love'.

To judge by the large number of known destructions (most presumably went unrecorded), at any moment in the 19th century someone, somewhere, was burning the papers of a homosexual relative. People who were almost certainly homosexual, like Thomas Gray or Thomas Lovell Beddoes, can now have no firm place in the record, especially since the standard of proof demanded of biographers is far stricter for homosexual than for heterosexual subjects. It is almost as if the surviving testimonies to forbidden love were written 2,000 years rather than four or five generations ago. Ancient Greek literature and 19th-century confessional gay literature probably survive in approximately the same proportions.

*

BY GATHERING THE EVIDENCE in one place, books like this tend to depict the Oceania of remote islands as a busy continent with well-established trade routes. Most writing on the subject – like the scene from *Le Rouge et le Noir* quoted as an epigraph to this chapter – was swathed in subtlety and would simply have passed unnoticed.

Most people came out to themselves, not in careful reading, but in unexpected moments and chance encounters. The vital moment could occur at school, in the armed forces, in other countries, or in cities where homosexual prostitutes, male and female, plied their trade (which accounts for most big cities in Europe and America). Institutions were especially important because they showed that homosexual relations could have a social context, however unpleasant. Information was suppressed, but it was also freely disseminated. Schoolboys were lectured on 'filth', schoolgirls were warned about inappropriate physical intimacy. The Austrian army gave its soldiers regular briefings on homosexuality. French soldiers in Algeria – especially 'those who were endowed with a pretty face' – 'had to reject the disgusting propositions of the Algerians'. Confessors' manuals, like the *Llave de Oro* – 'for opening the hearts of poor sinners' (Barcelona, 1857–83) – revealed the existence of homosexual attraction. They also contained lists of anatomically precise questions that might have inspired even the most experienced sinners.

Some men were alerted to their inclinations by a perceptive prostitute or girlfriend. A surprising number of people claimed to owe their enlightenment to animals: a woman known to Havelock Ellis 'had no idea at first that homosexual attractions in women existed', but then 'observations on the lower animals put the idea into my head'. Many people discovered their homosexuality only when the person they loved had gone away or died.

*

Once the hurdle of self-awareness had been overcome, the next step was to find a like-minded person. This was nearly always a dangerous affair. A man who approached the wrong person might be arrested, beaten up, blackmailed or disgraced.

Inevitably, the cases that came to public attention tended to be untypically dramatic: men mistaken for women, politicians ambushed in urinals, and so on. Most fiascos took place in private. Delicate friendships were destroyed by declarations of love or by the mere suspicion of homosexuality. Hans Christian Andersen's infatuation with his friend Edvard Collin lasted for years and never reached a happy resolution. When Collin told him to stop using the intimate 'Du' form, Andersen declared his love instead for Collin's sister and pretended to be a new man:

> I do not think that I am as passionate and soft as I used to be – that was a mistake and has been corrected. I wonder whether you will like me better?

Collin made a concession by offering to play an occasional game of chess, then closed the door for ever by getting married. Karl Heinrich Ulrichs seems to have suffered a similar misfortune. For a long time, he believed that Uranians could only fall in love with Dionings (heterosexuals).

The slow evolution of a friendship could hide a truth that seemed obvious in retrospect. In his twenties, Platen had become quite physically intimate with a young student called Schmidtlein. They sat on a park bench, amorously entwined and discussing art. Schmidtlein had read about romantic friendship and felt guilty that he could 'never feel the holy flame of friendship in my breast'. Finally, after one kiss too many, it dawned on him that Platen was a monster: 'From now on, I will avoid you like the plague.'

Embarrassing moments like this were a staple of moralistic British novels in which the repressed young man tried to enjoy his brotherly passion without 'soiling' himself. In the *Memoirs of Arthur Hamilton, B.A.* (1886) by Arthur Benson, the 'silent and languid' Arthur exemplifies the process of slowly coming out and suddenly going back in again:

Arthur seems not to have suspected it at first, and to have delighted in his friend's society; but such things as habits betray themselves, and my belief is that disclosures were made on November 8, which revealed to Arthur the state of the case. What passed I cannot say. I can hardly picture to myself the agony, disgust, and rage (his words and feelings about sensuality of any kind were strangely keen and bitter), loyalty fighting with the sense of repulsion, pity struggling with honour, which must have convulsed him when he discovered that his friend was not only yielding, but deliberately impure.

There is nothing like the po-faced English male romance to show the comic potential of illicit love. The wandering poet Albert Glatigny (1839–73) had a song on the subject that would have horrified the honourable Arthur. A man is asked why he has stopped seeing his friend Durand. He recalls the jolly times they had together: Durand, the joker, used to masturbate him and, just for a laugh, 'he ejaculated in my arse'. ('I laughed until I wept, I must confess.')

> *'Mais nous avons rompu. Nous sommes*
> *   brouillés à mort.'*
> *'Qu'a-t-il donc fait?'*
> *'On m'a dit qu'il était pour hommes!'**

Even if both partners turned out to be homosexual, the taboo could be just as effective. Love did not always have the last word. Many one-sided affairs survived the moment of realization only by mutual self-deception. In *Venus Urania* (1798), the Hanoverian diplomat Friedrich von Ramdohr told the bitter-sweet tale of two men who met in a famous German academy. (One was probably Ramdohr himself.)

> They lived together and seldom parted. [. . .] A subtle fire ran through their veins at every accidental touch.[†] Whenever they caught sight of one another unexpectedly, they were filled with inexplicable rapture. They stayed up all night together, and when the grey light of dawn forced them to seek the rest that the excited mind refused the exhausted body, their farewells continued on the doorstep in conversations that lasted hours. [. . .]

---

* 'But now we've broken up and we're deadly enemies.' / 'What did he do?' / 'They told me that he's homosexual!'

† Allusion to Sappho: 'Swiftly through all my veins a subtle fire runs' (tr. Bantock).

But those days soon disappeared like a beautiful dream! [. . .] Such crude symptoms of physical sexual sympathy manifested themselves in both men that these chaste and innocent (but not ignorant) young men were enlightened in a terrible way about the workings of unforeseen desires. They separated with a start, and that moment in which two souls appeared in all their purity seemed to them to be the blackest stain on their lives. In that instant, their passion ended. It was eventually replaced by tenderness founded on respect.

Sometimes – 'crude symptoms of physical sexual sympathy' notwithstanding – the point of realization was never reached. Novelists and doctors described homosexual relationships as if nothing could stop them, but it is almost a miracle that they ever started. In *Sodome et Gomorrhe*, Proust likened the coming together of two 'inverts' to the unlikely process by which a rare orchid in a Paris courtyard is pollinated by a Parisian bumble-bee. The seemingly impossible conjunction of flower and bee was not just a reference to lack of opportunities. Most of the obstacles to homosexual love were invisible. Ramdohr's reluctant lovers had no immediate, rational context, other than their own desires, in which to place their love. Irrational needs were not instantly translated into recognized forms of social behaviour. A whole society silently cheered on the heterosexual suitor, whereas homosexual people had to conduct their business in a void.

The separation of homosexual love from accepted norms explains why so many attempts to find a structure for that love seem so humorously incongruous: Joe Ackerley compared his illiterate sailor friend to 'the Ephebe of Kritios'; Natalie Clifford Barney sailed to Lesbos with Renée Vivien to found a new school of Sapphic poetesses:

> As we approached Mitilini, we heard the nasal whine of a gramophone in the harbour: 'Come, my little chicken, come to me!' Renée had been waiting on the bridge since dawn for this moment. She turned pale with horror!

Oxford aesthetes adored pimply urchins as incarnations of Ancient Greece. Frank Harris saw Oscar Wilde one day at the Café Royal telling two Cockney lads about the Olympic Games: ' "Did you sy they was niked?" "Of course", Oscar replied, "nude, clothed only in sunshine and beauty." '

The quest for what E. M. Forster called 'the Greenwood' – a special enclave where 'two men [could] defy the world' – was always vulnerable to the irruptions of the day-to-day. Normal reality was a greater threat than any modern Sheriff of Nottingham. If the miracle of a physically and emotionally fulfilling friendship occurred, a lastingly miraculous setting had to be found for it. Some of the coteries and countries described in the next chapter gave a glimmer of the Greenwood, though, as Ackerley pointed out, 'what was the good of making friends in other countries? One wanted them in one's own, one wanted them in one's home.' Even brothels could give intimations of a better life, precisely because, in Symonds' words, they were 'lawless' and 'godless'.

Coming out was almost meaningless without some prior rearrangement of the world. While some looked for a utopia where their love would be simultaneously normal and extraordinary – like Winckelmann in Rome or Oscar Wilde almost anywhere – others looked for the rationale and vindication of their love in the paranormal. 'All "abnormal" sex-acts', said W. H. Auden, 'are rites of symbolic magic.' According to Ulrichs, strange lights had sometimes been seen hovering around the erect penises of men on park benches. Since their affairs were acted out against a background of implausibility, it was almost logical to believe that they were not of this earth.

*

WITHOUT PARANORMAL ASSISTANCE, making contact with a like-minded person was an art that demanded even more finesse than heterosexual courtship.

The least subtle people learned to be allusive. Ideally, the text – of the conversation or the letter – would function like a *metafora di decettione* in which two objects are described simultaneously so that each reading is complete and coherent on its own. Anne Lister polished her love letters as craftily as a poet, adjusting her ambiguities and measuring out the precise quantity of passion. She analysed one of her letters to Maria Barlow in her diary: 'This ought not to be seen [. . .] Yet there is nothing, I think, I could not manage to explain away to warm friendship if I had the letter before me & was obliged to defend myself.'

Charlotte Brontë was just as cautious in her letters to Ellen Nussey, though the omissions made by Elizabeth Gaskell in her biography ('You tantalize me to death with talking of conversations by the fireside ~~and between the blankets~~') and the concerns of Charlotte's husband ('Arthur says such letters as mine never ought to be kept, they are dangerous as Lucifer matches') show that no allusion could be too obscure.

In Christopher Isherwood's *Mr Norris Changes Trains* (1935), Baron von Pregnitz practises the equally delicate art of ambiguous conversation. Like the messages of a secret agent, the Baron's exploratory talks with the narrator could pass, if need be, as idle chatter:

> 'Excuse me. Do you know Naples?'
> 'No. I've never been there.'
> 'Forgive me. I'm sorry. I had the feeling that we'd met each other before.'

> 'Excuse me, you were in London?'
> 'Part of the time, yes.'
> [. . .]
> 'And, excuse me, how are the Horse Guards?'
> 'Still sitting there.'
> 'Yes? I am glad to hear this, you see. Very glad . . .'

> 'Have you read *Winnie the Pooh*, by A. A. Milne?'
> 'Yes, I have.'
> 'And tell me, please, how did you like it?'
> 'Very much indeed.'
> 'Then I am very glad. Yes, so did I. Very much.'
> And now we were all standing up. What had happened? It was midnight. Our glasses touched.

The shared culture of gay men and women – their history, geography, literature, art and music – was not a passive store of knowledge. It was a vital means of communication. Anne Lister and her several lovers made their feelings known by referring to the rumours about Marie-Antoinette's lesbian antics and to the small number of texts in which lesbians were mentioned: Juvenal, Martial, Ovid, Petronius, Suetonius, the Bible and 'the Latin parts of the works of Sir William Jones'. They discussed the sex of the Moon –

female in some countries, male in others: 'I smiled & said the moon had tried both sexes, like old Tiresias, but that one could not make such an observation to every one.' A woman in Anne Lister's Paris pension passed her a note alluding to the period during which Achilles dressed as a woman and seduced King Lycomedes' daughter:

> 'I have a question to ask you. Êtes-vous Achilles?' I laughed & said she made me blush. [. . .] She said I was the only one in the house to whom she could have written it, because the only one who would have so soon understood it.

Men enjoyed a wider range of reference and were more likely to be able to find cheerful examples of male love: Achilles and Patroclus in *The Iliad*, the Theban band of warrior-lovers in Plutarch, Nisus and Euryalus in the *Aeneid*. References to Alexander the Great, Michelangelo, Frederick II and other eminent figures were increasingly understood as references to homosexuality. From the 1860s, in Britain and America, Walt Whitman was probably the commonest key to further intimacy, the 'password primeval' that could be 'flashed out' 'to such as alone could understand'.* Eventually, books on homosexual love – William Johnson's versions of Greek and Latin in *Ionica* (1858), Carpenter's *Ioläus: An Anthology of Friendship* (1902) – could be given as presents and tokens.

This furtive erudition was not entirely confined to cultured milieux. It could be found even in the stocking shop of the Western Penitentiary of Pennsylvania, where the young anarchist Alexander Berkman served his sentence from 1892 to 1906. A man called Red had decided to make Berkman his 'kid' (also known as a 'prushun' or a 'punk'):

> 'I don't know what you are talking about.'
> 'I know you don't. That's why I'm goin' to chaperon you, kid. [. . .] Moonology, my Marktwainian Innocent, is the truly Christian science of loving your neighbor, provided he be a nice little boy. Understand now?'

---

* Richard Le Gallienne's *The Book-Bills of Narcissus* (1891), alluding to Whitman's 'Song of Myself', 24: 'I speak the pass-word primeval [. . .] / Through me forbidden voices; / Voice of sexes and lusts, voices veil'd, and I remove the veil'.

'How can you love a boy?'

'Are you really so dumb? You are not a ref[orm school] boy, I can see that.'

'Red, if you'd drop your stilted language and talk plainly, I'd understand better.'

'[. . .] How can a self-respecting gentleman explain himself to you? But I'll try. You love a boy as you love the poet-sung heifer, see? Ever read Billy Shakespeare? Know the place, "He's neither man nor woman; he's punk."* Well, Billy knew. A punk's a boy that'll   '

'What!'

'Yes, sir. Give himself to a man. Now we'se talkin' plain. Savvy now, Innocent Abroad?'

Some of these conversations are a verbal equivalent of the extraordinary dance of gestures and expressions performed by Proust's Baron de Charlus in the vicinity of his beloved Jupien, 'like those questioning phrases of Beethoven's, indefinitely repeated at regular intervals'.

The trick was to build a retraction into the message, just in case. There are many examples of this two-steps-forward-one-step-back approach in private letters. Nikolai Gogol wrote to his 'tall, husky, and appetizing for the ladies Sobolevsky!', and offered to 'sunbathe in the nude' with another friend – 'and in addition I would marry you off to a pretty girl'. A similar trick consisted of condemning homosexuality and then watching the reaction. In Siegfried Moldau's play, *Wahrheit* ('Truth') (1907), a family friend broaches the subject with the Count's son:

'Do you know . . . do you remember ever hearing about what happened to Platen?'

'What of it?'

'That sort of thing, you know, happens more frequently – even today – than people realize.'

'Away with you, Baron! You don't mean to say that . . .'

'Yes, my poor boy, I'm afraid I do.'

---

* Cf. *Measure for Measure*, V, 1: 'Why, you are nothing then: neither maid, widow, nor wife?' 'My lord, she may be a punk; for many of them are neither maid, widow, nor wife.'

These superficially innocuous elaborations and interrupted propo-sitions also belong to the syntax of cruising. When Joe Ackerley went shopping for partners in London, he performed his circumvolutions on the pavement instead of on the page:

> I would hasten after him, pass without a glance (in the hope of not being noticed), and when I had reached what I considered to be an invisible distance ahead, turn about to retrace my steps for a head-on collision. If then I got a responsive look, a smile, a backward glance, if he then stopped to stare after me or to study the goods in the nearest shop-window (the more incongruous they were the safer I felt) I judged I might act, though still with caution in case he was luring me into some violent trap. The elaborateness of this maneuver often lost me the boy, he had gone into a house or disappeared up some side turning behind my back – and therefore remained in my chagrined thought as the Ideal Friend.

If the two potential partners already knew about each other, the degree of elaboration could render the message practically incompre-hensible to anyone else. When the schoolboy Arthur Rimbaud sent a selection of poems to Verlaine and promised to be 'less bother than a Zanetto' if Verlaine took him in, no one could accuse him of making obscene proposals – unless they noticed that all the poems had something to do with bottoms and knew that the character Zanetto – a seductive little vagrant played by the boyish Sarah Bernhardt – was a by-word for 'pederasty'.

These precautions made it relatively easy for later defenders of reputations to deny that a person was gay. Bland interpretations were always available, which, of course, was precisely the point.

Some fine examples of the routine finesse of gay men and women can be found in a new means of making contact that appeared towards the end of the century: the classified advertisement. The earliest example found so far was published in an Austrian newspaper, *c.* 1880:

> *Seeking* a friend who, like me, enjoys solitude and shuns company, especially that of women. Happy indeed the man who suffices unto himself. Happier still the man who has a like-minded friend. Whoever understands me should write to 'Mr Nature-Lover' at the newspaper offices.

Usually, the merest hint was enough. Without the inside knowledge of the sexologists who quoted them, some of the advertisements in German newspapers in the early 1900s would probably have passed unnoticed:

> Elderly gentleman, not a ladies' man, seeks acquaintance with like-minded gentleman.

> Young family man, 27, seeks friendly relations with energetic gentleman.

> Young man of pleasant appearance conversant with many languages seeks unpaid position as travelling companion. Offers to 'Uranus'.

> Gentleman, 23, seeks friend. Write please to 'Socrates'.

> Lady, 36, desires friendly relations. P.O. 16, 'Plato'.

> Actress with modern views desires to know rich lady with similar views, for friendly relations, etc.

Even without a tell-tale 'Plato', 'Socrates' or 'modern', the meaning was apparently quite clear. Richard von Krafft-Ebing and Albert Moll both claimed that whenever a woman advertised for a female friend, 'there could be no doubt about her intentions'. This economy of expression was shown by experiment in 1901. A homosexual philologist in Berlin known only as 'Dr B.' submitted a brief advertisement to thirty-six journals:

> [Male] friend, 17–21, seeks doctor, 25. 'Z', *Morgenpost*, Schiffbauerdamm, 2.

Eleven journals agreed to publish the text. (The others presumably understood.) Although it appeared only once, there were 140 replies. One hundred and eleven respondents were quite open about their desire for a homosexual relationship.

Whether or not the experiment ended there, we unfortunately have no further information on Dr B. and his 111 new friends.

*

THIS WAS NOT QUITE the life of fear and darkness associated with 'underworlds'. Deciphering coded messages was not just an inconvenience, it could be a pleasurable art in its own right. Even when the truth was out, there could be real satisfaction in the exercise of discretion and the sharing of secrets.

Colette, who signed her letters to Natalie Clifford Barney with significant phrases – 'I kiss you as skilfully as I know how' – found in the coteries of lesbian Paris a writer's dream of instant, profound communication:

> I enjoyed that wonderful promptness in silent language, in the exchange of threats and promises, as if, once dull-witted males were out of the way, every message from one woman to another became as clear as a flash of lightning, reduced as it was to a small number of infallible signs.

Henry James never aired the purposes of his writerly involutions in such a decisive fashion, but he too revelled in the necessary disguise. He wrote to J. A. Symonds from Paris on 22 February 1884, referring to his article on Italy:

> I sent it you because it was a constructive way of expressing the good will I felt for you in consequence of what you have written about the land of Italy – and of intimating to you, somewhat dumbly, that I am an attentive and sympathetic reader. I nourish for the said Italy an unspeakably tender passion, and your pages always seemed to say to me that you were one of a small number of people who love it as much as I do – in addition to your knowing it immeasurably better. I wanted to recognize this (to your knowledge); for it seemed to me that the victims of a common passion should sometimes exchange a look.

Either James was trying to make a simple thought last as long as possible ('I sent this to you because we both love Italy and I enjoy your Italian writings'), or he was being profoundly friendly. Almost everything in his letter to Symonds is a self-revelation: the love of Italy, the small number of people, the exchanged look, the 'victims of a common passion', and that key word, 'unspeakably', attached to 'tender'. James's book on Italy, *Italian Hours*, was also written for two audiences, one of which could always deny the other's existence: 'The arching body of the gondolier [. . .] suggests an image on a Greek frieze.' 'Most people, I think, either like their gondolier or hate him; and if they like him, like him very much.'

Even when intentions were quite open, old habits of obfuscation could give a sense of mystery to the proceedings. In July 1920, Thomas Mann wrote to Carl Maria von Weber, who had complained that *Death in Venice* gave a depressing view of homosexuality. Mann wanted to remove any impression that

> a mode of feeling which I respect because it is almost necessarily infused with *mind* (far more necessarily so than the 'normal' mode) should be something that I would have wanted to deny or, insofar as it is accessible to me (and I may say it is so with scarcely any reservation), would have wished to disavow.

It takes at least a minute to see this Russian-doll sentence as an admission of homosexuality, and at least another minute to see that it might not be an admission after all.

These phrases often have a peculiar beauty that comes from the petticoat layers of allusion around the central silence, the labyrinthine syntax, the pattern of allusions, the cloud that means nothing to some and that to others is a heavenly hieroglyphic.

Balletic beating about the bush was both a precaution and a ritual. It can be seen at its best in the *Dictionary of National Biography*, many of whose contributors were homosexual. Some entries are so coy as to appear insulting, but this was not necessarily the intention. The idea, sometimes, was to convey the precious information as it were under the counter:

> Beckford, William: noted for 'his oriental whims and his mysterious seclusion', which 'may have been partly owing to grave imputations upon his moral character'.

> Browning, Oscar (the disgraced Eton housemaster): 'assisted young Italians, as he had done young Englishmen, towards the openings they desired'.

> Carpenter, Edward: found his true 'pagan' mission in Italy where he developed 'a new enthusiasm for Greek sculpture'. His later works on a certain 'emotional state' 'had more vogue on the Continent than in England'.

> Solomon, Simeon: displayed 'signs of sentimental weakness'.

> Symonds, J. A.: 'No trait in his character was more marked than his readiness to fraternize with peasants and artisans.'

Wilde, Oscar, and Lord Alfred Douglas 'were extraordinarily complementary to one another'.

Some of these velvety circumlocutions are the sound of a door
closing softly against an ignorant world. Like *parlare* – the circus
slang that was adopted and modified by English gays in the mid-
20th century – secret vocabularies were more a celebration than a
practical device. Homosexual argot rarely played the same role as
thieves' slang. Words borrowed from prostitution – 'Mary-Ann',
'pouf', 'fairie', 'tante', 'tapette', etc. – were used in milieux from
which heterosexuals were excluded in any case.

Slang – or rather, a set of code words and euphemisms – was used
just as often by sneering heterosexuals: 'Is he *so*?', 'Is he one of them?'
or 'that way', 'Is he musical?', 'Is he a nonconformist?' The usual
complaint about homosexuals was not that they were hard to spot
but that they were too flagrant. Recondite terms were designed to
banish the subject from open conversation to the linguistic basement.
The most obscure terms relating to homosexuality belonged to a
heterosexual vocabulary: 'It smells of garlic here', in Paris, meant
'There are lesbians about' (from the supposed similarity of a garlic
clove to the clitoris). A 'chestnut gatherer' or 'pin-picker', in French,
was a sodomite (because they bend over). A French slang dictionary
of 1874 listed over forty insulting terms for a male homosexual. Gay
men and women tended to use more neutral or more loving terms:
'friend', 'brother', 'sister', 'father', 'mother', 'ganymede', 'Jonathan',
'Lesbian' (originally an erudite reference to the home of Sappho).

Even today, some of the most interesting and curiously Victorian
circumlocutions can be found in obituaries and literary companions
written by heterosexuals or closet gays. These phrases should be
collected and studied before they become completely incomprehensible: 'intensely private', 'complex personality', 'enigmatic', etc.

*

FOR MOST GAY PEOPLE, non-verbal argot was far more important
than a set of code words. Certain expressions and gestures were
almost universally understood: slightly prolonged eye contact, a flick
of the tongue, a particular way of smoking a cigarette or offering a

light, a style of dress. In the 1900s, red neckties and handkerchiefs were a clear signal in the United States, Brazil, Russia, Italy and probably throughout Europe. 'To wear a red necktie on the street', said Ellis's American correspondent, 'is to invite remarks from newsboys and others.'

Many signs, like the long velvet ties and red boots of St Petersburg homosexuals, came from the world of prostitution. Eventually, they were so widely known that they were used by heterosexuals to mock queers. In mid-19th-century London, 'poufs' were said to 'place their fingers in a peculiar manner underneath the tails of their coats and wag them about'. In 18th-century Holland, homosexual men signalled to one another by tapping the back of one hand with the other or by placing their hands on their hips.

Sometimes, tokens were used, like the beautifully primped poodles of Parisian lesbians or the green carnations of British aesthetes. The significant bouquet could also include tulips, lilies, orchids and any exotic, delicate, artificial bloom that was hard to propagate. These tokens often had long and complicated histories. The poodles were a reference to the supposed use to which frustrated 'tribades' put their lap-dogs. The carnation was a traditional symbol of the anus, and the colours red and green had a long association with homo-sexuality. Pinkness seems to have acquired consistently homosexual connotations only in the 1900s, but green had been a gay colour for centuries. Effeminate men in Ancient Rome were called *galbinati* because of their fondness for the colour green.

However useful they might be, secret signs are not peculiar to periods of repression. Webs of allusion are still spun – in conver-sations, letters, articles and photographs – when disguise is no longer necessary. This persistence of old habits is sometimes seen as a form of ghettoization – allowing gay life to be determined by its underworld past. But it can also be seen as a celebration of cultural wealth. This is partly a matter of taste and partly of generation. Like tradesmen ousted by machines, some people missed the chance to use their special skills. When the law was changed in 1967, Paul Bailey drank champagne with his partner to celebrate the fact that he was no longer a criminal.

Yet there were those – the painter Francis Bacon was one of them – who did not welcome the cautious move towards liberalism. 'I don't want to be tolerated', an ageing landscape gardener remarked to me. 'Tolerance is so boring.' He had enjoyed the 'thrill of the chase' for nearly half a century, and regarded the Labour government's modest bill as a 'terrible omen'.

In 1977, in his *Homosexuality and Literature, 1890–1930*, Jeffrey Meyers managed to present increasing tolerance as a cultural disaster. 'Subtlety, ambiguity and restraint' went out of the window along with injustice:

> When the laws of obscenity were changed [. . .], the theme surfaced defiantly and sexual acts were grossly described. The emancipation of the homosexual has led, paradoxically, to the decline of his art.

Most gay men and women – whether or not they were writers and however much they enjoyed the game – preferred to be able, when they wanted, to express themselves directly. In the 1920s, T. E. Lawrence, who had hardly dared evoke his rape by Turkish soldiers in *The Seven Pillars of Wisdom* ('the citadel of my integrity was irrecoverably lost'), was delighted by E. M. Forster's 'unpublishable' tales, 'The Life to Come' (1922) and 'Dr Woolacott' (1927). It was not the skilful reticence that excited him but the surprising openness:

> There is a strange cleansing beauty about the whole piece of writing ['Dr Woolacott']. [. . .] I must confess that it has made me change my point of view. I had not before believed that such a thing could be so presented – and so credited.

To Lawrence, Forster's simplicity was the herald of a happier age. As Philip Hensher pointed out in 2002, cunning innuendoes are no longer quite so crucial, at least in some milieux. Opportunities for wit must be set against the benefits of clarity:

> I've probably been insulted on the score of sexuality fewer than half a dozen times in my life and have never troubled to respond with anything more than 'Oh, fuck off.' Not exactly Oscar Wilde.

*

1. John Martin, *The Destruction of Sodom* (1832).

THE LIVES

OF

BOULTON AND PARK.

EXTRAORDINARY REVELATIONS.

THE TOILET AT THE STATION.

PRICE ONE PENNY.
Office : 5, Houghton Street, Strand.

2. 'The Toilet at the Station', from *Men in Petticoats. The Lives of Boulton and Park. Extraordinary Revelations* (1870).

3. 'Closing Scene at the Old Bailey', *The Illustrated Police News*,
4 May 1895.

4. Ambroise Tardieu

5. Johann Ludwig Casper

6. Carl Friedrich Otto Westphal

7. Albert Moll

8. Richard von Krafft-Ebing

9. 'Man–woman criminals', by Cesare Lombroso (1893): 'a couple I came upon in a prison', showing the characteristic 'disproportion in beauty and age'.

10. 'The Author Ready to Set Out on Life's Journey', from *Autobiography of an Androgyne* by Earl Lind (1900; published 1918).

11. George Catlin, 'O'n-daig, the Crow; a beau or dandy in full array, called by the Ojibbeways *sha-wiz-zee-shah-go-tay-a*, a harmless man' (1836).

12. Lord Arthur Clinton, MP, Frederick Park ('Fanny') and Ernest Boulton ('Stella, Star of the Strand'), c. 1868.

13. 'The Ladies of Llangollen': Sarah Ponsonby and Lady Eleanor Butler.

14. Anne Lister of Shibden Hall, Halifax (Yorkshire).

15. Edward Carpenter and
George Merrill at Millthorpe,
near Sheffield (Yorkshire).

16. 'Walt Whitman & his
rebel soldier friend Pete Doyle',
by Moses P. Rice (1865).
Walt Whitman:
'What do I look like here?'
Tom Harned:
'Fondness, and Doyle should be a girl.'

17. Radclyffe Hall and
Lady Una Troubridge.

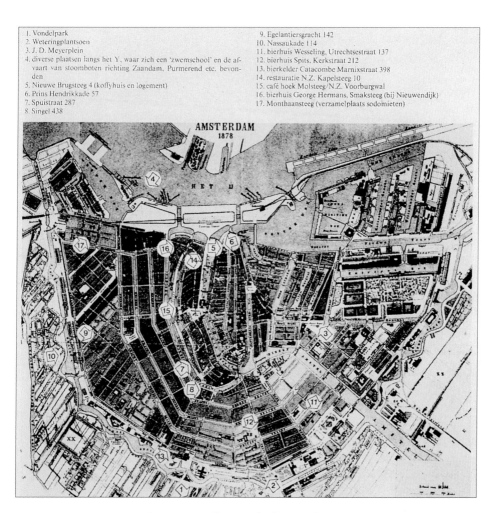

1. Vondelpark
2. Weteringplantsoen
3. J. D. Meyerplein
4. diverse plaatsen langs het Y, waar zich een 'zwemschool' en de af-
   vaart van stoomboten richting Zaandam, Purmerend etc. bevon-
   den
5. Nieuwe Brugsteeg 4 (koffyhuis en logement)
6. Prins Hendrikkade 57
7. Spuistraat 287
8. Singel 438
9. Egelantiersgracht 142
10. Nassaukade 114
11. bierhuis Wesseling, Utrechtsestraat 137
12. bierhuis Spits, Kerkstraat 212
13. bierkelder Catacombe Marnixstraat 398
14. restauratie N.Z. Kapelsteeg 10
15. café hoek Molsteeg/N.Z. Voorburgwal
16. bierhuis George Hermans, Smaksteeg (bij Nieuwendijk)
17. Monthaansteeg (verzamelplaats sodomieten)

18. Gay Amsterdam in the late 19th century.

19. The Rat Mort, a lesbian café (after 10 p.m.) on the Place Pigalle in Paris.

20. Unter den Linden, Berlin

21. Heinrich Hössli,
'the milliner of Glarus'

22. Karl Heinrich Ulrichs

23. Rosa Bonheur, in the
*Jahrbuch für sexuelle
Zwischenstufen*, 1900:
'famous French animal
painter, died in May 1899,
mentally and physically
distinct type of a sexual
intermediate stage'.

Rosa Bonheur (nach der letzten Photographie),
berühmte französische Tiermalerin, verstorben im Mai
1899, seelisch und körperlich ausgesprochener Typus
einer sexuellen Zwischenstufe.

24. Conrad Veidt as a persecuted Uranian and Magnus Hirschfeld as himself, in *Anders als die Anderen* (dir. Richard Oswald, 1919).

25. 'Berlin Census in a Thoroughly Modern Home', by Erich Wilke (1905).
'How many children?'
'Two daughters, one boy, three homosexual intermediates, and one Uranian.'

26. Havelock Ellis, from
The Birth Control Review
(New York, 1919).

27. Richard Burton in Arab dress.

"Had Shakespeare
asked me ..."

28. Max Beerbohm, caricature of Frank Harris:
'Had Shakespeare asked me, I should have had to submit.'

29. 'Merry Robin stops a Stranger in Scarlet': Howard Pyle, *The Merry Adventures of Robin Hood of Great Renown* (1883).

30. From the English translation of Adolphe Belot's *Miss Giraud, My Wife* (Chicago, 1891). *'Your strength will wear out against my will and you will exhaust yourself in useless struggles.'*

31. Sherlock Holmes (left) disguised as 'a Nonconformist clergyman' and Irene Adler as 'a slim youth in an ulster', by Sidney Paget. From Arthur Conan Doyle's 'A Scandal in Bohemia', *The Strand Magazine*, July 1891.

Merry·Robin·ſtops·a·Stranger· in·Scarlet :·

"GOOD-NIGHT, MR. SHERLOCK HOLMES."

32. Jean Delville, *L'École de Platon* (1898).

Any celebration of specifically gay forms of communication runs the risk of making love itself look like an accessory. The point of secrecy was not to declare the independence of a homosexual state but to find a means of expressing love. The circumstances were different, the disguises more subtle and the passion often intensified by difficulty or despair, but there is nothing fundamentally eccentric about gay love letters, whether they were written by an English aristocrat, a chaplain who performed homosexual marriages, the widow of a Lieutenant-Colonel or a self-educated man from the slums of Sheffield:

William Beckford to William Courtenay, Rome, 1 July 1782:

> I read your letter with a beating heart, my dearest Willy, and kissed it a thousand times. It is needless for me to repeat that I am miserable without you. You know I can scarcely be said to live in your absence. [. . .] What have we done, Wm., to be treated with such severity! I often dream after a solitary ramble on the dreary plains near Rome, that I am sitting with you in a meadow at Ford on a summer's evening, my arm thrown round your neck. [. . .] You will hardly be able to read this letter: it is blotted with my tears. My William, my own dear Friend, write to me for God's sake.

Rev. John Church to his friend Ned, 8 March 1809:

> [. . .] My heart is full, my mind is sunk, I shall be better when I have vented out my grief. Stand fast my dearest Ned to me I shall to you whether you do to me or no, and may we be pardoned, justified, and brought more to the knowledge of Christ. O help me to sing –
>
> > When thou my righteous Judge shall come
> > To fetch thy ransom'd people home, [etc.]
>
> > [. . .] I must close, I long to see your dear face again. I long for Sunday morning till then God bless you.

Maria Barlow to Anne Lister, August 1825:

> [. . .] You may command silence but to bid me cease to love you is vain & surely it will harm no one. Divided as we are doomed to be, you may be happy in making others so & those who are blessed with your friendship & affection can never fail to be so. I may love you to the latest

breath of my existence. That privilege cannot be taken from me, & that every blessing may attend you will be the often offered prayer of C.M.B.

George Merrill to Edward Carpenter, 8 November 1896:

Dear Ted [. . .] I shall be glad to see thy dear face again as I have such longings to kiss those sweet lips of thine. I will wait till I hear from you, first. So I must close dear heart as I am feeling a little low and lonesome. I'm always with thee every night in spirit, fondest love from your dear Boy G XXX.

Edmund Gosse's image of premature burial is unduly grim. Once over the obstacle of self-deception, it was a relatively short distance to the new world, some of whose colonies are described in the next chapter. Anne Lister enjoyed a varied sex life and probably had more fun than most of her contemporaries. Symonds and Housman managed to remain respectable while enjoying long affairs with their gondoliers. Even the cadaverous Gosse was seen at Browning's funeral in Westminster Abbey poring over Baron von Gloeden's popular photographs of naked Sicilian boys.

Coming out was not always just a matter of emotional fulfilment: it could also be part of a general liberation, a second coming-of-age. Long before anyone talked of a 'post-sexual' age, the lack of a homosexual heritage could be seen as a chance to disentangle love from convention and to experiment with new ways of being. For Margaret Fuller, homosexual love 'was a key which unlocked for me many a treasure which I still possess; it was the carbuncle which cast light into many of the darkest caverns of human nature'. For André Gide, it was the 'key' to his life's work, the 'sphinx' that led him to tackle all the other 'sphinxes of conformity, which my mind suspected of being the brothers and cousins of the first'. After meeting Una Troubridge in 1915, Radclyffe Hall discovered the happy irony that there could be greater freedom in a lesbian relationship than in a sanctioned alliance.

For pioneers like Whitman, Ulrichs and Carpenter, their time in the desert was a preparation for a better world. Whitman looked to 'adhesive love' for 'the counterbalance and offset of our materialistic and vulgar American democracy, and for the spiritualization thereof'. The determination to turn the tables on society and to throw its meagre tolerance in its face became increasingly obvious towards the end of the century. In this light, the lonely struggles of individuals look like contributions to a common cause. In Edward Carpenter's view, people who had undergone the arduous education of their desires were already, whether they knew it or not, 'the teachers of future society'.

6

Society of Strangers

Then, expressing my wish to have her, she answered, 'But we have had no priest but love. Do you not know the quotation?' I did not yet I said yes. Kissed her repeatedly, rather warmly. [...] Perhaps I shall have her yet before I go.

Anne Lister's diary, 13 November 1824

Once the Uranian nature of an individual has been certified, the individual should be officially registered as an Urning under a special name and should dress accordingly.

In the interests of morality, it would be advisable for the Urning, in nocturnal roaming of streets and public places in the town of residence, to refrain from visiting taverns unaccompanied and especially to behave in a decent and modest fashion befitting his womanly nature.

Heinrich Marx, *Urningsliebe* (1875)

W HEN WALT WHITMAN looked forward to a Uranian States of America, the existing forms of homosexual community resembled the rest of society as much as Dodge City and Tombstone resembled Boston and Philadelphia. None of the various homosexual groups and milieux of the 19th century seems to present a model for the future. They tend to confirm the popular impression that homosexuality was inseparable from prostitution and crime.

The main hope for would-be founders of a Uranian society appeared to lie in the sheer extent of the territory.

Anyone who approaches the subject from standard historical and literary sources in which homosexuality is practically non-existent might find the figures almost unbelievable. At the end of the century, homosexual male prostitutes in Berlin accounted for about 20 per cent of all prostitutes: a homosexual Berliner had approximately five times as many prostitutes to choose from as a heterosexual Berliner. Lesbian prostitutes in Berlin were said by different writers to represent between about 20 per cent and 25 per cent of the total. In 1836, a quarter of all female prostitutes in Paris were found to be lesbian. Half a century later, the proportion was thought to be even higher.

Some of these women were lesbians who earned a living by having sex with men. In brothels, as in prisons, female solidarity often took the form of lesbian 'marriages'. But many were catering to what was obviously a lively market. 'Tribade-prostitutes' were common on the streets of St Petersburg, where they were known as *koshki* (she-cats). In 1890s Paris, lesbian prostitutes solicited quite openly in the Bois de Boulogne and the Champs-Élysées. Some shops – especially haberdasheries, perfumeries, boulangeries and pâtisseries – operated as unregistered brothels. There was some concern in the 1890s (though mostly in unsubstantiated newspaper reports) that rival groups of upper-class lesbians were actively recruiting innocent girls from shops and factories.

Homosexual prostitution, both male and female, was often mentioned as a common fact of city life, not only in the big cities but also in places that were not usually thought of as ant-hills of vice: Bordeaux, Toulouse, Turin, Zurich, Breslau, Sofia, Dublin, etc. A wealthy man like Marcel Proust did not have to rely on chance encounters. He funded his own *'maison de garçons'* at 11, rue de l'Arcade in Paris. Tchaikovsky could travel all over Europe and always be sure of finding someone to have sex with. Roger Casement found rent boys in Lisbon, Las Palmas and Buenos Aires. Practically every port, from San Francisco to San Sebastián, was a haven for homosexuals.

Brothels were vulnerable to 'clean-up' campaigns, especially in England. There were more molly houses in London in the early

19th century than there were male brothels in the early 20th. But alternatives were always available. In Europe and America, bathhouses offered sex and companionship and were usually much safer than brothels. According to Dr Tarnovsky, 'blackmailing by bath-servants is unheard of, as they do the business in partnership, and share the proceeds'. The Bains de Penthièvre in Paris, which flourished in the 1890s, remained in business until the late 1960s. Procedures were sufficiently similar from one country to the next to be understood by any visitor. In pre-Revolution St Petersburg, for example, customers were shown an album of miniature photographs so that they could choose their attendant and his style of dress. The price list gave an additional measure of desirability.

Just as men in the novels of Balzac and Zola visit brothels to enjoy the sort of easy and intelligent female company that they claim not to find at home, bathhouse customers could relax in a world where secret signs were no longer necessary. In the bathhouse, the normal situation was reversed: it would have taken more ingenuity to *avoid* a homosexual encounter. Mikhail Kuzmin described a visit to a St Petersburg bathhouse in 1905:

> In the evening I thought I would go to the bathhouse just for style, for pleasure, for purity. [. . .] The man who met me at the door, on hearing that I required an attendant, a sheet, and soap, slowly turned and asked, 'Perhaps you want a good-looking attendant?' – 'No, no.' – 'Well alright then.' I do not know what came over me, for I was not even aroused. – 'No, just send an attendant.' – 'Then I'll send you a good-looking attendant', he said, with a persistent look. [. . .]
> [The young man] began to wash me unambiguously.

There were strenuous attempts to eradicate or regulate prostitution, but it was impossible to prevent the spread of homosexual districts. According to Rictor Norton, it was after the raid on Mother Clap's molly house in 1726 that the crime-infested area including Holborn and Saffron Hill became notorious as 'a molly district'. Certain parts of Manhattan, especially Broadway and Central Park, were known to be frequented by 'sodomites' as early as the 1840s. Before 1910, almost every American city had a community of 'sexual inverts' with its own cafés, dance-halls, clubs and churches, and 'certain streets where, at night, every fifth man is an invert'. By 1922, Earl Lind could talk of the boldness and 'political power' of sexual underworlds even in 'America's smaller cities west of the meridian of Kansas City'. The flourishing communities described in Edmund White's *States of Desire: Travels in Gay America* (1980) had long histories.

Districts often grew up around particular spots: in Paris, the 'tree of love' on the Avenue Gabriel, the wild boar statue in the Tuileries Gardens, the boulevard in front of Tortoni's restaurant, the foyer of the Comédie Française; in London, the statue of Achilles in Hyde Park was a favourite meeting place ('the things that go on in front of that work of art are quite appalling', says Mabel Chiltern in Wilde's *An Ideal Husband*). The appearance of gay communities is a constant feature of urbanization. The first small groups in Sweden (Stockholm in 1883, Gothenburg in 1917) coincided with increased mobility (bicycle and train). Railway stations, public urinals and parks, and more or less anywhere that afforded cover and an escape route, were likely to become cruising grounds and 'trysting places'.

The terms used by early observers – 'plague', 'infestation' and so on – suggest a natural, haphazard development, but these districts were not always unregulated. Visitor's guides to London and shrewd signs in pub windows warning the public to 'Beware of Sods!' suggest some rudimentary attempt to organize the market. In the rural Champs-Élysées of the 1830s, cruising areas were sectioned off by ropes and park chairs, and sentries were posted, as Victor Hugo discovered one evening. A polite voice came from the darkness: 'M. Victor Hugo is requested to pass this time on the other side of the avenue.'

The same effect was hugely magnified in Australia, which must have had the largest gay districts anywhere in the world in the 19th century. In some colonies, heterosexuality was the exception. Sydney had bars, hotels and drag shows for homosexual men several years before there was firm evidence of such things in the United States. The theory that new Australians were corrupted on convict ships and delivered to the continent in a state of sudden homosexuality hardly does justice to what was evidently a buoyant gay society. In 1839, the *Sydney Gazette* revealed – to the horror of some and for the convenience of others – that sodomites were 'obtaining companions' at the Victoria Theatre, 'both during performances and at the intermissions', and then 'drinking and supping with them at the hostelry across the way'.

*

THERE IS MUCH LESS evidence of lesbian organization. Early signs of social activity are suspiciously lurid and usually relate to particular individuals. The famous but probably non-existent 'Club des Anandrynes' in Paris (1770s) was a running joke that was used to discredit lesbians like the actress Mlle Raucourt. There may have been confederations of actresses – there were hundreds of smutty poems on the subject – but actresses had several reasons apart from sexual preference to band together. Most later evidence refers to institutions: brothels, prisons, factories, schools, hospitals and department stores. Almost none of the information comes directly from women, who tend in any case to be far less categorical than the men. The groups described by Radclyffe Hall in 1928 are either circumstantial (the women's ambulance brigade in the First World War) or remarkably genteel and discreet (Natalie Clifford Barney's Paris salon).

Most lesbians seem to have favoured 'marriages' rather than groups, though this may simply reflect the more restricted social life of women. Berlin prostitutes often shared a home: the 'father' earned money by selling sex to men; the 'mother' stayed at home to cook and clean. In *fin-de-siècle* Paris, lesbian couples were known as '*petites soeurs*' (little sisters) because they declared their bond by wearing identical clothes. It seems, however, that the effect of urbanization on the development of lesbian communities was delayed rather than profoundly different. The evidence for other cities is patchy, but the lesbian quarter in Paris was so well developed by the end of the 19th century that it is hard to believe that it was unique in Europe.

Montmartre – especially the lively zone on the lower slopes – was already popular with lesbians in the 1880s and had some embryonic features of a lesbian community. Lesbian couples 'took over' certain apartment blocks and restaurants. Cafés like the Souris and the Rat Mort were filled at night with noisy crowds of women wearing gaudy hats and oddly assorted clothes. 'One would have thought', said the novelist Catulle Mendès, 'that they had dressed in a hurry at a second-hand clothes shop while the police were battering down the door.' The fact that they stood rather than sat, wore no gloves and used the argot of artists and pimps was a sign of defiant independence. There was a wide range of ages and classes. The only men were the waiters (usually homosexual), a few sniggering tourists and some special friends of the house, the most famous being Toulouse-Lautrec.

Émile Zola and his wife made a study of the phenomenon for his novel *Nana* (1880). His research notes describe a lesbian restaurant at 17, rue des Martyrs, south of the Place Pigalle:

> Louise Taillandier. Summer at Asnières, a large and beautiful property. In Paris, three salons; smart day is Friday; up to 150 women and ten men. The women in pairs. All kiss Louise on the mouth. Mistresses of solemn bourgeois come to have fun. [. . .] Wine undrinkable. [. . .] Low-grade actresses. Fortunes made by romping* in town. An old tart, as soon as she finds a pretty novice, brings her along and all the fat ladies pay court to her. Fat ladies predominate.

The 'large and beautiful property' at Asnières, on the Seine north-west of Paris, was described to Edmond de Goncourt by a painter friend, who went there to paint the old ladies, as 'a peculiar lesbian brothel'. Further downstream, at a popular bathing spot painted by Renoir and Monet ('La Fournaise'), there was a well-known hotel-restaurant run by a former chorus girl. At this lesbian oasis, women could smoke, wear trousers, lean their elbows on the table and look for partners. Small waterside chalets were rented for the summer. After Maupassant described it in *La Femme de Paul* (1881), its fame must have spread far beyond the Seine.

*

SEPARATING EXPLOITATION from free exchange can be just as hard for us as it was for 19th-century policemen and novelists. The famously available and beautifully uniformed royal guardsmen in London for instance had a long tradition of prostituting themselves before

---

* Zola's verb *'gougnotter'* is derived from the derogatory slang term *'gougnotte'*. 'Romp' (noun and verb) was sometimes applied to lesbians.

settling down and marrying or emigrating – rather like the Oulad Naïl women of Algeria who, according to Gide, traditionally amassed a dowry by prostitution before returning to their village. In the early 20th century, soldiers in America and Europe could often be hired for sexual entertainment.

These arrangements are probably best described as mutual exploitation. There was an understanding that the customer (usually middle-class and well-off) would show appreciation if the relationship developed into an affair. An ungenerous 'twank' or 'bag', as London guardsmen called their clients, could always be punished or black-mailed into being reasonable. In 1849–50, the Victorian diarist and man-with-nothing-to-do, Edward Leeves, gave his guardsmen lovers little presents, took them to the seaside and submitted to some gentle extortion. The letters from his friend D. Paxton – known to his comrades as 'Screw' – were 'saucy' enough to be worth a few pounds. 'He & Tom do look stunning in their White Leathers!' 'What a set of fellows these Blues are!'

A similar situation prevailed in Venice, where Edward Leeves spent most of his time. Gondoliers, too, had a long tradition of prosti-tution. The aim of most gondoliers was to support their family by supplementing their wages, especially in the winter. A rigid code of honour and strict rules of conduct allowed them to keep their self-respect (passive intercourse was shameful; active intercourse was a source of income). Boys in most Italian cities also served foreign tourists, as did Tyrolean peasants, who offered special out-of-season rates.

'Subculture' is an inappropriately portentous term for these arrangements. Sex was – and still is in some parts of the world – a holiday trade comparable to giving guided tours and selling ice cream. Some of the young men known to lovers of Venice like Symonds, Leeves and Rolfe were taking advantage of an adventurous libido and a sense of moral freedom to acquire some little luxuries or to avoid what they considered to be more tedious or demanding work. Some of them might even have been gay. Most however were trapped by poverty and abused by pimps. The word 'tradition', applied to gondo-liers and guardsmen, does not preclude coercion and victimization.

Exotic scenery helped to maintain the idea of a sexual paradise in the mind of the paying customer, but desperate paupers could be found all over Europe and America. A seventeen-year-old boy called Ernest Thickbroom, who worked at the Cleveland Street brothel in London, was apparently quite unhampered by his morals, but then we know nothing of the life that had shaped his daily practice. When asked 'If I would go to bed with a man. I said "no". He said "you'll get four shillings for a time" and persuaded me.' Verlaine, who discovered London with Rimbaud in 1872, was quick to sniff out the opportunities:

> On leaving the urinal you fall into the hands of young boys who brush you from head to foot for two *sous*. I don't know what else they must do to people who know to pay a little extra, but they do look formidably suspect with their little tight-fitting suits and generally charming faces.

In New York, according to Earl Lind, two-thirds of 'unmarried toughs of the slums' between the ages seventeen and twenty-four would accommodate an invert if 'their sexual needs were not fully met by normal intercourse'. However poetic the middle-class customer cared to be – and however sex-starved the 'tough' – this was primarily a commercial transaction:

> 'O you are such a wonderful young fellow! Wonderful alone in your being brave enough to mount the sky-scraper skeletons! And still more wonderful in possessing the muscle necessary for wielding a sledge-hammer all day! May I feel your biceps?' [etc.]
> 'You said it! I've got the build of a pugilist. But it's meself as needs ter go ter the dentist ter git me teeth filled and have n't the price.'
> (Earl Lind, The Female-Impersonators)

The difference between prostitution and mutual exchange is sometimes more obvious. It has been suggested that some boys became Post Office messengers in order to enhance their gay life, but most young prostitutes were simply victims of exploitation. Jack Saul's 'happy hooker' narrative, *The Sins of the Cities of the Plain* (1881), is a work of pornography, not a disinterested personal account. Thousands of infant vagrants were recruited by pimps or served a gruesome apprenticeship. The real-life equivalents of Fagin's gang of urchins on Saffron Hill would not have stopped at picking gentlemen's pockets.

Very little reliable information presents the prostitute's point of view. The novels of Charles Dickens and Henry Mayhew's *London Labour and the London Poor* avoid the subject altogether. Middle-class customers who left accounts were either not interested or unaware of how the profession worked. According to 19th-century accounts that viewed prostitution as the natural vocation of degenerates, the ideal career for a male prostitute, at least in Paris, was to stay young as long as possible, then to set up as a kept man after giving his pimp away to the police. The boy prostitute, known as a 'petit jésus', would then become an adult 'jésus' and could either set about extorting money from his earlier customers or sell his address list to another 'jésus' in preparation for a comfortable retirement. This was known as 'going into politics'.

Most detectives and forensic doctors knew of prostitutes who had grown fat on the fruits of sodomy. One man had a house on the Champs-Élysées, a fabulous collection of paintings and a château in the Loire Valley. Another became chief of police in an American city. But these wealthy male courtesans were exceptions. There is a rare impression of the normal state of affairs in a letter written by Tchaikovsky in Paris in 1879. He described a pang of post-coital remorse in the garret of a 'petit jésus' from Lyon:

> A bed, a pitiful little trunk, a dirty little table with a candle-end, a few shabby trousers and a jacket, a huge crystal glass, won in a lottery – those make the room's only decorations.

*

THE CLOSE HISTORICAL TIES of homosexual groups with prostitution are misleading. Many heterosexual men with money resorted to prostitutes, but usually with simpler aims. For homosexual men, there were also social, practical and emotional reasons to descend into the underworld.

The only certain way to find a partner was to head for the red-light district. Heterosexual men could dispense with risky expeditions: at any social gathering, everyone could be presumed heterosexual and a certain amount of flirting was acceptable. Homosexual men could either rely on a dubious 'sixth sense' or go to places – clubs, brothels or private homes – where the selection of partners had already been made.

Sex was not always the prime motive. Some establishments became regular meeting places, either because the proprietors themselves were homosexual or because they knew how to exploit a special clientele. Profit was always more powerful than prejudice.

In New York, several bars followed the lead of Billy McGlory's 'Armory Hall' – a vast dance hall where, from the late 1870s, supposedly beautiful boys with squeaky voices and rouged cheeks indulged in 'disgusting badinage'. At the 'Golden Rule Pleasure Club' (1892) on West 3rd Street, each partition concealed a painted 'pansy'. The set-up was sufficiently obvious for the crusading Rev. Charles Parkhurst to turn on his heels and flee from the house 'at top speed'. Some proprietors made a deliberate attempt to achieve infamy by exploiting the most amusing or eye-catching features of gay life. New York 'fairies' and Philadelphia 'brownies' could attract both a homosexual clientele and the more daring brand of tourist. They also, increasingly, attracted doctors, sociologists, journalists, politicians and moral campaigners.

There were also some straight bars where homosexual men were tolerated and could form their own clubs. The 'Cercle Hermaphrod-itos' held its meetings in the 1890s at Paresis Hall in Manhattan – a bar with a small beer-garden and some furnished rooms on 4th Avenue south of 14th Street. In an ambience remarkable for the lack of spitting and tobacco smoke, about twenty men with names like 'Prince Pansy' and 'Manon Lescaut' chattered in pidgin French about their predicaments and passions. The group included a vaude-ville actor, a man who clothes-shopped for a famous actress, and the ubiquitous Earl Lind. At Paresis Hall, something like a normal conversation could be held. It must have been a cheerful release, despite the bleakness of the topics: bigoted employers, homophobic hooligans, mysterious disappearances.

Some venues eventually offered special services. A bar in Amsterdam in the 1890s that was adorned (unusually) with flowers and pictures of the royal family, ran a job exchange for young gay men and dispensed remedies for venereal disease. Some brothels offered medical assistance, and many cities seem to have contained at least one sympathetic doctor whose address was passed around. In Paris, and probably elsewhere, 'pederast' cafés employed female prostitutes to act as decoys in case the premises were raided.

The most popular public venues were balls, ranging from semi-private dances to the regular masked balls attended by hundreds of men – and sometimes women – in drag. The biggest European balls were those of Vienna, Berlin and Paris: at carnival time, the usual ban on transvestism was suspended. By the 1900s, 'invert balls' were being held about twice a week in Berlin.

These were not the 'orgies' of popular myth. The 'Viennese balls' in Berlin were held with the permission of the police, who used them to keep an eye on criminals. August Strindberg described one of them in *The Cloister* (1891):

> Everyone behaved ceremoniously, almost as if they were in a mad-house. Men danced with men, mournfully, with deadly seriousness, as if they were doing something they had been ordered to do, without pleasure, without a smile. [. . .]
>
> It seemed to him that the most horrible thing of all was that everything was done so seriously, and that it was all so respectable!

Many of the humbler balls must have been similarly dour. The Temperance Hall in Hulme (Manchester) was rented in 1880 by a private club which held drag balls in different parts of the country. The dancers were given a password ('Sister') and danced to the strains of a blind accordionist in front of blacked-out windows. The detective who raided the premises, however, identified the dance as the can-can, which can hardly be performed without some *joie de vivre*.

By far the commonest type of organization was the club or the coterie. Practically every town seems to have had small groups of homosexual men who either met at someone's home or travelled to the nearest city. Even this was a risky undertaking. A group of Frenchmen in the 1850s went on regular sprees to Lyon, but always on different trains, 'or else we'd be the talk of the town the next day'. Other shared interests could serve as a front. The Eagle Street College in Bolton (from the 1870s) was a reading group of Whitmaniacs. The 'Háfiz Tavern' in St Petersburg (1900s), which functioned as a private homosexual cabaret, could always claim to be a club for fans of medieval Persian poetry. The 'Lohengrin' in Berlin was ostensibly a Wagner admiration society. Some clubs hid behind euphemisms: the Réunion philanthropique in Brussels, the Club degli Ignoranti in Rome, or the Klub der Vernünftigen in Vienna.*

The rituals developed by some of these clubs helped to reinforce a sense of social identity. The parodies of childbirth and nursing performed in London molly houses seem to be a mostly 18th-century phenomenon. But marriages continued to be a common expression of love and sociality. A surprising number of priests and vicars were prepared to perform marriages for homosexual men or lesbians, and there were also many private arrangements. Anne Lister and her lover Marianne agreed to 'solemnize' their mutual vows 'by taking the sacrament together'. They routinely used the words 'marriage', 'mistress', 'wife' and 'divorce' without inverted commas.

These marriages were not always subterranean affairs. There is evidence from late-19th-century America, Britain, France and Germany of hotels rented for weddings, male brides in gorgeous gowns, exotic honeymoons (sometimes ruined by blackmailers) and bridal bouquets kept under glass in front parlours. These events were the feast days of small communities, dates in an otherwise blank calendar. The fact that they took place at all shows a remarkable degree of organization.

*

THE SHEER VARIETY OF these groups and coteries makes it hard to identify anything like a coherent 'gay community'. Some groups were exclusively working class; many were open to homosexual and bisexual men and women, others were tightly closed. Some of the most influential groups, like the Cambridge 'Apostles' or the coterie at Exeter College, Oxford, that published *The Chameleon* (p. 219), were groups of friends rather than spontaneous expressions of gay culture.

The importance of these groups is easily exaggerated. The

---

* *'Vernünftig'* (rational) and *'unvernünftig'* (irrational) were insiders' terms for 'homosexual' and 'heterosexual' respectively, as in Platen's poem, 'Was Vernünft'ge hoch verehren ...'

'homosexual underworld' described by Rolfe's biographer Symons consisted of a few 'simple little devils' who were prepared to have sex with foreigners. The gay 'subculture' in Copenhagen in 1815 seems to have consisted of a milliner from Paris and ten of his friends.

The most ambitious plans to found homosexual societies – Ulrichs' secret 'Urningsband' or George Ives' esoteric 'Order of Chaeronea'* – were unrealized or confined to small groups of friends. Perhaps the closest thing to a self-perpetuating gay community was the island of Capri. The discovery of the other-worldly Blue Grotto in 1826, its association with the pederastic Emperor Tiberius and the availability of local boys – but not the tolerance of the local authorities – made Capri one of the most popular homosexual sites in Europe, at least for those, like the arms manufacturer Krupp or the French aristocrat poet, Adelsward Fersen, who could afford to run a private pleasure palace.

Other utopias were even more exclusive: Frederick the Great's Sans-Souci, where a bronze Ganymede stood in front of the library window and where, said Frederick, 'ambition and hostility will be the only sins deemed "unnatural"'; Ludwig II's kitsch medieval castle, Neuschwanstein; Elisár von Kupffer's museum-temple devoted to boy love, the Sanctuarium Artis Elisarion near Locarno. These local paradises were magnified versions of private rooms decorated with significant photographs and souvenirs. They were blueprints for a future society only in the minds of their owners.

The only real homosexual 'subcultures' in which established customs survived from one generation to the next were institutional – prisons, brothels, navies, or the American hobo subculture. These mini-societies had their own initiation ceremonies, well-developed argots, including a language of tattoos (notably hearts and pansies), and recognized types of relationship. But they were also obviously defined by something other than sexuality.

Diversity is far more apparent than uniformity. The idea that gay culture is characterized in certain periods by certain kinds of

---

* Ives, who talked of 'the Cause', dated his letters from the Battle of Chaeronea (338 BC), where Philip of Macedonia slaughtered the Theban band of warrior lovers. Thus, AD 1900 was the year 2238.

relationship has proved to be vulnerable to fresh evidence. There are no lasting patterns of sexual activity based on age difference or sexual role. Even doctors noticed that the 'active' and 'passive' partners in a relationship were often interchangeable and that 'passivity' had no essential connection with 'effeminacy'. Much of the evidence of prevalent relationships relates to cross-dressing, but it is unclear whether the professional 'fairies' of New York and the 'petits jésus' of Paris were catering to a market, creating a need, or simply parodying existing types by trying to find a commercial common denominator.

The one feature that stands out is the relative unimportance of race, religion and class. Some drag balls in America were attended by blacks and whites. Adolfo Caminha's revolutionary novel *Bom-Crioulo* (Rio de Janeiro, 1895), in which a black sailor loves a young white cabin boy, was naturalistic, not fantastic. Throughout Europe and America, it was common for middle-class men to take a working-class lover. But this seems to have been largely a matter of circumstance. Class differences – like differences of religion and race – were overridden rather than abolished by desire. 'Equality' could become desperately tedious. Mikhail Kuzmin longed for a friend who could satisfy him both intellectually and physically: 'a comrade in tastes, reveries and delights'. The Cambridge 'Apostles' discussed 'the higher sodomy' but rarely had sex with one another.

Many gays and lesbians still feel marginalized by the notion of a 'gay and lesbian community', the coherence of which exists primarily in the minds of market researchers. It may be after all that the distinguishing features of homosexual groups will turn out to be more practical than fundamental. At the present rate of change, monogamy will soon be a primarily homosexual phenomenon.

It may be unprofitable in any case to look to the gay past for firm traditions. The most remarkable characteristic of these early forms of homosocial organization is not their coherence but their ability to survive in the diffuse manner of resistance groups or nomads. Some coteries had an astonishingly wide range. When clubs or homes were raided, extensive networks of friends often came to light. Many people had large collections of photographs, either personal or pornographic. Visiting cards with photo-portraits were exchanged like cigarette cards. Clubs corresponded with one another and operated as consulates and tourist information bureaux. Anyone travelling to another city could be given introductions and geographical information of the sort that was supplied in a less precise form by voyeuristic city guides.

There was even a kind of gay Grand Tour, the stages of which remained more or less mysterious until the 'pink' guidebooks of the late 20th century. (See the 'Map of Uranian Europe', p. 278.) Byron, for instance, was conscious of following in the wake of Beckford, 'the Martyr of Prejudice', when he sailed for the Continent in 1811, just as later travellers followed the Wilde trail to Berneval and Paris or the Rimbaud trail to London and Ethiopia. These new maps of martyrs' travels were superimposed on older routes with historical and mythological staging-posts: Chaeronea, where the Theban band perished; Leucadia, where Sappho jumped to her death; Mount Ida, where Zeus ravished Ganymede.

The public reaction to revelations of homosexual networks was always slightly hysterical. There was talk of a European 'freemasonry', an invisible web of vengeful, scheming perverts: 'Men of this breed are to be found everywhere', wrote the Berlin journalist Maximilian Harden, 'in the editorial offices of great newspapers, at tradesmen's and teachers' desks, even on the Bench.' Friedrich Engels was fascinated by the idea of a homosexual state within the State. When Marx sent him the Uranian pamphlet he had received from Karl Heinrich Ulrichs in 1869, Engels had a J. Edgar Hooveresque vision of 'pederasty' as a rival of international socialism:

> Pederasts are beginning to count themselves and are discovering that they are a power in the State. All they lacked was organization, but it looks from this [pamphlet] as though it already exists in secret. And they have such important men [. . .] in the old and even in the new parties that victory will certainly be theirs. '*Guerre aux cons, paix aux trous-de-culs*' ['War on cunts, peace to arseholes'] will be the cry. It's a good thing we're too old to have to worry about paying bodily tribute to the victors. But think of the young generation!

These ludicrous fears were not entirely detached from reality. Active urban 'pederasts' belonged to a very mobile and cosmopolitan society. Not all were bourgeois tourists taking a holiday from neighbours and policemen. Emotional as well as financial poverty was a good reason to emigrate. Mobility was not usually a matter of choice. In 1865, the Parisian police picked up signs of a homosexual diaspora. It was traced back to a raid on a flourishing club in the Grenelle area of Paris. Confiscated letters revealed a sparse but well-maintained communications network. One letter, dated 7 February 1865, was characteristically international: it had been sent by a Swiss businessman in London to a Swede who was in the service of a Russian aristocrat in Rome but who was temporarily in Paris staying with his lover and former master, an Italian count.

> I heard that you left for Africa. [. . .] The Boulevards or the Champs-Élysées would have been better, though they are not without danger.
>
> Be careful, my gazelle. The ladies have had so many mishaps in the last six months. [. . .] The Margrave of Saint-Léon has suffered greatly for her . . . political . . . opinions. Like many others, she was forced to leave Paris for several months. [. . .]
>
> If you have any news of all those darling people who are scattered to the four corners of Europe, be sure to tell me. Poor girls! What a struggle they have with people's prejudices!

It is easy to imagine the amazement of the detectives who read these letters. The 19th-century gay world is full of strange coincidences that make it look like a continental village: Earl Lind knew one of Whitman's 'adopted sons'; several people knew Karl Heinrich Ulrichs; the prostitute-author Jack Saul knew everyone. Familiar names turn up in unexpected places: Simeon Solomon, arrested at the *pissoir* outside the Paris Bourse; Proust's friend Raymond Laurent, found dead outside a Venice hotel by Wilde's son, Vyvyan Holland. Some men – described by Albert Moll as 'travelling international celebrities' – became famous for their beauty and were recognized throughout Europe.

Many people had so many partners that these coincidences are perhaps not surprising after all. Even in the 21st century, circles of acquaintance overlap at only a few removes. In a smaller society, and in a sub-population with powerful common interests, networks were bound to be extensive. Some of Krafft-Ebing's patients claimed to know large numbers of Uranians even in small towns (from eight in a town of 2,300, to more than eighty in a town of 60,000).

Clubs and cruising were the central nervous system of a dynamic and heterogeneous society. Its busy streets and anonymous connections can be seen in the few diaries and notebooks that have survived. Many of them seem at first to have been written by sex maniacs with a passion for accounting. Kenneth Searight's epic verse autobiography – 'The Furnace: an autobiography in which is set forth the secret diversions of a paiderast' – recorded sexual exploits throughout the British Empire and beyond. He had sex with at least 129 boys from 1897 to 1917. Roger Casement was equally wide ranging but more prolific. Earl Lind had known 800 men in twelve years (an average of one man every five and a half days) and was just as busy when he travelled to Europe.

These inventories of brief liaisons might suggest a degree of over-compensation, but they were also personal reminders that society was not as heterosexual as it thought. The records kept by John Maynard Keynes from 1906 to 1915 were like alternative roll-calls and registers, the sexual-economic figures from which the activity of a whole society could be deduced. This is part of one of his lists:

> Stable Boy of Park Lane
> Auburn haired of Marble Arch
> Lift boy of Vauxhall
> Jew Boy
> The Swede of the National Gallery
> The Young American of Victoria Sta
> The Young American near the British Museum
> The chemist's boy of Paris
> The clergyman
> David Erskine, M.P.
> The Blackmailer of Bordeaux

Whitman's notes of encounters in Manhattan are just as evocative but more obviously humane. His compressed jottings were the dry ingredients that could later be used to produce delicious memories and fill the future society of comrades with bodies and faces:

Saturday night Mike Ellis – wandering at the corner of Lexington av. & 32d st. – took him home to 150 37th street, – 4th story back room – bitter cold night

James Sloan (night of Sept 18 '62) 23rd year of age – plain homely, American

October 9, 1863, Jerry Taylor, (NJ.) of 2d dist reg't slept with me last night weather soft, cool enough, warm enough, heavenly.

*

THE FRAGILE SENSE of a gay community was based on experiences that seemed to preclude the possibility of a community. But then why should 'comrades' simply form another society like the old one? This apparent promiscuity was a life outside the society that had caused such grief and shame.

The men who flocked to alleyways and *pissoirs*, who offered themselves to strangers and explored dark *quartiers* they would otherwise never have seen, were being sociable, not subversive. Fleetingness was essential, not just for practical reasons. The poems of Constantine Cavafy celebrate transience as a liberation. The past could never stick to single, unrepeated moments of physical pleasure. History could be rewritten in the folds of a sheet and then smoothed out again. It was the revenge of chance on inevitability, sudden intimacy instead of endless anonymity, the memory of the body replacing the memory of the educated mind. And when they returned to the everyday world, all lovers could be certain in any case, like Cavafy's student Myrtias, in 'Dangerous Thoughts' (1911), to find the spirit as ascetic as before.

7

A Sex of One's Own

No virgin I deflower, nor, lurking, creep,
With steps adult'rous, on a husband's sleep.
I plough no field in other men's domain;
And where I delve no seed shall spring again.

Anon., Don Leon (1866)

Among the homosexuals there is found the most remarkable class of men, namely, those whom I call supervirile. These men stand by virtue of the special variation of their soul-material, just as much above Man, as the normal sex man does above Woman. Such an individual is able to bewitch men by his soul-aroma [. . .]. Names like Alexander the Great, Socrates, Plato, Julius Caesar, Michel-Angelo, Charles XII of Sweden, William of Orange, and so forth. [. . .] Consequently the German penal code, in stamping homosexuality as a crime, puts the highest blossoms of humanity on the proscription list.

Gustav Jaeger, Die Entdeckung der Seele (1880)
(tr. Edward Carpenter)

THE SENSE OF SOLIDARITY fostered by some of these groups could turn shame into self-respect and fear into defiance. Homosexual coteries and milieux were not just a happy convenience, they were a sign that things might change.

There was little sign, however, of any organized agitation until the end of the 19th century. Despite the revolutionary Code Pénal of 1791, the very notion of homosexual rights would simply not have occurred to most people. Even now, while specific rights are widely acknowledged, gay rights are still contentious. It was not until the mid-1990s that Amnesty International began to support prisoners who were persecuted for their sexual preference.

In the early 19th century, most gay people never wondered why homosexual relations were proscribed. Many never thought themselves innocent: they considered themselves weak, sick or freakish, and their dream was to be cured or left in peace. Uranians who were happy with their inclination were just as unlikely to demand reform, even privately. Just because a part of them belonged to a minority, it did not follow – any more than it does now – that they would be in favour of social change. Anne Lister was proudly lesbian and profoundly conservative. She found the idea of women's rights ridiculous and constantly reproached herself for talking to social inferiors. Her solutions were practical and lawful. She taught herself to ignore sarcastic comments and contrived a kind of marriage with her friend Marianne by insuring her life in Marianne's favour. In this way, she could offer her a husband's protection. She no more blamed society for the inconvenience than she thought of prosecuting the weather for making her house damp.

The history of the gay rights movement is, in fact, remarkably short, and any attempt to prolong its past life would only distort its true origins. Some of the texts that are used in college courses as examples of early gay militancy are plainly ironic. The petition of 'The Children of Sodom to the National Assembly' (1790), attributed to the pro-revolutionary Marquis de Villette, was an attack on the government that decriminalized sodomy: 'The Assembly of Buggers, Sodomites and Lesbians', which decrees complete freedom of action, 'even in the paths of the Luxembourg Gardens, despite what the legal owner says, and without hindrance by any other person', was not a real organization.* The 'Société des Émiles' (1860s) did exist and was popular with several members of the French government and the War Office, but its famous rule-book is a satire, not a confiscated document: 'Indecent relations with individuals of the female sex are banned'; 'The concierge is to keep two goats permanently at the disposal of military gentlemen who may be in a hurry', etc.

These spoofs are sometimes treated as genuine calls for equality, which only shows how little good evidence there is of organized homosexual protest. The lack of precedents also explains the peculiar prestige of the Marquis de Sade, whose *La Philosophie dans le boudoir* (1795) contains a detailed and rational defence of sodomy and lesbianism as natural forms of contraception. Between orgies, one of the main characters describes a passion for one's own sex as an innate disposition; he condemns the barbaric practice of killing people because 'they do not share your tastes', and notes the prevalence of the noble vice in all parts of the world, including 'the entire American continent'.

Sade represents a strand of Enlightenment thought that helped to show the way, but he makes a wretchedly sardonic pioneer. His defence of homicide in the same text is just as vigorous as his defence of homosexuality. As a recent sourcebook puts it with admirable moderation, 'No matter how one might want to embrace liberatory discourse about sexuality today, the philosophy upon which Sade based it shows his limits in his analysis of murder.'

The published writers who could, at a pinch, be described as early champions of gay rights would never have seen themselves in this light. Montesquieu, Voltaire, Beccaria and Condorcet were simply asserting the right of human beings not to be tortured and burned at the stake for a crime that had no victim. 'Sodomy violates the right of no man', said Condorcet. The same argument can be found throughout the 18th and 19th centuries and traced back at least to

---

* The carnival rhetoric of the Revolution (and of later French revolutions) thrived on sexual nonconformity. Villette, the 'retroactive citizen', was the object of several satires. Phrases such as 'for all ages and all sexes' were commonly used to poke fun at egalitarianism: e.g. the *Almanach lyrique* 'for democratic, aristocratic and impartial fuckers, or *The Three Sexes' Calendar*' (1790), which could be found 'At Sodom, Cythaera and especially in the pockets of those who condemn it'.

Thomas Aquinas, but it rarely amounts to a defence of homosexuality *per se*.

Most pleas for justice or tolerance were never published, though the fact that they were written at all shows that the idea existed. In 1811, Byron jokily proposed to write a pamphlet titled 'Sodomy simplified or Paederasty proved to be praiseworthy from ancient authors and modern practice'. In 1818, after translating Plato's *Symposium*, Shelley wanted to make his reader 'cast off the cloak of his self-flattering prejudices'. His 'Discourse on the Manners of the Antient [*sic*] Greeks Relative to the Subject of Love' (1818) cautiously hinted that sodomy could be an expression of love and that it was hardly 'more horrible than the usual intercourse endured by almost every youth of England with a diseased and insensible prostitute'. The complete text of the discourse was not published until 1931, in a private edition of 100 copies. Shelley himself was not prepared to cast off the cloak of prejudice. In a letter written four months after the Discourse, he expressed disgust at Byron's choice of companions in Italy: 'wretches who seem almost to have lost the gait and physiognomy of man, and who do not scruple to avow practices which are not only not named but I believe seldom even conceived in England'.

The real silent star of early gay rights is Jeremy Bentham, who wrote several hundred pages on the subject between 1774 and 1824. At first, his main point of attack was the law against that 'odious taste' and the busybody legislator who 'thrusts himself in between' two consenting adults. But half a century produced a change of emphasis. In the same rationalizing spirit that led to the creation of the word 'homosexuality', Bentham tried to devise a less tendentious vocabulary. He talked of 'regular' and 'irregular' rather than 'natural' and 'unnatural' forms of intercourse, and called homosexuality 'the improlific appetite' (because it does not produce babies).

Bentham's voluminous notes are probably the first such writing on the subject in English, yet they seem to sum up the general trend of the next 200 years, as if the collective mind would slowly follow the same argument to the same conclusion: humanitarian protest, informed relativism and, eventually, direct approval. Bentham finally came close to defending 'the improlific appetite' on its own terms: there were traces of it in the Gospels (see p. 242), it helped to prevent over-population, and it appeared to be universal. According to Bentham's anthropological information, only two tribes – one in New South Wales, the other in eastern Canada – were known to abuse women, and neither practised homosexuality.

The texts by Shelley and Bentham now look like milestones on the road to liberation, but they had to be excavated later on and were unknown at the time. Bentham's plan to collaborate with Beckford came to nothing. The sketch of a preface explains why: 'Never [. . .] did work appear [. . .] from which at the hand of public opinion a man found so much to fear, so little to hope.' The only effective work in Britain was done by a few active reformers like Edmund Burke, who twice sued newspapers, in 1780 and 1784, for hinting that his opposition to the pillorying of sodomites proved that he was one himself. The example was unlikely to push Bentham into print.

There was however one earlier defence of homosexuality in English which deserves to take pride of place if only because it was published. In Smollett's *The Adventures of Roderick Random* (1748), Earl Strutwell's defence of sodomy may be ironic but it presents the principal arguments of the next two centuries with the concision and humour that are painfully lacking in later disquisitions: the wisdom and excellence of famous homosexual men, the global prevalence of a supposedly unnatural taste, its tendency to diminish the number of bastards and venereal degenerates, and – something that makes Smollett a more inspiring pioneer than either Bentham or Shelley – its 'exquisite pleasure'.

*

ON THE CONTINENT, as every English moralist thought he knew, such matters were more freely discussed. Even before Goethe's essay on Winckelmann, German writers – who had at their disposal more editions and translations of classical texts than their neighbours – were debating the nature of Greek 'pederasty'. Comparisons were drawn between ancient and modern forms of homosexual love, notably in Ramdohr's *Venus Urania* (1798), which contained some real contemporary examples (see p. 140).

The culmination of these studies was a two-volume pot-pourri by a self-educated milliner in Glarus (Switzerland) called Heinrich

Hössli (1784–1864). *Eros. Die Männerliebe der Griechen* (1836–8 and 1840) might seem an obscure and chaotic work, but it had a lively effect on later developments. It was an inspiration to Ulrichs and a major source for Albert Moll's influential study of 1891.

Hössli, whose second son was homosexual, had been horrified by the torture and execution of a lawyer in Berne in 1817. Franz Desgouttes had murdered his young secretary, but the court's unusual cruelty was clearly motivated by Desgouttes's homosexual passion for his victim. Hössli asked the popular writer Heinrich Zschokke to write a novella on the subject but was disappointed with the result: *Der Eros*, 'a conversation about love', was a disquisition rather than a defence. Hössli decided to write his own *Eros*. His main ideas were that human laws were not the same as Nature's laws, that 'Greek love' had been maligned by Christian propagandists, and that 'sexual nature' is not a matter of choice. But the real force of his book lay in the anthology of texts which presented homosexuality as something civilized and beautiful: Aristotle, Socrates, Horace, Saadi, etc. Hössli's shopful of texts must have been a revelation to his readers.

From a historical point of view, the book itself is probably less significant than the fact that a man who made hats for a living and had no obvious talent for writing spent several years and a lot of money trying to write and publish it.

Writers tend to exaggerate the importance of the written evidence, but, even in Continental Europe, there is very little to exaggerate until the last third of the 19th century. The strongest hints of future movements are to be found, not in literary texts, but in a tone of defiance that becomes increasingly noticeable from the mid-18th century. There is something of this tone in the letters of Beckford and Byron, but it can also be heard in sodomite trials held in cities like Amsterdam or Paris where small communities offered daily confirmation that homosexual love was not essentially depraved.

It was in France, with its tradition of revolutionary violence, that the first stirrings of gay resistance were seen. At Riom prison in the Auvergne, in April 1848, the prisoners rioted, attacking warders and breaking open cells, when a young homosexual man was separated from his boyfriend. Cruising-grounds in Paris were tenaciously defended. In the 1840s, at the central markets, Les Halles, arrests

[179]

usually began at 9 p.m. Sometimes the market porters joined in. But the 'pederasts' would return the following evening with fresh recruits. When the wood partitions in the nearby toilets were replaced with metal sheets, they drilled new holes, and when pederasts were arrested, they showed a keen sense of their sexual rights. A café waiter, who had had to flee from mobs and policemen so many times that the prosecution was able to present five shoes as evidence against him, 'complained bitterly about police procedures, which he described as an attack on his freedom':

> He openly confessed to the purpose of his daily and nightly perambulations, but added, cynically: 'There are brothels of women, aren't there? Why shouldn't there be brothels of men? As long as this injustice persists, respectable fellows like myself will be in danger of getting themselves arrested.'

When the police decided to clean up the Champs-Élysées, there was armed resistance and blood was spilled. These pitched battles never acquired the symbolic importance of the Stonewall riots of 1969, but they do show that gay militancy was not a 20th-century invention.

An active sense of homosexual identity could also be detected in the use of more pleasant names than 'pederast' or 'sodomite'. Insulting words like *'tapette'** were defiantly adopted by some Parisian homosexuals, but other names implied a proud heritage. The commonly used term, *'chevaliers de la manchette'* ('Knights of the Sleeve') referred to the last of the Han emperors who, rather than wake his lover who had fallen asleep on his arm, cut the sleeve of his robe. The word *'spartiate'* ('Spartan'), used by Sade and the socialist visionary Fourier, referred to the Theban band of lovers and implied strength, loyalty and strict morality rather than the usual catalogue of vices.

Growing awareness of this bold heritage created a fertile ground for later movements. The cosmopolitan young man who wrote to

---

* A male prostitute. A *'tapette'* was a wooden paddle used to drive corks into bottles.

Dr Casper in 1852 was not only unrepentant, he almost felt sorry for heterosexuals:

> Believe me, we are generally better and more gifted than other people. [. . .] How can our sins be so great when they were committed by men like Plato, Julius Caesar, Frederick the Great, Gustav III of Sweden and many others? Were Winckelmann and Platen vulgar men? Most of us have beautiful eyes and the eye, after all, is the mirror of the soul!

By 1865, Karl Heinrich Ulrichs was able to look forward to a great change. Soon, Uranians would stop trying to fit in with society, society would have to adapt to them. Men in cafés would be appalled to see articles in their daily paper with titles like 'On Love Between Men'. But, said Ulrichs, 'you will just have to get used to it, like crabs to slow cooking. Hopefully, it will not be detrimental to your health.'

*

WE LAST SAW ULRICHS frightening his family with his circular letters (pp. 132–3). He eventually published twelve pamphlets on Uranian love, between 1864 and 1879. His proposals included a new civic and legal category for homosexual men and women and 'a Uranist Union', the aim of which would be 'to bring Urnings out of their previous isolation and unite them into a compact mass bound together in solidarity'.

This alone would make Ulrichs the founding father of gay rights, but he was not content with letters and pamphlets. In 1865, he proposed that the Congress of German Jurists debate a motion to demand equal rights for the third sex. The proposal was rejected. To judge by his later hesitations, he must have been relieved. Until 1868, all his pamphlets were published under a pseudonym, and the thought of defending such a motion in public was terrifying.

In 1866, one of his readers sent him a copy of Hössli's book. Ulrichs was haunted by the milliner's words: 'Two paths lay before me: to write this book and expose myself to persecution, or not to write and be riddled with guilt when I enter my grave.' The following year, Ulrichs returned to the Congress, which was held in Munich.

He had just left Hanover for the last time after being arrested for opposing the Prussian annexation. This seemed to give him the necessary combination of despair and determination. On the second day of the Congress, Ulrichs celebrated his forty-second birthday. On the third day, after changing his mind up to the last minute, he became the first person in history to come out in public. The speech, admittedly, contained no direct statement about his own sexuality, but the implication was clear to everyone in the hall.

> My heart was pounding in my breast as I mounted the podium on August 29th, 1867 in the Grand Hall of the Odeon Theatre, in front of an audience of more than 500 German jurists, which included some members of the German Parliament and a Bavarian prince. I mounted the podium with God!

He reached the part of his speech in which he claimed that there were thousands of Urnings in Germany and that this 'class of people' included 'many of the greatest and noblest intellects of our and other nations'. At this, there were calls to adjourn. But loud protests came from the other side of the hall: 'No, no, go on, go on!' The President asked Ulrichs to continue in Latin (in which he was fluent), but he left the podium without finishing his speech.

Ulrichs was already an experienced campaigner, and accounts of his historic speech that present him as a doomed martyr are an insult to his polemical skill. The reaction, during and after the speech, was not unanimous. Instead of running away, Ulrichs attended the closing banquet in the Glass Palace. Some people avoided him, but others 'freely and loyally engaged in conversation with me'. A few stunned and silent faces in the audience had shown that his words had not been wasted. For a supposedly futile gesture, the speech was remarkably successful.

*

THE GRAND HALL at Munich in 1867 stands at the junction of what seemed to be the two main roads to freedom: the public assertion of rights and their theoretical defence. The first road was to remain almost deserted until the mid-20th century; the second led through

endless conurbations and branched off so often that no one could be
sure that it was even heading in the right direction.

Most of the theories that were used to promote reform now sound
apologetic and self-defeating. The idea that homosexuality was natural
and innate might have been an argument for decriminalization but it
tended to be presented, even as recently as the 1960s, in a peculiarly
demeaning fashion. Homosexuality was compared, by its defenders,
to colour-blindness and congenital deformities like hare lips and club
feet. It was said to be common among primitive tribes and practically every species of animal, which only confirmed the impression
of moralists and policemen. The abiding image of Gide's *Corydon*
(1st edition, 1911; 12 copies) is that of two copulating male dogs on
a boulevard being separated by a *gendarme*. Even Ulrichs' theory of
'half-men' in whom a soul of one sex is 'trapped' or 'shut up' (*'inclusa'*)
in a body of the other, suggested some horrible mistake. Liberation, in
this case, would surely have consisted of a return to normality.

It is revealing that one of the commonest reference points for
late-19th-century campaigners was Schopenhauer's depressing
explanation of 'pederasty' in the second volume of *Die Welt als Wille
und Vorstellung* (1844). Like most people who gave the matter any
thought, Schopenhauer realized that so-called 'unnatural' desires were
a natural occurrence. Unlike most people, he associated the phenomenon with men who were either too young or too old – hence his
explanation: pederasty was Nature's way of 'obviating unsuccessful
procreations that might gradually deprave the entire species'.

Schopenhauer was fifty-six years old at the time and seems to have
had some personal experience of the phenomenon. His manner of
describing it, however, was scarcely flattering: the sex instinct, he
wrote, is led astray in pederasts, in the same way that the bluebottle
(*musca vomitoria*) is tricked by the smell of putrefaction given off by
the *arum dracunculus* into laying its eggs in the arum's flowers rather
than on rotting meat.

After Ulrichs and his notion of a third sex, this search for explanations and justifications opened up the subject to endless bickering
about causes and mental states. Worse still, it allowed the rest of
society to dictate the terms of the debate. Ulrichs himself gave up

the fight in 1880, when he emigrated to Italy. He eventually settled in L'Aquila and devoted himself to a journal written in Latin.*

The more pragmatic debate, which focused on the law against sodomy, ran into similar difficulties, though it produced an unprecedented spate of writing about homosexuality and a very active rights organization. Kertbeny's open letter to the Prussian Minister of Justice in 1869, which introduced the neutral term 'Homosexualität', and Heinrich Marx's *Urningsliebe* (1875) argued for the rights of an essentially moral and law-abiding section of the population. The problem here was that, while the sodomy law provided campaigners with a clear target, it also led them to reinforce the idea that homosexuality was largely a matter of sexual acts. The first open protest published in English – the anonymous poem, *Don Leon* (1866), falsely attributed to Byron – was practically a compendium of sodomy trials and appeared to be concerned above all with a certain kind of intercourse. The main arguments were that sodomites do not transmit syphilis and that their 'sport obscene', 'left unheeded, would remain unknown'. This was hardly an expression of pride.

Even the more progressive ideas – a separate State for Urnings, or the introduction of a new civil status – were acknowledgements that Uranians needed special treatment. Exactly the same ideas were espoused by people who wanted to control the 'problem' or solve it once and for all.

Looking back from the early 21st century, the most convincing arguments now seem to be the simplest – those that appealed to a basic sense of fairness or that held up a mirror to the accusers:

> Why, I wish to know, is it perfectly moral for me to copulate with a personage whose sexual organs are different from my own, and perfectly immoral for me to copulate with a personage whose sexual organs are not different? (Lytton Strachey (d. 1932), essay collected in *The Really Interesting Question*, 1972)

> We ought to think and speak of homosexual love, not as 'inverted' or 'abnormal' [...] or as an unhappy fault, a 'masculine body with a feminine soul', but as being in itself a natural, pure and sound passion,

---

* Ulrichs died in 1895. His home is now a pilgrimage site on the gay Grand Tour. A square in Bremen was renamed Ulrichsplatz in August 2002.

as worthy of the reverence of all fine natures as the honourable devotion of husband and wife, or the ardour of bride and groom. (James Millis Peirce, first dean of Harvard Graduate School, to J. A. Symonds, 1891; published posthumously in *Sexual Inversion*, 1897.)

Before the first gay rights organization was created at the turn of the century, the most effective contribution of theorizing writers was largely accidental. The flood of mostly German publications that followed Ulrichs' sixteen-year campaign – well over 1,000 books and articles on homosexuality from 1890 to 1914 – showed the astonishing size of the homosexual population. This, more than anything else, gave 'Urnings' a sense of their democratic rights – and the confidence to demand them – and awakened politicians to the existence of a powerful force.

The first estimates were extremely low. Ulrichs' first guess was 0.002 per cent and he never went higher than 0.5 per cent. Some campaigners, like Kertbeny and Magnus Hirschfeld, may have reduced their estimates so as not to alarm their readers: their figures hover around 2 per cent. But by the end of the century, figures of 4 per cent and above were commonly cited for Germany, Holland, all of Europe and 'middle-class England'. This is close to the average found by many modern surveys, including Kinsey's report of 1948 (4 per cent of white adult males exclusively homosexual throughout life).*

Even the meeker estimates made it possible to talk about millions of homosexual men and – after initial doubts – women. Variations were identified: an upward trend when heading East; a preponderance in certain professions and classes: hairdressers, waiters, aristocrats, etc. Otto de Joux claimed in 1893 that every third male servant was homosexual. According to an Italian study of 1900, 60 per cent of all inverts were musicians, indicating almost a million homosexual musicians in Italy alone. Edward Prime-Stevenson quoted what he

---

* The unusual figure of 0.02 per cent, triumphantly touted by Dr Marañón in 1930, was based on Madrid police records showing 687 inverts in all of Spain: 'The smaller number of inverts in Spain by comparison with Central European countries is notorious. This superiority of the Latin races is recognized by all writers on the subject.'

said was a 'psychiatric proverb', though it is hard to imagine anyone actually uttering it: 'So many Jews, so many similisexualists.'

These figures confirmed what many people already guessed from their own experience. Percentages are still eagerly discussed and used to gauge the likelihood of change. In 1997, Hugh David found the figure of 4 per cent of the adult male population depressingly low (it is equivalent, in Britain, to the population of Glasgow; in the United States, to the population of Los Angeles). But in the days when it was possible for people to think that they were unique, even 0.1 per cent would have been a comfort.

This cheerful demographic news was one of the highlights of the dazzling 'Pederasty' section in Richard Burton's 'Terminal Essay' to *The Arabian Nights* (1885). Burton cheekily identified a 'Sotadic Zone' lying between latitudes 30° and 43° north in which 'the Vice' was popular and endemic. This Zone, as if by chance, coincided with what was supposed to be the cradle of western civilization. It was clear in any case from Burton's planet-wide evidence that, when the ethnographic information was complete and all the other 'sotadic' parts were added, only a few poorly populated enclaves of endemic 'normality' would survive. An illustration of the Zone based on Burton's evidence would have looked something like the map opposite.

*

THE FIRST PART OF this chapter really belongs to the prehistory of gay rights. The modern story begins at the end of the 19th century with the creation by the Berlin doctor Magnus Hirschfeld of the 'Wissenschaftlich-Humanitäre Komitee' (Scientific and Humani-tarian Committee). It was the kind of name that could safely appear on a brass plaque or a letter-head without arousing any interest.

In 1895, Hirschfeld, a general practitioner, was shaken by a suicide letter from one of his patients: a young homosexual lieutenant who killed himself on the eve of his wedding. His dying wish was that Dr Hirschfeld, who was also homosexual, would help to improve the lot of people like himself.

A few days later, all of Europe seemed to be gloating over the

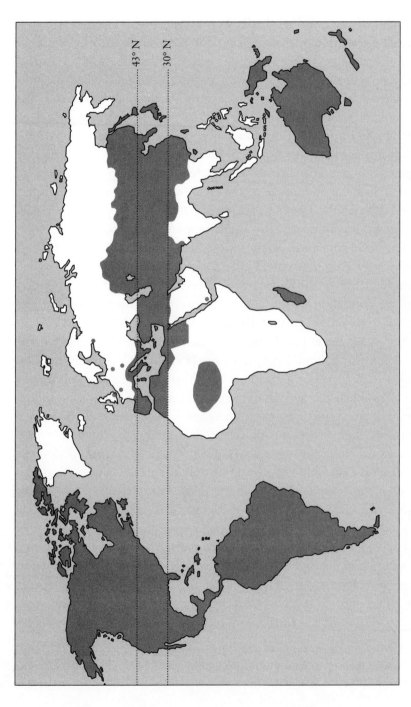

Richard Burton's 'Sotadic Zone', based on the 'Terminal Essay' in *The Book of the Thousand Nights and a Night*

downfall of Oscar Wilde. In Paris, the French-American poet Stuart Merrill drew up a petition asking for the sentence to be reduced. Almost everyone refused to sign, including Émile Zola. A British petition, prepared by More Adey, was even less successful. Magnus Hirschfeld had wider aims and a more diverse audience and was consequently more effective. He and his journalist friend Leo Berg sent letters of protest to the newspapers and Hirschfeld set to work on the first of his many books: *Sappho und Sokrates*, or 'How can one explain the love of men and women for people of the same sex?' It was published pseudonymously in 1896 by a young Leipzig publisher called Max Spohr. Spohr had already published two pro-homosexual works and was to prove remarkably resistant to prosecution.

The following year, while sitting in a train on his way to visit Spohr in Leipzig, Hirschfeld jotted down nine good reasons to repeal paragraph 175 of the German penal code. The result was a petition and the formation of the above-mentioned Committee on the day after Hirschfeld's twenty-ninth birthday: 15 May 1897.

Ten years later, the Committee had 500 members and correspondents throughout Europe. From 1899 to 1923, its journal, the *Jahrbuch für sexuelle Zwischenstufen* ('Yearbook of Sexual Intermediacy'), published hundreds of historical, literary and scientific studies, reviews, letters, pictures, news items and bibliographies. It effectively founded a new discipline and inspired or publicized the first serious outings of modern writers: Ludwig Frey's *Aus dem Seelenleben des Grafen Platens* (1899), C. H. Fahlberg's *H. C. Andersen: Beweis seiner Homosexualität* (1901), Hans Rau's *Franz Grillparzer und sein Liebesleben* (1904) and Eduard Bertz's *Der Yankee-Heiland (Walt Whitman): Ein Beitrag zur modernen Religionsgeschichte* (1906).*

Hirschfeld's Committee conducted polls, organized petitions, tried to secure visiting rights for jailed homosexuals and offered lesbians legal protection from violent husbands. It delivered medical certificates that allowed its cross-dressing members to obtain transvestism

---

* 'The Mental Life of Count Platen'; 'H. C. Andersen: Proof of his Homosexuality' (by 'Albert Hansen'); 'Franz Grillparzer and his Love Life'; 'The Yankee Saviour (Walt Whitman): a Contribution to the Modern History of Religions'.

permits from the police and worked with the 'Pederasty Division' of the Berlin police to combat blackmailers. It undertook a programme of public education with pamphlets like 'What the People should know about the Third Sex' (1902). Judges presiding at trials of homosexuals were bombarded with explanatory documents. Hirschfeld himself appeared at hundreds of trials as an expert witness. He also appeared as a therapist in one of the first gay films, *Anders als die Anderen* ('Not Like Other People'; dir. Richard Oswald, 1919), in which an imprisoned Conrad Veidt watches a long procession of homosexual kings, poets and philosophers passing under a banner marked 'Paragraph 175'.*

The Committee had a difficult life. Some of its more dramatic plans proved unworkable – like the idea of a mass self-denunciation by a thousand homosexuals who would inundate the police stations and demand to be prosecuted. Its meetings were often banned, especially after women (supposedly more corruptible) began to attend, and sometimes broke down when members suffered an emotional collapse or, on one occasion, attacked a doctor who accused them all of lacking willpower. Hirschfeld himself was fined 200 DM for disseminating obscene literature – specifically, a questionnaire sent to 3,000 medical students and 5,000 metal workers. In Munich, in 1919, he was beaten up by nationalist hooligans.

There were also the usual internal disputes. In 1902, a group led by Adolf Brand declared independence. The 'artistic' and paederastic 'Gemeinschaft der Eigenen' (Community of the Special) was inspired by snobbish pseudo-Greek ideals. Its motto might have been, 'Boys for pleasure, wives for convenience'. Their misogyny and occasional anti-semitism make them sound like a missing link between 1890s aesthetes and the Hitler youth. But their discomfort with Dr Hirschfeld is understandable. In his statement of secession in 1907, one of their leading figures, Benedict Friedländer, rejected the cowardly

---

* The first known gay film was Swedish: Mauritz Stiller's *Vingarne* ('The Wings') (1916), based on Herman Bang's novel about a sculptor and his pupil, Mikaël (1904). The wings refer to Carl Milles's sculpture of Ganymede and Zeus in the guise of an eagle.

notion that homosexuals were sick and effeminate. How could they expect to be treated as equals if they presented themselves as freaks and invalids?

Hirschfeld was well aware of the problem. He had tried, without much success, to neutralize the Committee's medical aura by canvassing the support, not just of doctors, but also of lawyers, politicians and clergymen. The scientific approach, especially when promulgated by the earnest 'Aunt Magnesia' (Magnus Hirschfeld), lent itself to parody. The cartoon that appeared in the Munich weekly *Jugend* in 1905 under the title, 'Berlin Census in a Thoroughly Modern Home', was not entirely unjustified:

> *Census Taker:* 'How many children?'
> *A Mother:* 'Two daughters, one boy, three homosexual intermediates, and one Uranian.'

The impression of pseudo-scientific debate and power struggles among the impotent is unfortunate but inevitable. With Magnus Hirschfeld's Wissenschaftlich-Humanitäre Komitee, the almost featureless night sky of earlier gay history gives way to the smaller, higher-resolution world of organizations, schisms, dates and egos. Even so, the world's first gay rights organization – what Thomas Mann called 'Dr Hirschfeld's ghastly "Committee" ' – not only did a lot of practical good, it was also a sign of progress.

The apparently absurd proliferation of scientific terms – 'similisexual' and 'alterosexual', 'homosexual' and 'heterosexual', 'allosexual' and 'normosexual', 'unisexual', 'monosexual', 'parisexual', 'feminosexual', 'philarrenic', 'androphile', 'ephebophile', 'commasculation', etc. – hinted at the future emergence of different sexualities from the previously undistinguished mass of 'sexual deviants'. Hirschfeld himself coined the term 'transvestite'. The sheer visibility and apparent decency of the Committee's activities were a confirmation and legitimation of something that was supposed not to exist. Questionnaires began to appear at the end of the century. For all their quirky precision, they suggested, like the later Kinsey Report, that sexuality in all its forms and 'intermediate stages' was a normal part of everyday life. Hirschfeld's questionnaire of 1899 eventually grew into a 137-question invitation to recognize oneself as a homosexual (1903):

- Do you have a preference for particular smells?
- Do you have a tendency to write anonymous letters?
- What do you usually carry in your pockets (knives, powder-box, matches, photographs, etc.)?*

The Committee's humourless but memorable propaganda also gave a recognizable, public context to what might otherwise have been very lonely defences of gay love: Gustav Jaeger's *Die Entdeckung der Seele* (2nd edition, 1880), Otto de Joux's *Die Enterbten des Liebes-glückes* (1893) and *Die hellenische Liebe in der Gegenwart* (1897), and Ludwig Frey's *Der Eros und die Kunst* (1896).† It amplified the almost silent voices of the last 100 years: Hössli's *Eros*, or Symonds' privately printed essays, *A Problem in Greek Ethics* (1883) and *A Problem in Modern Ethics* (1891). It also helped to prepare the way for studies that went far beyond the pleas for law reform and pity, like Edward Carpenter's *The Intermediate Sex* (1908), Iwan Bloch's social-anthropological studies (from 1902), and Charles Leland's *The Alter-nate Sex, or The Female Intellect in Man, and the Masculine in Woman* (London and New York, 1904), which insisted on the bisexuality of all remarkable people.

Above all, the Committee helped homosexual rights to be seen as a cause that civilized people should support. By 1923, its petition had been signed by thousands of people, including Albert Einstein, Sigmund Freud, Hermann Hesse, Rainer Maria Rilke, Thomas and Heinrich Mann, and Arthur Schnitzler.

It would be easy to list the Committee's failures. Its main aim was the abolition of paragraph 175, which was not fully repealed until 1994, and its international presence remained largely academic. The British Society for the Study of Sex Psychology, founded by Edward Carpenter and Laurence Housman in 1914, was mostly a vehicle for

---

* Samples of Prime-Stevenson's questionnaire (*c.* 1908), based on Hirschfeld's, are given in Appendix II.
† 'The Discovery of the Soul'; 'The Disinherited of Love's Happiness'; 'Hellenic Love in the Present'; 'Eros and Art'.

talks and publications, though it also functioned as a correspondence club for gay intellectuals and as an official front for George Ives's secret Order of Chaeronea (p. 168). The only American equivalent was the Society for Human Rights created by Henry Gerber in Chicago in 1924. It was broken up by the police after a few months.

Worst of all, to Hirschfeld's regret, the movement was never able to exploit its solidarity with women. This was a recurrent theme in early gay rights. Ulrichs had campaigned for the rights of women and unmarried mothers. The Swiss sexologist and entomologist, Auguste-Henri Forel, who called for a law allowing homosexual men to marry, also demanded complete equality of the sexes and a recognition that housework was just as important as paid work (in *Die sexuelle Frage*, 1905). The suffragette Johanna Elberskirchen published a pamphlet on 'The Love of the Third Sex' under the slogan, 'No Degeneration. No Guilt' (1904). But as the feminist Anna Rüling pointed out in a speech to the Committee in 1904, although 'the women's movement would not be where it is today' 'without the active support of the Uranian women', it was unwilling to attract more opprobrium than it already had to cope with. In Britain, too, the suffrage movement, which had roots in social purity campaigns, was inclined to oppose any form of illicit sexuality.

Anna Rüling also suggested that lesbians had suffered from the lack of anti-lesbian legislation: men could attack a well-defined law, women could only struggle with the hydra of prejudice. This alone does not explain why lesbian activism is almost totally confined to the later 20th century. Men with university degrees, a private income and an office were better able to found institutes and committees. Women contributed to the debate under men's umbrellas and tended to be even more respectably technical than the men. Edith Lees (Mrs Havelock Ellis) saw 'the invert' who avoids 'cheap physical expression' as the natural ally of the eugenicist. Stella Browne, who was also active in the British Society for the Study of Sex Psychology, called for social change, but on the grounds that 'female perversion' was an artificial result of oppression: women in a free society would naturally be heterosexual. Even the book that finally gave a face to lesbian rights

– Radclyffe Hall's *The Well of Loneliness* (published and prosecuted in 1928) – now seems remarkably tentative and apologetic.*

Despite its disappointments, and considering the almost total silence that preceded it, Hirschfeld's Committee was an amazing accomplishment. In the end, the fatal blow was struck, not by internal wrangling but by scandals and politics. Sordid attacks on the anti-imperialist diplomat Prince Philipp zu Eulenburg – one of the Kaiser's closest advisers – culminated in a series of embarrassing trials (1907–9). Hirschfeld's 'scientific' testimony looked ridiculous along-side the sensational revelations of high-ranking military officials prancing about in tutus and weeping into handkerchiefs. Hirschfeld further damaged his reputation by changing his diagnosis in a later trial to support a journalist, Maximilian Harden, who had been favourable to the Committee.

The trials and attempted cover-ups were perceived as a national humiliation and introduced the whole western world to the hilarious new German word, *'Homosexualität'*. Eulenburg's enemies in the Bismarck camp took full advantage. The subsequent replacement of doves with hawks in the Kaiser's entourage was later cited as a cause of the First World War.

The next time the German Parliament debated paragraph 175, in 1909, the official proposal was to increase the penalties and to crimi-nalize lesbian acts as well.

Hirschfeld's Committee made a partial recovery after the war. In 1919, Hirschfeld created his Institute for Sexual Research and spent much of his remaining sixteen years lecturing in Europe, America and Asia. He died in Nice in 1935, two years after the Nazis destroyed his Institute and burned his library.

The sinister imbeciles who thought that they were eradicating the work of a Jewish homosexual were of course deluded. Hirschfeld and

---

* The first national lesbian organization was 'The Daughters of Bilitis' (founded San Francisco, 1955), though women also played a role in the predominantly male Mattachine Society (founded Los Angeles, 1951). The only earlier sign of organized lesbian resistance is an isolated incident mentioned by Havelock Ellis: 'In a Spanish prison, some years ago [1890s?], when a new governor endeavored to reform the homosexual manners of the women, the latter made his post so uncomfortable that he was compelled to resign.'

his Committee had encouraged and recorded one of the most sudden and prolific flowerings of writing and debate on any single topic since the Reformation. After Hirschfeld, it was easier to imagine a society that might one day find hatred stranger than any kind of love and even fail to understand what all the fuss had been about. On the other hand, perhaps they simply made homosexuality look more exotic than ever. Pessimists could argue that rational agitation for reform only created more excuses for repression.

Hirschfeld himself might have tried to measure success by asking if his patient, the young lieutenant who killed himself in 1895, would have been less likely to do so a hundred years later. According to twelve different studies conducted in Europe and America between 1978 and 2000, young gays and lesbians are at least twice as likely as young heterosexuals to make a serious attempt at suicide. The experience of being gay might have changed much less than the history of the gay rights movement would suggest. Changes in etiquette are easily confused with changes in attitude. A hundred years on, the young lieutenant might still have killed himself, but the mourners at his funeral might have felt more at liberty to express their sympathy.

Part Three

8

Fairy Tales

Walking aimlessly, he came to the door of the house. He crossed the hall, climbed the stairs and took refuge in his room: he neither wanted to see nor to be seen. He opened the bookcase and closed it again at once, saying, 'So many books, and not a single line for me!'

Joseph Méry, *Monsieur Auguste* (1859)

I take this opportunity to mention the strange prejudice of Uranists regarding novelists or poets who, in whatever fashion, touch on the subject of love between men. The modern Uranist is immediately convinced that the writer has Uranist tendencies. [. . .] Uranists are usually incapable of taking a cold, objective view of anything that relates to their nature.

Albert Moll, *Die conträre Sexualempfindung* (1891)

THE LAST PART OF this book is an attempt to dispel an impression that the first parts have created: that homosexuality was practically absent from the rest of society and that everything would have gone on in much the same manner if men and women had never fallen in love with people of their own sex.

In the early 20th century, no one could plausibly claim (though many did, implausibly) that homosexuality had little or no effect on the supposedly normal order of things. But to say that it was a constant and vital influence was to invite disagreement and provoke disbelief. Some writers pointed to heroes of civilization like Socrates and Michelangelo and pleaded for tolerance on the grounds of discernible profit to the majority. This, however, drew attention to all the heroes who were clearly not homosexual and left the average non-genius in an uncomfortable position. Others, like Hans Blüher in *Die Rolle der Erotik in der männlichen Gesellschaft* (1917), claimed that homosexuality is not only natural but also the basis of all human society. This might have been true on a vast, theoretical plane, but it had little connection with daily life. Both arguments tended to ignore women altogether.

The argumentative approach turns facts into battlefields and has the same effect on historical evidence that armies have on populations: it creates political factions, diminishes individuals, invites retaliation instead of correction, and takes up a lot of space. The main aim of the following three chapters is mercantile rather than militant – to present the available evidence for a vital gay presence in three areas: literature, religion, and something more diffuse that might be called the art of living in the modern world.

*

UNTIL THE 1880s, very few modern literary works mentioned homosexuality directly. Even at the turn of the century, when 'Decadent' literature made the subject fashionable, only a small number of living faces lurked among the waxwork villains and perverts. A novel by Gautier and several novels by Balzac are sometimes made to represent the views of a whole period, but they are so unusual that their main role in a social history of homosexuality should be to show what was missing elsewhere.

Gautier's *Mademoiselle de Maupin, double amour* was published in 1835–6 when Gautier was twenty-four. The first volume (1835) ended with one of the first descriptions of a gay man coming out to himself and to a friend. D'Albert later discovers that his beloved 'Théodore' is a woman, but not until the second volume.

> 'I no longer know who I am, nor what other people are. [. . .] For a long time I have been listening to myself and observing attentively.

[. . .] And at last I have discovered the terrible truth . . . Silvio, I'm in love . . . No! I shall never be able to tell you . . . I'm in love with a man!'

The lesbian aspects of the novel were just as remarkable. Madeleine de Maupin's transvestism is logical rather than pathological: she wants to know what men say about women behind their backs and to find a more interesting pastime than 'pushing a bit of wool through the holes of a canvas ten million times'. Her own sexual feelings for women are adult, satisfying and sane.

Balzac's novels (1830s and 1840s) are even more extraordinary. *La Comédie Humaine* now looks like a whole prehistoric civilization where none was thought to exist. In Balzac, homosexual love takes several different forms. It is not explained away as depravity or madness. Even now, most gay characters carry psychological sandwich boards advertising their sexuality to the exclusion of all other traits. But Balzac's characters are never reduced to their sexual peculiarity. Their love, even when satisfied, does not inevitably lead to punishment and death. In Vautrin and Cousin Pons, homosexual love is not only a possible source of happiness, it is actually a redeeming feature.

Balzac and Gautier were practically unique in published literature for several decades. Towards the end of the 19th century, with the rise of literary realism and the resulting scramble for new subjects, references to homosexuality became more frequent, but the increase is negligible compared to the increase in the total number of books published.

In the present state of research, only about fifty works of western literature in the 19th century can be said to treat the subject of male homosexuality more or less openly. This figure includes several works that were known only later, like Melville's *Billy Budd* (published in 1924), or that treated the subject incidentally or imperceptibly. Parts of Rimbaud's *Une Saison en Enfer* were construed as a homosexual drama only by those who knew about his affair with Verlaine. Before the medicalization of the subject, nearly every recognizably homosexual male character was a type rather than a person who happened to be homosexual. George Sand's weedy Sylvinet in *La Petite Fadette* (1849) and Thomas Hardy's 'slack-twisted, slim-looking maphrotight fool', Christian Cantle, in *The Return of the Native* (1878) suffer from arrested development and are non-heterosexual rather than positively homosexual. Sand herself was not quite the sexual pioneer of literary legend. In *Histoire de ma vie*, she described her horror at discovering that certain paragons of 'ideal friendship' were in reality examples of 'insane or sickly deviance'. 'I was filled with disgust and saddened when I fully understood the tale of Achilles and Patroclus, Harmodius and Aristogiton.'

Most references went unnoticed in any case. Stendhal's notes for his unfinished novel *Lucien Leuwen* (1834–6) show him covering his tracks almost as soon as he conceives the character of Lord Link:

> Milord Link is a *Bishop of Clogher*, but don't say so. Milord Link is in exile from England and has four or five apartments in Montvallier, where he prefers to live because he is *too well known and discredited elsewhere*. But don't state the reason.

Even Balzac's descriptions were subtle enough to be fully appreciated only by a few. In 1891, in 'The Decay of Lying', Oscar Wilde was able to describe the death of Vautrin's lover Lucien de Rubempré as 'one of the greatest tragedies of my life' without giving too much away. *Le Père Goriot* was a set text in British schools for most of the 20th century, but the nature of Vautrin's attraction to his young protégé Eugène de Rastignac was as obscure to most readers (including this one) as it was to the character himself:

> 'Monsieur is siding with Collin', she replied, scrutinizing the student with an expression of venomous curiosity. 'And it's not hard to understand why.'
>
> Hearing this, Eugène sprang forward as if to pounce on the old maid and strangle her. Her treacherous meaning was written on her face and in that instant it cast a terrible light in his soul.

Lesbianism was mentioned far more frequently. But most 'lesbian' literature, like the fashionable paintings of sapphists lounging about in boudoirs, harems and Turkish baths, was created by men for male consumption. One of the best-known accounts of a physical lesbian relationship was Diderot's *La Religieuse*, written in 1760. But his tale of an astoundingly innocent novice preyed upon by a lusting Mother

Superior is more remarkable as an early realist novel than as a psychological study. The theme itself was an 18th-century commonplace. Like several other men who wrote about lesbians, Diderot was worried about the possible proclivities of his mistress and was not well placed to see beyond the clichés.

Serious depictions of lesbian love based on personal experience or careful thought were extremely rare. George Sand, whose friendship with the actress Marie Dorval was a common source of gossip, resorted to male clichés. In *Lélia* (1833), lesbianism was associated with misanthropy, incest and the dangerous sophistication of an ageing civilization. The daring scene of lesbian love between Lélia and her sister Pulchérie, like Coleridge's 'Christabel' (1797) and Baudelaire's 'Femmes damnées' (1857), came with the moral guarantee of guilt and wickedness (Pulchérie is 'the world's most famous courtesan'):

> 'I trembled as I kissed your arm. Then you opened your eyes and their penetrating gaze filled me with an unknown sense of shame. I turned away as though I had committed a guilty act. And yet, Lélia, no impure thought had entered my mind. How could that be? I knew nothing. Nature and God, my creator and master, were giving me my first lesson in love.'

Homosexuality in most literary works was an affliction rather than a virtue, a lack of something rather than a positive attribute. In English literature, it was confined almost entirely to school stories, where it signified either innocent enthusiasm or puerile depravity. The passion usually ended with the death of one of the friends or with the awakening of adult sensibility and the discovery of girls. The bestselling *Eric, or Little by Little* (1858) by the schoolmaster Frederic William Farrar – known to Swinburne as 'Dr Thwackum of Marlborough' – was deemed suspiciously effeminate by *The Saturday Review*: 'to the infinite indignation of all English readers, [the boys] occasionally kiss each other (principally however when they are *in articulo mortis* [at the point of death]) exchanging moreover such endearments as "dear fellow" and the like'. But even *Eric* drew a line between beastliness and passion. Eric and Edwin may '[squeeze] each other's hands, and [look] into each other's faces', but any boy who oversteps the mark is condemned as a servant of the Devil and a spreader of 'moral turpitude'. E. M. Forster deliberately reversed this cliché when he made Maurice's coming-of-age consist of embracing rather than shedding his homosexuality.

The later depiction of obviously homosexual characters was almost always defined by a specific concern – the sorry state of relations between men and women, the 'decadence' of the modern world, the scandal of prostitution or, later, the rise of a homosexual rights movement. Most novels on the subject that appeared in Britain and America were translations and could safely be regarded as studies of the moral climate in *other* countries. Current affairs were always more in evidence than psychology. In the 1880s and 1890s, several novels tackled the subject of sodomy and bullying in the French armed forces. The notorious case of Alice Mitchell (Memphis, 1892), who cut her lover's throat, produced a spate of tales about murderous lesbians. Many novels, by men and women, were inspired by fear of women's emancipation. Typically, the title character of Rhoda Broughton's *Dear Faustina* (London and Leipzig, 1897) is a home-destroying kidnapper of decent young girls. She visits slums, complains about the conditions of the workers, and has friends with 'wildly cropped grizzled hair and super-manly coats and waistcoats'. Her cutlery is never clean and she eats at the Aerated Bread Company instead of at a proper dinner table. Lesbianism, like socialism, atheism and vegetarianism, is a symptom rather than a state of mind.

These ideological caricatures were actually a sign of progress. Increasingly, fictional lesbians wore clothes and spent less time with their own bodies. Their Romantic sisters gazed at themselves in mirrors, stared out to sea, anticipated eternal damnation and, for an obscure reason, gnawed the bark of young trees. The *fin-de-siècle* lesbian was educated at a boarding-school or a convent. She was frighteningly self-possessed, wore dark colours, read novels, smoked cigars, injected morphine or inhaled ether, suffered from excess hair except on the head, spent too much time in conditions suitable for tropical plants, and was prone to horrible diseases. But at least, by the end of the century, she had developed other interests and had a social life.

*

A SIMPLE CHRONOLOGICAL list of poems and novels in which homo-sexuality was mentioned would suggest that a specifically homosexual category of literature emerged in the last two decades of the 19th century. But this was something quite different from what we now think of as gay literature.

First, the rise of the subject should be set against its continual repression. Balzac was often cited as the author of a melodramatic work about a lesbian, *La Fille aux yeux d'or* (1834–5), but his male homosexuals were ignored until the 1960s. A longer list could be drawn up of deliberately *non*-homosexual works: translations of classical and modern texts in which the boy-lover was changed into a girl (as in the first French translations of Whitman's *Leaves of Grass*); poems, novels and plays in which Sappho was depicted as the unhappy lover of a man. Countless poems were expurgated. A line in Goethe's famous song 'An den Mond' went through a typical series of changes like a stain through several washes: 'Blessed he who [. . .] holds a man to his breast'. Goethe changed 'man' to 'friend'; Charlotte von Stein changed the line to 'who keeps his soul pure'; and finally the whole stanza was expunged from the anthology, *Göthe als Lyriker* (1821).

Second, most books that treated the subject openly were also openly hostile. Tales of sodomy in 'investigative' works like *City Crimes, or Life in New York and Boston* (1849), by 'Greenhorn' (George Thompson), or *Sodom in Union Square, or Revelations of the Doings in Fourteenth Street*, 'by an ex-Police Captain' (1879), were obviously not supposed to be impartial. In the 1890s and 1900s, the commonest word in titles of novels on homosexuality is 'vice'. The best-known studies advertised themselves as warnings. Adolphe Belot's novel, *Mademoiselle Giraud, ma femme* (1870; US translation, 1891), about a furiously frigid lesbian, carried a stern preface by Émile Zola:

> Cease to hide this book; place it on all your tables, as our fathers placed the rods with which they chastised their children. And, if you have daughters, let your wife read this book before she separates herself from those dear creatures to send them away to school.

Zola's own male homosexual characters – Maxime in *La Curée* (1871) and Hyacinthe in *Paris* (1898) – were analysed as the human waste products of a sick society.

Most cautionary novels were addressed to husbands and fathers. Alfred Cohen's *A Marriage Below Zero* (New York, 1889) was a warning to the other sex. Elsie Bouverie ('Emma Bovary' with a twist) realizes too late that her husband Arthur, who wore rouge at their wedding, is a lover of men: 'As I look back now I wonder how I could have been so dense. It appears to me now that the veriest blockhead could have grasped the situation.'

Anyone, let alone a blockhead, might have failed to grasp the point of the pioneering *Monsieur Auguste* (1859) by Dumas's collaborator Joseph Méry. Addressing himself to prospective fathers-in-law, Méry claimed to be filling a gap in literature: of all the 'perverse, odious, eccentric or deadly individuals' described by novelists and playwrights, only one had escaped attention. Méry's hero was a male homosexual. But the author had 'preferred to commit the sin of obscurity rather than shed too much light', and as one reviewer pointed out, 'you have to concentrate very hard to find out what he is'. The fair-haired, falsetto-voiced painter Auguste, who has the blood of a water-lily in his veins, strangely refuses to marry Louise, who has a dowry of 500,000 francs. Readers who knew what Antinous, Girodet, Naples and a fondness for diluted champagne had in common would have understood. Everyone else would have read a tedious tale in which everything seemed to be significant without signifying very much.

Moral condemnation in these novels should not be taken too seriously. The subject of homosexuality, when it was broached, remained extremely popular with readers, and authors were generally rewarded for their daring. A book called *Les Intrigues de Molière* (1688), in which Molière was said to have been the lover of his pupil and principal actor, was republished by three different 19th-century editors before 1877. Sales of Dr Tardieu's forensic handbook on sex crimes and 'pederasts' (1857) would have thrilled a novelist. Méry's *Monsieur Auguste* had a new edition in 1860 and was republished in a cheap paperback series in 1867. Abel Botelho's *O Barão de Lavos* (Oporto, 1891) was the tale of a degenerate aristocratic 'pederast' and a beginner's guide to gay Lisbon: it sold out in two weeks and was translated into Spanish in 1907, making it one of the first modern works with a clearly homosexual subject to appear in Spain. In 1908, a French 'documentary and anecdotal' study of German homosexuality was reprinted nineteen times in three months. In 1909, Frederick Rolfe saw illustrated books about homosexual love as a lucrative alternative to gondoliering: 'Such books, privately published in Paris or Antwerp at £1 would sell like blazes.'

The growing prevalence of the subject in European and American literature was not primarily a result of moral campaigns or anxiety about the decline of standards. Nor, of course, was it a result of greater tolerance. Foucault's perception that even censorship was a way of generating 'discourse' about sex applies to novels as well as to medical works.

By the end of the 19th century, novelists had found new ways to write safely about homosexuality. Medical theories not only disseminated information, they also made the subject intellectually respectable. Case studies supplied ready-made characters whose every physical trait – dress, figure, gait and smell – exactly matched the inner self. 'Inversion' was a naturally dramatic subject: love against the law, decent people forced to live like criminals, individuals at odds with their own upbringing. It generated that most precious commodity: new plots. All the old tales of amorous misunderstanding could be retold with a different punchline. Some plots were so confused that the claim to be elucidating an obscure area of life looked extremely dubious. In *Weiberbeute* by 'Luz Frauman' (Budapest, 1901), a frustrated lesbian hypnotizes her girlish stepson into thinking himself a woman. She then induces a phantom pregnancy in him, fosters her own son on him and convinces him that he has given birth to a girl. Her death-bed confession is dismissed by the pseudo-mother as delirium. In Armand Dubarry's *Les Invertis* (1906), a homosexual Count woos his bride's lover by promising not to deflower the bride. The bride, meanwhile, is pursued by the Count's lesbian sister. This creates some original situations: a husband upset by the infidelity of his wife's lover; the adulterous couple fleeing to a life of respectability.

Many novels contained long 'scientific' passages to justify the titillation. Several different novelists copied Dr Tardieu's description of a male prostitute almost word for word. Admitting scientific principles to a work of villainy and virtue should logically have created difficulties, but notions of congenital inversion were rarely allowed to exonerate the 'perverts'. Almost a quarter of Dubarry's 'psychopathological novel' is taken up with a summary of the medical literature, but a higher power decides the fate of the evil pair: at the end of the novel, the Count and his sister are swept away by an avalanche in the Alps and, while clinging to a tree, are torn to shreds by eagles.

Joséphin Péladan's *La Gynandre* (1891), in which the androgyne Tammuz marries all the lesbians of Paris to replicas of himself and forces them to worship a giant phallus to the accompaniment of the 'Ride of the Valkyries', shows how little this literature had to with daily life, and how ripe it was for satire.

*

MANY THESE BOOKS were not really about homosexuality at all. Some gay writers – Melville, Whitman, Stoddard, Verlaine, Eekhoud and Kuzmin – returned to the subject again and again, but without trumpeting their intentions. Writers who broached the subject openly tended to treat homosexuality as a minor theme. In the same year that he wrote *Monsieur Auguste* (1859), Joseph Méry published ten other works, none of which had anything to do with homosexuality. George Thompson's underworld dragnet turned up thieves, conmen and gangsters as well as sodomites and lesbians. For Adolphe Belot, 'Miss Giraud, My Wife' was just one exotic bloom in a vast flower-bed of sex and crime: '500 Women for One Man', 'The Way of a Man with a Maid', 'The Mouth of Madame X***', 'The Parricide', 'The Stranglers', etc.

Perhaps the true ancestors of modern gay literature are not to be found in *belles lettres* at all but in homosexual pornography, where simple aims erased the clichés and injected some rudimentary realism and even a sense of humour.

Homosexual pornography was far more prevalent than it seems. Unfortunately, for obvious reasons, much of it is missing from library catalogues. Works like *Enthüllungen eines garçon d'hôtel* (Berlin, 1892), *Die Liebesfahrt eines Päderasten* (Nuremberg, 1908) or *Tagebuch eines Berliner Jungen* (date unknown)* survive only as titles in lists drawn up by the German police.

---

* 'Revelations of a Bellhop'; 'The Amorous Journey of a Pederast'; 'Diary of a Young Berliner'.

Pornographic books were as cosmopolitan as some of their readers. *The Power of Mesmerism. A Highly Erotic Narrative* (1891), supposedly printed in Moscow 'for the Nihilists', was probably published in Brussels and smuggled across the Channel. A copy of *Die Päderasten: Distraction de l'équipage* (1903),* in which two bored sailors called Jack and Bob explore each other's bodies with surgical precision, was rediscovered in Stockholm. Most large cities had secret distribution centres. A copy of the 1934 *Don Leon* (p. 184) – a limited edition published for subscribers in London – was stamped in blue ink on the title page, 'Palais Royal Beaujolais Library, Paris. NOT TO BE TAKEN INTO ENGLAND', and later bought in Dublin. In 1892, the US Post Office Department (as it was then called) was destroying French lesbian novels by the ton.

The audience for homosexual pornography was not necessarily homosexual. Lesbian scenes of vampirical women and their blushing victims were relatively common, but they catered to a male market. As Dr Hippolyte Homo (*sic*) discovered in 1872 in a study of prostitution in Château-Gontier, young men were 'avid for the spectacle of female homosexuality'.

In the simple, all-embracing world of pornography, shades of sexuality were insignificant. Most male homosexual scenes were part of a comprehensive survey of sexual possibilities. The hero of *The Power of Mesmerism* (1891) uses his power on men and women alike. The sexual education of Charlie Roberts in *The Romance of Lust, or Early Experiences* (4 vols, London, 1873–6) leaves no permutation untested and is still selling well in the 21st century.

The main difference between these pragmatic texts and their upmarket, moralizing equivalents is that the pornographic characters usually enjoyed themselves.† Genitals were the leitmotif and orgasm

---

* 'The Pederasts: A Crew's Diversion'.
† This is what distinguishes *Teleny* (1893; latest editions, 1986 and 1995), falsely attributed to 'Oscar Wilde and others', from other pornographic novels. *Teleny* has more to do with self-loathing than sex. It supports all the most humiliating theories. The narrator, who falls in love with a Hungarian pianist (Teleny), has hated women ever since discovering that they have digestive systems. He rapes a female servant in an attempt to become 'normal', but his first truly titillating experience is an agonizing train-ride during which he tries to postpone a visit to the toilet. Everything is fated to end badly. ('It was Kismet, as the Turks say.') Teleny stabs himself after being

the holy grail. Many of them also offered practical advice. *The Sins of the Cities of the Plain, or The Recollections of a Mary-Ann* (London, 1881) was typically cheerful and instructive:

> The writer of these notes was walking through Leicester Square one sunny afternoon, last November, when his attention was particularly taken by an effeminate, but very good-looking young fellow, who was walking in front of him, looking in shop windows from time to time, and now and then looking around as if to attract attention.
>
> Dressed in tight-fitting clothes, which set off his Adonis-like figure to the best advantage, especially about what snobs call the fork of his trousers, where evidently he was favoured by nature by a very extraordinary development of the male appendage [etc.]

Along with some pseudo-scholarly essays on sodomy and tribadism, *The Sins of the Cities of the Plain* gave information about London establishments, with their hours, rates and services, including a club off Portland Place run by a Mr Inslip – 'a rather suggestive name, you may think, considering the practices of the members of his club'. The main point however was to describe the jolly adventures of the 'mary-ann':

> 'You seem a fine figure, and so evidently well hung that I had quite a fancy to satisfy my curiousity [*sic*] about it. Is it real or made up for show?' I asked.
>
> 'As real as my face, sir, and a great deal prettier. Did you ever see a finer tosser in your life?' he replied, opening his trousers and exposing a tremendous prick, which was already in a half-standing state. 'It's my only fortune, sir; but it really provides for all I want, and often introduces me to the best of society, ladies as well as gentlemen. There isn't a girl about Leicester Square but what would like to have me for her man, but I did find it more to my interest not to waste my strength on women; the pederastic game pays so well, and is quite as enjoyable.'

*

---

found copulating with the narrator's mother: 'Though his face was covered with his hands, it was Tèleny. There was no mistake about it.'

GIVEN THE PREPONDERANCE of smut and prudishness, it is not surprising that when Méry's 'Monsieur Auguste' looks for something sympathetic to read, he finds the cupboard bare. Many of the texts that have since been exhumed were unknown to readers at the time. Even Verlaine, in 1888, saw nothing in modern literature but Balzac, Goethe, the 'ridiculous' and 'superficial' Joseph Méry and Henri d'Argis, whose novel, *Sodome*, he was prefacing. In 1914, Magnus Hirschfeld estimated that 75 per cent of homosexual men and women had never read a book about homosexuality.

This was not just a result of State censorship. Legal intervention was relatively rare, which, to judge by the fame of banned works like Baudelaire's *Les Fleurs du Mal* or Radclyffe Hall's *The Well of Loneliness*, was not necessarily a boon for homosexual literature. Eekhoud's *Escal-Vigor* (Paris, 1899), in which two noble lovers in the Hamlet-esque castle of Escal-Vigor (a partial anagram of 'Oscar Wilde') are murdered by a mob of local women, was banned in 1900, then translated into German and English (as *Strange Love*). Most gay novels never had the chance to be prosecuted. When Jacob Israël de Haan published his tale of two students, *Pijpelijntjes* (Amsterdam, 1904), his fiancée and the model for the main character, Dr Arnold Aletrino, who had defended Uranists at a medical conference, bought all the copies they could find and destroyed them.

Many gay writers repressed their own work. Georges Eekhoud asked his Belgian publisher to print no more than 200 copies of *Le Cycle patibulaire* (1892), to charge a high price, not to advertise it and not to display it in bookstores. For *Imre* (1906) – one of the first truly happy novels of gay love (p. 232) – Edward Prime-Stevenson used an obscure press in Naples whose typesetters could not read English. When the Scottish-German anarchist John Henry Mackay issued the first two books of his series on 'nameless love' in 1906, buyers were required to give their names and addresses and to sign a statement saying that they were disinterested 'lovers of art'.

Self-censorship went hand in hand with official censorship. The wretched end of most homosexual heroes was partly a precaution. Even in 1960, E. M. Forster felt that the relatively happy ending of *Maurice* condemned it to oblivion: 'If it ended unhappily, with a lad dangling from a noose or with a suicide pact, all would be well, for there is no pornography or seduction of minors. But the lovers get away unpunished and consequently recommend crime.'

Almost every scene of homosexual passion took place in or near the grave. In *La Maison de la vieille* (1894) by Catulle Mendès, a male soprano removes his clothes and lies on his friend's cold body in an ecstasy of passion, hoping to revive the corpse: 'He licked his eyes, his neck, his arms, his hands, his belly and his hips. [. . .] And, trying to double his weight, he crushed him with his body to make him rebound under the pressure [. . .].' It was effectively the first description in modern literature of a male homosexual orgasm, veiled in pathos and futility. In D. H. Lawrence's *The Prussian Officer*, written in 1913, the orderly and the officer lie together unclothed only on the mortuary slab. In Howard Sturgis's *Tim: A Story of Eton* (1891), Tim is allowed to see his beloved boyfriend Carol only when he is completely incapacitated and dying. Dickens' closest approach to a gay couple – Eugene and Mortimer in *Our Mutual Friend* – enjoy an unusually long death scene:

> 'Touch my face with yours, in case I should not hold out till you come back. I love you, Mortimer. Don't be uneasy for me while you are gone. If my dear brave girl will take me, I feel persuaded that I shall live long enough to be married, dear fellow.'
>
> Miss Jenny gave up altogether on this parting taking place between the friends [. . .]

Characters paid a heavy price for any episode of homosexual love. *Sodome* (1888) by Henri d'Argis had a preface by Verlaine, which was a way of advertising it to gay readers. They would have found a rare love scene – a visit to a mine followed by a soaping session in the pithead showers – but they would also have seen the hero end his life as a masturbating lunatic. In *Noodlot* (1890),* by the Dutch novelist Louis Couperus, a gay man sabotages his friend's marriage but later has his head smashed to a pulp by the would-be husband, who receives a token two-year prison sentence.

This epidemic of quasi-necrophilia was not just an attempt to placate the censor. The sheer extent of the epidemic suggests some-

---

* 'Destiny', translated as *Footsteps of Fate* (London, 1891).

thing more than authorial discretion. In twelve European and American novels (1875–1901) in which the main character is depicted, often sympathetically, as an adult homosexual man, six die (disease, unrequited love and three suicides), two are murdered, one goes mad, one is cured by marriage and two end happily (one after six months in prison and emigration to the United States). The same analysis applied to twelve lesbian novels (1870–1905) gives the following toll: four die (murder, suicide, meningitis and aphrodisiac abuse), four go mad (two are drug addicts), one has a nervous breakdown, one is cured by a man and two find satisfaction (revenge on a man and drowning of a husband).

Compassionate authors were just as likely to make their heroes die in torment. Karl Heinrich Ulrichs, who was so dauntless in his pamphlets, was dismal in his fiction. 'Manor', in *Matrosengeschichte* (1885), told the story of a young man who is adored by the ghost of a dead sailor. He drives a stake into the dead sailor's heart, then dies of longing. Liane de Pougy's bestselling *roman à clé*, *Idylle saphique* (1901) celebrates her affair with Natalie Clifford Barney but ends in failure, ruin and remorse.

Even if all the writers of these books could easily be divided into gay and straight, it would still be hard to find a single explanation for the fated misery: prudence, self-punishment or realism. In 1999, when happy endings were less implausible and censors less active, the novelist Colm Tóibín confessed to 'an urge to have gay lives represented as tragic', though he felt that the urge should be 'repressed'.

Death-bed scenes in modern gay literature have roots that go far beyond the advent of AIDS. Gay tragedy is a tradition, not just a circumstantial feature. This is one of the clearest signs that 19th-century gay literature was not a parasitic sub-section of 'serious' literature. It had a discreet life of its own and was far more influential than it seems.

It is often said that the great elegies of English literature were written by men about men. Perhaps the implicit disapproval of society sustained the quest for other meanings and consolations. Tennyson's *In Memoriam* (1850) was criticized in *The Times* (probably by the father of Gerard Manley Hopkins) for using language that 'might be addressed with perfect propriety, and every assurance of a favourable reception, to [a] young lad[y] with melting blue eyes and a passion for novels'. *In Memoriam* was a favourite with many gay readers but also with the general Victorian public. Tennyson's passionate love for Arthur Hallam – which he significantly toned down in the 1870 edition – had the usual homosexual markers: Michelangelo, Shakespeare and Socrates; clasped hands, the kiss of life and the poet himself repeatedly described as a 'widow'. But it was also, necessarily, turned into a metaphor. It was not just that this love could more easily be expressed now that Hallam was dead, but also that death and caution cast their love into a wider sphere and connected it with 'the deep pulsations of the world':

> Strange friend, past, present, and to be;
> Loved deeplier, darklier understood;
> Behold, I dream a dream of good,
> And mingle all the world with thee. *(cxxix)*

It may also be that, as Balzac's Vautrin and Proust's Charlus suggest, strange lovers were better adapted to states of chaos and decay. Charlus cheerfully turns his townhouse into a military hospital, but this is not just a reference to the sudden availability of handsome foreigners in uniform. It also has to do with the sudden fragility of the normal state of affairs. Without gay poets, the poetic record of the First World War in English literature would be much smaller and more forgettable.

Eliot's *The Waste Land* (1922) was in part an elegy to his young friend Jean Verdenal, who died in the War – though Eliot threatened to sue the scholar who first suggested it in 1952 – but it was also a tragi-comic celebration of that makeshift culture that spanned the continents and the centuries and thrived among the ruins. Verlaine's homosexual Parsifal and his seductive choirboys, Tiresias 'in whom the two sexes meet', and Sappho all appear in the same central section of *The Waste Land* (vv. 202–21 and corresponding notes), along with one of those model cosmopolitans who helped to keep international trade and literature alive:

> Mr. Eugenides, the Smyrna merchant
> Unshaven, with a pocket full of currants
> C.i.f. London: documents at sight,

Asked me in demotic French
To luncheon at the Cannon Street Hotel
Followed by a weekend at the Metropole.

*   *   *

MOST OF THE BOOKS mentioned in the first part of this chapter are just the shopfront of a very large and miscellaneous store. Parts of this store are now almost inaccessible. References to homosexuality were carefully encrypted and are becoming less decipherable as time passes.

To understand, for instance, why a character in Walter Scott's *Kenilworth* is called 'the infractor of the Lex Julia', it was necessary to know that this was the later name of a Roman law of 149 BC that imposed a fine on homosexual male intercourse. In *Le Cousin Pons*, Balzac used hints like secret marks of authentication. In his thick German accent, Schmucke tells the young man who helps him to bury his beloved Pons, '*Che bardacherai mon bain afec doi!*', which is supposed to mean, 'Je partagerai mon pain avec toi!' ('I'll share my bread with you!') But 'bread' becomes 'bath', and 'share' turns into a non-existent verb based on 'bardache' ('passive pederast').

Poems were an especially good medium for secret messages. Certain forms had private connotations: the Renaissance sonnet, associated with Shakespeare, or the Persian ghazel, associated with Háfiz. Heine even proposed '*ghaselig*' as a new word for 'pederast'. Verlaine and Renée Vivien used lines of thirteen syllables (the so-called *vers saphique*) for homosexual subjects. In poems to Rimbaud, Verlaine made all the rhymes feminine or placed the tercets above the quatrains – an arrangement called the '*sonnet inverti*' or, as Huysmans knowingly put it, the 'arse-in-the-air' sonnet.

In any genre, received ideas about sodomites and tribades could be used as a kind of code. Most of these notions were either incomprehensible or insulting enough to show that the author was not an apologist for vice. References to corrupt diplomats, a fondness for stable lads and grooms, beating up servants (see p. 90), destroying flowers, parting one's hair in the middle, or suffering from muscular spasms could all be signs of homosexuality. Edmond de Goncourt's

Georges Selwyn in *La Faustin* (1882) has a curious illness that causes him to crush any delicate, precious object that he holds in his hand, just as Dr Lombroso claimed to be able to detect lesbians by 'the continual, convulsive contraction of their hands'. These clichés had a long life. Virginia Woolf's Julia Craye was still behaving like a 19th-century lesbian in 1928: 'She crushed [the carnation], Fanny felt, voluptuously in her smooth veined hands.' 'What was odd in her, and perhaps in her brother, too, was that this crush and grasp of the finger was combined with a perpetual frustration.'

The commonest ruse was to alter the apparent sex of a character. A surprising amount of homosexual passion was portrayed by means of this simple device. The male objects of love in *Mademoiselle de Maupin*, Fenimore Cooper's *Jack Tier* (1850) or Rolfe's *The Desire and Pursuit of the Whole* (1909) may turn out to be female but, as far as emotional realities are concerned, this is a mere technicality.

Byron's *Lara* (1814) was the best-known and most powerful example of gender deception. As a teenager, André Gide found the first canto 'disturbingly interesting' and almost blamed it for his own peculiar feelings: 'the charm and the danger of these books is that one identifies oneself too closely with the hero and absorbs his passions'. By the time the luscious page Kaled is revealed to be a woman ('In baring to revive that lifeless breast, / Its grief seem'd ended, but the sex confess'd'), it is too late: the reader has had a true taste of homosexual passion. Even then, 'Kaled' keeps the secret of their love. 'Why did she love him? Curious fool! – be still – / Is human love the growth of human will?'

The increasingly common perception that biological sex was distinct from psychological gender made it possible to evoke this virtual homosexuality without changing the character's sex. In Rachilde's witty novel, *Monsieur Vénus* (1884), published when she was twenty-four, the amazonian Raoule ('the Christopher Columbus of modern love') seduces Jacques, who has the body of a girl and the soul of a woman. He is in effect a male lesbian and his seducer a female sodomite. In Howard Sturgis's *Belchamber* (1904), the puny Lord Charmington, known as 'Sainty', is as homosexual as it is possible to be without actually being gay.

A more risky device consisted of changing the sex of the author.

'Michael Field' was the joint pen-name of Katherine Bradley and her niece Edith Cooper, who, for thirty-five years, lived together 'the delicious adventure of the stranger nature'. Their love poems were well received until the author was discovered to be two women. Marc-André Raffalovich used a female persona for some of his early poems, *Cyril and Lionel* (1884), which allowed him to be quite explicit. But it did not prevent reviewers, including Oscar Wilde, from finding the poems 'unhealthy':

> Shall I never feel his mouth
> (Scarlet show the lips I love)
> Near as blossoms of the south,
> Blooms I kiss through scented hours
> Crushing sweetness from the flowers [. . .]

These devices were exact rhetorical equivalents of the inconveniences suffered by gay men and women in daily life: communicating with nods and winks, changing the loved one's gender for the purposes of conversation, pretending to share jokes about sexual deviance. Allegory, by contrast, operated on a different plane: it could create a separate world in which whole dramas were acted out and even brought to satisfactory conclusions.

*

ALLEGORY IS STILL a contentious aspect of gay writing. To read a work of literature as an expression of heterosexual desire is literary criticism; to read it as an expression of homosexual desire is 'appropriation' or 'prurience'. Associating it with something in one's own love life is either 'conscripting a writer for the cause' (gay) or 'demonstrating its universal relevance' (straight).

Gay fables take several forms – deliberate, unconscious, and strictly unrelated to the topic but conducive to gay readings. Some were barely fables at all. Nineteenth-century tales of male bonding are still being rediscovered and read as expressions of gay love. Theodore Winthrop's adventurer John Brent (1862) is a Wild West pin-up, 'the Adonis of the copper-skins!': 'What a poem the fellow is! I wish I was an Indian myself for such a companion; or, better, a squaw, to be made love to by him'. Bayard Taylor's *Joseph and His Friend* (1870) described 'a new world' beyond the Rocky Mountains 'where men might love each other without fear of conventional society'. It was dedicated to those 'who believe in the truth and tenderness of man's love for man, as of man's love for woman' (this phrase was omitted from the British edition). Owen Wister's 'irresistibly handsome' but uncommunicative *Virginian, A Horseman of the Plains* (1902) becomes a bosom buddy of the narrator when they adopt a lonely hen called Em'ly.

Female equivalents are harder to find, though there is something of these pioneer idylls in stories told about the Ladies of Llangollen (Wales was sufficiently remote and misty in the English imagination), living in their 'fairy palace' and 'Arcadian bowers' (Anna Seward).

The more exotic the setting, the more literal the dream. Charles Warren Stoddard's 'In a Transport', from *South-Sea Idyls* [*sic*] (1873), becomes ever more flagrant as the ship approaches Tahiti and eventually turns into something like a gay *South Pacific*:

> Who took me in his arms and carried me the length of the cabin in three paces, at the imminent peril of my life? Thanaron! [a French officer cadet] Who admired Thanaron's gush of nature, and nearly squeezed the life out of him in the vain hope of making their joy known to him? Everybody else in the mess! [. . .] And we kept doing that sort of thing until I got very used to it, and by the time we sighted the green summits of Tahiti, my range of experience was so great that nothing could touch me further. It may not be that we were governed by the laws of ordinary seafarers.

The crucial point – in fiction and, for Stoddard himself when cruising about the South Sea islands – was the absence of ordinary laws. This is why children's literature was such fertile ground for fabulists. The land of lost content was also a dream of future bliss.

Books ostensibly aimed at young readers could be surprisingly bold. Any attempt to tear away the veil of innocence might have harmed the accuser more than the perpetrator. Even now, gay readings of children's classics are generally accepted only if the author's life provides some corroborative evidence. Horatio Alger's tales of city urchins are thought to reflect the author's inclinations because Alger, a Unitarian minister, was chased out of Brewster, Mass., for practising 'deeds that are too revolting to relate' on two boys. *Winnie the Pooh*, on the other hand, which Christopher Isherwood's sleazy Baron von Pregnitz clearly enjoys (p. 143), is too entwined with presexual bliss to be readily associated with adult sexuality.

The same could be said of Kenneth Grahame's *The Wind in the Willows* (1908), in which nearly all the female characters are either unseen or non-speaking. The bachelor animals keep house, move in with each other – an occasion usually marked with the gift of a dressing-gown – but retain their independence: 'the Mole recollected that animal-etiquette forbade any sort of comment on the sudden disappearance of one's friends at any moment, for any reason or no reason whatever'. In the world beyond, there is a prison – from which Mr Toad escapes as a shapely washerwoman – but beyond that, according to a seafaring rat with gold earrings, there is Marseille, Venice, Sicily, Constantinople and the Greek islands. The god of this cosy and sometimes frightening universe is the satyresque Piper at the Gates of Dawn with his 'shaggy limbs', 'splendid curves' and 'rippling muscles'. ' "Afraid?" murmured the Rat, his eyes shining with unutterable love. "Afraid! Of *Him*? O, never, never! And yet – and yet – O, Mole, I am afraid!" '

The prime example of gay myth-making in childish fiction is Howard Pyle's *The Merry Adventures of Robin Hood of Great Renown, in Nottinghamshire* (1883). Forster saw the Merry Men as a domestic Theban band. Pyle saw them as handsome playmates in an all-male paradise. Maid Marion is absent and rarely mentioned. The main role of women is to bleed poor Robin to death. (He dies in 'Little John's loving arms'.) The real 'woman' of the Band is Allan a Dale who has the face of a maiden and a voice that 'charmeth all men'.

In the Greenwood, meetings between men invariably take the same form: a) sexual insults; b) stabbing, bashing, wrestling, etc.; c) friendship, death or humiliation (the Sheriff of Nottingham is last seen fleeing with an arrow in his bottom). Robin's aggressive flirting is oddly relentless:

> 'By my life!' quoth Robin Hood, laughing, 'saw ye e'er such a pretty, mincing fellow?'
> 'Truly, his clothes have overmuch prettiness for my taste', quoth

Arthur a Bland; 'but, ne'ertheless, his shoulders are broad and his loins are narrow.'

'Nay, but I do like thy words, thou sweet, pretty thing', quoth Robin. [. . .] 'Prythee, tell me, sweet chuck, why wearest thou that dainty garb upon thy pretty body?'

The death-bed scene with Little John is one of the best-known elegies of popular gay fiction, but the Greenwood is otherwise a happy place and Robin as desirable a bedfellow as any traveller might hope to meet:

The holy friar [. . .] held the light over Robin and looked at him from top to toe; then he felt better pleased, for, instead of a rough, dirty-bearded fellow, he beheld as fresh and clean a lad as one could find in a week of Sundays; so, slipping off his clothes, he also huddled into the bed, where Robin, grunting and grumbling in his sleep, made room for him. Robin was more sound asleep, I wot, than he had been for many a day, else he would never have rested so quietly with one of the friar's sort so close beside him.

Childish tales like these, with their celebrations of youth, their bold initiations and passionate friendships, have become indistinct with time. Novels and poems on the passing of boyhood – especially those that referred to hazy notions of Ancient Greek 'boy love' – had many themes and images in common with what now looks like plainly paedophile literature. The popular association of paedophilia with homosexuality made these similarities all the more misleading, and the confusion has since been aggravated by an academic variety of sexual relativism. An anonymous pamphlet on *Boy-Worship* (1880), for instance, in which a man tries to pick up two boys in an Oxford bookshop, was described recently as 'a wholly serious defence of romantic pederasty as a mode of male romantic attachment'.

The recurring characteristics of English 'boy-worship' are self-deception, trickery and bad poetry. The usual process is seduction by flattery or gift. The aim in almost every case is sexual though the object of desire is prepubescent: 'The Greeks who worshipped lovely boys [. . .] Deplored that sprouting hair destroys / The beauty that it mars.' (S. E. Cottam) 'In trousers now my boy's arrayed, / And in my heart I'm sore afraid / This manliness will interfere / With what to me has been so dear – My hand upon his bare knee laid.' (F. E. Murray) The justification by reference to 'the Greeks' is entirely spurious.

Most of these poets – notably Rev. E. E. Bradford, John Gambril Nicholson and Rev. S. E. Cottam – knew one another. Cottam, Bradford and Bloxam, founder of *The Chameleon*, were all at Exeter College, Oxford. They exchanged poems and photographs, and recycled the same clichés. Classical allusions and University degrees gave a surface respectability to the stalking of underage flesh:

> Smart-looking lads are in my line;
> The lad that gives my boots a shine,
> The lad that works the lift below,
> The lad that's lettered *G.P.O.* [. . .]

> When travelling home by tram or train
> I meet a hundred boys again,
> Behind them on the 'bus I ride
> Or pace the platform by their side. (Nicholson)

> I sat in the rector's study one night,
>   While the rector's wife conversed with me:
> And she mentioned her child, her heart's delight,
>   A boy I soon longed to see [etc.] (Cottam)

Rev. Cottam, who could imagine that a six-year-old boy on the beach at Worthing was looking at him 'wistfully', was quite open about his hobby. One of his *New Sermons for a New Century* (1900), on the subject of Christ's expressive eyes and pregnant glances, paints a surprising picture of his off-duty activities in London:

I meet a young man on Highgate Hill, and from the signals of his uplifted face I know he has caught the eye of someone at a window. I look round to see whether I am right, and there is a girl waving her hand. I overtake a small telegraph boy in Fleet Street, he seems as pleased as Punch; I interview him, and find that someone has just given him a big cigar.

*

MOST GAY FABLES were not deliberate attempts to describe the experience of being gay or even to appeal to gay readers. They were fantasies and recreations. Most of them have a small emotional repertoire and simply abolish the sinister world beyond instead of coming to terms with it. Perhaps only one 19th-century writer used the allegorical mask to explore the outside world. He eventually produced such a large body of consciously homosexual literature that he can fairly be called the Aesop of 19th-century homosexuality.

Hans Christian Andersen wrote fairy tales, not because he wanted to make children happy (he did not especially like them), but because the fairy tale was a magic cloak that allowed him to be himself in public. As 'Mother Fairy Tale' points out in 'The Little Green Ones': 'One should call everything by its right name; and if one dares not do it as a usual thing, one can do it in a fairy tale.'

The blundering naivety that made Hans Christian Andersen something of an international nuisance was part of his professional persona. He may have irritated his hosts with his tactlessness and hypochondria, but he was no more innocent than his crafty tales. For the benefit of his public, he conducted happily unrequited affairs with women who were in no danger of succumbing to his old-maidish charms. The 'Swedish Nightingale', Jenny Lind, wrote to a friend in exasperation after years of suffering Andersen's innocuous attentions: 'I need support! A man! A real, *strong, healthy* man!' His erotic feelings were reserved for men. Letters to his friend Edvard Collin might have been used in a romantic fairy tale: 'I long for you; yes, at this moment I long for you as if you were a lovely Calabrian girl with dark eyes and a glance of passionate flame.'

As an effeminate youth, Andersen had been humiliated by his fellow workers at the cloth-mill in Odense: they stripped him bare to find out if he was really a man. As an adult, he lived in a state of anxious frustration. In Denmark, the death penalty for sexual offences was not abolished until 1866, and although the last death sentence was passed in 1751, this effective abolition only made juries more eager to convict. The Danish writer who translated Andersen's first novel into German was forced into exile by rumours of his own homosexuality.

The point of 'The Emperor's New Clothes' is not that the emperor is pompous and gullible but that he feels himself to be an impostor: the clothes are supposed to be 'invisible to every person who was not fit for the office he held'. Even at the height of Andersen's popularity, there was always a chance that someone would draw attention to the obvious, like the child in the crowd or, in the real world, the parodist who portrayed him in 1841 as 'the Grand Eunuch'.

Many of the *Fairy Tales* were written as parables of his predicament. His first two novels had contained some plainly homoerotic scenes of cuddling and clutching that might have struck him later on as too revealing. The *Fairy Tales* showed a more cautious approach. Many of them refer to embarrassments or calamities caused by unusual sexual preference:

– an earthworm 'liked the boys better' – 'but then it couldn't see, poor, miserable creature that it was'.
– a snail's parents try to find him a wife (not realizing, presumably, that snails are hermaphroditic).
– a snowman, built around a stove-brush, suffers a self-destructive passion for the stove, which he incorrectly assumes to be 'of the female sex'.
– a flighty butterfly fails to choose a bride among the flowers, turns into 'an old bachelor', is caught in a net and 'stuck on a pin in a case of curiosities'.
– a windmill, whose mind is a composite of man and woman ('they are two, and yet one'), stands on the hill of 'public opinion'; despite the view, the windmill sees nothing like itself.

Abnormal desire leads either to death (the melting snowman, the bachelor butterfly, the little mermaid, who serves the handsome prince as a page-boy but will never be his bride), or disgrace (the old German bachelors of Copenhagen with their 'eccentric' thoughts and habits, who are mocked by little boys and carry knives to defend themselves against frequent attacks).

There are many other, less obvious allegories – some containing private references to friends – like 'The Silver Shilling', which, though made of silver, is not legal tender: 'It must be terrible indeed to have a bad conscience [. . .] if I, who am quite innocent, can feel so badly just because people think I am guilty.' Andersen himself was able to find subtle erotic meanings in other people's work. He objected to a statue of himself that would have shown a boy leaning against his groin 'because it reminds me of old Socrates and young Alcibiades'. His own works were later interpreted as gay fables, often by people who had no idea that Andersen himself was gay.

Apart from their sheer quantity, the *Fairy Tales* are unlike most other gay fables in their deliberate appeal to like-minded readers. 'The Little Mermaid' was written in the year of the marriage of Andersen's friend Collin, who would certainly have recognized the watery transvestite who stands over the prince and his bride with a knife in its hand. Andersen offered his readers a kind of confirmation in 'The Naughty Boy' (Christmas 1835). It was a version of a peder-astic poem by Anacreon, adapted by Byron in *Hours of Idleness* and later by Frederick Rolfe in *Stories Toto Told Me*. During a storm, a beautiful, naked boy carrying a cross-bow knocks at an old poet's door. The poet sits the boy on his lap, dries him off and the drooping bow-string becomes taut again. The boy then shoots an arrow through the old man's heart. The story ends with a warning about 'wicked little Cupid', but the obvious question remains unanswered: with whom does the poet fall in love? Since no women are mentioned, the boy is the only candidate.

Almost all these stories follow the tragic path of most gay fables. Once, however, Andersen managed to negotiate a happy ending with his imagination. 'The Ugly Duckling' (1842–3) may have been inspired by memories of his trip to Italy and his sudden delight in Naples, where Vesuvius erupted and the pimps offered customers a choice of boys or girls.

Like many of Andersen's tales, 'The Ugly Duckling' loses its complex iridescence in adaptations. Ugliness is not the duckling's only problem. Like Andersen at the cloth-mill, it encounters hostility not because of its supposedly repulsive appearance but because its gender is in doubt. The old woman who adopts the duckling is significantly confused:

> 'Now I shall have duck's eggs if only it is not a drake! We must find out about that!'

So she took the duckling on trial for three weeks, but no eggs made their appearance.

The farmyard in which the duckling tries to make a life for itself is divided into male and female, with no room for anything else:

> The cat was the master of the house and the hen the mistress, and they always spoke of 'we and the world', for they thought that they represented the half of the world, and that quite the better half.
>
> The duckling thought there might be two opinions on the subject, but the hen would not hear of it.
>
> 'Can you lay eggs?' she asked.
>
> 'No!'
>
> 'Will you have the goodness to hold your tongue, then!'
>
> And the cat said, 'Can you arch your back, purr, or give off sparks?'
>
> 'No.'
>
> 'Then you had better keep your opinions to yourself when people of sense are speaking.'

The duckling's peculiarity turns out to be the key to its identity. It discovers itself, not by acquiring a mate, but by seeing its own reflection. It finds happiness, not in a secret love-nest, but in a whole society of migratory birds. It does not simply learn to live with its oddness, it enters a world in which its supposed anomaly is a mark of its superiority. The farmyard is left to express its normality in egg-laying and aggressive displays. The duckling was not defective after all, it simply belonged to a different species, and the 'cure' for its apparent abnormality was the discovery of its ethnic roots.

Whether or not Andersen was able to spread his wings in the homosexual underworlds of Naples, Constantinople or 'that German Sodoma', Berlin, he was creating a virtual society by writing for its invisible members. At the same time, he was proving by his own success that homosexual snowmen, androgynous windmills and guilt-ridden shillings could be accepted and even honoured in the wider world.

The *Fairy Tales* are not reducible to Andersen's sexuality, and the idea that 'nobody can help his birth' is not just a coded plea for sexual tolerance. But they do show a homosexual sensibility illuminating subjects of universal interest. They were a personal vindication, but not, of course, a call for full equality. Gay pride was still a distant prospect:

> He felt quite shy, and hid his head under his wing; he did not know what to think; he was so very happy, but not at all proud; a good heart never becomes proud.

*

THE *FAIRY TALES* would be an excellent starting-point for anyone who wanted to show that gay writing has its own special characteristics. The slightly skewed quality of Andersen's writing, the phrases that sound like euphemisms, the worrying surfeit of significance, are often reminiscent of Kafka's techniques of self-analysis and concealment. Günter Mecke has shown that tales like 'Beschreibung eines Kampfes' (1903–4), in which the narrator falls in love with a man and attacks him from behind, are riddled with homosexual references, often of the sort that were instantly comprehensible to homosexual prostitutes and their clients. Later tales like *Der Prozeß* (1914–15) show a more intricate form of disguise.

The analogy could be extended to some of Melville's tales, like the bizarre 'I and My Chimney' (1856), in which, despite receiving threatening 'anonymous letters', a man refuses to allow his antique chimney to be investigated in case a 'secret closet' is revealed: 'Infinite sad mischief has resulted from the profane bursting open of secret recesses.'

Sexuality is not a skeleton key to the work of Andersen, Melville or Kafka. The sense of shame and strange excitement comes from the process of concealment rather than from the object that is being concealed. This is one of the problems faced by any sexually partisan form of criticism. Some writers, like Henry James, avoided the subject so completely that gay readings of their work have to operate on such deep or abstract levels that they could be applied to almost any writer. Others, like Robert Louis Stevenson in *Dr Jekyll and Mr Hyde* (1886), used homosexual references to create an atmosphere of unspeakable and mysterious depravity, but without intending the character to be seen as homosexual.

It is important in any case not to overemphasize the advantages of writing in the dark. For many gay writers, metaphor was not a decoration or a cunning device, it was a social necessity. Classical references could express a genuine perception of affinity with a past civilization, but they could also be awkward circumlocutions and marks of restraint. Custine's experiences in France may have helped him to see Russia as a despotism whose victims conspired in their own repression, a world in which 'everything is hidden but suspected'. The sexuality of Marcel Proust may, as some suggested, have given him insights into the mind of the opposite sex. Gay writers may be better at disguising the source of their emotions. (One of Custine's characters calls it 'the infernal art of deceiving without lying'.) It could make an otherwise banal story or poem mysteriously significant, like a spy's transmitter masquerading as a domestic radio. But writers generally prefer to choose their own restraints and to create dramatic tension in their own ways.

The benefits of concealment may be obvious to readers, and the disadvantages of disclosure just as obvious to writers. Thom Gunn felt that public knowledge of his homosexuality made some of his poems vulnerable to reductive readings. But he did not consider the Gay Movement a threat to his writing: 'In my early books I was in the closet. I was discreet in an Audenish way. If a poem referred to a lover, I always used "you". I figured it didn't matter, it didn't affect the poetry. But it did.' Colm Tóibín, who quotes this interview, finds the same liberation in his reading of the poems:

> I love what's hidden between the lines of these early poems. But then watching Gunn describe, with a freedom which is quite new, what it is like to be in bed with another man in, say, 'Jack Straw's Castle' is, from the gay point of view, like being there for the Annunciation.

* * *

'Gay literature', if such a thing existed, was not just literature produced by gay writers or devoted to the subject of homosexuality. It was also the body of writing in which gay men and women discovered themselves, regardless of the author's intentions or sexuality.

From 1899, evidence that gay literature did exist was provided, annually, by Magnus Hirschfeld's journal, the *Jahrbuch für sexuelle Zwischenstufen*. The 'Belletristisches' section of its bibliography listed a huge variety of books of possible interest to 'sexual intermediates'. The 1900 bibliography mentioned poems by Rimbaud and Schwinburne (*sic*), Tennyson's *In Memoriam*, the latest translation of Michelangelo's sonnets, the male prostitute episode in Huysmans' *À rebours* ('omitted from the German translation'), a novel in Czech by Jan Karadek (*Sodoma*, privately printed), volume II, chapter 7 of *Anna Karenina* ('sketch of the relations between two homosexual officers'), and several Japanese works, including M. Sasanoya's history of pederasty in Japan from earliest times to the introduction of western culture: *Nanskoku* (Tokyo, 1893–4).

Other lists appeared in the medical literature, at first as simple indications but increasingly as recommendations to interested readers. Havelock Ellis's list in *Studies in the Psychology of Sex* sounds like the catalogue of a pharmaceutical wholesaler: Whitman's *Leaves of Grass* 'may be of more doubtful value for general use', but 'furnishes a wholesome and robust ideal to the invert who is insensitive to normal ideals'.

By the end of the century, it was possible to create a distinctively homosexual interior that included a selection of significant books, not all of which had been written two thousand years ago. Edward Prime-Stevenson's character Dayneford, in 'Out of the Sun' (1913), has a small library in his villa on Capri, its walls 'tinted in the significant green', containing about thirty different titles: the old (Tibullus, Háfiz, Shakespeare, etc.) and the new (Whitman, Tennyson, Rachilde, Sturgis, etc.).

Apart from their particular interest, these books had a symbolic value. Wilde's interior, which was cruelly exposed at the sale of his belongings, might have appeared in a gay *Better Homes and Gardens*:

> [. . .] my Burne-Jones drawings: my Whistler drawings: my Monticelli: my Simeon Solomons: my china: my Library with its collection of presentation volumes from almost every poet of my time, from Hugo to Whitman, from Swinburne to Mallarmé, from Morris to Verlaine.

The Parisian home of the dandy Robert de Montesquiou gave several novelists ideas for homosexual settings: Persian and Japanese *objets d'art*, bonsai trees, old family portraits, antique furniture, engravings by Whistler, pictures of Baudelaire and Swinburne, 100 cravats in a glass case, and 'a slightly pederastic photograph of the gymnast from Mollier's Circus showing off his pretty ephebic shapes in a leotard'.

The most revealing items in gay libraries are the works that seem not to belong. Prime-Stevenson's ideal collection contained not only the obvious selection of American and European novels but also three novels by Dickens: *A Tale of Two Cities*, *David Copperfield* and *Our Mutual Friend*. (If his interest had extended to lesbians, he might have added *Little Dorrit*.)

The battle over Shakespeare's sonnets shows that these 'appropriations' were controversial long before journalistic misrepresentations of gay studies. The point is not that certain characters are or are not homosexual but that gay readers found their likeness in them. To an invisible man, any reflection is a consolation. In *A Tale of Two Cities* (1859), Sydney Carton, a bachelor consumed with self-loathing, redeems his lonely life with an act of self-sacrifice. In *Our Mutual Friend* and *David Copperfield*, Dickens quite deliberately left the door open. The description of 'Daisy' Copperfield's infatuation with the bewitching Steerforth, underlined with allusions to Smollett and the Arabian Nights, is plainly and, of course, purely homoerotic.

These adoptions were not, as Albert Moll believed, a case of arrogant self-delusion. No one thought that Victor Hugo was a closet homosexual, but his poems were popular with gay readers. Custine and Proust both saw reflections of homosexuality in Hugo's persona, 'Olympio', who returns to the scene of his former love to find that Nature herself is oblivious to his passion. Custine even wrote to tell Hugo: 'You will never know in what manner I applied your verse ['À Olympio'] to my own life, but you will know vaguely that there is a deeply suffering heart that felt itself return to life when it thought itself worthy of being consoled by you.' Similarly, Edith Simcox, who loved George Eliot 'lover-wise', identified herself with Maggie Tulliver in *The Mill on the Floss*.

Ironically, Platen's enemy Heinrich Heine was another favourite, as was Alfred de Musset. Their poems were copied out and memorized by courting couples, both gay and straight. As a child, Proust's character Baron de Charlus had created his own anthology by pretending that Musset's poems 'were addressed, not to a beautiful deceiver, but to a young man'. As Proust explains, 'Writers should not be offended that inverts give their heroines a male face. This slightly aberrant peculiarity is the invert's only means of giving what he reads its full universal import.' This 'peculiarity' is not after all exclusively gay: Verlaine's poems and Goethe's 'An den Mond' also served the romantic purposes of heterosexual lovers.

Some books were popular because of their subject: novels about married women living under cruel constraints, tales of illicit love, especially the legend of Tristan and Isolde. But the attraction was often a particular tone: a poignant sense of exclusion and ironic consolation, a protesting resignation, a turning of the world's hostility into the walls of a cosy retreat.

The instinctive perception of sympathy – even unintended – was especially strong in music. Gay tastes were remarkably consistent. The names of certain composers appear again and again in letters and novels: Beethoven (sonatas), Chopin (nocturnes), Wagner (*Lohengrin, Parsifal* and *Tristan*), Tchaikovsky (the *Symphonie pathétique*) and *fin-de-siècle* French composers: Debussy, Delibes, Gounod, Massenet.

The key ingredients seem to have been a melodious melancholy and something oxymoronic in the emotions: grandiose and senti- mental, ostentatious and discreet. The sexuality of the composer himself was not of primary importance, though both Forster and Prime-Stevenson suggest that Tchaikovsky's sexuality was audibly encoded in the bars of the *Symphonie pathétique*. Music could convey quite precisely what could never be said in print. According to Schubert's friend Josef Kenner, his music won him 'the heart of a seductively amiable and brilliant young man' (Franz von Schober) who dragged him down into 'the slough of moral degradation'. Wagner's music won him the love of Ludwig II, who, on one occasion, spoke to him through the mouth of Wagner's Brunhilda:

> You express to me your sorrow that, as it seems to you, each one of our last meetings has only brought pain and anxiety to me. Must I then remind my loved one of Brunhilda's words? 'Not only in gladness and enjoyment, but in suffering also Love makes man blest.'

The spontaneous translation of the dominant culture into more congenial terms can also be seen in the emergence of gay icons. Like Sarah Bernhardt and Judy Garland for later generations, Jenny Lind was a gay icon and a lesbian heart-throb. Hans Christian Andersen idolized her. J. A. Symonds looked at pictures of Jenny Lind in a bid to cure himself of homosexuality, and the author of *Autobiography of an Androgyne* called himself 'Jennie June' and 'Earl Lind' because the soprano was 'one of my models'.

Gay culture was not the exclusive product of professional writers and artists. A continually updated anthology of 'storiettes', as Frederick Rolfe observed, could be read in public lavatories at Victoria and South Kensington stations. J. A. Symonds found his feelings expressed in classical myths but also in obscene graffiti. Verlaine's unpublished poems might have graced (and probably did) the walls of any toilet.

> We two alone, in that café crammed with fools,
> Stood for the so-called loathsome vice of loving
> Men. Those blandly-smiling imbeciles, with their
> Normal romances and cheap moral standards,
> Had no idea: we shat on the bastards, while
> Jerking off and thrusting – to our heart's content,
> But also, it must be said, on principle [. . .]

Prison visitors were amazed to find homosexual love affairs openly celebrated on prison walls. Policemen found poems in the bedrooms and pockets of 'pederasts', perfectly scanned and indistinguishable from 'normal' love poems. The intricately obscene 'Sonnet du trou du cul' ('Arsehole Sonnet') by Rimbaud and Verlaine looks like an avant-garde joke, but a very similar ode to the anus was quoted by Prefect of Police Carlier. It had been sent by a valet to his master's friend: 'There is a thicket in my soul with bushy borders, the cage of a beautiful brown[-haired man], to whose confusèd song I harken. [. . .]'

It is often said that gay men and women are more adept at expressing themselves than heterosexuals, or more eager to do so. They were more likely to invent stories, to play roles, to rehearse a variety of relationships with the rest of society. Like Quentin Crisp,

[229]

they could find that estrangement imbued the everyday world with novelistic charm: 'Homosexuals have time for everybody. [. . .] Every detail of the lives of real people, however mundane it may be, seems romantic to them.'

There are surprising similarities between casual accounts of life as a homosexual and published literary works. Homosexual confessions generally seem to have been written much later than they actually were. Vampires, doppelgängers and weird metamorphoses were quite routine in interviews and autobiographies of homosexuals. J. A. Symonds was both a donnish scholar and a Gothic monster at large in Victorian London: 'And all the while the demon ravished my imagination with "the love of the impossible". Hallucination of the senses crowded in upon my brain together with the pangs of shame and the prevision of inevitable woes.' Existential alienation was a daily reality long before it became a literary theme. Krafft-Ebing's case 134 might have found the world of Franz Kafka almost naturalistic:

> But who could describe my terror when, the other morning, I woke with the feeling that I had undergone a complete transformation and turned into a woman? [. . .] When finally I dragged myself out of bed I sensed that an upheaval had taken place. Even during my illness, a visitor had said, 'He's very patient, for a man', and gave me a flower blooming in a pot, which struck me as rather strange but also made me glad.

*

IT WOULD BE EASY to give the story of 19th-century gay literature a happy ending. For all the ghastly tales of scheming inverts and vampirical lesbians, there were signs at the turn of the century of a more authentic literature and a wider choice of identities. Organs like Hirschfeld's *Jahrbuch*, Adelsward Fersen's neo-Grecian *Akadémos* and Charles Kains-Jackson's neo-chivalric *The Artist, or Journal of Home Culture* published the works of gay writers. Anthologies like Elisár von Kupffer's *Lieblingminne und Freundesliebe in der Weltliteratur* (1900) and Edward Carpenter's *Ioläus: An Anthology of Friendship* (1902) gave some canonical authority to texts and quotations that were already common currency among educated gays. Open celebrations of homosexual love were no longer quite so rare. The poet

Emmanuel Signoret was less inhibited, by himself or by censors, than most 20th-century poets: in *Le Livre de l'amitié* (1891), his lover's soul was as fragrant as a daffodil, he wanted their blood to mingle and their 'loins' to 'quiver', and their 'burning mouths remained pressed together for a long time'. In *Claudine à l'école* (1900) and the sequel, *Claudine en ménage* (1902), Colette showed that a witty, intelligent young woman could enjoy normal lesbian relations without becoming a mindless victim or a predatory fiend.

Colette's husband, Willy, encouraged her to spice up her novels for the male audience, but the references to hothouse atmospheres are clearly sarcastic. In one scene, Claudine talks to a 'psychological' novelist (based on Marcel Prévost, who had published a novel, *Chonchette*, about lesbians at boarding-school): 'Yes', he says, hoping to tease out her secret lesbian desires, 'the air outside has the intoxicating and dangerous staleness of a greenhouse.' Claudine answers in her rural accent: 'You're right there! The corn'll be up early, and the oats 'n' all!' The novelist, she suspects, will now go about telling people that Claudine likes only women, by which, in her opinion, he means 'she doesn't like *me*'.

This was more cheerfully realistic than fantasies like the hugely successful soft-porn *Chansons de Bilitis* (1900), supposedly 'translated from the Greek' by Pierre Louÿs. It was written for men like Marcel Prévost who peered though steamed-up windows and wondered what lesbians actually did with each other. The first poem described a lesbian, as usual, crushing flowers with her feet and making love to a tree.

Male homosexuality began to appear without its usual escorts. Robert Musil's *Die Verwirrungen des Zöglings Törleß* (1906) and D. H. Lawrence's *The White Peacock* (1911) present it as an aspect of human life instead of making it the prize exhibit. Thomas Mann's *Death in Venice* (1912) showed that the euphemisms applied to homosexual love could also be used to evoke other unnameable things – death, the unconscious mind, the murky origins of art.

Even in openly homosexual novels, happiness became slightly less unusual. Forster's *Maurice* (1913–14) may have been a sign of the times rather than a solitary dream. Two gay novels published in 1906 both had hopeful endings. Prime-Stevenson's *Imre* is a love story doubling as a gay travel guide and handbook. Passion is quite undisguised. An Englishman called Oswald meets a Hungarian lieutenant called Imre. They battle through the long process of self-revelation and are last seen blissfully strolling along the Danube to the nerve-thrilling sounds of a gypsy orchestra. In Kuzmin's *Wings*, the hero goes to Italy, decides to live with an older man, and, at the end of the novel, 'opens a window onto a street flooded with bright sunlight'.

That window would soon be closed. The grim trends in the legal and medical treatment of homosexuality are just as evident in literature. The extraordinary fuss made about Alec Waugh's *The Loom of Youth* (1917) shows how unbroachable the subject became, at least in Britain. Waugh's vague hints of 'ugly things' and 'friendships [. . .] too romantic to last' (Byron) were hardly a sign of growing confidence. A similar trend could be seen in lesbian literature. It says a lot about the lack of lesbian writing – and the self-image of lesbians – that the first national lesbian organization, the Daughters of Bilitis, took its name from the cliché-ridden sleaze of Pierre Louÿs.

As Lillian Faderman points out, Christina Rossetti's 'Goblin Market' (1862) and Thomas Hardy's *Desperate Remedies* (1871) contained exciting scenes of sexual passion between women, yet neither work was banned. In Radclyffe Hall's theoretically optimistic but depressing *The Well of Loneliness* (1928), which was banned, the joys of lesbian sex were crammed into a tiny half-sentence and denied the power of speech. Happiness and silence now went hand in hand:

> Stephen bent down and kissed Mary's hands very humbly, for now she could find no words any more . . . and that night they were not divided.

9

Gentle Jesus

'the love of Christ, which passeth knowledge'

Ephesians 3:19

EVEN IN RELIGIOUS MATTERS, the 19th century is much more recent than we think. We now know that not all Victorians were ardent church-goers. Many people were happy to lose their faith and embraced atheism without suffering any social consequences. Christianity still loomed large in most minds, and especially in homosexual minds, but it was not impossible, at least in private, to reconcile Christian belief with illicit love. A minister known to Magnus Hirschfeld saw no contradiction in his human and spiritual passions: if God had made him that way, he must have had a purpose. Ulrichs told his sister that it would be 'extremely unChristian' to ask God to perform a miracle and turn him into a lover of women.

Ironically, homosexual priests were less likely than most to consider themselves exceptional. According to Hirschfeld, every confessor knew 'thousands' of homosexuals. On the other hand, some people who were otherwise untroubled by religion were tortured by unanswerable questions: Why were only certain kinds of love acceptable to the religion of love? Why were they created with feelings that the Creator himself condemns?

The teaching of all Christian churches was unambiguous: sodomites were evil. They might even bring down the wrath of God on whole communities. The savage god who wiped out the Cities of the Plain did not launch his strikes with pinpoint accuracy. In 1750, the Bishop of London warned Londoners that the recent earthquakes felt in the capital had been caused by 'the unnatural Lewdness, of which we have heard so much of late'. Similar warnings are still being issued today. AIDS has often been described as a biblical scourge, and some right-wing evangelists in the United States held gays and lesbians partly responsible for the destruction of the World Trade Center.

These extreme expressions of conservative dogma now sound like paranoid delusions, though metaphysical fears were and still are widely reflected in private convictions. Many Christian homosexuals faced a wall of prejudice that began in the courtroom and ended in heaven. They lived and died with the contradiction of a God who made a certain kind of love a qualification for everlasting torment. But even the people officially referred to as 'sodomites' could have a profound effect on religious practice and belief, often in ways that still seem unacceptable to many Christians.

*

CHRISTIAN CONDEMNATIONS of homosexual love have always reflected the mores of a particular society. When Philo of Alexandria imagined the Sodomites indulging in 'strong liquor, dainty feeding and forbidden forms of intercourse', he was describing the Hellenistic ways of his contemporaries: 'They accustomed those who were by nature men to submit to play the part of women, and saddled them with the formidable curse of a female disease.'

Philo was not elucidating a passage of Old Testament scripture; he was attacking the sexual underworld of first-century Alexandria. Similarly, St Paul's allusions to homosexuality say more about life in certain parts of the Roman Empire than they do about the teachings of Christ:

> Their women did change the natural use into that which is against nature: And likewise also the men, leaving the natural use of the woman, burned in their lust one toward another. (Romans 1:26–7)

This was not the rural Judaea of the twelve disciples, it was the cosmopolitan playground described a few years later by Juvenal, Martial and Lucian:

> 'You're surely not a hermaphrodite', said I, 'equipped both as a man and a woman, as many people are said to be?' [. . .] 'No, Leaena', she said, 'I was born a woman like the rest of you, but I have the mind and the desires and everything else of a man. [. . .] Just give me a chance, and you'll find I'm as good as any man; I have a substitute of my own.' (Lucian, *Dialogues of the Courtesans*, 5)

Several different Jesuses coexisted in the early years of Christianity. The anti-sodomitical Christ of Paul and Philo was competing with alternative versions of himself. Paul, for instance, was not just chastising a group of versatile fornicators, he may also have been combating a belief held by some early Christians that sexual acts could serve a religious purpose. (As 19th-century missionaries and explorers discovered, this belief was not peculiar to early Christianity.)

Over a century later, Clement of Alexandria was trying to eradicate just such a heresy. A gnostic sect which prayed to images of Pythagoras, Plato, Aristotle, and a portrait of Jesus supposedly commissioned by Pontius Pilate had incorporated pederastic love into a baptismal rite. They justified their 'unspeakable teachings' with an expanded version of Mark's gospel dating from the first century (the so-called *Secret Gospel of Mark*). Clement quoted it in a letter (*c.* 180 AD):

> And going in immediately where the young man was, [Jesus] stretched out his hand and raised him up, taking him by the hand. The young man looked on him and loved him, and began to beseech him that he might be with him. They came out of the tomb and went into the young man's house, for he was rich. After six days Jesus laid a charge upon him, and when evening came the young man comes to him, with a linen robe thrown over his naked body; and he stayed with him that night, for Jesus was teaching him the mystery of the kingdom of God.

Clement was not doubting the authenticity of the Gospel; he was opposed to the dissemination of dangerous teachings which, in his view, were intended for an élite. This cautious, discriminating approach to divine wisdom is not peculiar to the early Church. In 1989, a report secretly commissioned by the House of Bishops of the Church of England found that there was no biblical justification for not supporting 'permanent homosexual relationships'. The report was suppressed, however, not because of theological disagreement, but because it was felt that the findings would be 'disturbing to the faithful'.

Biblical texts have always been tailored to fit social prejudice, especially in sexual matters. As the English barrister Humphry Woolrych pointed out in 1832, sodomy was always the great exception: 'The immediate execution of the Sodomite or unnatural person' is ordered by Leviticus, 'but in the very same chapter, there is an equal denunciation against adultery, cursing of mother and father, soothsaying, incantations and diviners'. Why, then, he wondered, were children who insulted their parents not also executed, along with fortune-tellers and adulterers?

Recent discussions in Britain of Section 28 of the Local Government Act (1988), which makes it illegal for schools and local authorities to 'promote homosexuality', have revealed a persistent belief that conservative public opinion and biblical teaching are more or less identical. It is still widely assumed, for instance, that Jesus condemned homosexuality.

*

DEPICTIONS OF A homosexual Christ are often seen as the ultimate act of gay impudence. Modern examples include the poem by James Kirkup in which a centurion makes love to the crucified Christ and which led to the prosecution of *Gay News* in 1977,* and Terrence McNally's play, *Corpus Christi* (1997), based on a real incident, in which the Jesus figure, a native of Corpus Christi, Texas, is crucified as 'king of the queers'.

Sexually ambiguous Messiahs belong to a tradition much older than the Christian Church. Relatively few have been the work of flippant provocateurs and sneering blasphemers. Most modern gay Christs were serious attempts by homosexual men and, more rarely, women to find a way in to the fortress of Christian dogma and to

---

* Kirkup's poem, 'The Love that Dares to Speak Its Name', is still banned in Britain and the United States. However, it can easily be found on the Internet, despite frequent changes of web address.

solve the painful riddle. Eloquent expressions of religious despair are common in letters and confessions:

> O God and Father, if You really exist, why are You doing this to me, and if this is the sin for which I must atone, why do You not forgive me? ('Sufferer from perverse sexual orientation', quoted by a German forensic doctor, 1873)

> I am hundreds of years old in this my wretchedness of every moment. I cannot battle against Love and crush it out – never! God has implanted the necessity of the sentiment in my heart; it is scarce possible not to ask oneself why has He implanted so divine an element in my nature, which is doomed to die unsatisfied, which is destined in the end to be my very death? (Ms. of an unknown 'Urning', quoted by Edward Carpenter, 1908)

For some, the answer was to abandon the Church. Edward Carpenter, who was ordained in 1869, 'unfrocked' himself five years later, partly to end the 'crucifixion' of his 'physical needs'. Clive Durham, in Forster's *Maurice*, also sheds the religion of his childhood like an old suit:

> He wished Christianity would compromise with him a little and searched the Scriptures for support. There was David and Jonathan; there was even the 'disciple that Jesus loved'. But the Church's interpretation was against him; he could not find any rest for his soul in her without crippling it, and withdrew higher into the classics yearly.

Not everyone could take comfort in a classical education, or forge a substitute faith, as Carpenter did, from the sunshine of Italy, the poetry of Walt Whitman and the conversation of friends like W. K. Clifford, whose 'inverted Doxology' sounded like a hymn of hope:

> O Father, Son and Holy Ghost –
> We wonder which we hate the most.
> Be Hell, which they prepared before,
> Their dwelling now and evermore!

Liberation from conformity was an intellectual luxury. For many, death seemed the only solution. 'The only exit for a soul thus plagued is suicide', wrote J. A. Symonds, who managed to adjust his faith and eventually felt more remorseful about his bogus marriage than about his sexuality. Men who took refuge in the Church, or who mistook their lack of sexual interest in women for a vocation, often found that they had simply turned themselves into hypocrites. The boy-loving curate of John Bloxam's tale, 'The Priest and the Acolyte', which was mentioned in the Wilde trials as 'a disgrace to literature', finds an ideal setting for his soul in the 'artistic beauty' of the High Church service, but peace of mind eludes him, as he tells his rector: 'In the sight of God my soul is blameless; but to you and to the world I am guilty of an abominable crime.'

The suicidal clergyman was – and still is – one of the commonest images of homosexual anguish. As Havelock Ellis wrote in 1897, everyone had heard of cases, or read about them in newspapers, 'in which distinguished men in various fields, not seldom clergymen, suddenly disappear from the country or commit suicide in consequence of some such exposure or the threat of it'. Their deaths were usually imputed to fear of discovery and interpreted as a tribute to normality, but they were surely in many cases the logical conclusion of a hopeless internal debate. Even the exceptional A. E. Forrest, who had sex with so many boys on Santa Cruz (Solomon Islands) in the 1890s that his bishop thought the mission utterly ruined, was eventually driven to suicide in 1908 and was 'remembered among the locals as the white man who was hounded to death by vindictive Christians'.

*

SOME INDEPENDENT SOULS, however, scoured the Bible, like W. C. Fields, 'looking for a loophole', and were surprised to find that Jesus never condemns sodomy. He does refer to the fiery fate of Sodom and Gomorrha, but only as a general reminder of the Day of Judgment or as a warning to those who fail to welcome the disciples:

> And whosoever shall not receive you, nor hear you, when ye depart thence, shake off the dust under your feet for a testimony against them. Verily I say unto you, It shall be more tolerable for Sodom and Gomorrha in the day of judgment, than for that city. (Mark 6:11)

For Jesus, as for a minority of later theologians, the Sodomites' sin was a breach of the law of hospitality rather than an unholy form of intercourse. This was not an original reading. In Genesis and Judges, the attempted homosexual gang rape of foreign visitors is the form that the crime of inhospitality happens to take. The story of Sodom is not, according to one view, a specific condemnation of sodomy, any more than the rape of the maids of Judah (Lamentations 5:11) implies a ban on heterosexual relations. According to Ezekiel, the Sodomites were proud, greedy, idle and selfish people, but not, apparently, sexual perverts. The Book of Wisdom defines their crime as 'bitter hatred towards strangers'.

The routine association of Sodom with the act of sodomy was a much later development and did not become widespread until the late 14th century. Even then, as Jeremy Bentham pointed out, referring to the Levite episode in Judges 19, there was surely some consoling precedent in the fact that 'the concupiscence of a whole male population' could be 'kindled to madness by a transient glimpse of a single man'. In such a country, 'is it possible that the nature of that love which had place between David and Jonathan would be matter of doubt?'

Careful readers of the Gospels might even detect signs of active tolerance or at least the glimmer of a compromise.

To some 19th-century readers, Jesus did appear to show unusual regard for men who were considered ridiculously or reprehensibly effeminate. In Matthew 19, after agreeing that some people will find it easier than others to avoid fornication, Jesus mentions three varieties of eunuch – those who were castrated, those who castrated themselves 'for the kingdom of heaven's sake', and an unidentifiable variety, perhaps hermaphroditic or simply impotent: 'eunuchs, which were so born from their mother's womb'. It is entirely defensible to see this as a reference to homosexuality. In the 2nd century, Clement of Alexandria and the gnostic philosopher Basilides defined this category of eunuch as men who naturally 'turn away from women'.

The more subtle or tenuous historical arguments seem to be quite recent, though they must have occurred to readers long before they were able to put the arguments in print. At Bethany, Jesus sends two disciples into the city to find the house where the Last Supper will take place. They are to look for 'a man bearing a pitcher of water' –

in other words a man who would be distinguished from the Passover crowd by his effeminate behaviour. (Only women fetched water.) At Capernaum, a Roman centurion begs Jesus to heal a sick servant 'who was dear unto him'. Marvelling at the centurion's faith, Jesus performs the miracle at a distance. Matthew calls the 'servant' *pais* (boy); Luke calls him *doulos* (slave). Both Gospels were probably written in Antioch of Syria, where the exceptional concern of a Roman centurion for a sick slave-boy would have had clearly erotic overtones.

None of this amounts to acceptance of homosexual love, and it would take an unusually determined anachronist to make a blind, backward leap of faith over 2,000 years of social change and to claim that Jesus himself was either homosexual or heterosexual. But it does show that the Gospels contained the elements of a rational, Christian defence of same-sex love. Church doctrine was not the final word. Earl Lind, in questioning St Paul's 'false sex doctrines', happily observed that

> Jesus made no such blunders in his sex teaching. He was the only biblical teacher apparently to recognize the existence of androgynes without thundering against them. As 'eunuchs from their mother's womb', he may of course have had in mind only anaphrodites [asexuals]. But apparently he was aware of the existence of androgynes, St John the Divine, apparently his favorite disciple, having possessed the earmarks, particularly 'softness' of disposition.

Along with David and Jonathan and their 'wonderful' love 'passing the love of women' (2 Samuel 1:26), the 'soft' apostle has always been the main focus of homosexual attention. John is repeatedly described (in John's Gospel) as 'the disciple whom Jesus loved'. At the Last Supper, he talks to Jesus while 'leaning on his bosom' or 'lying on his breast'. King James I had no doubt about the meaning of this love. In 1617, six years after the publication of the Bible that bears his name, James defended himself in the Privy Council against the charge of sodomy. His openly erotic relations with his 'sweet child and wife', George Villiers, were correctly thought to imply an even more shameful private life. James decided to invoke divine authority: 'Jesus Christ did the same, and therefore I cannot be blamed. Christ had his son John, and I have my George.'

Whatever its theological value, James's defence was not just a provocative personal fantasy. A few years before, Christopher Marlowe had been accused of claiming 'That St John the Evangelist was bedfellow to Christ and leaned alwaies on his bosom, that he used him as the sinners of Sodoma'. The notion that Jesus and John loved one another like husband and wife had been a theme of early medieval literature and iconography. This cheerful notion might have been driven underground by dogma and morality, but it was constantly being rediscovered.

*

THE 18TH AND 19TH CENTURIES saw the greatest proliferation of alternative Christs since the dawn of Christianity. Androgynous and even homosexual Jesuses emerged, along with many others, from the secular reassessment of the Gospels that culminated in David Friedrich Strauss's brutally forensic *Das Leben Jesu* (1835–6; translated by George Eliot in 1846), and Ernest Renan's more tactful *Vie de Jésus* (1863).

The historical approach to holy scripture is often associated with a devastating loss of faith: if Jesus was rooted in a particular culture, how could his teachings be universal? But for some, the secularization of Jesus had the effect of stripping away the layers of tradition to reveal a pristine, 'real' Jesus, who could then be dressed, of course, in other clothes: the socialist Jesus who fights for the oppressed, the capitalist Jesus who exploits the poor, the Messiah of material progress, or the Romantic atheist who prays to an empty sky.

Because of the inflammatory nature of the idea, the homosexual Jesus had a less public career than the others. But the fact that the idea was expressed at all suggests that there was a great deal of private meditation on the subject. A starting-point for some might have been a surprising passage in Diderot's *Essai sur la peinture* (1765; published in 1796). Diderot invited his readers to imagine how much warmth and beauty the Gospel figures would gain 'if our artists were not enchained and our poets constrained by those terrible words – sacrilege and profanation':

[. . .] if Christ, at the wedding at Cana, tipsy and a little nonconformist, had run his eye over the breasts of a harlot and the buttocks of Saint John, wondering whether or not he would remain faithful to the apostle whose chin bore the first wispy growth of beard [. . .] then you would see how differently we would regard the beauty to which we owe the grace of our redemption.

Diderot was not making claims on behalf of a repressed minority. He was trying to rescue religious subjects from censors and hypocrites. His sexually indecisive Messiah was a pleasantly normal human being, susceptible to the full range of human emotions.

Less public texts were more specific. Frederick the Great wrote in a poem that John had gained access to Jesus's bed by acting as his 'Ganymede'. Stendhal wanted to make this love affair the subject of a play in which Jesus – who 'never made his mother unhappy by preferring another woman' – would 'turn to his own advantage the doctrine of Socrates'.

In a more scholarly vein (but still in private), Jeremy Bentham observed that, like David's love for Jonathan, the love of Jesus and John was clearly presented as being 'of a different sort from any of which any of the other of the Apostles was the object'. Alerted by an intriguing reference in the *Monthly Magazine* of September 1811 to 'the episode of the cinaedus' (catamite) in the Garden of Gethsemane, Bentham suggested that the young man with a linen cloth over his naked body who flees from the soldiers (Mark 14:51–2) was a 'rival or a candidate for the situation of rival to the Apostle' John. This is interestingly reminiscent of the young man 'with a linen robe thrown over his naked body' in the *Secret Gospel of Mark*, which was not discovered until 1958.

By hinting at the erotic nonconformity of Jesus, Bentham was trying to remove 'that cloud of prejudice by which this part of the field of morals has to this time been obscured'. He was concerned, not with theological accuracy, but with 'the greatest happiness of the greatest number'.

Narrower political aims produced more lurid images. In a satire pretending to be a petition to the French National Assembly in 1790, the 'Children of Sodom' demanded the right to practise the science of 'antiphysics', 'which its detractors derisively call buggery'. This

'sweetest of mysteries' was after all revealed to mortals by the Son of
God:

> Has not [Jesus], moved by the most tender affection for his younger
> cousin, led us all, such as we are, down the path of knowledge? Has
> he not shown us the primary elements of this preference, which fools
> have called monstrous and bizarre, but whose divine essence we have
> recognized? [. . .] The dying Jesus, who suffered the same fate as our
> brother Paschal* – death on the bed of honour – used to say to St
> John: 'Come, my son; come, my beloved, rest your head on my chest.'
> Can we doubt the true essence of these tender expressions?

This was a sarcastic attack on the régime that was about to decrimi-
nalize sodomy, but the same idea was also expressed by supporters of
the Revolution. A brazen, priest-bashing text of 1790, *Bordel apostolique*, claimed, in the vigorous idiom of the Revolution, that 'St John
used to bugger the Virgin's son'. In his revolutionary phase, the
Marquis de Sade also referred to what was evidently a common theme
in some quarters, though only Sade, it seems, came up with the idea
that the boy Jesus had 'performed certain services – doubtless very
libertine – for the priests of the temple at Jerusalem'.

Antireligious blasphemies like these were not just devious inven-
tions of literary minds. There seems to have been a popular tradition
of innuendo which survived in homosexual slang until the early 20th
century. An *'apôtre'* (apostle) was a sodomite, a *'jésus'* or *'petit jésus'*
(roughly equivalent to 'pretty boy') was a male prostitute, and *'faire le
saint Jean'* was to make a discreet bow as a sign to other homosexuals.

Not all anticlericalism was irreligious. Many of the mystical sects
that sprang up in early-19th-century France associated the division
of humanity into male and female with social inequality and revived
the ancient Christian notion of androgynous perfection, for which
Paul himself could be quoted as an authority.† In the 1840s, devotees

---

* The last sodomite burned alive in France (1783).
† 'There is no longer male and female; for all of you are one in Christ Jesus'
(Galatians 3:28). The Gospel of Thomas (discovered in 1945) attributes the notion
to Jesus: 'Jesus said to them, "[. . .] when you make the male and the female one and
the same, so that the male not be male nor the female female [. . .] then you will
enter [the kingdom]." ' (Thomas 22)

of a new religion called Evadisme ('Eve' + 'Adam') worshipped a bisexual god and followed a man who called himself 'the Mapah' ('*maman*' + '*papa*'). Charles Fourier described an ideal society in which all forms of sexual congress would be practised, including 'monosexuality', and in which 'unisexual orgies' would be officially sanctioned. The Saint-Simonians thought that the Son of God should also be known as the Daughter of God.

It was under the influence of Saint-Simonian ideas that, in the mid-19th century, the painter Rosa Bonheur discovered striking evidence of Jesus's androgyny. It occurred to her (as it had a century before to the German pietist, Ludwig von Zinzendorf) that the red, tender wound in Jesus's side was a visual euphemism. This crucial image of Christian iconography was in fact a representation of the vagina, as some surprisingly detailed medieval paintings suggested. The masculinity of the adult Jesus was veiled by a loin-cloth, but his femininity was openly displayed.

An androgynous Christ was not, of course, a proto-homosexual, but the perception of his sexual ambiguity made it easier to find a place for homosexuality in Christian tradition. The historical continuities identified by Winckelmann's *Geschichte der Kunst des Altertums* (1764), Pater's *Studies in the History of the Renaissance* (1873) and Frazer's *The Golden Bough* (1890–1915) allowed imaginative bridges to be built between the Classical and Christian worlds. The effeminate features of Greek gods and heroes – Orpheus, Dionysus and Apollo – were seen to have survived in early images of Christ. To generations who began the school day with the Gospels and continued with Homer, Horace and Virgil, this was not entirely inconceivable.

Philosophical parallels confirmed artistic similarities. If Socrates could be seen as a pre-Christian, then Jesus could be seen as a latter-day Greek. In the Hellenistic Oxford of Benjamin Jowett and Walter Pater, the Christ-like qualities of Socrates – and the Socratic qualities of Christ – were a common theme, despite increasingly nervous awareness of what Gladstone called 'those shameless lusts, which formed the incredible and indelible disgrace of Greece'. In W. H. Mallock's satire on effete Oxford Hellenists, *The New Republic* (1877), an undergraduate's sonnet enfolds Narcissus, Venus and Christ in the same 'yearning': 'of these three / I knew not which was fairest'. Three years later, the sonnet was quoted in all seriousness in the pamphlet, *Boy-Worship* (Oxford, 1880). 'Our yearning tenderness for boys like these / Has more in it of Christ than Socrates', said the Rev. E. E. Bradford in *The New Chivalry and Other Poems* (1918). This was not just an academic theme. In poems written in the 1850s and 1860s, Walt Whitman associated Jesus with Hermes, Hercules, Socrates, 'the full-limb'd Bacchus', and a beautiful boy soldier.

The intercontinental sweep of Whitman's all-embracing odes was unusual for the time. Most consciously homosexual depictions of a 'Greek' Jesus date from the late 19th and early 20th centuries. The novelist Jean Lorrain imagined him in 1893 as a hermaphroditic Cupid, a beardless, heavy-lidded Adonis with 'a kind of ambiguous charm'. The American Catholic, 'R. S.', quoted in Havelock Ellis's *Studies in the Psychology of Sex*, thought that Jesus should look like 'some Praxitelean demigod or Flandrin's naked, brooding boy'.* He might have appreciated the soft-porn painting, *L'École de Platon* (1897), by the Belgian symbolist Jean Delville. Swathed in a pinkish robe and flanked by twelve nude disciples with body-builder muscles, 'Plato' is obviously supposed to be Jesus Christ.

Examples are too scarce to allow for much chronological precision, but there is some evidence for the earlier spread of the idea in a rearguard action. In *Amour et Mariage* (1858) and his Gospel commentaries (1866), Proudhon complained that an 'odious aspersion' had been cast on the love of Jesus and John. In his opinion, the Gospel love story was 'a Christian imitation of Greek love'. John was a dreamy, Platonic Jew who wanted to win a place for himself and Jesus in the pantheon of male lovers: Socrates and Alcibiades, Alexander and Hephaestion, etc. 'John is the Antinous of Christ.' As if alarmed by his own insight, Proudhon insisted however that their relations were pure: 'The Jews were lascivious, but not *pederastic.*'

Renan's *Vie de Jésus* (1863) also shows signs of a silent controversy. He claimed that Jesus's affection for John was exaggerated by John's acolytes, and denied, significantly, that Jesus had 'any knowledge of

---

* Hippolyte Flandrin's *Jeune homme nu assis sur un rocher* (1835–6) and photographs of Praxiteles' statue of Hermes, discovered in 1877, were common gay icons of the late 19th century.

Greek culture'. The 'Orient' was different in those days, according to Renan: men and women mixed more freely. 'Women, in fact, welcomed Jesus eagerly.' Jesus was such a perfect gentleman that he was able to establish 'a very tender intellectual union between the two sexes'. For Renan, a sensual, heterosexual Jesus was preferable to any sort of homosexual Christ.

*

THE ARTISTIC OSTENTATION and philosophical ingenuity of most paintings and published texts may be untypical of private fantasies, but they do suggest that Jesus was often the object of intense, personal communion. As Marc-André Raffalovich explained to the medical and legal readers of his *Uranisme et unisexualité* (1896): 'The sacred and tender love of one's fellow man, the love of the young, naked, bleeding god [. . .] fills Uranists [. . .] with understandable enthusiasm.'

The beautiful young man with long hair and loving gestures, whose passionate writhings adorned church walls and were admired in museums, was a ubiquitous image. As if by some extraordinary good fortune, this icon of male loveliness was mass-produced and publicly displayed by a society that was otherwise intent on reinforcing a heterosexual norm. And, as many people realized, the faces and bodies of some of the best-known Gospel figures had been objects of desire as well as models. A photograph of a Florentine or Sicilian boy might be compromising, but no one could easily object to a reproduction of one of Caravaggio's languorous Christs or of Andrea del Sarto's profoundly winsome John the Baptist.

The 'enthusiasm' referred to by Raffalovich was not necessarily profane. Homoeroticism was quite compatible with religious fervour. One day, after returning from the Bibliothèque Nationale to his room in Montmartre, Max Jacob had a vision of Christ and wrote a passionate ode to his dead body, reminiscent of the banned centurion poem by James Kirkup. In both cases, necrophiliac desire prefigures the Resurrection:

> Oh! if only I could bring you back to life, my beloved. You are even
> more handsome than before, my darling. I never want to leave you. I

like to feel your body in my arms. [. . .] Your stomach is hard – that's
what most surprises one in a corpse. I never noticed before what
delicate feet you had.

There was a similarly ecstatic blend of sexual and metaphysical
yearning in Gerard Manley Hopkins' earnest evocation of the physical
Jesus in a sermon preached at Leigh in Lancashire in 1879. High
Church Anglicanism might have allowed homosexual desire to be
sublimated, but it could still appear in public with very little disguise:

> In his body he was most beautiful. [. . .] They tell us that he was
> moderately tall, well built and tender in frame, his features straight
> and beautiful, his hair inclining to auburn, parted in the midst,
> curling and clustering about the ears and neck as the leaves of a filbert,
> so to speak, upon the nut. He wore also a forked beard and this as
> well as the locks upon his head were never touched by razor or shears;
> neither, his health being perfect, could a hair ever fall to the ground.
> [. . .] I leave it to you, brethren, then to picture him, in whom the
> fullness of the godhead dwelt bodily, in his bearing how majestic, how
> strong and yet how lovely and lissome in his limbs, in his look
> how earnest, grave but kind. In his Passion all this strength was spent,
> this lissomeness crippled, this beauty wrecked, this majesty beaten
> down. But now it is more than all restored, and for myself I make no
> secret I look forward with eager desire to seeing the matchless beauty
> of Christ's body in the heavenly light.

In earlier years, Hopkins had had 'evil thoughts' while sketching a
crucified arm. A crucifix belonging to his Aunt Kate had stimulated
him 'in the wrong way'. Yet the beautiful, never-balding Jesus of his
sermon was not a cynical, self-gratifying fantasy. It was part of a
lifelong attempt to find a liturgy through which his own kind of love
could be expressed and devoted to God.

Many examples of what would later be seen as crude appropriations
belong to this quest for accommodating rituals. In Frederick Rolfe's
Hadrian the Seventh (1904), George Arthur Rose, after long years in a
suburban lodging-house attic, is elected Pope and sets about renewing
Catholic ritual in line with his own peculiar tastes. Commissioning
a new cross, he shows the goldsmith the hermaphroditic Antinous
of the Belvedere (another popular gay icon): 'The cross will be of the

kind called Potent, elongate: the Figure will combine the body and limbs of the Apoxyomenos* with the head and bust of the Antinous.'

The Rev. Samuel Cottam, whose mind seems to have wandered quite freely during his sermons (see p. 219), thought of the official cult of Emperor Hadrian's drowned lover, 'the everglorious lad' Antinous (d. 122), as the religion that might have been: 'Antinoüs was within an ace of becoming the god of the modern world. We may say it was only the divinity of Christ which prevented this.'

'R. S.' had an even more ambitious arrangement in mind when he told Havelock Ellis of his personal theology. He appears to have been thinking of the Christian myth of male procreation, the all-male family of Father, Son and Holy Ghost, and the erotic connotations of holy communion:

> [...] when I realized that homosexually it was neither lawful nor possible for me to love in this world, I began to project my longings into the next.
>
> From the doctrines of the Trinity, Incarnation, and Eucharist, I have drawn conclusions which would fill the minds of the average pietist with holy horror; nevertheless I believe that (granting the premises) these conclusions are both logically and theologically defensible.

Theological argument was often quite irrelevant. Not all these remodellings of Christ were Christian. Anyone with the desire and the imagination could weave their own experiences into the story of Jesus. Prime-Stevenson wrote about Christ's 'vivid attraction to total strangers', as if the gathering of bachelor disciples had been an early form of cruising, with the characteristic indifference to class and status. In his view, Judas was the jealous lover who gave his boyfriend away to the police: 'We may also remember that Christ was a Jew, and that his apostles were of an Oriental race inclined to homosexual passions.' In *Une Saison en Enfer*, Rimbaud recast his adventure with Verlaine as a tale of the 'Foolish Virgin' and the 'Holy Bridegroom' – the charlatan Messiah and his weak disciple erotically entangled in a London bedsit. In *De profundis*, Oscar Wilde turned Jesus into

---

* Roman copy of a 4th-century BC Greek statue of an athlete scraping his arm with a strigil, in the Vatican Museum.

an 1890s aesthete with a criminal record: 'the scarlet figure of History', who exposed himself 'to all experience'; 'the dream of a Virgilian poet'; 'Socrates [might have] reasoned with him and Plato understood him.' Jesus and John appeared with growing frequency in lists of male lovers. Emmanuel Signoret's *Le Livre de l'amitié* (1891) placed Jesus and John – 'hair blowing in the breeze of sensual pleasure' – in the unlikely company of Verlaine and his young lover, Lucien Létinois.

In an age when most public heroes owed their prestige to acts of aggression, gentle Jesus remained a revolutionary presence. Jesus and the twelve apostles were a model homosocial community, a saintly equivalent of Robin Hood and his Merry Men. For those who lived in fear of persecution, in enforced chastity or in the company of a few like-minded friends, the select group of devoted young men was an inspiring example:

> The great framer of the world meant to create in Urnings a noble priesthood, a race of Samaritans, a severely pure order of men, in order to offer a strong counterpoise to the immoral tendencies of the human race. (Otto de Joux, *Die Enterbten des Liebesglückes*, 1893)

The language of the Gospels was used to express the suffering or happiness of a homosexual life – the abandonment by God or the revelation of the love 'which passeth knowledge'. The moment or process of coming out was a religious experience:

> I was overcome with real despair. I cried with shame, when the stranger turned to me in amazement: 'Why are you behaving like that? Hundreds of people do this!' Never in my life – may God forgive me! – have I heard such a blessed word. I felt as though I was waking to a new life and that I had been born again! (Testimony of 'an upper-class society man' published by J. L. Casper in 1863)

These were not parasitic exploitations of a supposedly fixed set of symbols. They were sincere attempts to escape from loneliness and despair, to share in the love that had been promised to all and reserved for a few.

Most yearnings for a church and a community found no immediate echo. They implied a religion that was mystical and personal rather than a public expression of shared beliefs. The huge angelic society of heaven was an implausible dream, or even a nightmare. Many years later, Quentin Crisp could imagine nothing better than eternal anonymity:

> By heterosexuals the life after death is imagined as a world of light, where there is no parting. If there is a heaven for homosexuals, which doesn't seem very likely, it will be very poorly lit and full of people they can feel pretty confident they will never have to meet again.

*

BY THE END OF the 19th century, the idea of Christian homosexuality was sufficiently well established to be used as a reason to reject Christianity. Many ideological attacks were based on an assumption that Jesus was effeminate and the Church a haven for inverts. It was partly to combat this association of Christian tenderness with effeminacy that Charles Kingsley developed the idea of 'muscular Christianity' and that Thomas Hughes (of *Tom Brown's Schooldays*) wrote *The Manliness of Christ* (1879 and 1894). Zola and other anti-clerical ideologues wrote of the 'devirilizing' effect of Jesus. Christian continence was widely held to be a cause of sexual perversion in men and women. According to Vasili Rosanov, in *People of the Moonlight* (1911), the 'wondrousness' of Christianity was simply the 'wonder' of 'inversion'. 'All New-Testament instructions, parables, images, similes, promises, and rules can be reduced to one: "Do not be attracted to women".'

The figure of the androgyne in art and literature also underwent a change. Androgynes had once been symbols of unity and hope, now they were nightmares of genital angst. Balzac's hermaphroditic angel on skis, Séraphîta-Séraphîtus (1835), is a model of loving omni-science. The Méphistophéla of Catulle Mendès (in an internationally best-selling novel of 1890) is a vampirical, cigarette-smoking trans-vestite who thinks that Jesus actively promoted lesbian sex. The angels of William Blake had embodied a religious idea. The swooning hermaphrodites of Burne-Jones and Gustave Moreau were eerily passive and consumed by an unknown disease. A similar degeneration occurred in homosexual interpretations of the Gospels. Aleister

Crowley's childish ode to sodomy in *White Stains* (1898) turned Luke 14:23 into a lewd innuendo: 'Go into the highways and hedges and compel them *to come in*' (Crowley's emphasis). A French journalist described Alfred Douglas as 'a gentleman who practises in his own fashion the injunction, "Suffer little children to come unto me." '

The theme was quickly taken up by 20th-century homophobia. If Gerard Manley Hopkins had preached his sermon thirty years later, his matinée idol Christ might have caused some discomfort in the pews. Homoerotic depictions of Jesus in the 20th century would often meet with organized opposition. This was the now familiar dilemma: social acceptance was impossible without recognition, but public recognition also brought public rejection.

For most of the 19th century, there had been a nervous, negative kind of freedom. Delville's Platonic Jesus, which visitors to the Musée d'Orsay now instantly recognize as a gay icon, passed without public protest, as did Simeon Solomon's homoerotic threesome, *The Sleepers and the One That Watcheth* (1870). This vertical bed scene on a starry background was not explicitly Biblical, but the title clearly alluded to the Garden of Gethsemane. Few enough bridges had been built between gay culture and the general public that Solomon's drawings could, without incurring instant opprobrium, circulate among the homosexual cognoscenti. (His drawing of *Love Talking to Boys* hung on the wall of Oscar Wilde's rooms at Magdalen.)

This uneasy state of affairs was a prelude to open combat. The crucified Christ, remarkable for its expressive loin-cloth, that Ralph Adams Cram supplied for All Saints' Episcopal Church in Boston, had been created under the homoerotic influence of 1890s aestheticism. When it was installed in 1911, 'it aroused enough ire to be threatened with replacement'. Duncan Grant's wall painting of *The Good Shepherd* (*c.* 1958), based on a Hermes in the Catacombs, adorned the Russell Chantry in Lincoln Cathedral until the 1960s, when the chapel was closed to the public and used as a store-room. Grant's noble, sensual Jesus was covered up by piles of ecclesiastical rubbish. (The mural is now on public display.)

It is typical of 19th-century gay traditions that the notion of a homosexual or sympathetic Jesus spread in such an obscure, rhizomatous fashion. Ideas arose independently and spontaneously, with few obvious signs of cross-fertilization. Yet this scattered minority gave new life to traditions that explicitly rejected it. Far from perverting holy scripture, most homosexual readings revealed inherent ambiguities and perhaps – to judge by the neurotic intensity of later reactions – the latent homosexuality of the established Church.

Most homosexual men and women who looked for warmth in the Church were not anticipating social liberation. They lived, like the early Christians, in a dark world of small spaces in which the only constant light came from a place beyond the grave. When Gerard Manley Hopkins administered First Communion to the blooming bugler boy at Cowley barracks –

> [. . .] so I in a sort deserve to
> And do serve God to serve to
> Just such slips of soldiery Christ's royal ration –

or when Verlaine pictured his ecstatic conversion as rough treatment at the hands of a Rimbaldian God, their religious passion was all the stronger for their experience of human love. And when Emily Dickinson longed for her beloved Sue Gilbert on Sunday mornings, her thoughts might have been sacrilegious in a strict sense, but there was probably no more fervent soul in the congregation.

> When [the pastor] said 'Our Heavenly Father', I said 'Oh Darling Sue', when he read the 100th Psalm, I kept saying your precious letter all over to myself, and Susie, when they sang – it would have made you laugh to hear one little voice, piping to the departed. I made up words and kept singing how I loved you, and you had gone, while all the rest of the choir were singing Hallelujahs. I presume nobody heard me, because I sang *so small*, but it was a kind of a comfort to think I might put them out, singing of you. [. . .] I think of love, and you, and my heart grows full and warm, and my breath stands still. The sun does'nt shine at all, but I can feel a sunshine stealing into my soul and making it all summer, and every thorn, a *rose*.
>
> [. . .] You won't cry any more, will you, Susie, for my father will be your father, and my home will be your home, and where you go, I will go, and we will lie side by side in the kirkyard.

10

Heroes of Modern Life

Be wary of the probable: start by believing the incredible.

Émile Gaboriau, *Monsieur Lecoq* (1869), chapter 8

When you have eliminated all which is impossible, then whatever remains, however improbable, must be the truth.

Arthur Conan Doyle, 'The Adventure of the Blanched Soldier', *The Case-Book of Sherlock Holmes* (1927)

T HE LOST HERITAGE of gay men and women was mislaid, not destroyed. Sexuality was never so obvious or so feared that it led to the suppression of an entire culture. Different standards are still applied to the lives and works of gay men and women, and a moralizing tone is still sometimes allowed when the subject is homosexuality, but the works of 19th-century gay writers are easy to obtain and widely read – even those that would otherwise have been forgotten.

The influence of gay men and women on European and American society was constant and profound, and there is no lack of evidence to prove it. But identifying specific influences – on literature and the arts, fashion, religion, law, medicine and psychiatry – might actually diminish their role by suggesting that gay experience can easily be separated from the rest of human life.

This final chapter, which forms a coda rather than a conclusion, is an attempt to detect, in a particular example, a more general influence. Much of this book has been devoted to extricating individuals from the mass. This is not a last-minute attempt to identify essential, common characteristics or to claim that gay men and women were fundamentally different from everyone else. Notions of profound superiority are just as suspect as notions of profound depravity. But the circumstances in which they lived *were* different and placed them in a special position.

The subject has been touched on at various points: Victorian society, like the 'primitive' cultures discovered by its missionaries and explorers, assigned a shamanic role to sexual strangers. The fascination with homosexuality – vulgarly expressed as prurient interest in bedroom behaviour – was the mark of an unconscious or grudging perception that gay men and women had special knowledge, that they formed a kind of existential avant-garde and were somehow more at home in the modern world than the protected majority. In a shy and silent part of the Victorian mind, 'Uranians' were the model citizens of a rapidly changing world.

This shamanic role is seen most clearly in the emergence of the private detective as a modern hero – hence the following few pages of literary analysis. But the significance of this figure and its amazing popularity go far beyond literary history. In this domain at least, a steady bridge existed between the fantasy world of popular perceptions and the real experience of gay men and women.

The end of this epilogue will have the not entirely incidental advantage of returning this history to its starting point – the criminal justice system – in more cheerful and intelligent circumstances.

*

IT IS GENERALLY AGREED that the myth of the private eye was invented by Edgar Allan Poe. The eccentric amateur sleuth, Auguste Dupin, was introduced in 1841 in *The Murders in the Rue Morgue*. He reappeared in *The Mystery of Marie Roget* (1842) and *The Purloined Letter* (1845). Although he then disappeared for ever, his footprints can be found in almost every detective tale that followed.

According to the narrator of *Marie Roget*, the gory mishap in the Rue Morgue was just a pretext. The idea was not to illustrate the homicidal propensities of the Bornese orang-utan but 'to depict some very remarkable features in the mental character of my friend, the Chevalier C. Auguste Dupin'. 'This depicting of character constituted my design; and this design was thoroughly fulfilled in the wild train of circumstances brought to instance Dupin's idiosyncrasy.'

The character of the world's first literary detective, in other words, is a puzzle cloaked in a mystery. When the tale appeared in *Graham's Magazine*, Poe, who edited the magazine, was running a cipher competition. Readers were invited to send in coded messages, which Poe then solved – all except one, which turned out to be a meaningless jumble of letters. His own cipher remained unsolved, despite the enticement of a year's subscription to the magazine.

Though no one seems to have noticed, *The Murders in the Rue Morgue* was another test of the readers' cryptic skills. The first part of the tale is a detailed exposition of Dupin's analytical methods, but it was also an invitation to apply the methods to the tale itself, to distinguish the large and irrelevant from the small and significant: 'The necessary knowledge', says Dupin, 'is that of *what* to observe.'

What then do we know about the enigmatic Dupin? Two kinds of information are offered: explicit and encrypted. The explicit information provides the clues and the encrypted information the proof.

First, the clues: Dupin belongs to an illustrious, aristocratic family, has written poetry, and admires Epicurus. He has a friend, known only as D., who is a renowned poet and a dandy, and whose servants are 'chiefly Neapolitans'. 'By a variety of untoward [and unspecified] events', Dupin has been reduced to poverty. He now goes out only at night and, despite having satisfied his creditors, is curiously vigilant: 'Observation has become with me, of late, a species of necessity.'

One evening, the narrator meets Dupin in 'an obscure library' and experiences something like love at first sight:

> I felt my soul enkindled within me by the wild fervor, and the vivid freshness of his imagination. Seeking in Paris the objects I then sought, I felt that the society of such a man would be to me a treasure beyond price; and this feeling I frankly confided to him. It was at length arranged that we should live together during my stay in the city.

The two friends make their home in 'a time-eaten and grotesque mansion' in the Faubourg St Germain. Their whereabouts are to remain a secret:

> Had the routine of our life at this place been known to the world, we should have been regarded as madmen – although, perhaps, as madmen of a harmless nature. [. . .]
>
> It was a freak of fancy in my friend (for what else shall I call it?) to be enamored of the night for her own sake; and into this bizarrerie, as into all his others, I quietly fell; giving myself up to his wild whims with a perfect abandon.

Dupin and his enthralled disciple spend their days behind closed shutters in the scent-laden gloom of their hideaway. Perfumed tapers burn in the unnatural darkness. At night, they prowl the streets, arm in arm, 'seeking, amid the wild lights and shadows of the populous city, that infinity of mental excitement which quiet observation can afford'.

One night, in a dirty street near the Palais Royal (the hub of Parisian prostitution), Dupin reveals his 'intimate knowledge' of the narrator's 'bosom':

> He boasted to me, with a low, chuckling laugh, that most men, in respect to himself, wore windows in their bosoms, and was wont to follow up such assertions by direct and very startling proofs of his intimate knowledge of my own. His manner at these moments was frigid and abstract; his eyes were vacant in expression; while his voice, usually a rich tenor, rose into a treble which would have sounded petulant but for the deliberateness and entire distinctness of the enunci-ation. Observing him in these moods, I often dwelt meditatively upon the old philosophy of the Bi-Part Soul, and amused myself with the fancy of a double Dupin – the creative and the resolvent.

Having now depicted his friend as a modern-day androgyne – tenor and treble, creator and analyst – the narrator feels the need to allay suspicions. In fact, he does the opposite:

> Let it not be supposed that I am detailing any mystery, or penning any romance. What I have described in the Frenchman was merely the result of an excited, or perhaps of a diseased, intelligence.

There is, of course, nothing essentially odd about the passionate, secretive and nocturnal friendship of two strange men in a crime-ridden city, even if one of them is a dandy with a 'diseased' mind and the other, later in the tale, finds a muscle-bound sailor (the owner of the orang-utan) 'not altogether unprepossessing'.

However, the details gradually form a human shape which few cultural detectives would expect to find at such an early date. Poe's description of two men burning perfumed tapers and keeping the shutters closed might not sound suspicious today, but it certainly did in 1841. Even half a century later, an identical domestic arrangement sent a little shiver of excitement through a London jury. Sir Edward Carson was cross-examining Oscar Wilde about his visits to the procurer, Alfred Taylor:

> *Carson:* It would not be true, then, to say that he always kept a double
>   set of curtains drawn across the windows and day and night
>   lighted the room with candles or gas?
> *Wilde:* Oh, I should think quite untrue.
> *Carson:* [. . .] Were they always highly perfumed, these rooms in
>   College Street?
> *Wilde:* [. . .] He was in the habit of burning perfume, as I am in my
>   rooms.
> *Carson:* As you are in your rooms?
> *Wilde:* As I am in mine – a very charming habit it is.

The jurymen, comments Montgomery Hyde, 'now began to show by the shocked looks on their faces what they thought of this establishment, so different from their own respectable habitations'. It was this peculiar arrangement that first excited the jury in the second trial: 'More than anything else perhaps they were influenced by the description of Taylor's rooms in Little College Street, with their heavily draped windows, candles burning on through the day, and the langorous atmosphere heavy with perfume.'

The criminal nuances of Poe's ménage help to thicken the foggy atmosphere, but they also reflect a precise intention. A handful of mythological allusions are scattered through the text, from the epigraph to the final paragraph. When these allusions are assembled, a pattern emerges:

– The epigraph, from Sir Thomas Browne's *Urn Burial* (via Suetonius's life of Tiberius), refers to the period when Achilles was dressed as a girl: 'What song the Syrens sang, or what name Achilles assumed when he hid himself among women, although puzzling questions, are not beyond *all* conjecture.'

– By closing the shutters in the daytime, Dupin and the narrator are said to 'counterfeit [the] presence' of the goddess of night.

– The two friends have 'often conversed' about a line of Latin: '*Perdidit antiquuum litera prima sonum*' ('The first letter has lost its former sound'). This refers to the belief that Orion was 'formerly written Urion'. 'From certain pungencies connected with this explanation', says Dupin, 'I was aware that you could not have forgotten it.' The nature of these 'pungencies' is revealed in the source of the quotation: Ovid's *Fasti*. Hyrieus, the founder of Hyria, was childless. He sought the help of the gods and was advised to urinate on the hide of a sacrificed bull and then bury it. Nine months later, a boy rose from the earth and was named Orion or Urion (from ουϱον, urine).

– Dupin compares his methods to the astronomer's trick of using peripheral vision: a sidelong glance at a star allows its light to fall on the more sensitive part of the retina, whereas, 'by a scrutiny too sustained, too concentrated, or too direct', 'it is possible to make even Venus herself vanish from the firmament'.

– The tale ends with Dupin's withering assessment of the Prefect of Police: 'In his wisdom is no *stamen*. It is all head and no body, like the pictures of the Goddess Laverna.' The Prefect is compared to the goddess of thieves and described as a unisexual organism, a flower without a pollen-bearing organ.

It now becomes clear that a hidden thread runs through the tale: the impersonation or elimination of the female or, in the Prefect's case, the male (the transvestite Achilles, the goddess of night 'counterfeited' by two men, the exclusively male procreation of Orion, the obliteration of Venus, and the stamenless Prefect-Laverna). To use Dupin's analogy, these classical allusions are the letters that form the largest word on the map – a word which, precisely because it stretches 'from one end of the chart to the other', escapes detection.

The murder story can now be seen as a symbolic reflection of the whole. Just as the 'man' who commits the murders is not a man, the man who solves them is not a man either in the normal sense of the word. Two 'wild' things are alive in the city (the adjective is applied twice to Dupin and twice to the ape): one of them has very large hands, tawny hair and the strength of a lunatic; the other is a nocturnal creature with heightened senses and unusual mating habits.

The Murders in the Rue Morgue turns out to be even more remarkable than it first appears. The world's first literary detective is also one of the first modern homosexual heroes. The painted fops of 18th-century satire and the creeping perverts of the penny dreadful are only distant cousins of Dupin. His closest living relative is the supernatural androgyne of Gothic fiction, but the androgyne now has an urban lifestyle, tastes in interior decoration and a like-minded friend. Unlike most later homosexual characters, he enjoys a passionate and stable friendship, uncontaminated by self-loathing or despair. He appears to be that rarest of birds in 19th-century literature: a happy homosexual.

The question then arises: where did he come from? We know that Poe met an orang-utan in Philadelphia in 1839, and it is not unreasonable to suppose that he also met a homosexual. Until now, the earliest known references to homosexuality in the urban United States (since Poe's fantasy Paris seems to be a transposition of New York) were sleazy exposés in the 1830s and 1840s on homosexual prostitution, foreign sodomites and a transvestite robber known as 'Beefsteak Pete' or the 'Man Monster'. Melville's *Redburn* (1849) refers to effeminate hookers 'with small feet like a doll's, and a small, glossy head like a seal's', 'standing in sentimental attitudes in front of Palmo's in Broadway'. In the same year, *City Crimes, or Life in New York and Boston* by 'Greenhorn' described the boy prostitutes who – as all New Yorkers apparently knew – sold themselves in the vicinity of Central Park to 'genteel foreign vagabonds'.

Dupin and his friend are a rare reminder that, despite the distorting weight of evidence, 19th-century homosexuality is not reducible to public prostitution any more than heterosexuality can be attributed to brothels. This twilight world also had its domestic, settled side. The prowling 'perverts' of the popular press were also hearth-rug homosexuals.

Poe's male ménage is neither a den of vice nor a cowering, apologetic anomaly. Far from corrupting society, Dupin rids it of a vicious threat. His mind may be 'diseased', but it would be hard to imagine a more useful citizen. In the factual writings of lawyers, doctors and journalists, the homosexual was a fictitious monster. In the dream world of literature, he was a real person and, more to the point, an improvement on the norm.

If Dupin and his friend had lived a century later, they might have been the subject of a police investigation or a medical inquiry. Normality would have been restored, but at what cost? The forces of order would have been left to their inadequate devices, and the city would still be terrorized by a hyperactive ape.

*

AN APPARENTLY straightforward case of influence can reveal a more profound connection. It is significant, for instance, that 'the introspective and pallid dreamer of Baker Street' inherited not only Dupin's methods but also, according to Dr Watson, his 'dual nature'.*

The following observations are not a sly attempt to ensnare the great detective in the elastic web of gay revisionism. Everyone already knows, instinctively, that Holmes is homosexual. Screen adaptations are a good test. The least convincing are always those that provide him with a girlfriend. The most convincing, like Billy Wilder's *The Private Life of Sherlock Holmes* (1970) – promoted as 'a love story between two men' – are those that exaggerate his camp behaviour. Without the tense, suppressed passion that binds him to his biographer, Holmes is just a man with an interesting hobby.

Conan Doyle himself was quietly ambivalent on the subject of homosexuality. In one of the medical tales collected in *Round the Red Lamp* (1894), an alienist called Charley Manson, 'author of the brilliant monograph, *Obscure Lesions in the Unmarried*', regrets that, while 'some of the richest human materials that a man could study' can be

---

* Émile Gaboriau's 'almost beardless, very pale' young bachelor detective, Lecoq, created in 1863, twenty-four years before Holmes, is another close relative. A 'naturally moral and honest young man, [he] spent much of his time in perpetrating – in fancy – the most abominable crimes'.

found in the field of medicine, these subjects are out-of-bounds to the novelist: for example, 'the singular phenomena of waxing and of waning manhood' and 'those actions which have cut short many an honoured career and sent a man to prison when he should have been hurried to a consulting-room'. This was Dr Doyle's view of the disgraced Oscar Wilde: 'I thought at the time, and still think [in 1924] that the monstrous development which ruined him was pathological, and that a hospital rather than a police court was the place for its consideration.' Or a writer's study. Doyle had once asked Roger Casement to provide him with information on sexual perversion among the natives of the Peruvian Amazon, and he supported him publicly even after the 'Black Diaries' had revealed Casement's own enthusiastic contribution to homosexual perversion in South America.

Holmes himself bears a striking resemblance to Oscar Wilde. Doyle first met Wilde at the Langham Hotel in August 1889, at a dinner given by the publisher J. M. Stoddart. The meeting led to the publication in *Lippincott's Magazine* of *The Picture of Dorian Gray*, 'a book which is surely upon a high moral plane', according to Doyle, and *The Sign of Four*, 'in which Holmes made his second appearance'.

Thirty-five years later, Doyle still remembered that 'golden evening'. Wilde's conversation had left 'an indelible impression' – his 'curious precision of statement', the 'delicate flavour of humour'. 'He towered above us all.' Doyle had in effect been dining with Sherlock Holmes. The two were easily confused. In 1923, during his ectoplasmic phase, Doyle received a message from beyond the grave and defied 'any man of real critical instinct to read that script and doubt that it emanates from Wilde': 'Being dead is the most boring experience in life, that is if one excepts being married or dining with a school-master!' If he had thought to insert the words, 'My dear Watson', it would have been obvious to him that the message had emanated, not from Wilde, but from the other leading wit and aesthete of the Decadent Nineties.

Sherlock Holmes, like Oscar Wilde, was one of the popular faces of Victorian aestheticism. The man on the Baker Street omnibus could peer through the fictitious windows of 221b and feel at home in the world of 'superior' minds. Like a true Decadent, Holmes enjoys 'introspective' German music and listens to it with 'languid, dreamy eyes'. 'Art for art's sake' is one of his mottoes – applied, not to poetry, but to the incongruously useful art of criminal detection. He possesses the prerequisites of any serious aesthete: 'extraordinary delicacy of touch', a 'catlike love of personal cleanliness', and artistic French blood. (His grandmother was the sister of the painter, Horace Vernet.) As Holmes tells Watson in 'The Greek Interpreter' (1893), 'Art in the blood is liable to take the strangest forms.' Proof of this is found in Sherlock's older brother, Mycroft – a brilliant and eccentric bachelor who spends his evenings at a club for unsociable men, observing the 'magnificent types' that tread its carpet: 'The Diogenes Club', explains Holmes, 'is the queerest club in London, and Mycroft, one of the queerest men.'*

As a lover of the artificial to whom country air is poison and London fog a tonic, Holmes abhors 'Nature' with a Baudelairian passion, though he is capable of falling into a long reverie whilst contemplating 'the drooping stalk of a moss-rose': 'What a lovely thing a rose is!' exclaims the great detective, astonishing the ever-observant Dr Watson: 'It was a new phase of his character to me, for I had never before seen him show any keen interest in natural objects.'

'Natural objects', of course, include women. 'As a lover', observes Watson, 'he would have placed himself in a false position.' The only woman he admires is Irene Adler, who dresses as a man. 'Male costume is nothing new to me', she tells her cerebral admirer.

Otherwise, the 'softer human emotions' in Holmes are reserved entirely for Watson. In the first story, *A Study in Scarlet* (1887), when Watson praises him for making criminal detection an exact science, Holmes 'flushed up with pleasure at my words, and the earnest way in which I uttered them. I had already observed that he was as sensitive to flattery on the score of his art as any girl could be of her beauty.' This delicate friendship is the subject of the second Holmes story, *The Sign of Four* (1890). The interest lies not in the feeble mystery but in the enigma of the Holmesian brain. Early in

---

* In 1894, 'queer' had already acquired its modern sense. Wilde's persecutor, the Marquis of Queensberry, referred that year to 'the Snob Queers like Roseberry' [sic]. The words 'earnest' and 'languid', applied below to Holmes, also had homosexual connotations.

the investigation, Dr Watson inconsiderately falls in love with the distressed client:

'What a very attractive woman!' I exclaimed, turning to my companion.

He had lit his pipe again and was leaning back with drooping eyelids. 'Is she?' he said languidly; 'I did not observe.'

'You really are an automaton – a calculating machine', I cried. 'There is something positively inhuman in you at times.'

He smiled gently.

The human calculating machine tries to woo Watson away from his beloved Mary. Summoning up a meal of grouse and oysters, he chides his friend, 'You have never yet recognized my merits as a housekeeper.' He even tries to impress him with his bedside manner:

'Look here, Watson; you look regularly done. Lie down there on the sofa and see if I can put you to sleep.'

He took up his violin from the corner, and as I stretched myself out he began to play some low, dreamy, melodious air – his own, no doubt, for he had a remarkable gift for improvisation. I have a vague remembrance of his gaunt limbs, his earnest face and the rise and fall of his bow. Then I seemed to be floated peacefully away upon a soft sea of sound until I found myself in dreamland, with the sweet face of Mary Morstan looking down upon me.

His wifely virtues spurned, Holmes loses his friend to marriage with 'a most dismal groan'.

Happily, Mrs Watson never materializes and has the grace to be dead by 1904. 'Old times' return, with many moments of fervent intimacy: Watson's hands are clutched, his knees patted, and his ears brushed by Holmes's whispering lips. When the trail leads out of London, they sleep in 'double-bedded' rooms. In the following scene, Watson has been shot and feels a searing pain in his thigh. The 19th-century man of forensic investigation meets the 19th-century man of medicine in a loving embrace:

My friend's wiry arms were round me, and he was leading me to a chair.

'You're not hurt, Watson? For God's sake, say that you are not hurt!'

[263]

It was worth a wound – it was worth many wounds – to know the depth of loyalty and love which lay behind that cold mask. The clear, hard eyes were dimmed for a moment, and the firm lips were shaking. For the one and only time I caught a glimpse of a great heart as well as of a great brain. All my years of humble but single-minded service culminated in that moment of revelation.

A writer who could tease his readers with untold tales like that of the Giant Rat of Sumatra ('for which the world is not yet prepared'), was certainly capable of toying with the subscribers of *The Strand Magazine* and their amazing infatuation with Holmes. Between 1886 and 1927, the great detective becomes increasingly patriotic, but also increasingly camp. 'I trust that age doth not wither nor custom stale my infinite variety', he prompts his sidekick. On separate occasions, he greets Inspector Gregson and a 'tremendously virile and yet sinister' criminal with the Shakespearean refrain, 'Journeys end in lovers' meeting'.

In 1908, Baden-Powell held up this camping aesthete as a role model in his *Scouting for Boys*. The title has since acquired an accidental ambiguity which suits Holmes quite well. He nurtures young detectives, trains a gang of little urchins, and, in *The Hound of the Baskervilles* (1901), adopts a fourteen-year-old telegraph boy as his valet, which was hardly an innocent act after the Cleveland Street scandal (p. 26). Sherlock's little helpers not only run errands, they also help to 'fill up the gap of loneliness and isolation which surrounded the saturnine figure of the great detective'.

Holmes's sexuality, like Dupin's, is not just an exotic embellishment to match the Persian slippers, the Stradivarius violin and the hypodermic needles: it is an essential part of his character, which might explain why Doyle 'recognized' Sherlock Holmes in the American actor, William Gillette – a man described as 'very handsome', 'eccentric' and 'no longer interested in women'. Like Dupin, Holmes has a distinctly homosexual lifestyle. He sits with his friend in the Northumberland Avenue Turkish baths, for which 'both Holmes and I had a weakness'. A simple Venn diagram of his readings would show them to have homosexuality as their common denominator: Horace, Catullus, Háfiz and Thoreau; anthropology, medicine, scandal sheets and police records. Instead of asserting his manliness in 'amateur sport, which is the best and soundest thing in England', he frequents Chinese opium dens, consorts with 'rough-looking men', and has 'at least five small refuges in different parts of London, in which he was able to change his personality'. He stalks his prey, at various times, as a groom, a sailor, a nonconformist clergyman, a rakish young workman, a French *ouvrier* and an old woman:

> 'You've seen me as an old woman, Watson. I was never more convincing. [Count Sylvius] actually picked up my parasol for me once. "By your leave, madame", said he – half-Italian, you know, and with the Southern graces of manner when in the mood, but a devil incarnate in the other mood. Life is full of whimsical happenings, Watson.'

This hazardous underworld is Holmes's natural habitat. He first appeared two months after the Labouchere Amendment. He next appeared in February 1890, at the height of the Cleveland Street scandal. He thrives in the world of impending disgrace that the Baker Street files so amply record:

> There are the dispatch-cases filled with documents, a perfect quarry for the student, not only of crime, but of the social and official scandals of the late Victorian era. Concerning these latter, I may say that the writers of agonized letters, who beg that the honour of their families or the reputation of famous forebears may not be touched, have nothing to fear.

Watson never tries to 'force a confidence', though, as a reader of 'modern French psychologists' and the *British Medical Journal*, he clearly has suspicions. Why, for instance, does Holmes speak 'with such intensity of feeling' of the blackmailer, Milverton, who 'purrs' and has a hairless face? Why does he suddenly beg Watson to run away with him to the Continent after almost losing his life in Vere Street – a name notorious in the annals of homosexual scandal? And what are we to make of his evil pursuer, Moriarty? What were those 'dark rumours' that forced him to resign his Chair at a provincial university? And to what is Holmes referring when he says that Moriarty suffers from 'hereditary tendencies of the most diabolical kind'?

These too, no doubt, were tales 'for which the world was not yet prepared'.

*

THE EXTRAORDINARY SUCCESS of Dupin and Holmes, both as crime-solvers and as fictional characters, is directly related to their sexuality. Corroboration can be found in the long line of sexually ambiguous sleuths that followed in their velvety footsteps: E. W. Hornung's Raffles and his adoring ex-fag and biographer, Bunny, who finds him 'irresistible' and feels 'an almost staggering sense of safety' in his 'masterful' presence (from 1899); Maurice Leblanc's Arsène Lupin, 'gentleman burglar', and his young accomplice, Gilbert (from 1907); Agatha Christie's Hercule Poirot (from 1920), the little dandy with a 'cherub-like face' whose friends include dustmen and dukes, and who has a housekeeper's eye for detail: he notices stray threads, fusses about the positioning of teacups, uses cosmetics, and criticizes his companion, Captain Hastings, for being interested only in women: 'Ah, *mon ami*, one can have romance without golden-haired girls of matchless beauty.'

Dorothy L. Sayers' Lord Peter Wimsey (from 1933) is theoretically heterosexual but matches the typical medical profile of an 'invert': 'a colourless shrimp of a child', born of 'exhausted stock'. 'All nerves and nose', he grew up with a passion for books and music, was known to his fellow Etonians as 'Flimsy' and is still a bachelor at the age of forty-five.

Many other detectives – Miss Marple, Father Brown, Ellery Queen – lead similarly pregnant, celibate lives. S. S. Van Dine's languid aristocrat detective, Philo Vance (from 1926) – 'New York's leading flâneur and art connoisseur' – lives with an English butler and eats with his inseparable friend the author. Rex Stout's happily unmarried, hippo-sized sleuth, Nero Wolfe (from 1934), lives with his 'futile and sterile' orchids and his young friend Archie Goodwin in an all-male household.

The persistent ambivalence of the literary sleuth can hardly be attributed to conscious imitation, since neither Dupin nor Holmes was recognized as homosexual, except by casual humorists. Balzac, significantly, created a homosexual detective at almost the same time as Poe: Vautrin, the convict who becomes Head of the Sûreté and who is both a danger to society and 'a great doctor of the soul'. Neither writer knew of the other's detective. They were acting, independently, on the same insight. Both Poe and Balzac saw in the city-dwelling homosexual the outline of a much older type: the berdache or shaman, the sexually ambiguous warlock (or sherlock?) who knows how to live on the night-side of life and to decipher its secrets.

The anthropological association of clairvoyance with homosexuality may correspond in part to certain practical characteristics of gay life. The fact that detective fiction represents a disproportionately large amount of modern gay fiction does suggest a special affinity with these ambiguous heroes who owe their strange power to secrets. In his *Intermediate Types Among Primitive Folk* (1911), Edward Carpenter suggested that the 'Uranian', like the shaman, possesses unusual powers of observation. He or she may even represent a more advanced stage of evolution: 'This interaction in fact, between the masculine and the feminine, this mutual illumination of logic and intuition, this combination of action and meditation [. . .] may give the mind a new quality, and a new power of perception.' Something similar had been observed more than 2,000 years before by Herodotus in the men-women of the Scythians.

It is tempting to associate the modern survival of transvestite 'twin-spirits' in the tribes of North and Central America with the prevalence of these homoerotic detective partnerships in American literature. Passionate male friendships associated with uncanny deductive powers and a desire for social justice are a common theme, from the 'Leather-Stocking Tales' of Fenimore Cooper to the masked Lone Ranger and his uncannily perceptive sidekick Tonto, who, for the first two years of his existence, rode behind his partner on the same horse, and, of course, the 'dynamic duo', Batman and Robin, who have a cosy home life as Bruce Wayne and Dick Grayson but who also cruise the slimy streets of Gotham City, nervously disguised and dressed in tights. Noting the large number of homosexual Batman devotees at the Quaker Emergency Service Readjustment Center in New York City, Fredric Wertham described the caped crusaders' friendship in 1955 as the typical pederastic relationship, 'a wish dream of two homosexuals living together'.

This is not just a matter of archetypes and the collective unconscious. For the berdaches of the modern world, a double life on the fringes of respectable society was simply an everyday reality. The New York transvestite, Earl Lind, described his nocturnal activities in terms very similar to those used by Poe's narrator:

> Because of my innate appetencies and avocation of female-impersonator, I was fated to be a Nature-appointed amateur detective. I enjoyed entrée to the hearts of both male and female denizens of the Underworld, my stamping-ground when I surrendered my bisexual body to the feminine side of my dual psyche.

The wearing of masks, the street-wise reading of signs, the ability to operate in different milieux: these were the qualifications of the urban homosexual and the private detective. Sexual singularity was a key to the world of crime and the secret configurations of the city, as Sherlock Holmes discreetly implied in the 'magnum opus' to which he devotes his later years: *Practical Handbook of Bee Culture, with Some Observations upon the Segregation of the Queen* – 'behold the fruit of pensive nights and laborious days when I watched the little working gangs as once I watched the criminal world of London'. By the same token, J. Edgar Hoover's clandestine transvestite activities were perhaps not unrelated to his grotesque efficiency as director of the FBI. As he wrote in 1947, with personal, inside knowledge, 'depraved human beings, more savage than beasts, are permitted to rove America almost at will'.

The astounding commercial success of the homosexual detective represents a kind of recuperation of the scapegoat by an apparently homophobic society. Just as the American Indian berdache was allowed to break taboos – to wear women's clothes and even to be sodomized in public ceremonies – the homosexual sleuth was a special case. In the dream world of literature, the scapegoat was not only readmitted to society, he was idolized and imitated.

The detective figure also shows a direct and positive influence of gay culture on the majority culture. It is noticeable that both Edward Carpenter and Earl Lind attribute the Uranian's unusual percipience, not to the acquired habit of avoiding detection and identifying fellow homosexuals, but to an innate quality. It was this heightened awareness that fascinated the first sexologists and turned their readers into amateur detectives. Pseudo-informative works like *Woran erkennt man Homosexuelle?** (1908) served the same function as detective stories. What was the secret sense that allowed these alien creatures to recognize one another at a glance and yet remain undetected? Was it innate or acquired? Could a normal person learn to identify them?

The strange race of Uranians seemed to cross social and national boundaries with ease and to thrive in that unfathomable environment, the modern megalopolis. They retained their identity in the face of aggressive conformity. While the average alienated citizen ran like a tram from home to work and back again through uncharted zones of danger, the homosexual was a true denizen of the city. He found friends among the faceless masses. He knew how to converse with strangers. His domestic arrangements were always open to change. He had already adapted to the strange new world.

To most gay men and women, this fantasy would have seemed both familiar and remote. Most would have been happy to exchange their heroic special powers for respectability and affection.

*

THE INCREASING VISIBILITY of 'the homosexual' in the 20th century impaired the crime-solving abilities of the gay detective. The article on 'Mystery and Detective Fiction' in the *Encyclopedia of Homosexuality* (1990), which says nothing about Dupin, Vautrin and Holmes, claims that gay men did not appear in the detective novel until the 1930s. But these were just the seedy stock-characters of earlier, melodramatic fiction, like the eerily mincing Joel Cairo in *The Maltese Falcon* (1930). Homosexuality was once again a mark of villainy and associated, not with love, but with sinister genital intentions.

The 19th-century 'sherlock' probably died out before the Second World War. The figure was already collapsing into farce when it had a splendid late flowering in a film called *The Arsenal Stadium Mystery* (1939), adapted from an unremarkable novel by Leonard Gribble.

---

* 'How to Recognize Homosexuals'.

Inspector Slade (played by Leslie Banks) is seen enjoying himself in a variety of compromising positions: interviewing a member of the pre-War Arsenal football team in a steaming bath, reading a newspaper that covers the naked bottom of a player. To his Sergeant's disgust, he finds the case a thrilling prospect: 'Well, all these outdoor fellows with their er . . . shorts on.'

Slade's campness is the key to his deductive genius: 'You know, everybody has two sides to their nature', he tells his bemused Sergeant. 'We've all been indiscreet in our time.' In the opening and closing scenes, the Inspector, wearing a beret and a buttonhole, is rehearsing a chorus-line of sturdy policemen dressed in tutus: 'Ladies, ladies', he cries, 'these skirts weren't provided for you by Nature. They're meant to enhance your beauty, to allure. You must swish 'em about a bit and make 'em look attractive. [. . .] The fair name of the Metropolitan Police beauty chorus is at stake.' When Sergeant Clinton holds up a ballet dress, the Inspector observes with interest: 'You know, Sergeant Smithers is getting a bit broad in the hips. That's the second time he's split that.'

Like the sherlocks before him, Slade is not a public enemy but the man who delves into the sewers of society and notices what others cannot or will not see. He even has a civilizing influence on those brutal enforcers of public morality, the Metropolitan Police. As long as Slade is on the case, it is hard to believe that it will all end in tragedy:

> Sergeant Clinton (watching the tutued policemen prance across the stage):
>   'You know, you oughtn't to be doing all this, Sir. These men will never be the same again.'
> Inspector Slade: 'Well, that's something to be thankful for.'

Appendices

I. Criminal Statistics

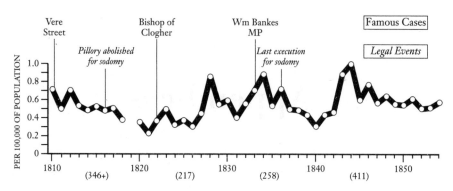

1. Indictments for sodomy and related offences in England and Wales
per 100,000 of population, 1810–1900

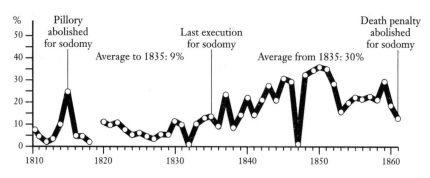

2. Percentage of convicted sodomites sentenced to death in England
and Wales, 1810–1861

1810–35: of 78 sentenced to death, 46 were executed.
Figures unavailable for 1819. No death sentences in 1832 and 1847.

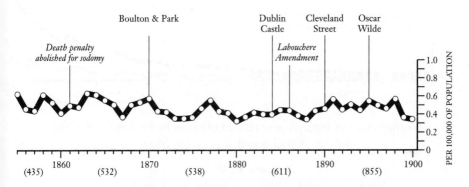

Death penalty
abolished for sodomy

Boulton & Park

Dublin
Castle

Cleveland
Street

Oscar
Wilde

Labouchere
Amendment

PER 100,000 OF POPULATION

(435)   1860   (532)   1870   (538)   1880   (611)   1890   (855)   1900

Includes indecency after 1892. Figures unavailable for 1819.
Numbers in parentheses show actual numbers convicted, by decade.

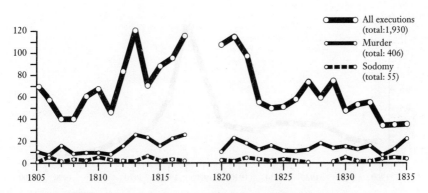

All executions
(total:1,930)

Murder
(total: 406)

Sodomy
(total: 55)

3. Executions for sodomy in England and Wales, 1805–35

Figures unavailable or incomplete for 1818 and 1819.

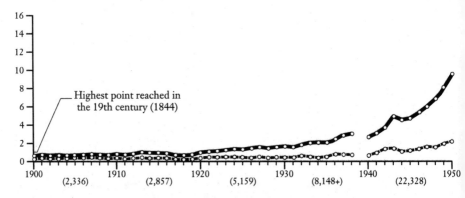

Highest point reached in
the 19th century (1844)

(2,336)   (2,857)   (5,159)   (8,148+)   (22,328)

4. Recorded cases of buggery and related offences in England and Wales
per 100,000 of population, 1900–2000

No figures for 1939.
Numbers in parentheses show total number of cases, by decade.

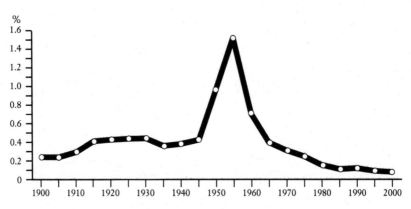

5. Buggery and related offences in England and Wales as a percentage of
total recorded crime, 1900–2000

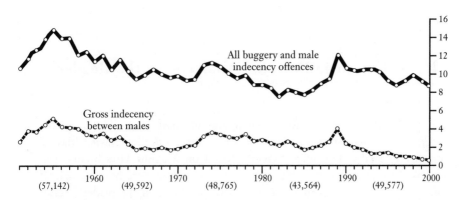

(57,142)   1960   (49,592)   1970   (48,765)   1980   (43,564)   1990   (49,577)   2000

NOTE: *The contrast between Graph 1 (1810–1900) and Graph 4 (1900–2000) should probably be slightly greater. The 19th-century figures represent indicted individuals. The later figures record offences, which usually involved two people. However, since the indictment rate for 1810–1900 was approximately 50 per cent, the two sets of figures are roughly consistent.*

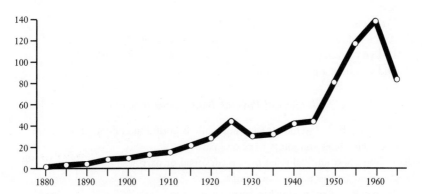

6. Arrests for sodomy and related offences in twelve American cities, 1875–1965

Each point represents the annual average, per city, for the five years to that point.

II. 'A Categoric Personal Analysis for the Reader'

The following questions are selected and adapted from *The Intersexes. A History of Similisexualism as a Problem in Social Life*, by 'Xavier Mayne' (Naples, *c.* 1908). The questionnaire, based on Magnus Hirschfeld's, was supposed to help readers decide whether or not they were homosexual. 'It can be filled out and taken to a confidential psychiater if the reader intends to visit one.'

A. Heredity and Early Youth

1. Do any of your parents or relatives have similisexual traits?
2. Are there any unscrupulous intriguers, eccentrics, liars or kleptomaniacs in your family?
3. Did your father or mother (especially your mother) want a child of the other sex?
4. Was your teething normal and timely?
5. As a child, were you mocked as a sissie or a tomboy?
6. Did you develop an early taste for music, drawing and other arts?
7. Did you have a good memory?

B. General Physical Traits, Capacities, Etc.

8. Was your body (excluding face) unusually beautiful in childhood or youth?
9. Are your bones and joints large or small?
10. Is your chest unusually flat or curved, broad or narrow?
11. Are your fingers pointed or blunt?
12. Is your handwriting small or large?
13. Are your feet large or small, broad or narrow? Do you have a high instep?
14. Can you easily separate your big toe from the other toes by its own force?

C. Physiognomy and Kindred Details

15. Is your skin soft or rough, sensitive or insensitive?
16. Do you give off an odour, especially when warm?

17. Are you unusually sensitive to pain? Do wounds heal quickly?
18. Do you experience difficulty in coughing, spitting and swallowing?
19. Are you a good whistler and do you like to whistle? Can you sing, and does it come naturally?
20. Are you comfortable wearing clothes intended for the opposite sex? When so dressed, do you make a convincing man or woman?

D. *Distinctively Sexual Characteristics*

21. Do you have an ideal sexual companion? If so, have you met your ideal?
22. Does your attraction depend partly on intellectual qualities or is it purely physical?
23. Do you consider yourself sexually potent to a marked degree?
24. How often must you have sexual intercourse in order to feel at ease?
25. Which is your preferred form of similisexual sex: *coitus inter femora, coitus ani, amplexus sine coitu, onanismus mutuus, onanismus buccalis*, etc.?
26. During intercourse, do you imagine performing the act with another person?
27. Are you given to loving people whom you do not respect?
28. Did you ever feel that a mere glance had revealed another person's homosexuality to you, or betrayed your own?

E. *Various Moral, Temperamental, Habitual Traits, Etc.*

29. Are you talkative?
30. Are you logical?
31. Are you artistic, and especially: do you like music and does it seem to contain a mysterious personal message? Does music affect you sexually?
32. In painting, do you most admire landscapes or figures? If the latter: male or female, clothed or nude?
33. Do you prefer to read prose or poetry; history, biography, travel and other more solid literature? Or do you 'like nothing so much as a good novel'?
34. Do you have a talent for acting?
35. Do you like prize-fights, bull-fights, dog-fights and football matches?
36. Do you see yourself as 'a part of wild Nature', as 'a sort of tree, beast, bird, torrent'?
37. Are animals particularly attracted to you?
38. Do you smoke, or care for strong drinks? Do you gamble? Do you instinctively use strong language?
39. Do you believe that the Similisexual is a higher or a lower form of human nature?

III. Uranian Europe

Acknowledgements

This book would not have existed without the work of Martin Duberman, Lillian Faderman, Evelyn Hooker, Jonathan Katz, Rictor Norton and most of the writers whose names appear in the bibliography.

I am happily indebted to Gill Coleridge, Starling Lawrence, Becky Senior and Peter Straus for their support and good advice. Camilla Elworthy, Andrew Kidd, Therese Mahoney, Simon Phillips and Alison Robb also helped to make this a strangely merry adventure.

Stephen Roberts comprehensively improved the original draft.

Margaret wrote the book with me.

Notes

For full references, see the list of works cited.

JfsZ = Jahrbuch für sexuelle Zwischenstufen

1. PREJUDICE

1. 'that most horrid . . . crime': McCormick, 285.
2. Baron de Charlus: Proust, III, 429. E.g. Pushkin on his friend Filipp Filippovich Vigel: 'I shall put his portrait *behind* all the others', etc.: Pushkin, 616.
3. 'This sin is now so frequent', etc.: Anselm to Archdeacon William; Trumbach in Duberman (1989), 131 (cf. Pepys, 1 July 1663); Matthews, 13 January 1811, in Crompton (1985), 161; Wilson, in Reade, 6; Martineau, in Lacassagne, 'Pédérastie', 250; Adler, vi.
5. 'abnormal conditions': Lydston, 34.
7. Lilith: G. S. Viereck, *The Candle and the Flame* (1912), in Gifford, 89–90.
7. sexually undifferentiated organisms: Gley (1884), in *JfsZ*, VI (1904), 477; Kiernan (1884) and Lydston (1888), in Weininger, 56–7; Ellis, 312–15 (summary); Proust, III, 31; Chevalier (1893), 410.
7. Xq28 region of the X chromosome: e.g. Hamer–Copeland, 144–8.
7. Napoleonic Wars: Crompton (1985), 167.
7. Marquis de Boissy: Burton, 190; see also Bleys 112 and 127.
7. 'came to them from Europe': Gide (1924), 47.
7. *The Whip*: Katz, in Duberman (1997), 223.
8. French dictionary: La Châtre, II ('Pédéraste').
8. tendency to live in London: Wellings et al., 227.

10. 'unisexuals': Raffalovich, 77–8.
10. Himmler's theory: Mosse, 167.
12. anal intercourse also commonly practised: e.g. Benkert, in Blasius, 75; Casper (1881), 120; Ellis, 283; Krafft-Ebing, 258; Lacassagne, in Raffalovich, 18–19 n.; Moll, 134; Pouillet, 12–13; 'Risks for Sexually Transmitted Diseases – A Pilot Study' (U. of Chicago, November 1996).
12. 'homos' + 'sexus': e.g. discussion in L'Intermédiaire des chercheurs et curieux (1907), 774, 822, 878–9, suggesting 'homéosexuel', 'homéophyse' and 'homophysique'.
12. Spain and Canada: see Eisenberg (Spain) and Maynard (Canada).
13. 'attitudes of a particular society': Field Marshal Montgomery, Daily Mail, 27 May 1965; Mary Whitehouse, Whatever Happened to Sex? (1977); The Star, 2 and 9 September 1986 (last three from Davenport-Hines).
14. Mansfield Park: ch. 6. J. Bate, in TLS, 4 August 1995; Woods, 138.

2. In the Shadows

17. laws, court records, etc.: see especially: Chauncey, Cocks, Coward, D'Emilio – Freedman, Engelstein, Eskridge, Gilbert, Greenberg, Harvey, Hekma, Higgs, Hirschfeld (1914), Hitchcock, Hocquenghem, Krafft-Ebing, Meer (1984), Merrick, Moran, Nabokov, Norton (1997), Prime-Stevenson (1908), Sibalis, in Merrick–Ragan, Walmsley, Weeks (1989). Some figures for England and Wales are available at: homeoffice.gov.uk/rds/pdfs/100years.xls
18. 'lesbians also suffered': Cf. L. Crompton's 1980 article, 'The Myth of Lesbian Impunity', questioned, e.g., by Kord, in Kuzniar, 229; see also Meer (1991).
18. 'false and deceitful practices': in Faderman (1994), 155.
19. Vere Street case: Holloway; Norton (1992), 187–98.
20. village of Faan: L. J. Boon and T. van der Meer, in Gerard–Hekma; L. von Römer, in JfsZ, VIII (1906), 365–511.
20. pragmatic, secular view: Monter (on Suisse romande).
20. If Wilde had been convicted: Norton (1997), 141.
21. ewe (1834): Hyde (1970), 91–2.
21. fowl (1877): PRO HO 45/9427/61018.
22. naval court-martials: Harvey; also Gilbert.

23. last execution for sodomy: A. H. Huussen, in Maccubbin; cf. T. van der Meer, in Gerard–Hekma, 268 (last execution in 1765).
23. gay 'genocide': e.g. Crompton (1978).
23. Jefferson and others: Katz (1976), 24.
25. 'sodomy arrests': Eskridge, 25.
25. In British India: Khanna.
25. 'a hoary miscreant': Harvey, 942.
26. community in Chartres: M. Sibalis, in Merrick–Ragan, 91–2.
26. 'Pearce unbutt'd my Breeches': Harvey, 942.
26. Cleveland Street: Chester et al.; Hyde (1976).
26. Conspiracy theory: Aronson.
26. As Harry Cocks suggests: Cocks, 222.
27. Code Pénal of 1791: Not the work of an individual, though Napoleon's famously homosexual arch-chancellor Cambacérès is often given the credit.
27. *'abusos deshonestos'*: Eisenberg.
27. 'traces of habitual pederasty': Lalande; Robb (2000), 223–4.
28. diaspora of 'pederasts': Carlier, 444–7 and table.
28. 'Normal' prostitutes: Carlier, 277.
29. 'A wealthy foreign gentleman': Canler, 122–3.
29. files of the Préfecture: Gunther.
29. a well-known pianist: Gury, 124.
30. toilets in Toronto: Maynard.
30. Madrid, Barcelona, Copenhagen, etc.: Hirschfeld, in Bland–Doan, 229; Casper (1871); D. Healey and G. Hekma, in Higgs; W. van Rosen, in Gerard–Hekma.
30. 'Pederasty Division': Haas, II, 1. Obituary of Meerscheidt-Hüllessem: *JfsZ*, IV (1902), 947–55.
30. 'Pink Lists': Müller, 321.
31. 'orgies in private homes': Carlier, 471.
32. 'exterminating them in herds': Crisp, 76.
32. United States (Graph 6): based on Eskridge.
32. sodomy prosecutions in France: Lever; M. Rey, in Gerard–Hekma and Maccubbin; summary by C. Courouve (1999): http:// jgir.multimania.com/procsod.htm
32. 'Brigade Mondaine': 'Fichier général de la Brigade Mondaine', Préfecture de Police, Paris, March 1968: rpt. C. Courouve.
32. In Germany, paragraph 175: e.g. Mondimore, 214; Müller, 321–3.
33. The Soviet Union: Engelstein. Swedish figures in Rydström, 246.

33. 'snowball' effect: Norton (1997), 139.
35. 'Your Lordship's delicacy': 13 January 1811, Crompton (1985), 161.
35. 'booby-trap': Wilde (2000), 690.
35. 'unnatural habits, tastes and practices': Holland, 39.
36. 'rose-leaf lips': Holland, 105; Hyde (1973), 116.
36. 'Did you ever kiss': Holland, 207–8.
36. 'Never was Paris so crowded': Harris (1916), 146.
36. Medieval legend: e.g. Ashbee (1879), 69.
37. *Daily Telegraph* reporter: 6 April 1895: in Goodman, 75.
37. Anglican clergyman: Ellmann, 441–2; Hyde (1973); Sinfield; etc.
37. Louise Jopling: *Twenty Years of My Life* (1925), 82: in Reade.
37. 'the Love that dare not speak its name': Douglas's poem, 'Two Loves'; Hyde (1973), 201.
37. W. T. Stead: *The Review of Reviews*, June 1895: Hyde (1973), 340–1.
37. *Illustrated Police Budget*: Goodman, 130.
38. 'too low to appreciate': Hyde (1973), 258.
38. 'public school colours': Hyde (1973), 146.
38. 'the rage against Wilde': Hyde (1973), 164 n.
38. 'unnatural union' with Ireland: McCalman, 149.
38. Dublin Castle affair (1884): e.g. Hyde (1970), 127–33.
38. troublesome Irish MP: Hyde (1970), 137.

3. COUNTRY OF THE BLIND

40. 'The psychoanalytic press': Adler, 49.
40. 'There is more variety': Brouardel, in Lacassagne, 'Pédérastie', 256.
42. 'The sodomite had been a sinner': Foucault, 59. See, e.g., D'Emilio–Freedman, in Nye, 110; Trumbach, 3. The best informed application of the construction theory is Greenberg's: e.g. 407–8.
42. 'hermaphrodism of the soul': L. J. Boon, in Gerard–Hekma, 246 ('hermaphrodites in their minds', 1734); also Casper (1881), 118 ('hermaphrodisme moral', i.e. 'mental'). Early studies of mental and hereditary 'perversion': Brière de Boismont (see also G. Hekma, in Bremmer); P. Lucas; Moreau, 159 (referring to father's memoir in *L'Union médicale*, 1850); Moreau de Tours (1859); Morel.
43. 'There was light': Thoinot, 297–8.
43. ancient authors: Chevalier, 72–3 and 84 (Parmenides and Herodotus); Schrijvers (Soranus); Beard, 66 (Hippocrates).

44. Pueblos of New Mexico: Chevalier, 280; Katz (1976), 304.

44. Hippocrates as authority: e.g. Morel (1852–3).

44. genital anomalies: e.g. Drs Ottolenghi (1888) and Virgilio (1889), in Hofmann, 180.

44. over-developed clitorises: Parent-Duchâtelet; Beaude ('Hermaphrodisme'); Debay, 45; Larousse ('Tribade'; also 'Clitorisme'); Delvau ('Anandryne'); Christian, 371 (rare).

45. 'masculine type of larynx': Theodor Simon Flatau, in Ellis, 255; also Krafft-Ebing, 301 (from Moll).

45. 'I have encountered': Cabanis, 311.

45. Lucien de Rubempré: Balzac, V, 145–6.

46. 'The distinctive characteristics': Walker, 154. On A. Weil: Hodann, 53–4.

46. 'infundibular' anus before Tardieu: e.g. Cullerier, in Reydellet (1819), 45; Lauvergne (1841), 289.

46. 'I have seen one pederast': Tardieu, 178.

46. 'Curled hair': Tardieu, 173.

47. 'succubus' and 'incubus': Tourdes–Metzquer, 222.

47. whistling: Ellis, 143, 191 and 256; also 'Earl Lind' (1918), 37; Ulrichs (1994), 152 and 384.

48. inability to urinate: e.g. Tardieu, 189.

48. 'I must show myself': Ulrichs (1994), 550.

48. Uranists become heavy smokers: Moll, 92.

48. bone-crushing handshake: Proust, IV, 388; Rivers, 73.

48. Throw an object: Hirschfeld (1914), 194.

49. 'sidereal pendulum': Hirschfeld (1914), 196.

49. 'But just as the fellow': Dio Chrysostom, 329.

49. Raphael Kirchner: Müller, 318.

49. *Sunday Mirror*: David, 197–8.

49. 'It is not necessary to be homosexual': Allen, in Plummer, 181.

50. caustic Dead Sea: Le Baillif de la Rivière, 34.

50. 'If several women': Lombroso–Ferrero, 403.

50. typical show of revulsion: Fodéré, IV, 574.

50. 'cerebro-spinal': Colin, 216–7 (Magnan's classification).

50. 'self-respect': Walker, 162.

51. Giraud's 'ragged fundament': Basilius, quoted in Anon. (1866?), 74.

51. 'the Ganymedes' syphilis': Ashbee (1879), 405; Littré ('Cristalline').

51. Paresis: Katz (1976), 367; and see p. 165.

51. 'cancers in the womb': Tissot, 52; also 'Saphisme', by 'D.', in *Dictionnaire encyclopédique des sciences médicales*, XV (addenda) (1885).

51. tuberculosis, dropsy and typhoid: Henke, 105–6; also Wildberg, in F. Dohrn, 'Zur Lehre von der Päderastie', *Revue trimestrielle de médecine légale* (Berlin, 1855).

52. Sir Alexander Morison: Norton (1992), 261.

52. 'Adhesiveness' in *The Lancet*: Lynch, 84.

52. *The Principles and Practice*: Taylor, 1018; 3rd ed.: II, 458–61.

52. *British Medical Journal*: Porter–Hall, 162–3.

53. widespread homosexual culture: prostitutes: Parent-Duchâtelet, 1836; convicts: Lauvergne, 1841; criminals: Tardieu, 1857; Canler, 1862.

53. 'an enthusiastic love': In Moritz's *Magazin für Erfahrungsseelenkunde*, VIII (Berlin, 1791).

53. disciplinary lines: Beyond France and Germany, the first major medical studies specifically devoted (at least in part) to what was later called homosexuality appeared as follows: Italy, 1878 (Tamassia); Britain, 1882 (article on 'Perverted Sexual Instincts' in *Brain*, by J. Krueg, a Viennese doctor); USA, 1882 (Blumer and Kiernan); Holland, 1883 (Donkersloot); Russia, 1884 (Tarnovsky); Denmark, 1891 (Pontoppidan); Portugal, 1896 (Silva); Spain, 1929 (Marañón).

54. Sándor Ferenczi: Fernandez, 91–3.

55. 'contrary sexual feeling': *'Conträre Sexualempfindung'* implied a misdirection of the sexual instinct. The Italian equivalent, *'inversione sessuale'*, first used by Arrigo Tamassia in 1878, was eventually preferred. The English 'sexual inversion' appeared in the title of Symonds' pamphlet of 1883. The French *'inversion'* was used by Charcot and Magnan in an article of 1882. A common Dutch term was *'verkeerde liefhebbers'* (wrong or mistaken lovers: cf. Westphal's 'Verkehrung'). Ulrichs' 'Urning' (English: 'Uranian' or 'Uranist': see p. 53) reflected a similarly conservative view of sexuality (true men like women, true women like men) but defined the difference in constitutional rather than pathological terms: 'That an actual man would feel sexual love for a man is impossible. The Urning is not a true man. He is a mixture of man and woman.' Ulrichs, *Araxes* (1870). Tr. J. Steakley, in Blasius–Phelan, 64.

55. Pleas of insanity: case of William North, 22 November 1822: Orr, 'Public Opinion in London . . .'.

55. a 'third sex': Lauvergne, 288 ('un sexe douteux'); Gautier, 144; Balzac, VI, 840 (variant: 'le dernier sexe'); Chevalier, 486.

55. '*homo mollis*': Fränkel; Kennedy, 59–60.

56. '*Examination of Pederasts*': Vibert, 334.

56. 'lubricated fingers': in Müller, 109.

56. cold hands: in Lacassagne, 'Pédérastie', 254–5.

57. 'the Government's penis': Corbin, 134 n.

58. 'Urnings near and far': Ulrichs (1994), 549.

58. 'attained its enormous popularity': in C. White, 316.

59. 'He confesses': Chevalier, 321–3.

60. 'I was so unhappy': Casper (1881), 119.

61. 'I could write volumes': Krafft-Ebing, 279.

61. 'like husband and wife': Krafft-Ebing, 236.

61. 'commoner than I imagine': Symonds (1984), 281; for texts by Symonds, see also Norton, comp.

61. '*No one* suspects': Müller, 209.

61. 'First, I must beg': Krafft-Ebing, 249.

61. 'a born homosexual': Hirschfeld (1905), 44.

62. 'Father, Mother, forgive me!': Otto de Joux: Müller, 238–9.

62. de Rode and Strassmann: Müller, 258–9.

62. 'Novel of a Born Invert': Saint-Paul, 89.

63. 'Books like yours': G. Hérelle, 'Lettre-préface pour une réponse au questionnaire du docteur Laupts': Lejeune, 90.

63. French prospectus: Pollard, 90.

63. 'lewd, wicked, bawdy': Pearsall, 239; Weeks (1977), 60–1.

65. Edmund White and Martin Duberman: e.g. P. Robinson, 335–6.

65. 'a perpetual discord': Symonds (1984), 283.

65. 'Is it right to chastise': 'Earl Lind' (1922), 23.

65. 'Miss L.': Krafft-Ebing, 308.

66. 'Be in no doubt': Lejeune, 90.

67. 'They had to, of course': Rivers, 166.

67. Ulrichs' neologisms: His main categories are 1. *Dioning* (heterosexual, including the *Uraniaster*, or 'faute-de-mieux' homosexual); 2. *Urning* (abnormal man), including the *Männling* (attracted to effeminate men), *Weibling* (attracted to masculine men) and *Zwischen-Urning* (attracted to adolescents); 3. *Uranodioninge* (attracted to both sexes); 4. *Hermaphrodite*. All these categories have female equivalents: *Urningin*, *Dioningin*, etc.

67. Kertbeny: real name, Karl Maria Benkert: Haas, I, 2; trans. in Blasius–Phelan. Benkert is an important figure in the history of comparative literature. Baudelaire (II, 959) received a poorly spelt

letter from him in 1864 and wrote on it: 'The man who knows 52 languages. Obviously he only knows 51.' However, the attribution of the word 'homosexuality' to Benkert is uncertain. Jaeger's source, 'Dr M.', really was a doctor, unlike Benkert, and was born in about 1820: *JfsZ*, II (1900), 53–9. (Benkert was born in 1824.) A little-known predecessor of the word was used by Proudhon in 1858: *'homoiousien'*, usually applied to the Trinity ('of the same essence'): Courouve (1985), 130.

67. 'Thereafter he adopted': Ellis, 272.
68. anal intercourse: see note 12 on p. 282.
69. 'A physician is not blamed': Karlinsky, 274.
69. Katherine Mansfield: Alpers, 96; Boddy, 29 and 40.
69. cold baths: Katz (1976), 134–5; Acton, 203; Austen, ch. 1.
69. Wellington School: Hyam, 67; see also Lyttelton, 17.
69. drastic cures: Moll, 273; Magnan (1885), in Chevalier, 509.
70. 'Many even lack awareness': Krafft-Ebing, 260.
70. 'I seek no remedy': Krafft-Ebing, 280.
70. incidence of nervous complaints: Saint-Paul, 230.
70. 'I have often had occasion': Tardieu, 169.
70. A medical encyclopedia: L. Blumenstok, in *Real-Encyclopädie der gesammten Heilkunde*, 2nd ed.: H. Kennedy, in Rosario, 36–7.
71. 'omosessualismo' and 'uranismo': Morselli, 680–2.
71. 'One would certainly not': Charcot; Magnan, 184.
71. 'Uranists weeping': Moll, 113; also Mantegazza (1886), in Dallemagne, 509.
71. 'Oh, dear sad memories!': Garnier, 388.
71. 'one can, without much risk': in Saint-Paul, 253.
72. 'sexual perversion can coexist': Ball, 140; also Féré, 444.
72. 'Ever since I gave free rein': Müller, 223.
72. 'innate inversion': Westphal, 324.
72. laws against transvestism: facsimile of 'Transvestism Permit' (for Rosa Bonheur) in Stanton, 364. On Bonheur: Cooper, 47–9; Van Casselaer, 41.
73. 'in whose domain they belong': Westphal, 352.
73. 'lucid psychopaths': Chevalier, 457.
73. *'chastise* or *sequester'*: Chevalier, 474.
73. Heinz Tovote: J. Jones, 132.
74. 'double inversion': Saint-Paul, 313.
74. bladder washing: Katz (1976), 149.

74. 'pull up my socks': Westwood, 41 (Michael Schofield: Higgins, 135).
74. 'Get married': Gide (1947), 29–30.
75. a tax on bachelors: Aldrich ('Tardieu').
75. boudoirs and harems: Müller, 144; Hirschfeld (1914), 497.
75. 'I can do it!': Goncourt, II, 1003.
75. patient who fled in horror: Moll, in Saint-Paul, 318 n.
75. the dentist's chair: Hartland, 67.
75. 'But tell it in England': Hyde (1973), 311.
76. 'When a contrary-sexual': Krafft-Ebing, 345.
76. treated by Krafft-Ebing: Müller, 143–4; Krafft-Ebing, 341.
76. 'spontaneous erections': Bernheim, 338–9.
77. Dr Quackenbos: Hale, 244; Katz (1976), 144–5.
77. Edmund Bergler: in David, 180.
77. a 'poisonous' effect: Katz (1976), 135.
78. 'therapeutic nihilism': Schrenck-Notzing, ch. 9.
78. Frank Lydston: Katz (1976), 590 n. 5
78. F. E. Daniel: Katz (1976), 136.
78. *No sexual pervert*: Lydston, 51.
80. 'Homosexuality is assuredly': Freud, in E. Jones, III, 195–6.
80. *Die conträre Sexualempfindung*: 2nd ed., 1893. Translated into French in 1893 (6th ed., 1897) and eventually English: *Perversions of the Sex Instinct: a Study of Sexual Inversion Based on Clinical Data and Official Documents* (Newark, 1931).
80. 'One is no more likely': Moll, 213.
81. 'Man generally performs': Moll, 289.
82. 'One can easily see': Moll, 190.
82. 'Since abstinence': Moll, 295.
82. 'To make a complete study': Moll, 186.

4. OUTINGS

86. 'Ever since I came': 27 July 1818: Luppé, 72.
86. 'Sitting on the ruins': 11 November 1818: Luppé, 73.
86. 'the only feelings': Duras, 148.
86. 'Few people': Luppé, xiii. On Varnhagen von Ense: *Eldorado*, 133.
86. 'Is this misfortune?': 25 November 1820: Luppé, 85.
87. 'As long as we speak': Custine, 29.
87. Edward Sainte-Barbe: Muhlstein, 174.

87. In November 1824: *L'Étoile*, 6 November 1824; then in *Le Moniteur*, *La Quotidienne*, *Le Journal des Débats*.
87. 'My God, what a sordid combination': Luppé, 100.
88. 'a stranger to everything': Muhlstein, 184.
88. 'black depths': Luppé, 259–60.
89. 'Any friendship that lasts': Courouve (1985), 31.
89. 'They were barely in the street': Delécluze, 343.
89. 'Sgricci is here improvising': Crompton (1985), 245.
89. under surveillance in Florence: E. Del Cerro, in Dall'Orto.
90. '*Des soins divers*': Viel-Castel, I, 206.
90. Julie Candeille: Delécluze, 181.
91. Foucault pointed out: Foucault, 97.
92. 'That his affinity with Hellenism': *Westminster Review*, January 1867: D. Donoghue, 47.
92. 'those who are observant': quoted by Pater: Gay (1984–98), II, 240. On Winckelmann and Goethe: Derks; S. Richter and R. Tobin, in Kuzniar.
92. experiments with sodomy: Casanova, II, 270–4; Gay (1959), 290–1 (Voltaire); Flaubert, I, 572 and 638 (15 January and 2 June 1850).
93. Winckelmann's private letters: Derks, 179 ff.
94. Carl Justi's biography: Gay (1984–98), IV, 177–8.
94. *L'Amitié antique*: Dugas, 94; see also Delepierre.
94. some British scholars: see Dowling; Turner.
94. skin temperature and *Galanterien von Berlin*: Derks, 90 ff.
95. Heine and Platen: Bumm, 533; Derks, 505.
96. investigation of Iffland: Derks, 436; also Kleist, 448 and Heine's attack on Platen ('der gaselige Iffland').
96. Even Havelock Ellis: Ellis, 179.
96. 'My tastes incline me': Moers, 270; see also Goncourt, I, 323; Barbey d'Aurevilly.
97. Marquess of Anglesey: *JfsZ*, III (1901), 544; also Bloch, 413; Hyde (1970), 153–4.
97. Fred Barnes: P. Bailey.
98. North American Indians: e.g. Bancroft; Bleys, 18, etc.; D'Emilio–Freedman, 7; Karsch-Haack; Katz (1976), 292–318; J. Grahn, in Kehoe 43 (lesbianism); A. Robinson, 32–3; Roscoe, in Duberman (1997).
98. unfortunate and hilarious aberration: Macintosh (1981), 35.
98. In the 1830s: Catlin, I, 15 and 111–13.

98. Trial of Boulton and Park: N. Bartlett in Goldberg; Cohen, 78–117; Farrer; Hyde (1970), 95; Roughead, 149–83.
100. 'minstrelization': Weeks (1989), 111.
101. division of labour, etc.: Greenberg, 356.
101. 'Crimes of the Clergy': by William Benbow: Ashbee (1879), 46–50; Crompton (1985), 308–9; also McCalman, 149; Norton (1992).
101. 'unnatural practices': Rowse, 126.
101. 'My Lord Gomorrah': Chester et al., 177.
102. Gibbon found it 'astonishing': Crompton (1985), 233.
102. 'even the law-abiding citizens': Norton (1992), 117; see also Greenberg, 340.
102. 'Ninety-nine normal men': Ellis, 351. Similar tolerance in 18th-century Paris: Coward, 239.
103. Druids' Hall drag ball: Cocks, 89–90.
103. Saul was interviewed: Weeks (1989), 114.
103. Voyeuristic tours: e.g. Paris (M. Wilson, in Epstein–Straub, 210); New York ('Earl Lind').
104. 'Jack the Ripper': *The Illustrated Police News*, 26 October 1889: Bartlett, 110.
104. Beckford at Fonthill: Mowl, 207.
104. '*favourite Propensity*': Thrale, II, 799.
104. 'Ah! Mr. FitzGerald': Blyth, 80.
104. Carpenter at Millthorpe: Carpenter (1916); also Weeks (1977), 79.
105. Edward Shelley: Hyde (1973), 191.
106. 'simulated and hypocritical': Murray, 309. Other examples of public sympathy (once the victim had died or been punished): Roger Casement, after his arrest as a spy and the surreptitious circulation of the 'Black Diaries' – now known to be genuine; Friedrich Krupp and 'Fighting Mac' Macdonald, after suicide (1902 and 1903); the radical German lawyer Jean Baptiste von Schweitzer, jailed for indecent behaviour but later President of the Workingmen's Association and member of the North German Reichstag (Gay (1984–98), II, 245; Steakley, 1–3.) On Johannes von Müller (later denounced as 'unGerman'): Bumm, 189; Derks, 247, 344, etc.
106. black-balling Sodomites: Proust, III, 33.
106. 'the antipathy itself': Bentham, 'Offences Against One's Self'.
107. Lincoln and Speed: Katz (2001), 14.
107. Edward McCosker: Katz (1976), 29–32.
108. Thomas Jefferson Withers: Duberman (1986), 5 ff.

108. Albert Dodd: Gay (1984–98), II, 208–12.
109. 'stubbornly ambiguous objects': Deitcher, 14. See also Bush.
109. 'A man crying': Cohen, 177.
109. In a communal bed: Chateaubriand, I, 7, 6.
109. '[T. A. said]': McCormick, 275.
110. 'wooden-walled Gomorrahs': *White-Jacket*, quoted by H. Beaver in Melville (1985), 43.
110. mining camps: Chauncey (1994), 91 n.; Hyam, 98; Johnson.
110. old American sailor: Katz in Duberman (1997), from B. R. Burg.
110. 'sexual cocytus': Ellis, 121.
111. Katharine Davis: D'Emilio–Freedman, 193.
111. Willy and Parsifal: Courouve (1985), 130.
112. *Daily Telegraph*: Cohen, 94.
112. new . . . persecution complex: Legrand du Saulle, 119 and 462–3.
112. 'Who is he': Crain, 171.
112. Coleridge on Shakespeare: *Marginalia*, 2 November 1803: see Woods, 104.
112. dreams of being sexually assaulted: *Marginalia*, 13 December 1803; see also Paglia, 342–3.
113. 'Discourse on the Manners': Notopoulos, 413.
113. 'I began to be apprehensive': Smollett, ch. 51.
114. 'The kiss of friendship': Bloch, 398–9; also Greenberg, 341; Spencer, 234.
114. Whitman's salute: 'Behold this swarthy face'.
114. William Cobbett: Crain, 130.
115. 'We agreed it was a scandal': Lister, *No Priest*, 32.
115. 'That's a man', etc.: Lister, *I Know*, 49; *No Priest*, 37–8.
115. 'Brought on the subject': Lister, *I Know*, 156.
116. whirligigs and John Lockhart: Mavor, 162.
117. 'Three o'clock dinner': Mavor, 40.
117. 'damned Sapphists': Norton (1997), 203.
117. Anne Lister to Llangollen: Lister, *I Know*, 210.
117. Byron and Edlestone: Crompton (1985), 102.
117. 'Two women': Colette, 617–18.
118. *General Evening Post*: Mavor, 136.
119. 'even doubtful if it can exist': Faderman (1985). On the supposed non-existence of lesbians: Castle; E. Donoghue.
121. 'The facts that will cure': Murdoch, 6.

5. MIRACULOUS LOVE

125. Peter Doyle: Kaplan, 311–12.
126. Tchaikovsky to his brother: Poznansky, 12.
126. 'various manipulations'; love life and legend: Poznansky, 16, 13, 19–28, 196 and 213–20.
128. examples of cross-dressing: Morgan (200–1) cites non-sexual reasons for cross-dressing: freedom, employment, economy, fear of being arrested as a prostitute.
128. 'position of a young person': Gosse to Symonds, 5 March 1890: Grosskurth, 282.
129. 'Two years ago': Ellis, 134.
129. Lytton Strachey: Askwith, 53.
129. 'Miss Right': Ackerley, 153.
129. Mikhail Kuzmin: Malmstad–Bogomolov, 30.
129. understanding parents: Prime-Stevenson (1908), 183; Hirschfeld (1905), 45.
129. Christmas: Hirschfeld (1905), 50–2.
129. 'she ran away from home': Krafft-Ebing, 317.
129. pining for a woman: Krafft-Ebing, 319.
130. 'Frau von T.': Krafft-Ebing, 313–15.
130. Sackville-West: Nicolson, 140, etc. On lavender marriages: article by Hirschfeld in *JfsZ*, III (1901), 37–71.
130. An army doctor: Müller, 352.
131. *My Life*: C. White, 275.
131. 'carefully hid' and *Les Faux-Monnayeurs*: Gide (1947), 19 and 111.
132. Karl Heinrich Ulrichs: Kennedy; Steakley; Ulrichs (1994).
132. 'My dear sister' and replies: Ulrichs (1899), 40–51.
133. 'My dear ones' and replies: Ulrichs (1899), 49–57.
134. 'stimulate a romantic feeling': Symonds (1984), 135 and 141.
134. 'shoals of painted . . . youths': Chauncey (1994), 116 and 179.
135. 'I will be the robust husband': 'A Woman Waits For Me'.
135. Hilda Maria Käkikoski: T. Juvonen, in Aldrich–Wotherspoon, 237.
135. Minnie Benson: Askwith, 134, 192, etc.
135. Carl Pontus Wikner: A. Norström, in Aldrich–Wotherspoon, 485–6. Author's translation.
136. into the river Avon: Symonds (1984), 195.
136. 'FEVERISH, *fluctuating*': Kaplan, 316; cf. Bullough, 49.

136. 'a great big hearty': Kaplan, 313.

136. Whitman to Symonds: Kaplan, 47.

137. 'I have never professed': Lucien, 152–3.

137. London Library: Ann Thwaite, in Norton (1997), 162.

137. destroyed by his widow: Lovell, 791.

137. 'a packet of letters': Askwith, 209.

137. 'thwarted, frustrated': Noakes, 131.

138. Austrian army: Ulrichs, *Memnon*, in Ellis, 23.

138. French soldiers in Algeria: Duchesne, 41.

138. *Llave de Oro*: Ashbee (1879), 69.

138. 'observations on the lower animals': Ellis, 241.

139. 'I do not think': Prince, 118.

139. Platen and Schmidtlein: Bumm, 210–19; Derks, 492–6.

140. Albert Glatigny: 'L'Honnête scrupule', in Larivière (1998), 141–2.

140. 'They lived together': Ramdohr, II, 104–7.

141. *Sodome et Gomorrhe*: Proust, III, 9.

141. 'the Ephebe of Kritios': Ackerley, 164.

141. 'As we approached Mitilini': Barney, 78.

141. 'Did you sy they was niked?': F. Harris, in Dowling, 145.

142. 'the Greenwood': Forster, *Maurice*, 120 and 221.

142. 'what was the good': Ackerley, 173.

142. 'lawless' and 'godless': Symonds (1984), 254.

142. 'All "abnormal" sex-acts': in Ackerley, xiv.

142. strange lights: in *Formatrix* (1865) (Müller, 197): this and similar passages omitted by Hirschfeld from his edition of Ulrichs' writings (1898).

142. 'This ought not to be seen': quoted by Norton (1997), 166.

143. Charlotte Brontë: E. Miller, in Lesbian History Group.

143. Baron von Pregnitz: Isherwood, 26, 109 and 27.

143. 'Sir William Jones': Lister, *No Priest*, 32.

144. 'like old Tiresias': Lister, *I Know*, 235–6.

144. 'I have a question to ask': Lister, *No Priest*, 26.

144. Alexander Berkman: Berkman, II, ch. 10; Katz (1976), 532.

145. 'like those questioning phrases': Proust, III, 7.

145. Nikolai Gogol: Karlinsky (1834 and 36).

145. 'Do you know . . .': J. Jones, 183–4.

146. 'I would hasten after him': Ackerley, 173.

146. 'less bother than a Zanetto': Murphy, *Rimbaud* (1991), 73; Robb (2000), 100.

146. '*Seeking* a friend': Carlier, 451.

147. classified ads: Hirschfeld (1905), 60–1; Näcke, in *JfsZ*, V, 2 (1903), 319–50; Katz (1976), 48.

147. 'Socrates' or 'modern': e.g. Lorrain (1929), 72: 'a very ... modern though timid boyfriend'.

147. 'there could be no doubt': Krafft-Ebing, 302; Moll, 315.

147. A homosexual philologist: *JfsZ*, V, 2 (1903), 950–1, from *Frührot, freiradikale Zeitschrift*, 8–13 (1901); Hirschfeld (1914), 535–6.

148. 'I kiss you as skilfully ...': Pichois–Brunet, 111.

148. 'I enjoyed that wonderful promptness': Colette, 597 (*Le Pur et l'Impur*).

148. James to Symonds: quoted from L. Edel's edition.

148. *Italian Hours*: James (1992), 18.

149. Mann to Weber: Reed, 85 (Reed's translation). Generally: Heilbut.

150. *parlare*: also 'parlary', 'polari', 'parlyaree'. Hayes; I. Lucas; Macintosh (1973); Norton (1997), 115–18; Weeks (1989), 111 and (1990), 138.

150. 'It smells of garlic': Chevalier, 250.

150. 'chestnut gatherer': Courouve (1985); Lacassagne–Devaux ('Pédéraste').

150. French slang dictionary: Delvau.

151. red neckties: Ellis, 298–9; also Anon. (1893), 32; Healey, 40 and 281 n. 90.

151. velvet ties and red boots: Healey, 39.

151. 'poufs': Anon. (1850), in Ashbee (1877), 405.

151. tapping the back of one hand: T. van der Meer, in Gerard–Hekma, 288: also, in 1689, by kicking one another's feet.

151. Parisian poodles: Taxil, 263.

151. *galbinati*: or *galbanati*. Chevalier, 90; Ellis, 298; Martial, 3, 82, 5. On green, also: Winn, 182–3.

152. 'Yet there were those': P. Bailey, 29–30.

152. 'Subtlety, ambiguity': Meyers, 3.

152. 'There is a strange': 21 December 1927 (Lawrence, 38–9; see also 262).

152. 'I've probably been insulted': Hensher.

153. Beckford to Courtenay: Haggerty, 147–8.

153. Church to Ned: McCormick, 261–2.

153. Barlow to Lister: Lister, *No Priest*, 116.

154. Merrill to Carpenter: quoted by N. Greig, in Carpenter (1984), 41.

154. Gosse at Browning's funeral: Pearsall, 452.

154. Margaret Fuller: Katz (1976), 466.

154. 'sphinxes of conformity': Gide to R. Fernandez, 1934: Courouve (1985), 166.

154. 'adhesive love': a phrenological concept: Whitman, *Democratic Vistas* (1871), para. 111, note 2; also Stern, 105.

155. 'teachers of future society': Carpenter, *The Intermediate Sex*, 1.

6. SOCIETY OF STRANGERS

157. 20 per cent of all prostitutes: Prime-Stevenson (1908), ch. 6.

157. 20 per cent and 25 per cent of the total: Moll, 309; Chevalier, 233; Prime-Stevenson (1908), ch. 6; Rüling, also in Blasius–Phelan, 149; see also Elisabeth Dauthendy, in *JfsZ*, VIII (1906), 285–300; Zimmerman.

157. *koshki*: Healey, 53.

157. lesbian prostitution in Paris: Chevalier, 236–7; Corbin, 214; Taxil, 263.

158. 'blackmailing by bath-servants': Tarnovsky, 146.

158. Bains de Penthièvre: M. Sibalis, in Higgs, 25.

158. St Petersburg bathhouses and Kuzmin's visit: Healey, 34.

158. Holborn and Saffron Hill: Norton (1992), 72.

159. 'every fifth man is an invert': Ellis, 352.

159. 'meridian of Kansas City': 'Earl Lind' (1922), 6.

159. particular spots: Delcourt, 285–9; Ariès–Duby, 588; Citron, I, 381–2; Coward, 239; Fournier-Verneuil, 281, 314 and 337; Merrick, 288; M. Sibalis, in Higgs, 16–17; McCormick, 356; Wilde, *An Ideal Husband*, II.

159. groups in Sweden: Rydström, and thesis: 'Sinners and Citizens: Bestiality and Homosexuality in Sweden, 1880–1950' (U. of Stockholm).

159. 'Beware of Sods!': Anon. (1850), 405.

159. Victor Hugo: Ashbee (1879), 407–10.

159. Sydney: Norton (1997), 259–60; also Ellis, 185.

159. *Sydney Gazette*: M. Smith, 'Australia's Gay Heritage', in Bob Hay, 'The Sodomites' Guide to Colonial Sydney': http://members.ozemail.com.au/~vombatus

160. Mlle Raucourt: e.g. Coward, 246. See also Stambolian–Marks, 359–60.

160. poems on actresses: Robb (1993), 178–82.

160. lesbian apartment blocks: Chevalier, 237.

160. lesbian cafés: Frey, 374–5; Taxil; etc.

160. 'One would have thought': Mendès (1890), 493.

161. Louise Taillandier: Zola (1880), 205–6.

161. lesbian brothel at Asnières: Goncourt, II, 741.

161. London guardsmen: Ackerley, 174–5; Leeves, 27–29 April 1850; also Lorrain (1922), 176; Porter–Weeks, 32.

163. Ernest Thickbroom: Weeks (1989), 113.

163. 'On leaving the urinal': September 1872: *Arthur Rimbaud*, no. 54.

163. 'unmarried toughs': 'Earl Lind' (1918), 63.

163. 'O you are such . . .': 'Earl Lind' (1922), 134–5.

164. 'going into politics': Chevalier, 185.

164. fruits of sodomy: Canler, 126; Macé, 169.

164. a 'petit jésus' from Lyon: Poznansky, 21.

165. Armory Hall: Chauncey (1994), 37; Katz (1976), 574–5.

165. Rev. Charles Parkhurst: Katz (1976), 40.

165. 'brownies': J. Kiernan (1916), in Chauncey (1982–3), 142; 'Earl Lind' (1922), 89.

165. Paresis Hall: 'Earl Lind' (1922), 146 ff.; also Katz (1976), 47 and Chauncey (1994), 34. On commercial exploitation in US cities, see also Lydston (1892), in Nye, 153.

165. A bar in Amsterdam: G. Hekma, in Higgs, 70.

166. 'Everyone behaved ceremoniously': Strindberg (1891), 12; see also Strindberg (1885).

166. Temperance Hall: Cocks, 90–2.

166. A group of Frenchmen: Carlier, 442–3.

166. Eagle Street College: C. White, 218.

166. 'Háfiz Tavern': Malmstad–Bogomolov, 103–5.

167. The 'Lohengrin': Hirschfeld (1905), 53.

167. Some clubs hid: O. de Joux, in Müller, 80.

167. homosexual marriages: e.g. Carlier, 349–50 and 457; Ellis, 250; Norton (1992), 199.

167. 'taking the sacrament': Lister, *I Know*, 160.

168. 'simple little devils': Rolfe (1974) and introduction.

168. Copenhagen in 1815: W. von Rosen, in Gerard–Hekma, 198–9.

168. 'Order of Chaeronea': Stokes; Conner, 257; Weeks (1977), 118.

168. Blue Grotto, Capri: Gregorovius, 756–8.

168. Adelsward Fersen: Beurdeley, 211–13; Ogrinc.

168. 'ambition and hostility': J. Steakley, in Gerard–Hekma, 168.
168. Neuschwanstein: e.g. Fernandez, 49–54.
168. Elisár von Kupffer: e.g. Haas, III, 3.
168. American hobo subculture: F. Willard, in Ellis, 360–7; Rev. F. C. Laubach, in Chauncey (1994), 397 n. 56.
168. language of tattoos: Lacassagne, 'Tatouage', 124–5; also Kurella, 112.
169. blacks and whites: Katz (1976), 49, on a 'miscegenation dance' in Saint Louis.
169. 'a comrade in tastes': Malmstad–Bogomolov, 145.
169. Cambridge 'Apostles': e.g. Dickinson; Felix; Furbank; Skidelsky.
170. 'Martyr of prejudice': Crompton (1985), 126.
170. 'Men of this breed': Quoted by R. Lewinsohn: Rivers, 170.
170. Engels to Marx: Manchester, 22 June 1869: Müller, 57.
171. club in the Grenelle area, and letter: Carlier, 447.
171. Solomon at the Bourse: W. A. Peniston, in Merrick–Ragan, 134.
171. dead outside a Venice hotel: 'In Memoriam', in *Akadémos*: Ogrinc.
171. 'travelling international celebrities': Moll, 148.
171. large numbers of Uranians: Krafft-Ebing, 267 and 288.
172. 'The Furnace': Hyam, 128–31; C. White, 328–30 and 339–40.
172. 'Stable Boy of Park Lane': Felix, 108.
172. 'Saturday night Mike Ellis': Norton (1999).

7. A SEX OF ONE'S OWN

175. Lister insuring her life: Lister, *I Know*, 309.
175. 'Children of Sodom': Gunther (1995).
176. 'Société des Émiles': Courouve (1871).
176. *La Philosophie dans le boudoir*: Sade (1795), 'Troisième Dialogue'.
176. 'analysis of murder': Blasius–Phelan, 48.
176. 'Sodomy violates . . .': Larivière (1998), 96.
177. Thomas Aquinas: *Summa theologica*, 2.2.154 ('unnatural vice' compared to adultery, seduction and rape).
177. 'Sodomy simplified': Crompton (1985), 126.
177. 'Discourse on the Manners': Notopoulos, 404–13.
177. Byron's choice of companions: Shelley, II, 58 (to Peacock, Naples, December 1818).
177. Jeremy Bentham: Bentham; also Crompton (1985), 20 ff.
178. 'Never [. . .] did work appear': Crompton (1985), 255 (July 1816).

178. Burke twice sued newspapers: Crompton (1985), 32–3; Mavor, 136.

178. 'exquisite pleasure': Smollett, ch. 51; see also chs 34–35.

178. German writers: G. Hekma, in Gerard–Hekma, 437; Norton (1997), 172; Derks, 79. E.g. J. G. Hamann, *Sokratische Denkwürdigkeiten* (1750), J. M. Gesner, *Socrates Sancta Paederasta* (1769), Herder, 'Ueber die Schaamhaftigkeit Virgils' (1769).

179. Riom prison: Perrot, 288.

180. 'He openly confessed': Carlier, 302; also Hirschfeld (1905), 115; Huysmans, *Là-bas* (1891), ch. 12; Taxil, 264.

180. clean up the Champs-Élysées: Ashbee (1879), 407–10.

180. '*tapette*': Courouve (1985), 212. Cf. later adoptions: 'schwul', 'queer', etc.

180. '*chevaliers de la manchette*': e.g. Larivière (1998) ('Ai-Ti'); Littré ('Manchette'); Rousseau, *Les Confessions*, I, 2.

180. '*spartiate*': Fourier, 212; Sade (1791), 281.

181. 'Believe me . . .': Casper (1863).

181. 'like crabs to slow cooking': *Ara spei* (1865); Kennedy, 81.

181. Ulrichs at Congress of German Jurists: *Gladius furens* (1868).

183. copulating male dogs: Gide (1924), 95–6.

183. *Die Welt als Wille und Vorstellung*: Schopenhauer, 620 and 643–51.

184. Ulrichs in L'Aquila: On Ulrichs today: www.angelfire.com/fl3/celebration2000

184. 'sport obscene': Anon. (1866), 7.

184. 'Why, I wish to know': Summers, 688.

184. 'We ought to think': H. Kennedy, in Rosario, 32.

185. 'middle-class England': Ellis, 64.

185. 'smaller number of inverts in Spain': Marañón, 176.

185. every third male servant: Joux, 193.

185. inverts were musicians: Calesia (1900), in Ellis, 295; see also Kraepelin, 781.

186. 'psychiatric proverb': Prime-Stevenson (*c.* 1908), 76.

186. 4 per cent of adult male population: David, ix.

186. Wissenschaftlich-Humanitäre Komitee: e.g. Haas; Hirschfeld; *JfsZ* (1899, etc.); Müller, 300 ff.; Steakley; Wolff.

188. French petition: Ellmann, 463; Fernandez, 81; Goncourt, III, 1199; Lucien, 78.

188. British petition: Ellmann, 463; Hyde (1973), 291–2.

189. Community of the Special: J. Jones, 97–8; Müller, 306–9.

189. Benedict Friedländer: in Blasius–Phelan, 152–61.

190. 'ghastly "Committee" ': To C. M. von Weber, Munich, 4 July 1920.
192. Henry Gerber: Chauncey (1994), 144.
192. Johanna Elberskirchen: Haas, IV, 2.
192. Anna Rüling: ed. Faderman and Eriksson; see Blasius–Phelan, 143 ff.
192. the suffrage movement: Tickner, 222–3.
192. 'cheap physical expression': 'Eugenics and Spiritual Parenthood' (1911), in C. White, 115.
192. Stella Browne: Blasius–Phelan, 186 ff.
193. 'In a Spanish prison': Ellis, 209.
193. Eulenburg trials: Haas, III, 1; also Grand-Carteret; Rivers, 188 ff. French reaction: Mirbeau.
193. cause of First World War: Baumont.
194. studies on suicide, 1978–2000: the 1989 report that revealed an epidemic of gay teen suicides was widely publicized partly because it was so easy to discredit. For a summary of studies: www.sws.soton.ac.uk/gay-youth-suicide/04-gay-bisexual-suicide-studies.htm

8. Fairy Tales

198. basis of all human society: Blüher, 166.
200. Christian Cantle: Woods, 13; *The Return of the Native*, I, 3 and III, 7.
200. 'insane or sickly deviance': Sand (1971), II, 125–6 (IV, ch. 13).
200. 'Milord Link is a *Bishop of Clogher*': Stendhal (1968–74), IX, 318: *Lucien Leuwen*, IV, 1; Thompson; also J.-J. Labia's introduction to Stendhal (1994).
200. 'Monsieur is siding with Collin': Balzac, III, 222.
201. Diderot and possible proclivities: Faderman (1981), 44.
201. 'I trembled as I kissed your arm': Sand (1833), 189.
201. *Eric, or Little by Little*: Chandos, 298–9; Hyde (1970), 112–14 (*Saturday Review*).
202. in *other* countries: e.g. the novels by Adolphe Belot (p. 203), Louis Couperus (p. 210), Georges Eekhoud (p. 209) and Adolf von Wilbrandt: *Fridolin's Mystical Marriage* (1875; New York, 1884), based on the theories of Ulrichs.
202. French armed forces: e.g. Darien; Descaves; Hermant; see also Gury, 87. Others: Diraison-Seylor, *Les Maritimes, moeurs candides* (s.d.); Jean Bosco, *Le Vice marin* (1905), in Millward, 166–7; Gury, 87.

202. Alice Mitchell (Memphis, 1892): Dubarry (1906), 151; Ellis, 201; Eskridge, 20; Faderman (1981), 291 and (1994), 139.

203. Sappho as lover of a man: Robb (1993), 172 and 176.

203. Goethe's 'An den Mond': Derks, 479–81; *JfsZ*, II (1900), 67.

203. *City Crimes*: Woods, 152–3.

203. *Sodom in Union Square*: Katz (1976), 574 n. 40.

203. 'Cease to hide this book': from translation by 'A. D.' (Chicago, 1891), 12–13.

204. *A Marriage Below Zero*: Gifford, 27; Mitchell–Leavitt, 196.

204. 'you have to concentrate very hard': Larousse, XI, 473.

204. *Les Intrigues de Molière*: Livet.

204. 'documentary and anecdotal': H. de Weindel and F. P. Fischer, *L'Homosexualité en Allemagne* (Juven, 1908): Rivers, 128.

205. 'Such books': Rolfe (1974), 25–6 and 48.

205. *Weiberbeute*: Hirschfeld, *Die Transvestiten* (1910); Foster, 221.

206. Joséphin Péladan: *La Gynandre* (1891) and Birkett, 153, 317, etc.

206. lists drawn up by the German police: Müller, 289.

207. *The Power of Mesmerism*: Summers.

207. *Die Päderasten*: Müller, 289.

207. lesbian novels by the ton: Dr Irving C. Rosse, in Katz (1976), 72.

207. vampirical women: see Dyer.

207. Dr Hippolyte Homo: Corbin, 187.

208. *The Sins of the Cities*: on Jack Saul, see Kaplan.

209. 75 per cent of homosexual men and women: Hirschfeld (1914), 395.

209. *Escal-Vigor*: Eekhoud (1899); Lucien, 116.

209. series on 'nameless love': J. Jones, 272; Popp, 32–40.

210. In *La Maison de la vieille*: Mendès (1894), 398.

210. *The Prussian Officer*: Woods, 222.

211. 'gay lives represented as tragic': Tóibín, 28.

211. elegies of English literature: e.g. Crompton (1985), 187; Woods, ch. 9.

211. *In Memoriam* and *The Times*: Crompton (1985), 190; Reade, 9; Spencer, 260.

212. Charlus's military hospital: Proust, IV, 387. On 'lovely war': e.g. Porter–Weeks, 78.

213. *Kenilworth*: Anon. (1866), 68.

213. '*Che bardacherai mon bain afec doi!*': Murphy, ed., 148 n. 88.

213. private connotations: e.g. Mann, 39.

213. Heine proposed '*ghaselig*': Derks, 554; also Bumm, 254.

213. 'arse-in-the-air' sonnet: Huysmans, ch. 14.
213. stable lads and grooms: e.g. Roger de Beauvoir's 'David Dick', the groom who wears rouge (Beauvoir, II, 127–65); Balzac's lads (Robb (1994), 260–1); Lorrain's 'bougres d'écuries' (Winn, 102–3).
214. 'continual, convulsive contraction': Lombroso, 402 and fig. 8.
214. Woolf's Julia Craye: Woolf, 104–5.
214. Gide reads *Lara*: *Journal*, 18 February 1888; Pollard, 268.
214. 'Christopher Columbus of modern love': Rachilde, 94.
215. *Cyril and Lionel*: Arch Smith, 30–1.
215. Winthrop, Taylor and Wister: excerpts in Mitchell–Leavitt.
216. these pioneer idylls: e.g. Winifred Mercier writing to 'Donald' about 'the great wide west', 'where perhaps there might be more chance of finding out what manner of being you were' (Vicinus, 205).
216. Charles Warren Stoddard: Higgs, 168; Katz (1976), 501; Mitchell–Leavitt, 69; also Austen.
217. 'deeds that are too revolting to relate': Katz (1976), 33.
217. *The Wind in the Willows*: see also Mitchell–Leavitt, 296.
217. Robin's aggressive flirting: Pyle, 114 and 325.
218. 'The holy friar': Pyle, 315.
218. 'wholly serious defence': B. A. Inman, in Dowling, 111.
218. 'The Greeks who worshipped': 'The Problem of the Face', Cottam (1930), 39.
218. 'In trousers now': *Rondeaux of Boyhood* by 'A. Newman' (1923): Arch Smith, 165.
219. 'Smart-looking lads': 'Your City Cousins', Nicholson.
219. 'I sat in the rector's study': Cottam (1930), 78.
219. 'I meet a young man': Cottam (1900), 181.
220. Jenny Lind wrote to a friend: Prince, 222.
220. 'I long for you': Prince, 166.
221. 'The Grand Eunuch': Prince, 195.
222. 'it reminds me of old Socrates': Wullschlager, 424; also Mayer, 227.
224. *Dr Jekyll and Mr Hyde*: Showalter, 107 ff.
225. 'infernal art of deceiving': Custine (1971), 67.
225. Thom Gunn and Colm Tóibín: Tóibín, 231–2.
226. Whitman's *Leaves of Grass*: Ellis, 339.
226. 'Out of the Sun': *Her Enemy, Some Friends – and Other Personages: Stories & Studies Mostly of Human Hearts* (Florence, 1913): see Mitchell–Leavitt.
226. 'my Burne-Jones drawings': Wilde (2000), 713.

226. Montesquiou's interior: Goncourt, III, 604.

227. battle over Shakespeare's sonnets: e.g. Barnstorff; Crompton (1985), 5–6, 189 and 327–8; Harris (1909); Rau, 203 (also Schönholzer); Shakespeare, 117; Wilde (1889); Woods, 72.

227. Hugo's 'Olympio': Luppé, 191 (27 August 1837); Proust, II, 437–8.

227. 'lover-wise' and Maggie Tulliver: 2 and 18 January 1881: P. Johnson, in Lesbian History Group, 67–71.

227. Charlus and Musset's poems: Proust, IV, 178 and 489; also II, 747.

228. Tchaikovsky's sexuality audibly encoded: *Maurice*, ch. 32; *Imre*, 111.

228. Schubert's friend: Newbould, 179.

228. Ludwig II and Brunhilda: Carpenter (1902), ch. 5 (2 November 1865).

229. Jenny Lind as icon: Andersen (see p. 220); Symonds (1984), 135; 'Earl Lind' (1922), 94. Also Marie-Antoinette: Saint-Paul, 88; Fernandez, 52 and 68.

229. 'storiettes' in lavatories: Aronson, 22.

229. obscene graffiti: Symonds (1984), 187–8.

229. 'We two alone': 'Dans ce café bondé d'imbéciles . . .' (1891): Verlaine (1985).

229. 'There is a thicket': Carlier, 287.

230. 'Homosexuals have time for everybody': Crisp, 45.

230. 'the love of the impossible': Symonds (1984), 188.

230. 'But who could describe my terror': Krafft-Ebing, 243.

231. 'You're right there!': Colette, 449.

232. 'opens a window': Engelstein, 388; Malmstad–Bogomolov, 95.

232. *Loom of Youth*: e.g. Porter–Weeks, 49.

232. Rossetti and Hardy compared to Hall: Faderman (1981), 172; Hall, 316.

9. GENTLE JESUS

233. 'thousands' of homosexuals: Hirschfeld (1914), 537.

234. Bishop of London: Davenport-Hines, 101.

234. Philo of Alexandria: D. Bailey, 22.

235. Lucian, *Dialogues of the Courtesans*: tr. M. D. Macleod.

235. *Secret Gospel*: Smith (with photographs of ms); also Ehrman, 131–2.

235. House of Bishops: J. John, 12–23.

236. Humphry Woolrych: 'Sodomy and Bestiality', in C. White, 28–9.

237. 'O God and Father': Scholz, in Müller, 237.

237. 'He wished Christianity': Forster, *Maurice*, 68; see John 20:2; 21:7 and 20.

237. W. K. Clifford: Carpenter (1916), ch. 3.

238. A. E. Forrest: Hyam, 104.

239. 'In Genesis and Judges': Genesis 18–19:28; Judges 19.

239. Sodom is not, according to one view: e.g. Prime-Stevenson (1908), 43–4. Same and similar texts quoted by Bentham and D. Bailey. See also Boswell, 93 ff; J. John, 15; 'Homosexualität und Bibel' ('by a Catholic priest'), *JfsZ*, IV (1902), 199–244.

239. 'According to Ezekiel . . . Book of Wisdom': Ezekiel 16:49; Book of Wisdom 19:13.

239. Clement and Basilides: Clement, *Miscellanies*, III, 1, 1.

239. subtle or tenuous historical arguments: e.g. Smith; T. Horner, 'Jesus', in Dynes et al. See Luke 7:1–10; Matthew 8:5–13.

240. 'Jesus made no such blunders': 'Earl Lind' (1922), 15.

241. Christopher Marlowe: Richard Baines, in Norton (1992), 20.

241. medieval literature and iconography: Boswell, 105.

241. *Essai sur la peinture*: Diderot, 1143–4.

242. Frederick the Great: Larivière (1997), 148–9.

242. Stendhal: Del Litto, 272; Mérimée, *HB* (1850).

242. Bentham and the *Monthly Magazine*: Crompton (1985), 280–2.

242. 'Children of Sodom': Gunther (1995).

243. *Bordel apostolique*: Courouve (1999).

243. Sade and temple at Jerusalem: Sade (1795), 'Troisième Dialogue'.

244. Rosa Bonheur: Cooper, 49.

244. Zinzendorf: Busst, 7.

244. Gladstone and 'shameless lusts': Dowling, 78.

245. Lorrain and hermaphroditic Cupid: 'Sur un Dieu mort', in *Buveurs d'âmes* (1893); Birkett, 198–9.

245. 'a Christian imitation': Proudhon, 382.

246. 'The sacred and tender love': Raffalovich, 30; see also Faber.

246. Max Jacob's vision of Christ: *La Défense de Tartuffe* (1919).

247. Hopkins' sermon of 1879: Hopkins (1967), 35–6; N. White, 317.

247. 'evil thoughts' and 'in the wrong way': N. White, 114.

247. *Hadrian the Seventh*: Rolfe (1904), 177–8.

248. Samuel Cottam: Cottam (1960), 68 n.; Arch Smith, 175.

248. 'R. S.': Ellis, 114.

248. 'vivid attraction' and Judas as lover: Prime-Stevenson (1908), 82 and 258; Arch Smith, 175.

250. eternal anonymity: Crisp, 150.

250. 'muscular Christianity': Hughes (1879 and 1894); Dowling, 44.

250. anticlerical ideologues: Zola (1898), 228, 382, 433; George Moore, *Mike Fletcher* (1889), in Birkett, 36; Mendès (1890), 46–7; Rimbaud, 'L'air léger et charmant de la Galilée . . .' and 'Les Premières communions'; Paul Scheerbart, *Tarub. Bagdads berühmte Köchin. Arabischer Kulturroman* (1897), in J. Jones, 291 n. 3; see also G. Rousseau on Richard Payne Knight, in Rousseau–Porter, 108–9.

250. *People of the Moonlight*: Blasius–Phelan, 205–13.

250. The figure of the androgyne: Busst, 10.

251. 'Suffer little children': E. Rouzier, in *Le Journal*, 26 October 1900: Arch Smith, 48.

251. Ralph Adams Cram: Shand-Tucci.

251. Duncan Grant: Watney, 70–72.

252. Rimbaldian God: Verlaine, *Sagesse*, II, 1.

252. Emily Dickinson to Sue Gilbert: Late April 1852: Faderman (1994), 49.

10. HEROES OF MODERN LIFE

254. 'primitive' cultures: See note on North American Indians on p. 290.

257. Carson cross-examines Wilde: Holland, 155–6, 124.

257. 'The jurymen': Hyde (1973), 124.

259. 'Beefsteak Pete' et al.: Duberman (1997), 223–30.

259. 'Palmo's in Broadway': Melville (1982), 301.

259. 'Greenhorn': Woods, 153.

260. 'introspective and pallid dreamer': Doyle (1981), 547.

261. 'hurried to a consulting-room': 'A Medical Document'.

261. disgraced Oscar Wilde: Doyle (1989), 79–80.

261. Doyle on *Dorian Gray*: Doyle (1989), 79.

261. dinner with Wilde at the Langham: Doyle (1989), 79.

261. 'dining with a school-master!': Booth, 342.

262. 'The Snob Queers': Ellmann, 402.

264. 'no longer interested in women': Booth, 244.

265. Vere Street: A different Vere Street: Clare Market, not Oxford Street.

266. 'Ah, *mon ami*': *The Lost Mine* (1925).

266. 'colourless shrimp': *Murder Must Advertise* (1933).
267. Lone Ranger and Tonto: Rothel, 58.
267. homosexual Batman devotees: Wertham, 190–2.
268. 'Because of my innate appetencies': 'Earl Lind' (1922), 4–5.
      Comparable remarks in Sennett.
268. Hoover and 'depraved human beings': 'How Safe is Your Daughter?',
      American Magazine, July 1947: in Eskridge, 60.
268. *Woran erkennt man Homosexuelle?*: By Raphael Eugen Kirchner (Wald,
      1908): Müller, 318.
269. 'Mystery and Detective Fiction': J. B. Levin, in Dynes et al.

Works Cited

(Unless otherwise indicated, the place of publication is London, New York or Paris.)

Ackerley, J. R. *My Father and Myself* (1968). Intro. W. H. Auden (1969). New York Review Books, 1999.

Acton, William. *The Functions and Disorders of the Reproductive Organs in Youth, in Adult Age, and in Advanced Life*. Churchill, 1857.

Adler, Alfred. *Das Problem der Homosexualität: erotisches Training und erotischer Rückzug*. 1917; Leipzig: Hirzel, 1930.

Aldrich, Robert and G. Wotherspoon, eds. *Who's Who in Gay and Lesbian History from Antiquity to World War II*. Routledge, 2001.

Allen, Clifford. *A Textbook of Psychosexual Disorders*. 2nd ed. Oxford UP, 1969.

Alpers, Antony. *The Life of Katherine Mansfield*. 1980; Oxford UP, 1982.

Anon. *Yokel's Preceptor, or More Sprees in London! being a regular and Curious Show-Up of all the Rigs and Doings of the Flash Cribs in this Great Metropolis* [etc.]. Dugdale, *c*. 1850.

Anon. *Don Leon: a Poem by Lord Byron [. . .] forming part of the private journal of His Lordship*. 1866?; Fortune Press [1934].

Anon. *Boy-Worship*. Oxford, 1880.

Anon. *Teleny*. 1893; ed. J. McRae. GMP, 1986.

Arch Smith, Timothy d'. *Love in Earnest: Some Notes on the Lives and Writings of English 'Uranian' Poets from 1889 to 1930*. Routledge & Kegan Paul, 1970.

Argis, Henri d'. *Sodome*. Piaget, 1888.

Ariès, Philippe and Georges Duby, gen. eds. *Histoire de la vie privée. IV. De la Révolution à la Grande Guerre*. Seuil, 1987.

Aronson, Theo. *Prince Eddy and the Homosexual Underworld*. John Murray, 1994.

Arthur Rimbaud. Paul Verlaine. Manuscrits et lettres autographes. [. . .] Succession Jean Hugues. Drouot, March 1998.

Ashbee, Henry Spencer ('Pisanus Fraxi'). *Index librorum prohibitorum: being Notes Bio- Biblio- Icono-graphical and Critical, on Curious and Uncommon Books*. Privately printed, 1877.

Ashbee, H. S. *Centuria librorum absconditorum [etc.]*. Privately printed, 1879.

Askwith, Betty. *Two Victorian Families*. Chatto & Windus, 1971.

Austen, Roger. *Playing the Game. The Homosexual Novel in America*. Bobbs-Merrill, 1977.

Bailey, Derrick Sherwin. *Homosexuality and the Western Christian Tradition*. Longmans, 1955; Hamden Coun., 1975.

Bailey, Paul. *Three Queer Lives. An Alternative Biography of Fred Barnes, Naomi Jacob and Arthur Marshall*. Hamish Hamilton, 2001.

Ball, Benjamin. *La Folie érotique*. Baillière, 1888.

Balzac, H. de. *La Comédie Humaine*. 12 vols. Ed. P.-G. Castex. Pléiade, 1976–81.

Bancroft, Hubert Howe. *The Native Races of the Pacific States of North America*. I. *Wild Tribes*. Appleton, 1875.

Barbey d'Aurevilly, Jules. *Du dandysme et de Georges Brummell*. Caen, 1845; 2nd ed. Lemerre [1879].

Barney, Natalie Clifford. *Souvenirs indiscrets*. Flammarion, 1960.

Barnstorff, D. *A Key to Shakespeare's Sonnets*. Tr. T. J. Graham. Trübner, 1862.

Bartlett, Neil. *Who Was That Man? A Present for Mr. Oscar Wilde*. 1988; Penguin, 1993.

Baudelaire, Charles. *Oeuvres complètes*. 2 vols. Ed. C. Pichois. Pléiade, 1975–6.

Baumont, Maurice. *L'Affaire Eulenburg et les origines de la guerre mondiale*. Payot, 1933.

Beard, George Miller. *La Neurasthénie sexuelle: hygiène, causes, symptômes et traitement*. New York, 1884; 3rd ed. 1894. Tr. P. Rodet: Société d'éditions scientifiques, 1895.

Beaude, Jean-Pierre. *Dictionnaire de médecine usuelle*. 2 vols. Didier, 1849.

Beauvoir, Roger de. *Histoires cavalières*. 2 vols. Brussels: Hauman, 1838.

Beckford, William. *Vathek*. Ed. R. Lonsdale. Oxford UP, 1983.

Belot, Adolphe. *Mademoiselle Giraud, ma femme*. Pref. É. Zola. 1870; *Mademoiselle Giraud, My Wife*. Tr. A. D. Chicago: Laird & Lee, 1891.

Benson, Arthur Christopher. *Memoirs of Arthur Hamilton, B.A., of Trinity College, Cambridge [. . .]*. Kegan Paul & Co., 1886.

Bentham, Jeremy. 'Offences Against One's Self'. Ed. L. Crompton. *Journal of Homosexuality*, III, 4 (1978) and IV, 1 (1978).

Berkman, Alexander. *Prison Memoirs of an Anarchist*. 2nd ed. Mother Earth, 1920.

Bernheim, Hippolyte. *Hypnotisme, suggestion, psychothérapie*. Doin, 1891.

Beurdeley, Cécile. *L'Amour bleu*. Tr. M. Taylor. Cologne: Benedikt Taschen, 1994.

Birkett, Jennifer. *The Sins of the Fathers. Decadence in France 1870–1914*. Quartet Books, 1986.

Bland, Lucy and L. Doan, eds, *Sexology Uncensored. The Documents of Sexual Science*. Polity Press, 1998.

Blasius, Mark and S. Phelan, eds. *We Are Everywhere. A Historical Sourcebook of Gay and Lesbian Politics*. Routledge, 1997.

Bleys, Rudi C. *The Geography of Perversion: Male-to-Male Sexual Behaviour Outside the West and the Ethnographic Imagination*. Cassell, 1996.

Bloch, Ivan. *Sexual Life in England Past and Present*. Tr. 1938; Royston: Oracle, 1996.

Blüher, Hans. *Die Rolle der Erotik in der männlichen Gesellschaft. Eine Theorie der menschlichen Staatsbildung nach Wesen und Wert*. Jena, 1917; ed. H.-J. Schoeps. Stuttgart: Klett, 1962.

Blyth, James. *Edward Fitzgerald and 'Posh', 'herring merchants' [. . .]*. John Long, 1908.

Boddy, Gillian. *Katherine Mansfield, the Woman and the Writer*. Penguin, 1988.

Booth, Martin. *The Doctor, the Detective and Arthur Conan Doyle: A Biography of Arthur Conan Doyle*. Hodder & Stoughton, 1997.

Boswell, John. *Christianity, Social Tolerance, and Homosexuality. Gay People in Western Europe from the Beginning of the Christian Era to the Fourteenth Century*. Chicago UP, 1980.

Botting, Douglas. *Alexander von Humboldt: Biographie eines grossen Forschungs-reisenden*. 1973. Tr. A. Hohenemser. Prestel, 1989.

Bradford, Edwin Emmanuel. *The New Chivalry, and Other Poems*. Kegan Paul & Co., 1918.

Bremmer, Jan, ed. *From Sappho to De Sade. Moments in the History of Sexuality*. Routledge, 1989; 1991.

Brière de Boismont, Alexandre. *De la folie raisonnante et de l'importance du délire des actes: pour le diagnostic et la médecine légale.* Baillière, 1867.

Broughton, Rhoda. *Dear Faustina.* Leipzig: Tauchnitz; London: Bentley, 1897.

Bullough, Vern. *Homosexuality: A History.* New American Library, 1979.

Bumm, Peter. *August Graf von Platen. Eine Biographie.* Schöningh, 1990.

Burton, Richard. 'Terminal Essay'. *The Book of the Thousand Nights and a Night.* 2 vols. Privately printed, 1885.

Bush, Russell. *Affectionate Men: A Photographic History of a Century of Male Couples, 1850s to 1950s.* St Martin's, 1998.

Busst, A. J. L. 'The Image of the Androgyne in the 19th Century'. In Ian Fletcher, ed. *Romantic Mythologies.* Routledge & Kegan Paul, 1967.

Cabanis, Georges. *Rapports du physique et du moral* (1802). In *Oeuvres philosophiques.* I. Ed. C. Lehec and J. Cazeneuve. PUF, 1956.

Canler, Louis. *Mémoires.* 2 vols. Roy, 1882.

Carlier, François. *Études de pathologie sociale. Les Deux prostitutions.* Dentu, 1887.

Carpenter, Edward. *Love's Coming of Age* (1896; 1902; enlarged ed., 1906, with *Homogenic Love*); *Ioläus: An Anthology of Friendship* (1902; enlarged ed., 1906); *The Intermediate Sex* (1908); *Intermediate Types Among Primitive Folk: A Study in Social Evolution* (1911; 1914); *My Days and Dreams* (1916): see Simon Dawson.Com, 'The Edward Carpenter Archive' <http://www. simondsn. dircon.co.uk/ecindex.htm>; also 'People with a History: An Online Guide to Lesbian, Gay, Bisexual and Trans History', ed. Paul Halsall, 1997 <http://www.fordham.edu/halsall/pwh/index-eur1.html>

Carpenter, E. *Selected Writings.* I. *Sex.* Ed. N. Greig. GMP, 1984.

Casanova, Giacomo. *Mémoires.* Ed. R. Abirached and E. Zorzi. 3 vols. Pléiade, 1958–60.

Casper, Johann Ludwig. *Practisches Handbuch der gerichtlichen Medicin.* 1858; 5th ed., rev. Carl Liman. 2 vols. Berlin: Hirschwald, 1871; 7th ed. 1881. *Traité pratique de médecine légale, rédigé d'après des observations personnelles.* 2 vols. Tr. G. Baillière. Baillière, 1883. *A Handbook of the Practice of Forensic Medicine, Based Upon Personal Experience.* 4 vols. Tr. G. W. Balfour. The New Sydenham Society, 1865.

Casper, J. L. *Klinische Novellen zur gerichtlichen Medicin.* Berlin: Hirschwald, 1863.

Castle, Terry. *The Apparitional Lesbian: Female Homosexuality and Modern Culture*. Columbia UP, 1993.

Catlin, George. *Letters and Notes on the Manners, Customs, and Conditions of the North American Indians, Written during Eight Years' Travel (1832–1839) amongst the Wildest Tribes of Indians in North America*. 1844; Dover, 1973.

Cavafy, C. P. *Collected Poems*. Tr. E. Keeley and P. Sherrard. Chatto & Windus, 1990.

Chandos, John. *Boys Together: English Public Schools 1800–1864*. 1984; Oxford UP, 1985.

Charcot, Jean-Martin and V. Magnan. 'Inversions du sens génital'. *Archives de neurologie*, January–February 1882.

Chateaubriand, François-René de. *Mémoires d'outre-tombe*. 2 vols. Ed. M. Levaillant and G. Moulinier. Pléiade, 1951.

Chauncey, George. 'From Sexual Inversion to Homosexuality: Medicine and the Changing Conceptualization of Female Deviance'. *Salmagundi*, 58–9 (1982–3), 114–46.

Chauncey, G. *Gay New York. The Making of the Gay Male World, 1890–1940*. 1994; Flamingo, 1995.

Chester, Lewis, D. Leitch and C. Simpson. *The Cleveland Street Affair*. Weidenfeld & Nicolson, 1976.

Chevalier, Julien. *Une maladie de la personnalité: l'inversion sexuelle; psycho-physiologie; sociologie; tératologie*. Pref. A. Lacassagne. Storck; Masson, 1893.

Christian, J. 'Onanisme'. *Dictionnaire encyclopédique des sciences médicales*. 2nd series (1869–89), XV, 359–85.

Citron, Pierre. *La Poésie de Paris dans la littérature française*. 2 vols. Éditions de Minuit, 1961.

Cocks, Harry. *Abominable Crimes: Sodomy Trials in English Law and Culture, 1830–1889*. PhD thesis, Manchester, 1998.

Cohen, William A. *Sex Scandal: The Private Parts of Victorian Fiction*. Duke, 1996.

Colette. *Oeuvres*. Ed. C. Pichois. I. Pléiade, 1984.

Colin, Henri. *Essai sur l'état mental des hystériques*. Pref. J. Charcot. Rueff, 1890.

Conner, Randy P. et al. *Cassell's Encyclopedia of Queer Myth, Symbol, and Spirit*. Cassell, 1997.

Cooper, Emmanuel. *The Sexual Perspective. Homosexuality and Art in the Last 100 Years in the West*. 1986; Routledge, 1994.

Corbin, Alain. *Les Filles de noce. Misère sexuelle et prostitution (19ᵉ siècle).* 1978; Flammarion, 1982.

Cory, William (Johnson). *Ionica.* 1858; ed. A. C. Benson. George Allen, 1905.

Cottam, Samuel E. *New Sermons for a New Century.* Skeffington, 1900.

Cottam, S. E. *Cameos of Boyhood and Other Poems.* Stockwell [1930].

Cottam, S. E. *Friends of My Fancy, and Other Poems.* Eton: The Shakespeare Head Press, 1960.

Couperus, Louis. *Noodlot,* 1890. Tr. C. Bell. *Footsteps of Fate. A Novel.* Heinemann, 1891.

Courouve, Claude. 'La Société des Émiles. Chanson de J. Duflos (A. Glatigny)' (1871) www.multimania.com/jgir/emiles.htm

Courouve, C. *Vocabulaire de l'homosexualité masculine.* Payot, 1985.

Courouve, C. 'Compléments à mon ouvrage *Vocabulaire de l'homosexualité masculine.* Paris: Payot, 1985.' 13 December 1999. (website)

Coward, David. 'Attitudes to Homosexuality in 18th-Century France'. *Journal of European Studies,* 10 (1980), 231–55.

Crain, Caleb. *American Sympathy. Men, Friendship, and Literature in the New Nation.* Yale, 2001.

Crisp, Quentin. *The Naked Civil Servant.* 1968; Quality Paperback, 2000.

Crompton, Louis. 'Gay Genocide: from Leviticus to Hitler'. In L. Crew, ed. *The Gay Academic.* Palm Springs: ETC, 1978.

Crompton, L. *Byron and Greek Love. Homophobia in 19th-Century England.* Faber, 1985.

Crompton, L. 'The Myth of Lesbian Impunity: Capital Laws from 1270 to 1791'. *Journal of Homosexuality,* VI, 1–2 (1980–1); and in *The Gay Past. A Collection of Historical Essays.* Eds S. J. Licata and R. P. Petersen. Binghamton: Harrington Park, 1985.

Custine, Astolphe de. *Aloys ou le Religieux du Mont Saint-Bernard.* Ed. P. Sénart. 10/18, 1971.

Dallemagne, Jules. *Dégénérés et déséquilibrés.* Alcan; Brussels: Lamertin, 1895.

Dall'Orto, Giovanni. 'Sodoma all'Improvviso'. *Babilonia,* 133 (May 1995), 68–70.

Darien, Georges (G.-H. Adrien). *Biribi.* 1890; Martineau, 1966.

Davenport-Hines, Richard. *Sex, Death and Punishment. Attitudes to Sex and Sexuality Since the Renaissance.* Collins, 1990.

David, Hugh. *On Queer Street. A Social History of British Homosexuality, 1895–1995.* HarperCollins, 1997.

Debay, Auguste. *Hygiène et physiologie du mariage: histoire naturelle et médicale de l'homme et de la femme mariés, dans ses plus curieux détails. Hygiène spéciale de la femme enceinte et du nouveau-né.* Dentu, 1862.

Deitcher, David. *Dear Friends: American Photographs of Men Together, 1840–1918.* Abrams, 2001.

Delcourt, Pierre. *Le Vice à Paris.* Piaget, 1888.

Delécluze, Étienne-Jean. *Journal de Delécluze, 1824–1828.* Ed. R. Baschet. Grasset, 1948.

Delepierre, Octave-Joseph ('M. Audé'). *Dissertation sur les idées morales des grecs et sur le danger de lire Platon.* Rouen: Lemonnyer, 1879.

Del Litto, Victor. *En marge des manuscrits de Stendhal.* PUF, 1955.

Delvau, Alfred. *Dictionnaire érotique moderne, par un professeur de la langue verte.* 1864; 2nd ed. Neuchâtel: Société des Bibliophiles cosmopolites, 1874.

D'Emilio, John and E. B. Freedman. *Intimate Matters. A History of Sexuality in America.* Harper & Row, 1988.

Derks, Paul. *Die Schande der heiligen Päderastie. Homosexualität und Öffentlichkeit in der deutschen Literatur, 1750–1850.* Rosa Winkel, 1990.

Descaves, Lucien. *Sous-offs: roman militaire.* Tresse & Stock, 1890.

Dickinson, Goldsworthy Lowes. *The Autobiography of G. Lowes Dickinson and Other Unpublished Writings.* Ed. D. Proctor. Duckworth, 1973.

Diderot, Denis. *Oeuvres.* Ed. A. Billy. Pléiade, 1951.

Dio Chrysostom. *Dio Chrysostom.* Tr. J. W. Cohoon and H. Lamar Crosby. III. Heinemann; Harvard UP, 1951.

Donoghue, Denis. *Walter Pater: Lover of Strange Souls.* Knopf, 1995.

Donoghue, Emma. *Passions Between Women. British Lesbian Culture, 1668–1801.* Scarlet Press, 1993.

Dowling, Linda. *Hellenism and Homosexuality in Victorian Oxford.* Cornell, 1994; 1996.

Doyle, Arthur Conan. *The Penguin Complete Sherlock Holmes.* Ed. C. Morley. Penguin, 1981.

Doyle, A. C. *Memories and Adventures.* 1924; Oxford UP, 1989.

[Drysdale, George.] *The Elements of Social Science; or, Physical, Sexual and Natural Religion.* By a Graduate of Medicine. 7th ed. Truelove, 1867.

Dubarry, Armand. *Les Invertis (Les Déséquilibrés de l'amour).* Daragon, 1906.

Duberman, Martin. *About Time. Exploring the Gay Past.* 1986; Meridian, 1991.

Duberman, M., ed. *A Queer World. The Center for Lesbian and Gay Studies Reader.* New York, 1997.

Duberman, M., M. Vicinus and G. Chauncey, eds. *Hidden from History. Reclaiming the Gay and Lesbian Past*. 1989; Penguin, 1991.

Duchesne, Édouard-Adolphe. *De la prostitution dans la ville d'Alger depuis la conquête*. Baillière, 1853.

Dugas, Ludovic. *L'Amitié antique d'après les mœurs populaires et les théories des philosophes*. Alcan, 1894; 1914. Arno Press, 1976.

Duras, Duchesse de. *Olivier ou le secret*. Ed. D. Virieux. Corti, 1971.

Dyer, Richard. 'Children of the Night: Vampirism as Homosexuality, Homosexuality as Vampirism'. In *Secret Dreams. Sexuality, Gender and Popular Fiction*. Ed. S. Radstone. Lawrence & Wishart, 1988.

Dynes, Wayne, et al. *Encyclopedia of Homosexuality*. 2 vols. Garland, 1990.

'Earl Lind' (a.k.a. 'Ralph Werther' and 'Jennie June'). *Autobiography of an Androgyne*. Ed. A. W. Herzog. New York: The Medico-Legal Journal, 1918; Arno Press, 1975.

'Earl Lind'. *The Female-Impersonators. A Sequel to the Autobiography of an Androgyne and an account of some of the author's experiences during his six years' career as instinctive female-impersonator in New York's Underworld; together with the life stories of androgyne associates and an outline of his subsequently acquired knowledge of kindred phenomena of human character and psychology*. Ed. A. W. Herzog. New York: The Medico-Legal Journal, 1922; Arno Press, 1975.

Eekhoud, Georges. *Escal-Vigor. Roman*. 1899; Mercure de France, 1901.

Ehrman, Bart D., ed. *The New Testament and Other Early Christian Writings*. Oxford UP, 1998.

Eisenberg, Daniel. ' "La Escondida Senda": Homosexuality in Spanish History and Culture'. In D. W. Foster, ed. *Spanish Writers on Gay and Lesbian Themes. A Bio-Critical Sourcebook*. Greenwood Press, 1999.

Eldorado. Homosexuelle Frauen und Männer in Berlin 1850–1950. Berlin, 1984.

Ellis, Havelock. *Studies in the Psychology of Sex*. II. 1910; New York: Random House, 1936.

Ellis, H. On *Sexual Inversion* (1896, with J. A. Symonds), see p. 52.

Ellmann, Richard. *Oscar Wilde*. Hamish Hamilton, 1987.

Engelstein, Laura. *The Keys to Happiness. Sex and the Search for Modernity in Fin-de-Siècle Russia*. Cornell, 1992.

Epstein, Julia and K. Straub, eds. *Body Guards. The Cultural Politics of Gender Ambiguity*. Routledge, 1991.

Eskridge, Jr, William N. *Gaylaw. Challenging the Apartheid of the Closet*. Harvard, 1999.

Faber, Geoffrey. *Oxford Apostles: A Character Study of the Oxford Movement*. Faber, 1933.

Faderman, Lillian. *Scotch Verdict. Miss Pirie and Miss Woods v. Dame Cumming Gordon*. Quartet, 1985.

Faderman, L. *Surpassing the Love of Men. Romantic Friendship and Love Between Women from the Renaissance to the Present*. Morrow, 1981; Women's Press, 1985.

Faderman, L., ed. *Chloe Plus Olivia. An Anthology of Lesbian Literature from the Seventeenth Century to the Present*. 1994; Penguin, 1995.

Farrer, Peter, ed. *Men in Petticoats. A Selection of Letters from Victorian Newspapers*. Liverpool: Karn, 1987.

Felix, David. *Keynes. A Critical Life*. Greenwood Press, 1999.

Féré, Charles. *La Pathologie des émotions: études physiologiques et cliniques*. Alcan, 1892.

Fernandez, Dominique. *Le Rapt de Ganymède*. Grasset, 1989.

Flaubert, Gustave. *Correspondance*. 4 vols. Ed. J. Bruneau. Pléiade, 1973–.

Fodéré, François-Emmanuel. *Traité de médecine légale et d'hygiène publique ou de police de santé*. 6 vols. Mame, 1813.

Forster, E. M. *The Life to Come*. Arnold, 1972.

Forster, E. M. *Maurice*. Ed. P. N. Furbank. Penguin, 1972.

Foster, Jeannette H. *Sex Variant Women in Literature. A Historical and Quantitative Survey*. Frederick Muller, 1958.

Foucault, Michel. *Histoire de la sexualité. I. La Volonté de savoir*. Gallimard, 1976.

Fourier, Charles. *Le Nouveau monde amoureux*. 2nd ed., 1845. Ed. S. Debout-Oleszkiewicz. *Oeuvres complètes*. VII. Anthropos, 1971.

Fournier-Verneuil. *Paris, tableau moral et philosophique*. Chez les principaux libraires, 1826.

Fränkel, Hieronymous. 'Homo mollis'. *Medicinische Zeitung vom Verein für Heilkunde in Preußen*, XXII (1853), 101–3.

Freud, Sigmund. *A Case of Hysteria, Three Essays on Sexuality, and Other Works*. In *The Standard Edition of the Complete Psychological Works*. VII. Gen ed. J. Strachey. Hogarth Press, 1953–74.

Frey, Julia. *Toulouse-Lautrec. A Life*. Weidenfeld and Nicolson, 1994.

Furbank, P. N. *E. M. Forster. A Life*. 1977–8; Sphere Books, 1988.

Garnier, Paul. *La Folie à Paris: étude statistique, clinique et médico-légale*. Baillière, 1890. Parts in *Les Fétichistes*. Baillière, 1896.

Gautier, Théophile. *Mademoiselle de Maupin*. 1835; ed. J. Robichez. Imprimerie Nationale, 1979.

Gay, Peter. *Voltaire's Politics: the Poet as Realist*. Princeton UP, 1959.

Gay, P. *The Bourgeois Experience: Victoria to Freud*. 5 vols. Oxford UP, 1984–98.

Gerard, Kent and G. Hekma, eds. *The Pursuit of Sodomy: Male Homosexuality in Renaissance and Enlightenment Europe*. Haworth, 1988. (= *Journal of Homosexuality*, XVI, 1–2.)

Gide, André. *Corydon. Quatre dialogues socratiques*. Gallimard, 1924. 1st ed. (ends in 3rd Dialogue): *C.R.D.N.* (Bruges, 1911); 2nd ed., 1920.

Gide, A. *Si le grain ne meurt*. Nouvelle Revue française, 1926.

Gide, A. *Et nunc manet in te, suivi de Journal intime*. Ides et Calendes, 1947.

Gifford, James. *Dayneford's Library. American Homosexual Writing, 1900–1913*. U. of Massachusetts, 1995.

Gilbert, Arthur N. 'Buggery and the British Navy, 1700–1861'. *Journal of Social History*, X, 1 (Fall 1976), 72–98.

Goldberg, Jonathan, ed. *Reclaiming Sodom*. Routledge, 1994.

Goncourt, Edmond de. *La Faustin*. Flammarion-Fasquelle, 1882.

Goncourt, E. and Jules de. *Journal. Mémoires de la vie littéraire*. 3 vols. Ed. R. Ricatte. Laffont, 1989.

Goodman, Jonathan, ed. *The Oscar Wilde File*. Allison & Busby, 1988; 1995.

Grand-Carteret, John. *Derrière 'Lui' [the Kaiser]: l'Homo-sexualité en Allemagne*. 1908; Lille: Cahiers Gai-Kitsch-Camp, 1992.

Greenberg, David F. *The Construction of Homosexuality*. Chicago, 1988.

Gregorovius, Ferdinand. *Wanderjahre in Italien*. 1856–77; ed. F. Schillmann. Jess, 1928.

Grosskurth, Phyllis. *John Addington Symonds: A Biography*. Longmans, 1964.

Gunther, Scott. 'La Construction de l'identité homosexuelle dans les lois aux États-Unis et en France'. DEA de Sciences Sociales (mémoire principal). École des Hautes Études en Sciences Sociales, September 1995.

Gury, Christian. *L'Honneur musical d'un capitaine homosexuel en 1880. De Courteline à Proust*. Kimé, 1999.

Haas, François. *Per scientiam ad justitiam? L'opposition à la répression pénale de l'homosexualité dans l'Allemagne de Guillaume II*. (Thesis)

Haggerty, George. *Men in Love: Masculinity and Sexuality in the Eighteenth Century*. Columbia UP, 1999.

Hale, Nathan G. Jr. *Freud and the Americans. The Beginnings of Psychoanalysis in the United States, 1876–1917*. Oxford UP, 1971.

Hall, Radclyffe. *The Well of Loneliness*. 1928; ed. A. Hennegan. Virago, 1982.

Hamer, Dean and P. Copeland, *The Science of Desire: The Search for the Gay Gene and the Biology of Behavior*. Simon & Schuster, 1994.

Harris, Frank. *The Man Shakespeare and his Tragic Life-Story*. Frank Palmer, 1909.

Harris, F. *Oscar Wilde*. 1916; Robinson, 1992.

Hartland, Claude [pseud.]. *The Story of a Life: for the Consideration of the Medical Fraternity*. St Louis, 1901; San Francisco: Grey Fox, 1985.

Harvey, Arnold D. 'Prosecutions for Sodomy in England at the beginning of the 19th Century'. *Historical Journal*, XXI, 4 (1978), 939–48.

Hayes, Joseph J. 'Gayspeak'. *The Quarterly Journal of Speech*, LXII, 3 (October 1976), 256–66.

Healey, Dan. *Homosexual Desire in Revolutionary Russia: the Regulation of Sexual and Gender Dissent*. Chicago, 2001.

Heilbut, Anthony. *Thomas Mann. Eros and Literature*. Macmillan, 1995; 1996.

Hekma, Gert. 'Homosexual Behaviour in the 19th-Century Dutch Army'. *Journal of the History of Sexuality*, II, 2 (October 1991), 266–88. Also in John Fout, ed. *Forbidden History*. Chicago, 1992.

Henke, Adolph Christian Heinrich. *Lehrbuch der gerichtlichen Medicin*. Stuttgart: Wolters, 1832.

Hensher, Philip. 'Gay art lite'. *Prospect Magazine*, March 2002.

Hermant, Abel. *Le Cavalier Miserey, 21e Chasseurs: moeurs militaires contemporaines*. 1887; Ollendorff, 1901.

Hichens, Robert S. *The Green Carnation*. Heinemann, 1894.

Higgins, Patrick, ed. *A Queer Reader*. Fourth Estate, 1993.

Higgs, David, ed. *Queer Sites. Gay Urban Histories Since 1600*. Routledge, 1999.

Hirschfeld, Magnus. *Berlins drittes Geschlecht. Schwules und lesbisches Leben im Berlin der Jahrhundertwende*. 1905; ed. M. Herzer. Rosa Winkel, 1991. Tr. *Le Troisième sexe, Les Homosexuels de Berlin* (1908).

Hirschfeld, M. *Die Homosexualität des Mannes und des Weibes*. Berlin: Marcus, 1914. *The Homosexuality of Men and Women*. Tr. M. A. Lombardi-Nash. Prometheus, 2000.

Hirschfeld, M., *see* Wissenschaftlich-Humanitäre Komitee.

Hitchcock, Tim. *English Sexualities, 1700–1800*. Macmillan, 1997.

Hocquenghem, Guy. *Homosexual Desire*. 1972; tr. D. Dangoor, 1978; Duke UP, 1993.

Hofmann, Eduard Ritter von. *Lehrbuch der gerichtlichen Medizin, mit gleichmäßiger Berücksichtigung der deutschen und österreichischen Gesetzgebung*.

1878; 10th ed. Ed. A. Haberda. Berlin and Vienna: Urban & Schwarzenberg, 1919.

Holland, Merlin. *Irish Peacock & Scarlet Marquess. The Real Trial of Oscar Wilde*. Fourth Estate, 2003.

Holloway, Robert. *The Phoenix of Sodom, or the Vere Street Coterie, Being an Exhibition of the Gambols Practised by the Ancient Lechers of Sodom and Gomorrah, embellished and improved with the Modern Refinements in Sodomitical Practices, by the members of the Vere Street Coterie, of detestable memory*. London, 1813.

Home Office and Scottish Home Department (Sir John Wolfenden, Chairman). *Report of the Committee on Homosexual Offences and Prostitution*. HMSO, September 1957.

Hopkins, Gerard Manley. *The Sermons and Devotional Writings*. Ed. C. Devlin. 1959; Oxford UP, 1967.

Hössli, Heinrich. *Eros. Die Männerliebe der Griechen, ihre Beziehungen zur Geschichte, Literatur und Gesetzgebung aller Zeiten. Oder Forschungen über platonische Liebe, ihre Würdigung und Entwürdigung für Sitten-, Natur- und Völkerkunde*. 1836, 1838; 2nd ed. Münster i.d. Schweiz: beim Herausgeber [1840].

Hughes, Thomas. *The Manliness of Christ*. Macmillan, 1879; 1894.

Huysmans, Joris-Karl. *À rebours*. 1884; ed. P. Waldner. Garnier-Flammarion, 1978.

Hyam, Ronald. *Empire and Sexuality. The British Experience*. Manchester, 1990; 1991.

Hyde, H. Montgomery. *The Trials of Oscar Wilde*. 1962; Dover, 1973.

Hyde, H. M. *The Other Love. An Historical and Contemporary Survey of Homosexuality in Britain*. Heinemann, 1970.

Isherwood, Christopher. *Mr Norris Changes Trains*, 1935; Penguin, 1961.

James, Henry. *Italian Hours*. Ed. J. Auchard. 1992; Penguin, 1995.

James, H. *Letters*. 4 vols. Ed. L. Edel. Harvard UP, 1974–84.

John, Rev. Dr Jeffrey. 'The Bible and Homosexuality'. *Christian Action Journal* (Summer 1990), 12–23.

Johnson, Susan Lee. *Roaring Camp. The Social World of the California Gold Rush*. Norton, 2000.

Jones, Ernest. *The Life and Work of Sigmund Freud*. 3 vols. Basic Books, 1953–57.

Jones, James W. *'We of the Third Sex'. Literary Representations of Homosexuality in Wilhelmine Germany.* Peter Lang, 1990.

Joux, Otto de. *Die Enterbten des Liebesglückes oder Das dritte Geschlecht.* Leipzig: Spohr, 1893.

Kaplan, Justin. *Walt Whitman: A Life.* Simon and Schuster, 1980.

Karlinsky, Simon. *The Sexual Labyrinth of Nicolai Gogol.* Harvard, 1976.

Karsch-Haack, Ferdinand. 'Uranismus oder Päderastie und Tribadie bei den Naturvölkern'. *JfsZ*, III (1901), 72–201.

Katz, Jonathan. *Gay American History. Lesbians and Gay Men in the U.S.A. A Documentary.* Thomas Y. Crowell, 1976.

Katz, J. *Love Stories. Sex Between Men Before Homosexuality.* Chicago, 2001.

Katz, J., ed. *Documents of the Homosexual Rights Movement in Germany, 1836–1927.* Arno Press, 1975.

Kehoe, Monika, ed. *Historical, Literary and Erotic Aspects of Lesbianism.* Harrington Park, 1986.

Kennedy, Hubert. *Ulrichs. The Life and Works of Karl Heinrich Ulrichs, Pioneer of the Modern Gay Movement.* Boston: Alyson, 1988.

Khanna, Shamona. 'Gay Rights'. *The Lawyers*, June 1992.

Kleist, Heinrich von. *Sämtliche Werke und Briefe.* IV. *Briefe von und an Heinrich von Kleist, 1793–1811.* Ed. K. Müller-Salget and S. Ormanns. Deutscher Klassiker Verlag, 1997.

Kraepelin, Emil. *Psychiatrie: ein Lehrbuch für Studirende und Aerzte.* 5th ed. Leipzig: Barth, 1896.

Krafft-Ebing, Richard von. *Psychopathia sexualis. Mit besonderer Berücksichtigung der konträren Sexualempfindung. Eine medizinisch-gerichtliche Studie für Ärzte und Juristen.* 1886; 14th ed. 1912; Matthes & Seitz, 1997.

Kurella, Hans. *Naturgeschichte des Verbrechers: Grundzüge der criminellen Anthropologie und Criminalpsychologie.* Stuttgart: Enke, 1893.

Kuzniar, Alice, ed. *Outing Goethe and His Age.* Stanford, 1996.

Lacassagne, Albert. 'Pédérastie'. *Dictionnaire encyclopédique des sciences médicales.* 2nd series (1869–89), XXII, 239–59; 'Tatouage'. 3rd series (1874–87), XVI, 124–5.

Lacassagne, Jean and P. Devaux. *L'Argot du 'milieu'.* New ed. Albin Michel, 1948.

La Châtre, Maurice. *Nouveau Dictionnaire universel.* 2 vols. Docks de la Librairie, 1865–70.

Lacroix, Paul. *Histoire de la prostitution chez tous les peuples du monde: depuis l'Antiquité la plus reculée jusqu'à nos jours*. III. Seré, 1852.

Lalande, Françoise. 'L'Examen corporel d'un homme de lettres'. *Parade sauvage*, 2 (April 1985), 97–8.

Larivière, Michel. *Homosexuels et bisexuels célèbres: le Dictionnaire*. Delétraz, 1997.

Larivière, M. *Pour tout l'amour des hommes: anthologie de l'homosexualité dans la littérature*. Delétraz, 1998.

Larousse, Pierre. *Grand Dictionnaire universel du XIXe siècle*. 1866–79.

Laupts, *see* Saint-Paul, Georges.

Lauvergne, Hubert. *Les Forçats considérés sous le rapport physiologique, moral et intellectuel: observés au bagne de Toulon*. Baillière, 1841.

Lawrence, T. E. *The Selected Letters*. Ed. M. Brown. Dent, 1988.

Le Baillif de La Rivière, Roch. *Premier traicté de l'homme, et de son essentielle anatomie avec les elemens, & ce qui est en eux*. Langelier, 1580.

Leeves, Edward. *Leaves from a Victorian Diary*. Intro. J. Sparrow. The Alison Press / Secker & Warburg, 1985.

Le Gallienne, Richard. *The Book-Bills of Narcissus*. 1891; Lane, 1895.

Legrand du Saulle, Henri. *Le Délire des persécutions*. Plon, 1871.

Lejeune, Philippe. 'Autobiographie et homosexualité en France au XIXe siècle'. *Romantisme*, 56 (1987), 79–100.

Leland, Charles Godfrey. *The Alternate Sex, or The Female Intellect in Man, and the Masculine in Woman*. Wellby, 1904.

Lesbian History Group. *Not a Passing Phase. Reclaiming Lesbians in History 1840–1985*. The Women's Press, 1989; 1993.

Lever, Maurice. *Les Bûchers de Sodome: histoire des infâmes*. Fayard, 1985.

Lind, Earl, *see* 'Earl Lind'.

Lister, Anne. *I Know My Own Heart. The Diaries of Anne Lister 1791–1840*. Ed. H. Whitbread. New York UP, 1992. [Excerpts from 1817–1824.]

Lister, A. *No Priest But Love. Excerpts from the Diaries of Anne Lister, 1824–1826*. Ed. H. Whitbread. Otley: Smith Settle, 1992.

Littré, Émile. *Dictionnaire de la langue française*. Hachette, 1873–5.

Livet, Charles-Louis. *Les Intrigues de Molière et celles de sa femme ou La Fameuse comédienne. Histoire de La Guérin*. Isidore Liseux, 1877.

Lombroso, Cesare and Guglielmo Ferrero. *La Donna delinquente, la prostituta e la donna normale*. Turin and Rome: Roux, 1893. *La Femme criminelle et la prostituée*. Tr. L. Meille. Alcan, 1896.

Lorrain, Jean. *Le Vice errant*. II. *Les Noronsoff*. Ollendorff, 1922.

Lorrain, J. *Correspondance*. Ed. G. Normandy. Baudinière, 1929.

Louÿs, Pierre. *Les Chansons de Bilitis, traduites du grec*. Mercure de France, 1898.

Lovell, Mary S. *A Rage to Live: A Biography of Richard and Isabel Burton*. Little, Brown, 1998.

Lucas, Ian. 'The Color of His Eyes: Polari and the Sisters of Perpetual Indulgence'. In A. Livia and K. Hall, eds. *Queerly Phrased: Language, Gender and Sexuality*. Oxford UP, 1997.

Lucas, Prosper. *Traité philosophique et physiologique de l'hérédité naturelle dans les états de santé et de maladie du système nerveux*. 2 vols. Baillière, 1847 and 1850.

Lucien, Mirande. *Eekhoud le rauque*. P. U. du Septentrion, 1999.

Luppé, Albert, comte de. *Astolphe de Custine*. Éditions du Rocher, 1957.

Lydston, G. Frank. *Impotence and Sterility with Aberrations of the Sexual Function and Sex-Gland Implantation*. Chicago: Riverton Press, 1917.

Lynch, Michael. 'Here is Adhesiveness: from Friendship to Homosexuality'. *Victorian Studies*, XXIX, 1 (Autumn 1985), 67–96.

Lyttelton, Edward. *The Causes and Prevention of Immorality in Schools*. Social Purity Alliance. Privately printed, 1877; 1887.

Maccubbin, Robert Purks, ed. *'Tis Nature's Fault: Unauthorized Sexuality During the Enlightenment*. Cambridge UP, 1987.

Macé, Gustave. *La Police parisienne. Le Service de la Sûreté*. Charpentier, 1885.

Macintosh, Mary. 'The Homosexual Role'. *Social Problems*, XVI, 2 (Fall 1968), 182–92. In K. Plummer, ed. *The Making of the Modern Homosexual*. Hutchinson, 1981.

Macintosh, M. 'Gayspeak'. *Lunch*, 16 (January 1973), 7–9.

Magnan, Valentin. *Recherches sur les centres nerveux: alcoolisme, folie des hérédit-aires dégénérés, paralysie générale, médecine légale*. II. Masson, 1893.

Malmstad, John E. and N. Bogomolov. *Mikhail Kuzmin. A Life in Art*. Harvard, 1999.

Mann, Thomas. Lecture on Platen (1930). In *Schriften und Reden zur Literatur, Kunst und Philosophie*. Fischer, 1968. II, 33–43.

Marañón, Gregorio. *La Evolucion de la sexualidad y los estados intersexuales* (1930). *The Evolution of Sex and Intersexual Conditions*. Tr. Warre B. Wells. Allen & Unwin, 1932.

Marx, Heinrich. *Urningsliebe. Die sittliche Hebung des Urningthums und die Streichung des §175 des deutschen Strafgesetzbuchs*. Leipzig, 1875.

Mason, Michael. *The Making of Victorian Sexuality*. Oxford UP, 1994.

Maupassant, Guy de. *La Femme de Paul*. In *La Maison Tellier* (1881). Ed. L. Forestier. Folio, 1973.

Mavor, Elizabeth, ed. *A Year with the Ladies of Llangollen*. Penguin, 1984; 1986.

Mayer, Hans, *Aussenseiter*. Suhrkamp, 1975.

Maynard, Steven. 'Through a Hole in the Lavatory Wall: Homosexual Subcultures, Police Surveillance, and the Dialectics of Discovery, Toronto, 1890–1930'. *Journal of the History of Sexuality*, V, 2 (October 1994), 207–42.

McCalman, Iain. *Radical Underworld. Prophets, Revolutionaries, and Pornographers in London, 1795–1840*. Oxford: Clarendon Press, 1993.

McCormick, Ian. *Sexual Outcasts*. II. Routledge, 2000.

Mecke, Günter. *Franz Kafkas offenbares Geheimnis. Eine Psychopathographie*. Wilhelm Fink, 1982.

Meer, Theo van der. *De wesentlijke sonde van sodomie en andere vuyligheeden. Sodomieten vervolgingen in Amsterdam 1730–1811*. Amsterdam: Tabula, 1984.

Meer, T. van der. 'Tribades on Trial: Female Same-Sex Offenders in Late 18th-Century Amsterdam'. *Journal of the History of Sexuality*, I, 3 (January 1991), 424–45.

Melville, Herman. *Redburn. His First Voyage*. Ed. H. Beaver. Penguin, 1982.

Melville, H. *Billy Budd, Sailor and Other Stories*. Ed. H. Beaver. Penguin, 1985.

Mendès, Catulle. *La Maison de la vieille. Roman contemporain*. 1894; ed. J.-J. Lefrère et al. Champ Vallon, 2000.

Mendès, C. *Méphistophéla. Roman contemporain*. Dentu, 1890.

Merrick, Jeffrey. 'Commissioner Foucault, Inspector Noël, and the "Pederasts" of Paris, 1780–3'. *Journal of Social History*, XXXII, 2 (1998), 287–307.

Merrick, J. and Bryant T. Ragan, eds. *Homosexuality in Modern France*. Oxford UP, 1996.

Méry, Joseph. *Monsieur Auguste*. 1859; Lévy, 1871.

Meyers, Jeffrey. *Homosexuality and Literature, 1890–1930*. Athlone Press, 1977.

Miller, D. A. *The Novel and the Police*. U. of California, 1988.

Miller, Neil. *Out of the Past: Gay and Lesbian History from 1869 to the Present*. Vintage, 1995.

Millward, Keith. *L'Oeuvre de Pierre Loti et l'esprit 'Fin de siècle'*. Nizet, 1955.

Mirbeau, Octave. *La 628-E8*. 1907; Charpentier, 1918.

Mitchell, Mark and David Leavitt, eds. *Pages Passed from Hand to Hand. The Hidden Tradition of Homosexual Literature in English from 1748 to 1914*. 1997; Vintage, 1999.

Moers, Ellen. *The Dandy. Brummell to Beerbohm*. Secker & Warburg, 1960.

Moll, Albert. *Die conträre Sexualempfindung*. 1891; 2nd ed., 1893. Tr. Drs Pactet and Romme. *Les Perversions de l'instinct génital. Étude sur l'inversion sexuelle basée sur des documents officiels*. Carré, 1893.

Mondimore, Francis Mark. *A Natural History of Homosexuality*. Johns Hopkins UP, 1996.

Monter, E. William. 'La Sodomie à l'époque moderne en Suisse romande'. *Annales*, 29, 4 (July–August 1974), 1023–33.

Moran, Leslie J. *The Homosexual(ity) of Law*. Routledge, 1996.

Moreau, L. *Les Aberrations du sens génésique*. n.p., 1887.

Moreau (de Tours), Jacques-Joseph. *La Psychologie morbide dans ses rapports avec la philosophie de l'histoire ou De l'influence des névropathes sur le dynamisme intellectuel*. Masson, 1859.

Morel, Bénédict-Auguste. *Traité théorique et pratique des maladies mentales: considérées dans leur nature, leur traitement, et dans leur rapport avec la médecine légale des aliénés*. 2 vols. Baillière, 1852–3.

Morel, B.-A. *Traité des dégénérescences physiques, intellectuelles et morales de l'espèce humaine et des causes qui produisent ces variétés maladives*. Baillière, 1857.

Morgan, Fidelis. *The Well-Known Trouble-Maker: A Life of Charlotte Clarke*. Faber, 1988.

Morselli, Enrico. *Manuale di semejotica delle malattie mentali: guida alla diagnosi della pazzia per i medici, i medico-legisti e gli studenti*. II. Vallardi, 1885.

Mosse, George L. *Nationalism and Sexuality. Respectability and Abnormal Sexuality in Modern Europe*. Fertig, 1985.

Mowl, Timothy. *William Beckford. Composing for Mozart*. John Murray, 1998.

Muhlstein, Anka. *Astolphe de Custine: the Last French Aristocrat*. Tr. T. Waugh. Duckworth, 2001.

Müller, Klaus. *Aber in meinem Herzen sprach eine Stimme so laut. Homosexuelle Autobiographien und medizinische Pathographien im neunzehnten Jahrhundert*. Rosa Winkel, 1991.

Murdoch, Iris. 'The Moral Decision About Homosexuality'. *Man and Society*, 7 (Summer 1964), 3–6.

Murphy, Steve. *Rimbaud et la ménagerie impériale*. CNRS; P. U. de Lyon, 1991.

Murphy, S., ed. A. Rimbaud, *Un Cœur sous une soutane*. Musée-Bibliothèque Arthur Rimbaud, 1991.

Murray, Douglas. *Bosie. A Biography of Lord Alfred Douglas*. Hodder & Stoughton, 2000.

Musil, Robert. *Die Verwirrungen des Zöglings Törleß* (1906). In *Gesammelte Werke*. Ed. A. Frisé. VI. Rowohlt, 1978.

Nabokov, Vladimir. 'Die Homosexualität im Russischen Strafgesetzbuch'. *JfsZ*, V, 2 (1903), 1159–71.

Newbould, Brian. *Schubert. The Music and the Man*. Gollancz, 1997.

Nicholson, John Gambril. *A Garland of Ladslove*. Privately printed, 1911.

Nicolson, Nigel. *Portrait of a Marriage*. Weidenfeld and Nicolson, 1973.

Noakes, Vivien. *Edward Lear. The Life of a Wanderer*. Collins, 1968.

Norton, Rictor. *Mother Clap's Molly House. The Gay Subculture in England 1700–1830*. GMP, 1992.

Norton, R. *The Myth of the Modern Homosexual. Queer History and the Search for Cultural Unity*. Cassell, 1997.

Norton, R. 'Walt Whitman, Prophet of Gay Liberation'. 'The Great Queens of History'. 18 November 1999 <http://www.infopt.demon.co.uk/whitman.htm>.

Norton, R., comp. 'The John Addington Symonds Pages'. 1997; 2000 <http://www.infopt.demon.co.uk/symindex.htm>.

Notopoulos, James A. *The Platonism of Shelley. A Study of Platonism and the Poetic Mind*. Duke UP, 1949.

Nye, Robert A. *Sexuality*. Oxford UP, 1999.

O'Brien, M. D. *Socialism and Infamy. The Homogenic or Comrade Love Exposed: An Open Letter in Plain Words for a Socialist Prophet*. 3 eds. Sheffield: privately printed, 1909.

Ogrinc, Will H. L. 'A Shrine to Love and Sorrow. Jacques d'Adelswärd-Fersen (1880–1923)'. semgai.free.fr/contenu/textes/fersen/W__Ogrinc__Fersen.html

Orr, Dave. 'Sex in the City: Social Responses to Same-Sex Sex Between Men in Early Nineteenth-Century London'. Institute of Historical Research, U. of London Seminar, October 2001.

Paglia, Camille. *Sexual Personae. Art and Decadence from Nefertiti to Emily Dickinson*. Yale UP, 1990.

Parent-Duchâtelet, A.-J.-B. *De la prostitution dans la ville de Paris, considérée sous le rapport de l'hygiène publique, de la morale et de l'administration.* 1836; 3rd ed. 2 vols. Baillière, 1857.

Pearsall, Ronald. *The Worm in the Bud: the World of Victorian Sexuality.* 1969; Pimlico, 1993.

Perrot, Michelle. '1848. Révolution et prisons'. In *L'Impossible prison: recherches sur le système pénitentiaire au XIXᵉ siècle.* Ed. M. Perrot. Seuil, 1980.

Pichois, Claude and Alain Brunet. *Colette.* De Fallois, 1999.

Plummer, Kenneth. *Sexual Stigma: an Interactionist Account.* Routledge, 1975.

Pollard, Patrick. *André Gide, Homosexual Moralist.* Yale UP, 1991.

Popp, Wolfgang. *Männerliebe. Homosexualität und Literatur.* Metzler, 1992.

Porter, Kevin and J. Weeks, eds. *Between the Acts. Lives of Homosexual Men, 1885–1967.* Routledge, 1991.

Porter, Roy and L. Hall. *The Facts of Life. The Creation of Sexual Knowledge in Britain, 1650–1950.* Yale UP, 1995.

Pougy, Liane de (Marie Chassaigne). *Idylle saphique.* La Plume, 1901.

Pouillet, Thésée. *De l'onanisme chez l'homme.* Vigot, 1897.

Poznansky, Alexander. *Tchaikovsky's Last Days. A Documentary Study.* Oxford: Clarendon Press, 1996.

Prime-Stevenson, Edward Irenaeus. *The Intersexes. A History of Similisexualism as a Problem in Social Life.* By Xavier Mayne. Naples: privately printed, *c.* 1908.

Prime-Stevenson, E. I. *Imre: A Memorandum.* Edited [i.e. written] by Xavier Mayne. Naples: The English Book-Press, 1906; Arno Press, 1975.

Prince, Alison. *Hans Christian Andersen. The Fan Dancer.* Allison & Busby, 1998.

Proudhon, Pierre-Joseph. *Les Évangiles.* Lacroix, 1866.

Proust, Marcel. *À la recherche du temps perdu.* Ed. J.-Y. Tadié. Pléiade, 1987–89.

Pushkin, Alexander. *The Letters of Alexander Pushkin.* Ed. and tr. J. T. Shaw. U. of Wisconsin, 1967.

Pyle, Howard. *The Merry Adventures of Robin Hood of Great Renown, in Nottinghamshire.* Sampson, Low & Co., 1883.

Rachilde (Marguerite Eymery). *Monsieur Vénus.* 1884; Brossier, 1889.

Raffalovich, Marc-André. *Uranisme et unisexualité. Étude sur différentes manifestations de l'instinct sexuel.* Storck; Masson, 'Bibliothèque de criminologie', 1896.

Ramdohr, Friedrich Wilhelm Basilius von. *Venus Urania. Über die Natur der Liebe, über ihre Veredlung und Verschönerung.* 3 parts. Leipzig, 1798.

Rau, Hans. *Franz Grillparzer und sein Liebesleben*. Barsdorf, 1904.

Reade, Brian, ed. *Sexual Heretics: Male Homosexuality in English Literature, 1850–1900*. Routledge, 1970.

Reed, T. J. *Death in Venice. Making and Unmaking a Master*. Twayne, 1994.

Reydellet, Pierre. 'Pédérastie'. *Dictionaire* [sic] *des sciences médicales*. Ed. Adelon et al. XL. Panckoucke, 1819. Pp. 37–45.

Rivers, J. E. *Proust and the Art of Love. The Aesthetics of Sexuality in the Life, Times, and Art of Marcel Proust*. Columbia UP, 1980.

Robb, Graham. *La Poésie de Baudelaire et la poésie française, 1838–1852*. Aubier, 1993.

Robb, G. *Balzac: A Biography*. Picador; Norton, 1994.

Robb, G. *Rimbaud*. Picador; Norton, 2000.

Robinson, Alfred. *Life in California During a Residence of Several Years in That Territory*. 1846. Ed. A. Rolle. Peregrine, 1970.

Robinson, Paul. *Gay Lives. Homosexual Autobiography from John Addington Symonds to Paul Monette*. U. of Chicago, 1999.

Rolfe, Frederick ('Baron Corvo'). *Hadrian the Seventh*. 1904; Chatto & Windus, 1950.

Rolfe, F. *Stories Toto Told Me, or A Sensational Atomist. In His Own Image*, by Baron Corvo. Lane, 1901.

Rolfe, F. *The Venice Letters*. Ed. C. Woolf. Cecil and Amelia Woolf, 1974.

Rosario, Vernon A., ed. *Science and Homosexualities*. Routledge, 1997.

Rothel, David. *Who Was That Masked Man? The Story of the Lone Ranger*. 1976; San Diego and New York: Barnes; London: The Tantivy Press, 1981.

Roughead, William. *Bad Companions*. Edinburgh: W. Green & Son, 1930.

Rousseau, G. S. and Roy Porter. *Sexual Underworlds of the Enlightenment*. Manchester UP, 1987.

Rowse, A. L. *Homosexuals in History. A Study of Ambivalence in Society, Literature and the Arts*. Dorset Press, 1977.

Rüling, Anna. 'Welches Interesse hat die Frauenbewegung an der Lösung des homosexuellen Problems?' *JfsZ*, VII, 1 (1905), 129–51.

Ruggiero, Guido. *The Boundaries of Eros: Sex, Crime and Sexuality in Renaissance Venice*. Oxford UP, 1985; 1989.

Rydström, Jens. ' "Sodomitical Sins are Threefold": Typologies of Bestiality, Masturbation and Homosexuality in Sweden, 1880–1950'. *Journal of the History of Sexuality*, IX, 3 (July 2000), 240–76.

Sade, Donatien-Alphonse-François de. *Justine, ou Les Malheurs de la vertu*. 1791; Pauvert, 1966.

Sade, D.-A.-F. de. *La Philosophie dans le boudoir*. 1795; ed. J.-J. Pauvert. La Musardine, 1997.

Saint-Paul, Georges. *Tares et poisons, perversion & perversité sexuelles: une enquête médicale sur l'inversion: notes et documents; Le roman d'un inverti-né: Le procès Wilde: La guérison et la prophylaxie de l'inversion*, par le Dr Laupts. Pref. É. Zola. Masson, 1896; 2nd ed.: *L'Homosexualité et les types homosexuels*. Vignot, 1910.

Sand, George. *Lélia*. 1833; Calmann-Lévy, 1958.

Sand, G. *La Petite Fadette*. 1849; ed. P. Salomon and J. Mallion. Garnier, 1981.

Sand, G. *Histoire de ma vie*. In *Oeuvres autobiographiques*. Ed. G. Lubin. II. Pléiade, 1971.

Sand, G. and Marie Dorval. *Correspondance inédite*. Ed. S. André-Maurois. Gallimard, 1953.

[Saul, Jack.] *The Sins of the Cities of the Plain, or The Recollections of a Mary-Ann. With Short Essays on Sodomy and Tribadism*. London, Leicester Square, 1881.

Schönholzer, Jakob, ed. *Franz Grillparzer. Sein Leben in Tagebüchern, Briefen und Erinnerungen*. Aehren, 1952.

Schopenhauer, Arthur. *Die Welt als Wille und Vorstellung*. In *Sämtliche Werke*. Ed. J. Frauenstädt and A. Hübscher. III. Brockhaus, 1949.

Schrenck-Notzing, Baron Albert von. *Die Suggestionstherapie bei krankhaften Erscheinungen des Geschlechtssinnes, mit besonderer Berücksichtigung der conträren Sexualempfindung*. Stuttgart: Enke, 1892.

Schrijvers, P. H. *Eine medizinische Erklärung der männlichen Homosexualität aus der Antike*. Amsterdam: Gruner, 1985.

Sennett, Richard. *The Fall of Public Man*. Cambridge UP, 1977.

Shakespeare, William. *Les Sonnets de William Shakespeare*. Tr. F.-V. Hugo. Lévy, 1857.

Shand-Tucci, Douglass. *Ralph Adams Cram: Life and Architecture*. I. U. of Massachusetts Press, 1995.

Shelley, Percy Bysshe. 'A Discourse on the Manners of the Antient [*sic*] Greeks Relative to the Subject of Love'. July–August 1818; 1931. In Notopoulos, 404–13.

Shelley, P. B. *The Letters of Percy Bysshe Shelley*. 2 vols. Ed. F. L. Jones. Oxford: Clarendon Press, 1964.

Showalter, Elaine. *Sexual Anarchy. Gender and Culture at the Fin de Siècle.* 1990; Virago, 1992.

Signoret, Emmanuel. *Le Livre de l'amitié: poèmes en vers et en prose. Mirzael – Myrtil.* Vanier, 1891.

Sinfield, Alan. *The Wilde Century: Effeminacy, Oscar Wilde and the Queer Moment.* Cassell, 1994.

Skidelsky, Robert. *John Maynard Keynes.* I. *Hopes Betrayed, 1883–1920.* Macmillan, 1983.

Smith, Morton. *The Secret Gospel. The Discovery and Interpretation of the Secret Gospel According to Mark.* 1973; Aquarian Press, 1985.

Smollett, Tobias. *The Adventures of Roderick Random.* 1748, Ed. D. Blewett. Penguin, 1995.

Spencer, Colin. *Homosexuality. A History.* Fourth Estate, 1995.

Stambolian, George and Elaine Marks, eds. *Homosexualities and French Literature. Cultural Contexts/Critical Texts.* Cornell UP, 1979.

[Stanton, Theodore.] *Reminiscences of Rosa Bonheur.* Melrose, 1910.

Steakley, James D. *The Homosexual Emancipation Movement in Germany.* 1975; Ayer Company, 1993.

Stendhal. *Armance, ou quelques scènes d'un salon de Paris en 1827.* Ed. J.-J. Labia. Garnier, 1994.

Stendhal. *Oeuvres complètes.* Geneva: Cercle du Bibliophile, 1968–74.

Stern, Madeleine B. *Heads & Headlines. The Phrenological Fowlers.* U. of Oklahoma, 1971.

Stokes, John. 'Wilde at Bay: the Diaries of George Ives'. *English Literature in Transition, 1880–1920,* XXVI, 3 (1983), 175–86.

Strindberg, August. 'Nature the Criminal' (1885). In *Getting Married.* Tr. M. Sandbach. Victor Gollancz, 1972.

Strindberg, A. *The Cloister.* 1891. Tr. M. Sandbach. Secker & Warburg, 1969.

Sturgis, Howard O. *Belchamber.* Constable, 1904.

Summers, Claude J., ed. *The Gay and Lesbian Literary Heritage. A Reader's Companion to the Writers and their Works, from Antiquity to the Present.* Henry Holt, 1995.

Symonds, John Addington. *A Problem in Greek Ethics, being an inquiry into the phenomenon of Sexual Inversion addressed especially to medical psychologists and jurists.* Privately printed, 1883; 1901; 1908.

Symonds, J. A. *A Problem in Modern Ethics, being an inquiry into the phenomenon of Sexual Inversion.* Privately printed, 1891; 1896.

Symonds, J. A. *The Memoirs of John Addington Symonds.* Ed. P. Grosskurth. Hutchinson, 1984.

Symonds, J. A., *see* Norton, comp.

Tardieu, Ambroise. *Étude médico-légale sur les attentats aux mœurs*. Baillière, 1857; ed. G. Vigarello. Grenoble: Millon, 1995.

Tarnovsky, Veniamin. *The Sexual Instinct and its Morbid Manifestations from the Double Standpoint of Jurisprudence and Psychiatry*. 1885; tr. W. C. Costello and A. Allinson. Carrington, 1898.

Taxil, Léo. *La Corruption fin-de-siècle*. Noirot, *c*. 1909.

Taylor, Alfred Swaine. *The Principles and Practice of Medical Jurisprudence*. Churchill, 1865; ed. T. Stevenson. 2 vols. Churchill, 1883.

Thoinot, Léon-Henri. *Attentats aux mœurs et perversion du sens génital*. Douin, 1898.

Thompson, C. W. 'Les Clefs d'Armance' and 'Stendhal connaisseur de l'"improper" '. *Stendhal Club*, 100 (1983) and 114 (1987).

Thrale, Hester Lynch. *Thraliana. The Diary of Mrs. Hester Lynch Thrale (Later Mrs. Piozzi), 1776–1809*. Ed. K. C. Balderston. 2 vols. Oxford: Clarendon Press, 1942.

Tickner, Lisa. *The Spectacle of Women. Imagery of the Suffrage Campaign, 1907–14*. Chatto & Windus, 1987.

Tissot, Samuel-Auguste-André-David. *L'Onanisme: essai sur les maladies produites par la masturbation*. 1758; Garnier, 1905.

Tóibín, Colm. *Love in a Dark Time. Gay Lives from Wilde to Almodóvar*. Picador, 2001.

Tourdes, Gabriel et Edmond Metzquer. *Traité de médecine légale théorique et pratique*. Asselin et Houzeau, 1896.

Trumbach, Randolph. *Sex and the Gender Revolution*. I. *Heterosexuality and the Third Gender in Enlightenment London*. U. of Chicago, 1998.

Turner, Frank M. *The Greek Heritage in Victorian Britain*. Yale UP, 1981.

Ulrichs, Karl Heinrich. 'Vier Briefe'. *JfsZ*, I (1899). In Katz (1975).

Ulrichs, K. H. *Forschungen über das Räthsel der mannmännlichen Liebe*. Ed. H. Kennedy. Berlin: Rosa Winkel, 1994.

Ulrichs, K. H. *The Riddle of "Man-Manly Love": the Pioneering Work on Male Homosexuality*. 2 vols. Tr. M. A. Lombardi-Nash. Buffalo: Prometheus Books, 1994.

Van Casselaer, Catherine. *Lot's Wife. Lesbian Paris, 1890–1914*. Liverpool: Janus Press, 1986.

Verlaine, Paul-Marie. *Femmes. Hombres.* Ed. J.-P. Corsetti and J.-P. Giusto. Le Livre à venir, 1985.

Vibert, Charles-Albert. *Précis de médecine légale.* Intro. P. Brouardel. 3rd ed. Baillière, 1893.

Vicinus, Martha. *Independent Women: Work and Community for Single Women, 1850–1920.* Virago, 1985.

Viel-Castel, Horace de. *Mémoires sur le règne de Napoléon III.* 6 vols. Chez tous les libraires, 1883.

Walker, Kenneth. *The Physiology of Sex and its Social Implications.* 1940; revised, 1954; Pelican, 1965.

Walmsley, Roy. 'Indecency Between Males and the Sexual Offences Act 1967'. *The Criminal Law Review* (1978), 400–7.

Watney, Simon. *The Art of Duncan Grant.* John Murray, 1990.

Waugh, Alec. *The Loom of Youth.* Richards, 1917.

Weeks, Jeffrey. *Coming Out. Homosexual Politics in Britain, from the Nineteenth Century to the Present.* Quartet Books, 1977; 1990.

Weeks, J. *Sex, Politics and Society. The Regulation of Sexuality Since 1800.* 2nd ed. Longman, 1989; 1994.

Weininger, Otto. *Geschlecht und Charakter. Eine prinzipielle Untersuchung.* 1903; Munich: Matthes & Seitz, 1980.

Wellings, Kaye et al. *Sexual Behaviour in Britain. The National Survey of Sexual Attitudes and Lifestyles.* Penguin, 1994.

Wertham, Fredric. *Seduction of the Innocent.* Museum Press, 1955.

Westphal, Carl Friedrich Otto. 'Die conträre Sexualempfindung, Symptom eines nevropatischen (psychopatischen) Zustandes'. *Archiv für Psychiatrie und Nervenkrankheiten*, II, 1 (1870), 73–108. Rpt in *Gesammelte Abhandlungen.* Ed. A. Westphal. Berlin: Hirschwald, 1892.

Westwood, Gordon. *A Minority. A Report on the Life of the Male Homosexual in Great Britain.* Longmans, 1960.

White, Chris, ed. *Nineteenth-Century Writings on Homosexuality. A Sourcebook.* Routledge, 1999.

White, Edmund. *States of Desire. Travels in Gay America.* 1980; Picador, 1986.

White, Norman. *Hopkins. A Literary Biography.* Oxford UP, 1992.

Wilde, Oscar. *The Complete Letters of Oscar Wilde.* Ed. M. Holland and R. Hart-Davis. Fourth Estate, 2000.

Wilde, O. 'The Portrait of Mr W. H.' *Blackwood's Edinburgh Magazine*, July 1889.

Winn, Phillip. *Sexualités décadentes chez Jean Lorrain: le héros fin de sexe.* Rodopi, 1997.

Wissenschaftlich-Humanitäre Komitee. *Jahrbuch für sexuelle Zwischenstufen, mit besonderer Berücksichtigung der Homosexualität.* Leipzig and Berlin: Max Spohr, 1899–1923.

Wissenschaftlich-Humanitäre Komitee. *Was muss das Volk vom dritten Geschlecht wissen? Eine Aufklärungsschrift.* Leipzig: Spohr, 1901.

Wolfenden, *see* Home Office.

Wolff, Charlotte. *Magnus Hirschfeld. A Portrait of a Pioneer in Sexology.* Quartet Books, 1986.

Woods, Gregory. *A History of Gay Literature. The Male Tradition.* Yale UP, 1998.

Woolf, Virginia. 'Moments of Being. "Slater's Pins Have No Points".' In *A Haunted House and Other Short Stories.* 1944; GraftonBooks, 1982; 1991.

Wullschlager, Jackie. *Hans Christian Andersen. The Life of a Storyteller.* Allen Lane, 2000.

'Xavier Mayne', *see* Prime-Stevenson.

Zimmerman, Bonnie, ed. *Lesbian Histories and Cultures. An Encyclopedia.* Garland, 2000.

Zola, Émile. *La Curée.* 1871; ed. H. Mitterand. Folio, 1981.

Zola, É. *Nana.* 1880; ed. C. Becker. Garnier, 1994.

Zola, É. *Paris.* 1898; ed. M. Le Blond. *Oeuvres complètes.* XXXV. Bernouard, 1929.

Zola, É, *see* Belot and Saint-Paul.

Index

Monaco 27
Monet, Claude 161
Montesquieu, Charles de Secondat,
  Baron de 176
Montesquiou, Robert de 226
Monticelli, Adolphe 226
Moreau, Gustave 250
Morison, Sir Alexander 52
Moritz, Karl Philipp 53
Morris, William 226
Morselli, Enrico 71
Moscow 30
Mother Clap 158
Müller, Johannes von 291
Munich 181–2, 189
Murdoch, Iris 121
Murray, F. E. ('A. Newman') 219
Musil, Robert 231
Musset, Alfred de 227, 228

Nabokov, Vladimir 33
Naples 7, 30, 93, 96, 143, 204, 209, 222,
  223, 255
Napoleon I 22, 26, 88
Nazis 10, 32–3, 83, 193
Neuschwanstein 168
Newlove, clerk 27
New York 7, 8, 30, 51, 103, 134, 158,
  163, 165, 169, 172–3, 259, 267
Nice 193
Nicholson, John Gambril 219
Nicolson, Harold 130
Norton, Rictor 102, 158
Nussey, Ellen 143

O'Brien, M. D. 105
'Order of Chaeronea' 168, 192
Orion 258
Orpheus 244
Oswald, Richard 189
Ovid 143, 258
Oxford 141, 167, 218–9

Paget, Henry (5th Marquess of
  Anglesey) 97
Palermo 60

Paris 7, 8, 28, 30, 31, 51, 60, 97, 151,
  157, 158, 159, 160–1, 164, 166, 169,
  171, 175, 179–80, 255–6
Park, Frederick (a.k.a. 'Fanny') 98–101,
  109, 112, 119
Parkhurst, Rev. Charles 165
Parmenides 43
Paschal, convicted sodomite 243
Pater, Walter 92, 244
Patroclus 144, 200
Paul, St 133, 233, 234, 235, 240, 243
Paxton, D. ('Screw') 162
Pearce, defendant 26
Peirce, James Millis 185
Péladan, Joséphin 206
Pepys, Samuel 3
Périé, Hilaire 91
Persia 7
Pétain, Philippe, Maréchal 32
Petronius 143
Philadelphia 165, 259
Philip II (of Macedonia) 168
Philo Judaeus (Philo of Alexandria)
  234, 235
Pilate, Pontius 235
Platen, Count von 94–6, 97, 139, 167,
  181, 188, 227
Plato 44, 53, 80, 174, 177, 181, 235,
  245, 249
Plutarch 144
Poe, Edgar Allan 254–60, 266–7
Ponsonby, Sarah 116–18, 216
Pontoppidan, Knud 286
pornography 58, 206–8
Portugal 27, 33, 157, 204
'Posh', friend of E. Fitzgerald 104
Pougy, Liane de (Marie Chassaigne)
  211
Praxiteles 245
Prévost, Marcel 231
Prime-Stevenson, Edward Irenaeus
  ('Xavier Mayne') 129, 185–6, 191,
  209, 226, 227, 228, 231–2, 248, 276
prostitution 57, 74–5, 142, 157–9,
  162–4
Protheroe, Edward, MP 101